Moral Time

Moral Time

Donald Black

OXFORD
UNIVERSITY PRESS

OXFORD
UNIVERSITY PRESS

Oxford University Press, Inc., publishes works that further
Oxford University's objective of excellence
in research, scholarship, and education.

Oxford   New York
Auckland   Cape Town   Dar es Salaam   Hong Kong   Karachi
Kuala Lumpur   Madrid   Melbourne   Mexico City   Nairobi
New Delhi   Shanghai   Taipei   Toronto

With offices in
Argentina   Austria   Brazil   Chile   Czech Republic   France   Greece
Guatemala   Hungary   Italy   Japan   Poland   Portugal   Singapore
South Korea   Switzerland   Thailand   Turkey   Ukraine   Vietnam

Copyright © 2011 by Oxford University Press

Published by Oxford University Press, Inc.
198 Madison Avenue, New York, New York 10016

www.oup.com

Oxford is a registered trademark of Oxford University Press

Library of Congress Cataloging-in-Publication Data
Black, Donald J.
Moral time / Donald Black.
   p.   cm.
Includes bibliographical references and index.
ISBN 978-0-19-973714-7 (cloth : alk. paper)
1. Social conflict—Philosophy. 2. Conflict—Philosophy. I. Title.
HM1121.B53   2011
303.601—dc22   2010027115

1 3 5 7 9 8 6 4 2

Printed in the United States of America
on acid-free paper

*To
Roberta*

Contents

Preface xi

CHAPTER 1: INTRODUCTION 3
THE NATURE OF SOCIAL TIME 4
THE ORIGIN OF CONFLICT 5
    Crime as Social Time 6
    Punishment as Social Time 9
    Luck as Social Time 10
RIGHT AND WRONG 11
    Law 12
    Dislike 13
    Virtue 15
    Injustice 15

PART I: RELATIONAL TIME

CHAPTER 2: OVERINTIMACY 21
OVERINVOLVEMENT 22
    Rape as Relational Time 23
    Filthy Involvements 25
    The Crime of Touching 29
    The Crime of Looking 30
    Social Contamination 32
    Overinvolvement as Bad Manners 34
OVEREXPOSURE 36
    Nakedness as Relational Time 37
    The Crime of Being Noticed 38
    Overintimate Art 40
    Overexposure as Bad Manners 42

CHAPTER 3: UNDERINTIMACY 43

UNDERINVOLVEMENT 44

Adultery as Relational Time 44

The Crime of Saying Goodbye 46

Underinvolvement as Bad Manners 50

UNDEREXPOSURE 51

Secrecy 51

Lying 52

Underexposure as Bad Manners 54

PART II: VERTICAL TIME

CHAPTER 4: OVERSTRATIFICATION 59

OVERSUPERIORITY 60

Success as Witchcraft 61

The Enforcement of Equality 63

The Crime of Doing Too Well 66

OVERINFERIORITY 71

Social Castration 71

Hard Times 74

Violence as Vertical Time 76

Health as Wealth 79

CHAPTER 5: UNDERSTRATIFICATION 82

UNDERSUPERIORITY 82

Misfortune as Witchcraft 83

The Evil Eye 84

Theft as Vertical Time 87

UNDERINFERIORITY 89

Rebellion as Vertical Time 90

The Crime of Being Uppity 92

Equality as Bad Manners 95

PART III: CULTURAL TIME

CHAPTER 6: OVERDIVERSITY 101

OVERTRADITIONALISM 102

Savages 102

Race as Culture 106

The Crime of Being Different 108

OVERINNOVATION 109

    Heresy as Cultural Time 109

    Overcreativity in Art 112

    Overcreativity in Science 115

    Insanity as Culture 117

CHAPTER 7: UNDERDIVERSITY 120

UNDERTRADITIONALISM 121

    Conversion as Cultural Time 122

    Going Native 125

    Gender as Culture 127

UNDERINNOVATION 129

    Conservatism as Cultural Time 130

    Bad Faith 133

    The Crime of Being Old-Fashioned 135

CHAPTER 8: CONCLUSION 137

THE GEOMETRY OF SOCIAL TIME 138

TRIBAL TIME 140

    The Right to Intimacy 141

    The Right to Equality 143

    The Right to Purity 144

MODERN TIME 144

    The Right to Privacy 145

    The Right to Opportunity 146

    The Right to Diversity 147

POSTMODERN TIME 147

    The Right to Happiness 148

    The Right to Rights 149

    The Global Self 149

Notes 153

References 201

Name Index 265

Subject Index 277

Preface

Conflict is everywhere. Clashes of right and wrong occur in all human relationships in all societies. Someone always regards someone else as evil, wrong, unjust, dangerous, or just rude. The result might be anything from an angry stare or frown to criticism, ostracism, fighting, or killing. And conflicts are a central concern of everyone—as much as health or wealth or anything else.

I have studied conflict of a moral nature for many years. I first looked at law, and developed a theory to explain why people call the police or go to lawyers, why some legal cases are more successful, and why some crimes receive more punishment. Then I examined other ways people handle conflict, such as mediation, gossip, avoidance, and violence—from fighting and feuding to terrorism and war. I discovered that the management of conflict depends on its location and direction in social space, including the social distance between those involved, such as their degree of intimacy, inequality, and cultural diversity. Justice is geometrical: It varies with the shape of social space.

But as I studied the handling of conflict, I often wondered what explains conflict itself. Why is it so common? What causes it? And why are some conflicts worse than others? It is not enough to say that deviant behavior or immorality is whatever people define it to be—a social construction—as if it were arbitrary or random. Nor is it enough to say that conflict derives from the violation of rules, such as laws or customs. Why are those the rules? And why do people violate them? An adequate answer to these questions is not something merely psychological, such as frustration, disgust, or a need for justice. Why do these feelings arise in the first place? It also adds little to say that conflict results from what people learn. Why do they learn what they learn? Why is crime criminal, immorality immoral, or rudeness rude? No one has satisfactorily answered these questions. Few have even tried.

What, then, causes conflict? The answer begins with time. Everyone is familiar with various kinds of time, including physical time (such as the motion of Earth around the sun) and biological time (the aging of organisms). But here I propose a new and entirely sociological concept of time: *social time*—the dynamic dimension of social space. Social space continually fluctuates, and every fluctuation is a movement of social time. Social time includes relational time, vertical time, and cultural time. Moreover, I have discovered that the fundamental cause of conflict is the movement of social time. And because conflict itself is a movement of social time, conflict causes still more conflict. Social time is moral time.

The purpose of the theory of moral time is scientific: to explain conflict. Although the theory is not perfect or final, I believe it is extremely powerful. It clearly and simply explains the vast majority of the conflicts I have examined over the years, not only in modern societies but across the world and throughout history. It pertains to conflict in literally every kind of human relationship, whether between relatives, friends, colleagues, strangers, groups, or nations. It orders a wide range of facts about conflict described by scholars in such fields as sociology, criminology, anthropology, and history, and addresses everything from mild dislike and bad manners to crime, litigation, massacres, and wars. It answers questions seldom asked scientifically at all, such as what is deviant about deviant behavior, what is the origin of morality, and what gives rise to accusations of wrongdoing that never even happened. The book concludes with a theory that explains why conflict differs from one social location to another, and why it changes over the course of human history.

The theory of moral time has practical value as well. Because it tells us when conflict is likely to occur and when one conflict will be more serious than another, it allows us to prevent conflict to some degree—whenever we are willing and able to alter the course of social time. Often, however, we cannot stop social time, and can only prepare for its consequences. But whether or not we can prevent or prepare for conflict, we might still want to know why these clashes occur, and why they will forever be our fate. And because the theory of moral time explains the content of morality and reveals the factual basis of moral judgment, it might also be relevant to the judgment of moral judgment.

I am pleased to thank some of those who have contributed to this book. First I thank the University of Virginia for my uniquely luxurious position of University Professor, which has long given me the freedom to pursue my work without distractions. For making this possible, I thank the late dean of the Faculty of Arts and Sciences Hugh P. Kelly, former president of the university Robert M. O'Neil, and outgoing president John T. Casteen III. I thank the university's Alderman Library for its peerless service (called "Library Express on Grounds"), which hand delivers any publication requested by a faculty member at any time—another luxury that has greatly advanced my work. I thank the numerous scholars whose research has educated me so much about the nature of human conflict. I am likewise grateful to the many colleagues and students who have shared my excitement about the power and promise of pure sociology, and who have devoted their own work to its development.

I thank those at Oxford University Press who made my manuscript into a book— especially my wonderful editor James Cook, who was enthusiastic about the theory of moral time from the beginning and who always made me feel fortunate to have Oxford as my publisher. I thank Jacqueline Doyle for her excellent editing of the manuscript, Christine Dahlin and Michael O'Connor for all their help during the book's production, and Jessica Heslin and Brady McNamara for its elegant design. I also thank the three anonymous scholars who generously took the time to read and evaluate an early version of the manuscript for Oxford.

I particularly wish to thank Mary Patricia Baumgartner for meticulously reading and greatly improving the manuscript page by page and sentence by sentence—and for her countless contributions to my work over the years. I thank my poet son Malachi for encouraging my efforts on this book for much of his life. I even thank my magical cat Katherine the Great for keeping a smile on my face, and for making sure I never sleep too late.

And finally I thank the one who contributed more to this book than I can adequately communicate, who was present for the birth of the theory and who lived with it every day for years I do not wish to count, who shared in the excitement of its development and participated in my many decisions and revisions as it matured, who found so much evidence relevant to its application and evaluation, and who commented so crucially on everything—from the concepts, formulations, and illustrations to the clarity of the writing and the design of the dust jacket—adding so much that she is part of every page of the book and part of whatever beauty it might possess. I therefore dedicate this book to my perfect wife: Roberta Senechal de la Roche.

Flag Day 2010
Free Union, Virginia

Moral Time

1 | Introduction

A man rapes a woman. A wife leaves her husband. Nations go to war. Black American teenagers criticize a schoolmate for acting white. A young man attacks someone for insulting him. An African blames his illness on witchcraft. American whites in the Old South scold a black for being uppity. New Guinea tribesmen torture and eat a foreigner. Scientists ridicule a new theory. A Muslim man beats his daughter for not wearing her headscarf. Japanese crucify Christians. Germans kill millions of Jews.

Conflict is a clash of right and wrong. It is crime and punishment in the broadest sense—what sociologists call deviant behavior and social control.[1] Some conflict is both. Violence might be a crime, for example, but also a punishment.[2] Other conflict pertains to someone considered dangerous: an enemy to attack or avoid.[3] Or it might merely be a matter of discourtesy or dislike. But all conflict concerns something defined as wrong or bad or otherwise undesirable, whether illegal, immoral, improper, or impolite.[4]

This book contains a theory of why conflict occurs, and why some conflicts are worse than others.[5] It also explains what is wrong, whether according to law, ethics, etiquette, or other rules. Central to the theory is a new concept of *social time*—a distinctively and purely sociological form of time: *Social time is the dynamic dimension of social space.* Social space constantly fluctuates, and every fluctuation is a movement of social time. These fluctuations cause clashes of right and wrong:

> *The fundamental cause of conflict is the movement of social time.*

Conflict occurs throughout the social universe. It is inevitable and inescapable. And everywhere it attracts as much or more attention than any other feature of human life.[6] People consider conflict a problem, and try to minimize it as much as possible. But conflict is ubiquitous because the movement of social time is ubiquitous, and it is inevitable because the movement of social time is inevitable.[7] Every conflict is itself a movement of social time, and conflict therefore causes more conflict. Social time is *moral time.*

THE NATURE OF SOCIAL TIME

Space is the geometry of reality, and social space is the geometry of social reality. Social space is multidimensional, with relational, vertical, and cultural dimensions. Each dimension has its own geometry, measured by its own kind of social distance. Relational distance is a degree of intimacy, such as the involvement of one person or group in the life of another. Vertical distance is a degree of inequality, such as a difference in wealth or authority. Cultural distance is a degree of diversity, such as a difference in religion or ethnicity.[8]

Social space differs considerably from physical space. Whereas a physical distance is always the same in each direction (such as from London to Paris and from Paris to London), for example, a social distance is not: My social closeness to you might be greater than your closeness to me, for instance, such as when I know more about your life than you know about mine.[9] Also unlike physical space, social space is a zero-sum game: When I increase my closeness to you I reduce my closeness to others, and vice versa. And social space constantly fluctuates. Its geometry is never more than a moment in social time.

Time is the dynamic dimension of reality, and social time is the dynamic dimension of social reality. Social time includes the fluctuation of every dimension of social space: *Relational time* is an increase or decrease of intimacy (relational distance). *Vertical time* is an increase or decrease of inequality (vertical distance). *Cultural time* is an increase or decrease of diversity (cultural distance). Any such change is a movement of social time, whether a rape, divorce, achievement, loss, contact with a foreigner, or the creation of something new.[10]

Eighteenth-century philosopher David Hume said that physical time is observable: a "perceivable succession of changeable objects."[11] Social time is observable as well.[12] Physicist Hermann Minkowski said that physical time and space are part of a single reality: "Henceforth space by itself, and time by itself, are doomed to fade away into mere shadows, and only a kind of union of the two will preserve an independent reality."[13] Social time is likewise inseparable from social space.[14] Physicist Amrit Sorli said that "change does not 'happen' in time," but rather "change itself *is* physical time."[15] And social time is social change. But social time also differs from other forms of time: For example, social time does not normally recur in cycles like Earth's movement around the sun or the moon's movement around Earth. Nor does it always have a single direction like the aging of plants and animals.[16] Social time is multidimensional, and moves at different speeds and in different directions from one social location to another.[17]

Social time moves when someone increases or decreases intimacy with someone else, achieves more or less than someone else, or accepts or rejects an idea of someone else. It moves when someone allows a relationship to weaken, disobeys an authority, or converts to another religion. It moves when strangers become acquaintances, when a marriage begins or ends, when a business hires or fires an employee, and when a nation rises or falls. It moves when someone gains or loses wealth, gives birth or dies, commits a crime or punishes a criminal, creates or criticizes a work of art, or introduces or ignores a new theory. Social time is the ceaseless motion of the social universe.[18]

THE ORIGIN OF CONFLICT

Every conflict is an event. Someone hurls an insult, snubs a friend, slaps a face, calls the police, kills an enemy, or explodes a bomb in a public place. Every conflict has a history: It arises with a movement of social time, whether an increase or decrease of intimacy, inequality, or diversity. If social space were frozen forever, conflict would never occur. But social space constantly fluctuates. The movement of social time is the cause of all conflict.[19]

Just as lighting a match might ignite an explosion, so a movement of social time might immediately cause a conflict. But social time also causes conflict the way smoking causes cancer: slowly and subtly, in a manner sometimes difficult if not impossible to detect. Just as each puff of a cigarette does not result in lung cancer, so each movement of social time does not result in a conflict. And just as the likelihood of cancer increases if smoking continues, so the likelihood of conflict increases with each movement of social time. It is all a matter of degree: The greater and faster the movement of social time, the greater is the likelihood of conflict and the greater the conflict is likely to be.

Social time causes conflict in all human relationships—between family members, lovers, friends, acquaintances, strangers, organizations, tribes, and nations. But a movement of social time is not always something someone regards as wrong or bad. On the contrary, it might be something considered entirely acceptable or even desirable, such as a new relationship or a major achievement. Or it might be something completely nonhuman in origin, such as a disease or disaster.[20] Yet all movements of social time cause conflict.

Every movement of social time that causes conflict is an increase or decrease of social closeness:

Conflict is a direct function of overcloseness.

And:

Conflict is a direct function of undercloseness.

But what is too much or too little closeness depends on how much closeness exists in the first place.[21] Too much or too little closeness in one location might be normal in another. Too much intimacy between strangers might not be too much in a family, for instance, and too much inequality or diversity in a simple tribe might not be too much in a modern society. Yet everywhere the same movements of social time cause conflict, including movements of relational time, vertical time, and cultural time. In particular, conflict results from *overintimacy* and *underintimacy*; *overstratification* and *understratification*; and *overdiversity* and *underdiversity*. We shall see, for example, that all these movements of social time have caused a great deal of violence in many places across the world.

Note, however, that conflict does not result from the mere existence of more or less intimacy, inequality, or diversity. Nothing static causes conflict. Conflict always results from something dynamic: the movement of social time.

CRIME AS SOCIAL TIME

What is deviant behavior? What is criminal about crime, immoral about immorality, or bad about bad manners? Why does punishment occur? Why does criticism, ostracism, gossip, or other social control occur? Sociologist Howard S. Becker famously said that deviant behavior is "behavior that people so label."[22] But what does the labeling of deviant behavior tell us about the nature of deviant behavior? It tells us nothing at all. The question remains: Why is anything labeled deviant? Is it arbitrary? Random? Why, for example, is rape or robbery deviant, apart from being labeled as such? Why is anything regarded as wrong? Some might say that what is wrong is whatever violates a rule. But why does the rule exist? Why is anything criminal? Why is anything a sin? What is evil or rude or crazy? In short, what is deviant about deviant behavior?

Deviant behavior is a movement of social time. It is a deviation of social space from its previous shape.[23] And the greater and faster the movement of social time, the greater is the seriousness of the deviant behavior and the more conflict it causes.[24]

Crime is a movement of social time. Sin is a movement of social time. Rudeness is a movement of social time. Anything wrong is a movement of social time. Consider rape: Why is rape wrong? It is wrong because it is a drastic movement of relational time, a radical and rapid increase of intimacy: sexual intercourse without consent.[25] It is overintimacy. Moreover, because rape is a greater increase of intimacy than, say, an unwanted touch or a trespass on someone's property, it causes more conflict.[26] Leaving a spouse or lover is a movement of relational time in the opposite direction: It is underintimacy. And it too causes conflict.

Movements of vertical and cultural time cause other conflicts. For instance, disrespect toward an equal introduces inequality between the parties (overstratification), and rebellion against a superior reduces (or threatens to reduce) inequality between the parties (understratification)—and both cause conflict. A new religion increases diversity (overdiversity), and its repression rejects diversity (underdiversity)—and both cause conflict as well. Rape is thus a relational crime, disrespect a vertical crime, and heresy a cultural crime.

But crime does not occur in a social vacuum. Because different crimes often involve different movements of social time, their legal nature alone does not tell us how much conflict they will cause. For instance, stranger rape is a greater movement of relational time than spousal rape—because the spouses were already intimate before the rape. So stranger rape is worse: It attracts more social control.[27] The movement of social time entailed by a crime also typically radiates beyond the victim: If you kill someone, for example, you usually alter the lives of other people at the same time. If you kill a physician or teacher, you destroy whatever that person was contributing to other people, and you do more social damage than if you kill a homeless person who contributes little or nothing to anyone else. Likewise, if you ridicule my religion or ethnicity, you ridicule not only me but everyone else with my religion or ethnicity, possibly even people in other parts of the world. The farther and faster social time radiates, the more conflict it causes.[28]

Sociologists have long explained crime with social conditions such as inequality, a lack of opportunity, the existence of a subculture, or the absence of social bonds.[29] But all these conditions are static rather than dynamic, and nothing static causes crime or anything else. Something must happen before any crime will occur: *The cause of crime is always a movement of social time.*

A radical and rapid movement of social time might cause a violent crime, such as a beating or killing. We shall see that sudden losses of intimacy (such as when a woman leaves her husband) sometimes lead to violence, for example, and the same is true of sudden losses of social status (such when a man loses his job). Look for social locations where social time moves in large and fast steps and you will find more violence than where social time moves more gradually. And because violence itself is often a radical and rapid movement of social time, violence often causes more violence.[30]

Multidimensional movements of social time are especially dangerous, like one explosive substance added to another. On Christmas Eve in 2008, for instance, a California man dressed as Santa Claus entered a party and killed his ex-wife and eight of her relatives. Later he shot himself, bringing the number of dead to ten. Why did this happen? What caused these killings? They occurred six days after his wife finalized a divorce, which ended not only his relationship with his wife but with his stepdaughter and others in his wife's large family. His wife also obtained a court order requiring him to support her in the future, to make a lump sum payment of ten thousand dollars to her, to allow her to keep the diamond wedding ring he had bought for her, and even to give her the family dog (his last remaining close companion). He had recently lost his job as well, making it difficult for him to meet expenses such as the support payments to his ex-wife, his legal fees, and his house payments.[31] All these movements of social time together caused the Christmas Eve explosion.

Conventional theories in criminology cannot tell us what causes particular crimes such as the one described above. Was it inequality or a lack of opportunity? A subculture of violence or an absence of social bonds? No. Static conditions cannot cause crime. Static conditions are not even dangerous. What is dangerous is the movement of social time. The greater and faster the movement of social time and the more dimensions of social space it alters, the more dangerous it becomes.

The theory of moral time thus tells us why crime is criminal, why one crime is more serious than another, and why crime occurs. It is all a matter of social time.

PUNISHMENT AS SOCIAL TIME

Punishment is also a movement of social time. Every reaction to deviant behavior alters social space: *Social control is a movement of social time.* For example, banishment and imprisonment are movements of relational time that alter intimacy. Fines and payments of compensation are movements of vertical time.[32] Executions of heretics and massacres of ethnicities are movements of cultural time. Some applications of social control involve more than a single movement of social time at once. But always the most severe forms of social control are the greatest movements of social time.

Deviant behavior and social control are reciprocal movements of social time. Just as crime is a movement of social time, so the punishment of crime is a movement of social time that corresponds to the movement of social time to which it reacts. The most serious forms of deviant behavior—those involving the greatest movements of social time—therefore cause the most severe forms of social control. Because a stranger rape is a greater movement of social time than an intimate rape, for example, the social control of a stranger rape attracts more punishment.

But social control does not occur in a social vacuum. If you send my father to prison for killing my mother, for instance, I lose not only my mother but also my father and whatever he contributes to my life and family. If you send a stranger to prison for killing my mother, however, I lose only my mother. If you fire me from my job, you deprive my family of my earnings.[33] If you discipline a football star by not letting him play, you deprive his team and fans of his talent. If you attack a member of my ethnic group, you attack other members of the same group, including me. Social control thus radiates into social space and may entail different movements of social time from one case to the next.

Because every form of social control is a movement of social time, social control also causes conflict. Punishment might cause more crime by a criminal, for instance, or it might cause someone else to retaliate against those who inflicted the punishment.[34] Conflict causes more conflict, possibly continuing far into the future.[35]

LUCK AS SOCIAL TIME

Although crime and punishment are always movements of social time, not all movements of social time are matters of right and wrong. Even if we could live in a utopian world where no one ever does anything wrong, conflict would still occur. Some conflict results from movements of social time regarded as entirely normal (such as the beginning of a close relationship), and some results from movements of social time regarded as highly admirable (such as economic or other success). Other conflict might result from movements of social time that are completely unintentional, or possibly just a matter of luck. Some movements of social time (such as accidental injuries) might result from human carelessness, and still others (such as diseases and disasters) have no human cause at all. People suffer diverse reversals of fortune that are no fault of their own—or anyone else's. But they still cause conflict.

Death, for example, is an unavoidable event that is both sociological and biological. It destroys relationships, possibly redistributes wealth, and rearranges social space in other respects. And all deaths are not equal: They differ in their sociological significance. For instance, the death of someone with many close relationships and responsibilities is a greater movement of social time than the death of someone who is isolated and poor. The former therefore causes more conflict than the latter.

Some deaths cause more deaths. In the Suku tribe of Congo, a single killing might ignite a "chain of killings" (known as *kembi*). When someone in clan A kills someone in clan B, members of clan B might kill someone in clan C, whose members then kill someone in clan D, who kill someone in clan E, and so on—the killings "extending" into "the surrounding social universe" until they "disappear over the horizon."[36] A related phenomenon (called "running amok") occurs in parts of Southeast Asia: After suffering a romantic rejection, gambling loss, or other reversal of fortune, a man might grab a machete or other weapon and indiscriminately attack people in a public place.[37] In a similar scenario (called *juramentado*) in the southern Philippines, a Muslim man might attack a crowd of Christian strangers completely unrelated to his problem.[38] Movements of social time in modern societies sometimes have similar results, including running amok. In a 1984 case in California known as the "McDonald's Massacre," for example, a man who had recently lost his job walked into a McDonald's restaurant and shot forty people, killing twenty-one.[39]

Movements of social time also cause suicide. Recall, for instance, the California man who killed himself (after killing others) immediately after his wife ended their marriage. Movements of social time cause predatory crime such as rape and robbery as well.[40] A teenager might thus steal something, rob someone, or join a gang and begin participating in killings and other crime after losing a parent or failing in school.[41] Or a man might commit a theft such as embezzlement after suffering a financial loss from a bad investment or stock market crash. Some movements of social time may be difficult to observe, but it is not difficult to see their consequences.

If you wish to prevent conflict, you must prevent movements of social time. But if you cannot prevent a movement of social time that is likely to cause a conflict, you can at least anticipate and prepare for the consequences. And if you wish to initiate a major movement of social time (such as leaving your spouse, firing your employee, or replacing your religion), you should know that it is likely to cause trouble, possibly even violence. Social time is dangerous, and you must handle it with care.

RIGHT AND WRONG

Morality includes all rules of conduct—what sociologists call "norms."[42] Many philosophers and others have tried to understand the origin of morality: Why is anything considered wrong or bad or improper? Some say morality is arbitrary, without any rational basis, or that it derives from tradition or religion and has no other justification. Others say it merely reflects subjective opinions or emotional reactions such as disapproval, disgust, and indignation.[43] Still others say it prohibits whatever is harmful, though what is harmful might also be a matter of opinion.[44] But the answer is actually a matter of fact, entirely observable: *The origin of morality is the movement of social time.*[45]

The theory of moral time explains what rules of conduct define as wrong: What is wrong is always a movement of social time. For example, rape is wrong because it is a radical seizure of intimacy—a movement of relational time. Desertion is wrong because it is a radical reduction of intimacy—a movement of relational time as well. Killing is wrong because it is a radical and multidimensional movement of social time—relational, vertical, and cultural at once. Morality is not arbitrary, nor is it merely a matter of opinion or emotion. It has a social logic: It forbids the movement of social time.[46] The fundamental norm is to preserve the shape of social space, and every moral judgment judges social time itself.[47]

Moral rights imply a duty not to alter social space.[48] Relational rights protect relational space, and vertical and cultural rights protect vertical and cultural space.

My right to privacy protects me from invasions by you, and implies that you have a duty to keep your distance and to leave me alone. My right to property protects my wealth, and implies that you have a duty not to steal or damage or otherwise molest whatever I possess. My right to freedom of expression protects my culture, and implies that you have a duty to be tolerant.

Morality does not forbid every movement of social time, but everything morality forbids is a movement of social time. The movement of social time makes immorality immoral, crime criminal, and rudeness rude. The theory of moral time thus explains such prohibitions and prescriptions as the Ten Commandments of the Bible and the Sharia law of Islam; the legal codes of ancient Babylonia, classical India, dynastic China, and the Germanic and Celtic tribes of early Europe; the taboos and customs of tribal societies in Africa, Asia, Oceania, and the Americas; the criminal and other laws of the modern world; the rules and regulations of organizations; the expectations of families, friends, and strangers—every standard by which anyone judges anyone else's conduct. Everywhere morality forbids the same movements of social time, including too much or too little intimacy, too much or too little inequality, and too much or too little diversity. In this sense, morality is universal.

Yet the precise nature of morality differs from one place to another and changes over time.[49] People with different social locations in different historical periods defend different rights and impose different duties. Whereas rights to privacy, property, and freedom of expression are important in a modern society such as the United States, for instance, those rights have little or no relevance in a simple tribe with little or no privacy, property, or diversity. What is too much intimacy in a modern society might likewise be normal in a simple tribe, and what is too much inequality or diversity in a simple tribe might be normal in a modern society. We shall see that the movement of social time varies with the shape of social space, and that morality varies accordingly.

LAW

Law forbids various movements of social time, but the handling of legal cases does not merely depend on what is written in the formal law. It also depends on the sociological reality of the cases, including the actual movement of social time entailed by each. The formal law of modern societies ignores the sociological reality of the cases, however, and so does the ideal of equality before the law: that like cases should be handled in like fashion. Justice is not actually blind, however, nor do the scales of justice ignore the sociological reality of the cases. Equality before the law is a legal fiction, and so is the rule of law itself.[50]

Formal law ignores the sociological reality of particular cases of crime and other illegality. It defines each rape only with the technical elements of the crime such as sexual intercourse and a lack of consent, for example, while it ignores who rapes whom. Yet because stranger rapes are greater movements of social time than spousal or other intimate rapes (where closeness was already present), stranger rapes attract more punishment than intimate rapes.[51] Formal law similarly defines homicide only according to the technical elements of the crime such as the killer's malice and deliberation prior to the killing, while it ignores who kills whom. Yet because killings of prominent citizens with many responsibilities are greater movements of social time than killings of homeless people who live by scavenging or charity, the former attract more punishment than the latter.[52] Punishment thus corresponds to the movement of social time entailed by each crime.

The ideal of equality before the law also ignores the sociological reality of punishment and other remedies. Whereas a prison term for someone who kills a fellow family member (such as a spouse) is technically the same as a prison term for a stranger who kills the family member, for instance, the punishment of each is a different movement of social time. One difference is that the imprisonment of the killer of a family member removes a second family member from the same family, while the imprisonment of a stranger for killing the same person does not. Yet family killings attract less severity than stranger killings.[53] A prison term for a prominent citizen with many responsibilities similarly entails a different movement of social time (such as a greater loss of income and other forms of social status) than the same punishment for someone such as a homeless person at the bottom of society, and crimes by prominent citizens with many responsibilities receive less punishment than the same crimes by those at the bottom of society.[54]

The ideal of equality before the law says that like cases should be handled in like fashion, then, but the ideal does not describe the reality: *Like cases are treated in like fashion only when the cases entail the same movements of social time.* Law is relative, not universal. It varies with the movement of social time.[55]

DISLIKE

But most clashes of right and wrong do not involve law. They are part of everyday life, and arise whenever anyone does anything that someone else dislikes. Many offenders are not even aware of the hostility their behavior attracts. Gossip is a common feature of everyday life, for example, yet by nature it is secret, unknown to those whose reputations it might tarnish. So is the chronic complaining ("griping" and "whining") found in some walks of life. Others simply reduce contact or conversation with those they dislike. In any case, the source of their hostility is always the same: *What everyone dislikes is the movement of social time.*

Because social time usually moves in small steps, most dislike is mild. But whether we regard these little movements of social time as matters of bad manners, bad judgment, or bad character, they continually damage our relationships as we travel the social universe. Some people get too close with "nosy" questions about our personal lives or talk too much about themselves (overintimacy). Others do not display enough interest in us or do not return our favors or thank us for our kindnesses (underintimacy). We call them vulgar or selfish, "egotistical" or "cold," ungrateful or uncivilized. Another is arrogant or "heavy-handed" or has a "big head" and seems to think he is "better" than us (overstratification). Another is a "loser" who is lazy and does poorly at everything (understratification). Still another has peculiar ideas (overdiversity) or lacks tolerance of anyone who is different (underdiversity). Some repeatedly commit these little crimes, and we dislike them intensely.

People sometimes express their dislike for others by accusing them of wrong-doing that never even happened. After suffering a loss (such as being fired or experiencing a financial reversal), for example, the losers might gossip or grumble about being betrayed ("stabbed in the back") or otherwise victimized, when the loss actually resulted from their own misconduct, incompetence, lack of effort, or something else unconnected to those they criticize. Or they might blame their loss on "crooks" and "thieves" on "Wall Street" or somewhere else far away, when the real cause was their own bad judgment, if it was anyone's fault at all.

Some also attribute bad motives (such as greed or selfishness) to people who have actually behaved in a completely acceptable or even admirable fashion. When an associate achieves more than they do, for instance, they might secretly condemn the achiever for being a "social climber" or "careerist" or an otherwise unsavory or self-interested person who cares only about getting ahead or making money and who will do anything to succeed. Others similarly accuse successful political figures or others who acquire authority of doing whatever is necessary to gain power, even though it is impossible to know whether the accusations are true.[56] People even attribute bad motives to entire groups. For example, some say that Jews and Americans are successful only because they are power hungry and greedy and willing to use any means (including cheating and lying) to get what they want.[57] But the real cause of the dislike is at least partly that Jews and Americans have been *too* successful—which we shall see is a cause of conflict everywhere. In each case the cause of dislike is the same: the movement of social time.

VIRTUE

Virtue is the opposite of what we dislike: It is what we admire. Philosophers have long distinguished virtue from mere conformity to moral rules.[58] Virtue pertains to ideals, to being what we should be instead of merely *not* doing what is prohibited. It pertains to character instead of misbehavior. But exactly what is the sociological nature of virtue? Who is the ideal person? It is the one who best preserves and defends the shape of social space: *Virtue minimizes the movement of social time.*

Look at the many virtues: integrity, generosity, responsibility, loyalty, modesty, friendliness, politeness, helpfulness, respectfulness, trustworthiness, prudence, reverence, tolerance, justice, courage, bravery. The same traits are celebrated everywhere.[59] We all praise those who display these characteristics, and eulogize them when they die.[60] Yet all virtues have the same sociological significance: They maintain the shape of social space.[61]

For example, loyalty and friendliness are relational virtues that preserve the closeness of relationships. Respectfulness and modesty are vertical virtues that preserve the distribution of social status. Reverence is a cultural virtue that preserves whatever is sacred. Virtuous people do not get too close to those who are distant or too far from those who are close. They achieve as much as anyone else, but not significantly more or less. They conform to a golden mean between too much and too little of anything.[62]

Virtue sometimes requires actively doing what is best—whatever is needed to maintain the shape of social space. Virtuous people defend their group and culture, possibly with bravery and self-sacrifice. They defer to their superiors, but defend their own social position as well, including their honor and respectability. They are polite and pleasant, kind and generous. They help those in need. They are devout. For all these reasons, they are admirable. They have character. And we like them.

INJUSTICE

A false accusation blames someone for something that never happened.[63] Everyone considers false accusations unjust, especially when those accused are killed or otherwise punished. Why then do these accusations occur? Why would anyone claim that someone did something that never even happened? The answer again is social time: *False accusations result from movements of social time that are not themselves defined as wrong.*

Recall that some movements of social time are misfortunes of everyday life, others are increases of cultural diversity, and still others are instances of achievement or good fortune. Although such events are not regarded as immoral or otherwise wrong in themselves, all sometimes cause false accusations. And they dramatically illustrate the moral nature of social time.[64]

People in many societies make false accusations of witchcraft, for example, and kill the alleged witch. An innocent person might thus be accused of using witchcraft to cause a misfortune such as an injury or disease—when the misfortune is actually what causes the accusation. Christians have likewise made various false accusations against Jews, leading to countless killings and other forms of anti-Jewish hostility throughout much of European history. In medieval Europe during the great epidemic known as the Black Death, for instance, many Christians accused Jews of poisoning their wells to spread the disease, massacred thousands, and forced thousands more to flee to other countries. Some tribal people similarly blame epidemics on the black magic of weaker tribes.

Religious and other cultural clashes also lead to false accusations, illustrated by various allegations of sexual promiscuity against members of Christian sects in medieval Europe and Christian missionaries in nineteenth-century China. Cultural differences between Christians and Jews have contributed to false accusations against Jews as well, including allegations that they kidnapped, crucified, and consumed the blood of Christian children—resulting in numerous executions and massacres of Jews across much of Europe. Twentieth-century German leaders falsely accused Jews of various evils, such as a conspiracy to start World War II and to exterminate the German population, and killed millions.[65]

Another cause of false accusations is too much success. People in some tribal societies accuse prosperous people of using witchcraft and other black magic to attain their wealth, for example, when their increase of wealth is what actually causes the accusations.[66] The rise of modern America to a position of global domination in the late twentieth century attracted many false accusations too, including a claim by radical Muslims that the United States was leading a crusade against the entire Islamic world—which justified mass killings of American and other Western civilians.[67] But false accusations always make sociological sense: They result from movements of social time that are not wrong in themselves.

The following chapters elaborate the theory of moral time and show how it explains various forms of conflict across the world and over the centuries. Part I pertains to relational time, Part II to vertical time, and Part III to cultural time. The chapters apply the theory to such topics as crime of various kinds, incest and other sexual immorality, violence, secrecy, blasphemy, lying, witchcraft, rudeness, rebellion, desertion, exhibitionism, racism, anti-Semitism, conservatism, honor, heresy, homosexuality, obscenity, infidelity, creativity, and insanity. The book concludes with a theory that explains the evolution of conflict and morality from the tribal to the modern age and beyond.

I | Relational Time

2 | Overintimacy

Intimacy is a relational distance: a degree of participation in the life of someone else.[1] How much contact do people have? How many activities do they share? How long have they done so? People are also more or less intimate with nonhumans, such as animals and objects. And they are more or less intimate with themselves: How much time do they spend alone? What do they do alone?[2]

Intimacy constantly fluctuates—gradually or suddenly, in small or large steps. I increase my intimacy with you when I enter more of your life or reveal more of my life to you, and I decrease my intimacy with you when I reduce contact or conceal more of my life from you. Any such change is a movement of *relational time*: the dynamic dimension of relational space. A decrease of relational distance is *overintimacy*, and an increase is *underintimacy*.

Relational distance is two-directional: I might be closer to you than are you to me.[3] I might learn more about your life than you learn about mine, or I might reveal more of my life to you than you reveal to me. And intimacy is a zero-sum game: An increase of closeness with one person reduces it with another. A man who begins an extramarital romance thereby reduces his closeness to his wife, and any other romance similarly reduces the closeness of each partner to others. According to a study in modern England, for example, people who begin romantic relationships lose an average of two close friendships with others.[4] Those who end romances or friendships become closer to others, however, and those with fewer friends have closer friendships than those with more.[5] People with fewer close relationships are also closer to themselves.

Moreover, intimacy varies with its location and direction in social space. For instance, downward intimacy (with a social inferior) is greater than upward intimacy (with a social superior). When blacks were a lower caste in the American South, whites might freely ask blacks personal questions, such as where they lived or whether they were married, but blacks who asked whites similar questions were considered too "familiar."[6] A marriage might likewise be closer in one direction than the other. In the highly patriarchal Pashtun tribe of Pakistan and Afghanistan, for example, a husband is able to learn a great deal about his wife's daily life (partly because she is usually confined to their home), but she learns little about his, and must not even ask.[7]

Although people commonly consider intimacy a positive feature of human life, increases of intimacy cause trouble. And the greater and faster these increases occur, the more trouble they cause:

Conflict is a direct function of overintimacy.

People regard some intimacy as dirty and disgusting.[8] Some, such as rape or incest, is criminal. Public kissing is a crime in parts of the Muslim world. And some intimacy, such as touching or staring, might be impolite.

Intimacy includes both involvement and exposure. Whereas involvement occurs when we enter someone's life, exposure occurs when we reveal our lives to someone else. My involvement in you increases my closeness to you, while my exposure to you increases your closeness to me. Too much of the former is *overinvolvement*, and too much of the latter is *overexposure*.

OVERINVOLVEMENT

Too much involvement is a trespass, and might include anything from an overly personal question to a taboo sexual relationship, a burglary, a rape, or an invasion.[9] All such movements of relational time cause conflict: *Conflict is a direct function of overinvolvement.*

Some tribes kill any stranger who enters their territory.[10] Arctic Eskimos (also known as Inuit) have an "obstinate and hostile suspicion of strangers," for example, and any unknown individual who approaches an Eskimo camp without an invitation risks attack.[11] One nation's intrusion into another's territory might cause a war, and a nation's occupation of another nation might cause other violence, such as sabotage, assassinations, or terrorism.[12]

Because all physical contact is a form of involvement, it is always a form of intimacy as well. Even violence is a form of intimacy, and all the more when it inflicts pain.[13] Spanking a child is a form of intimacy and so is slapping a wife, beating a prisoner, or whipping a slave. So is torture, which might include additional intimacy, such as stripping or raping the prisoner.[14]

RAPE AS RELATIONAL TIME

Why does rape cause conflict? Rape causes conflict because it is a radical and rapid movement of relational time, a seizure of closeness: sex by force. It is an extreme case of overintimacy. It might be painful and injurious as well. Yet it is a matter of degree: The more relational distance a rape crosses and collapses, the greater it is. And the greater the rape, the more conflict it causes.

A rape between strangers is a greater movement of relational time than a rape between intimates such as spouses or friends—and is therefore worse: It causes more conflict, legal and otherwise. In modern America, for example, the rape of a stranger is more likely to result in legal action, a conviction, and a severe punishment.[15] The rape of someone who has never been sexually intimate with anyone (such as a virgin, child, or nun) is all the worse. In medieval England the punishment for raping a stranger (especially a virgin) might be castration, blinding, or death.[16] In Renaissance Venice the rape of a prepubescent girl doubled the punishment, and the rape of a nun was also worse.[17] And because a married woman has an exclusive sexual relationship with her husband, the rape of a married woman by someone other than her husband received "considerably more" punishment than the rape of an unmarried woman.[18] In colonial America the rape of a married or engaged woman or a girl under the age of ten might be death.[19] But in many societies the rape of one's own wife is not even a crime.[20]

An upward rape (of a superior) is worse than a lateral or downward rape (of an equal or inferior).[21] Among the Burgundians of early Europe, for instance, a slave who raped a free woman was killed, but a slave who raped another slave received only a flogging (150 blows of a stick).[22] In colonial North Carolina a black slave convicted of raping a white woman might receive a harsher punishment than a white ever received for anything. For example, one court hanged two slaves convicted of raping a white woman, severed their heads, displayed the head of one at the fork of a road, and placed the other's on the end of a pole while his body was burned.[23] Later, during racial segregation in the American South, blacks who raped whites were more likely to be executed than blacks who raped blacks or whites who raped whites or blacks.[24] In late nineteenth- and early twentieth-century America, whites might lynch a black for raping a white woman, possibly adding torture and mutilation (such as castration) as part of the punishment.[25] In Springfield, Illinois, in 1908, white crowds attacked numerous blacks (killing two) and burned black-owned homes after a white woman reported being raped by a black man.[26]

People in other places and times handle rape with other forms of social control. The ancient Assyrians allowed a raped virgin's father to rape the rapist's wife.[27] The Germanic tribes of early Europe required the rapist to pay compensation to the victim's husband, father, or (if the victim was a slave) owner.[28] The Ifugao of the Philippines require a married man who rapes a married woman to pay compensation to her husband, his kin, the victim, her kin, and (because the rape is a form of adultery) to his own wife.[29] The Gusii of Kenya attack and kill the rapist and any of his clansmen they can find.[30] A rape between New Guinea tribes might cause a war.[31]

Some victims handle the rapist themselves. In one Chinese case during the Qing Dynasty (1644-1912), a servant bit off her master's tongue when he tried to rape her.[32] Another Chinese woman cut off the rapist's penis, causing him to bleed to death.[33] In North America, Kiowa Indian women once ambushed a known rapist (who had victimized some of them), held him to the ground, pressed their genitals to his face, and spread menstrual blood over his mouth (causing him to vomit).[34]

But nothing can undo a rape. It is an irreversible movement of relational time that collapses the relational space between those involved, stigmatizes the victim, and changes her relationship with others. And the greater the social distance it crosses, the greater is the damage. Just as a stranger rape or upward rape is worse, so is rape by a cultural outsider or by a group ("gang rape").

Blame might also fall on the victim. The ancient Babylonian Code of Hammurabi equated a married woman's rape with adultery and applied the same penalty: Both parties were bound and thrown into a river to drown.[35] In modern Egypt, Bedouin tribesmen might still kill both parties.[36] Modern Pakistani courts might sentence a rape victim to a public whipping or imprisonment (if no eyewitnesses can prove her lack of consent), and police officers might rape her at the police station as a further degradation.[37] In Imperial China raped virgins were expected to commit suicide.[38]

Other victims of rape suffer social death.[39] In ancient Athens, for example, a raped woman had "no opportunity to proclaim her innocence," and her husband was "legally compelled" to divorce her. She became a social outcast, prohibited from wearing jewelry and participating in public ceremonies, and she could rarely find another husband.[40] An American high school student described how being raped changed her life: "None of the girls were allowed to have me in their homes, and the boys used to stare at me on the street when I walked to school." In modern societies such as the United States, "one of the victim's main concerns may be whether people will find out what has happened."[41] Most victims do not call the police, and some actively pretend that the rape did not even occur (such as by continuing whatever they were doing before the attack).[42] Although involuntary, then, the intimacy of rape is still a disgrace.[43]

FILTHY INVOLVEMENTS

Some intimacy is only taboo in particular relationships, such as between close relatives (incest), members of the same gender (homosexuality), married people and others (adultery), unmarried couples (fornication), authorities and subordinates, professionals and clients, buyers and sellers (prostitution), adults and children, people and animals (bestiality), and people and themselves (masturbation). Intimacy in the wrong relationship is sometimes condemned as "filthy," "dirty," or "unnatural"—not even human.[44]

Consider incest:

> The incest taboo is universal in human culture. Though no single definition of the taboo applies among all peoples, no known culture permits unrestricted sexual union among kin. Almost all cultures prohibit intercourse and marriage within what is known as the nuclear family, that is, between parents and children [or] brothers and sisters. The particular forms of the incest taboo, the types of behavior forbidden, the range of persons to whom the prohibition applies, and the punishments that attend its violation vary endlessly from one society to another. What is common to most cultures, however, is the seriousness with which the taboo is regarded. It is commonly understood as a fundamental rule of social order.[45]

Many social scientists (especially anthropologists) have tried to understand why incest is so widely prohibited: "Explaining the incest taboo has been a central preoccupation of anthropology for the past hundred years."[46] But the incest taboo is not a mystery, nor is its universality. Something is overintimate everywhere, and incest is simply a form of overintimacy in a family. Although every family is intimate to some degree, every family also limits the intimacy it allows. And incest is just too much.

In many societies people regard homosexuality ("being gay") as filthy and unnatural. The Roman emperor Justinian said it caused earthquakes.[47] In seventeenth-century Massachusetts, where homosexuality was known as "sodomy" and said to be "contrary to the very light of nature," it was punishable by death. Elsewhere homosexuals have been burned at the stake.[48] But the taboo against homosexuality is not a mystery either: It simply prohibits too much intimacy within a gender.

In Western countries male homosexuality has always attracted more hostility than female homosexuality ("lesbianism").[49] In England as recently as the mid-twentieth century, for instance, male homosexuality was a crime while female homosexuality was not.[50] The reason is that male homosexuality is often more overintimate than female homosexuality: Women normally share more of their lives and feelings with each other and have more physical contact of an affectionate nature—a difference between the genders that has apparently increased in recent centuries.[51] In addition, fewer homosexual women than homosexual men have sexual relations with strangers, which is a greater movement of relational time than sexual relations with a friend.[52] Because male homosexuality commonly entails more overintimacy than female homosexuality, then, it causes more conflict.

In the Netherlands the first wave of criminal trials for male homosexuality began in 1730, but the prosecution of female homosexuality came somewhat later, resulted in less severity, and was relatively rare.[53] Criminal cases against male homosexuals have also been more frequent in modern America. So have violent attacks.[54] In one case at the University of Virginia in 2009, for example, five young men "yelled homophobic slurs" at two young men and then physically attacked them—because they were holding hands while walking late at night.[55] Negative nicknames for male homosexuals (such as "fairy" or "cocksucker") are likewise more numerous and "virulent and contemptuous" than those for female homosexuals (such as "dyke" or "butch").[56] Yet lesbians may encounter considerable hostility as well, such as when a California woman who "lived openly with a female partner" (and had a "gay pride" sticker on her car) was "jumped by four men, taunted for being a lesbian, repeatedly raped, and left naked outside an abandoned apartment building."[57]

Some forms of homosexuality are taboo in all societies, but other forms may be permissible or even obligatory.[58] Although male homosexuality is "universal" in the tribes of southwestern New Guinea and common in 10 to 20 percent of other New Guinea tribes, for example, every tribe that allows or encourages some forms of male intimacy prohibits others.[59] In one tribe men thus introduce all boys to homosexual fellatio (oral intercourse) at about the age of eight during their initiation into adulthood, but who fellates whom is strictly regulated: Initiates may serve only as fellators, and later they may only be fellated—without exception. All other homosexual behavior is taboo, and some is particularly so. For instance, "the idea of fellatio with one's father or biological brothers is completely abhorrent and not discussed," and "ideally all male kin, including cross-cousins, are taboo." And a man who fellates anyone after he is married is considered "crazy."[60]

In ancient Greece it was permissible for an older man to have a sexual relationship with a young man or boy; but their intimacy could not extend beyond intercrural copulation (in which the older man inserted his penis between the younger person's thighs), and could not occur at all with a slave.[61] Ancient Romans similarly allowed some sexual intimacy between a man and his male slave, but only if the master was the active partner.[62] In late Imperial China a young man caught being the passive partner in a homosexual relationship might commit suicide (apparently to avoid the "unbearable disgrace" of being labeled a male prostitute).[63] Male homosexuality of any kind is illegal everywhere in modern Africa, and is sometimes classified as an "unnatural act" or an act "against the order of nature" and punished with a prison term or death.[64] In modern Iraq Muslim clerics commonly make public statements condemning male homosexuals (known as "puppies"), and each month at least one male homosexual is killed by private citizens (sometimes members of his own family).[65]

Fornication is another crime in the Islamic world. The Koran prescribes a beating of "a hundred stripes" for both offenders, but modern Muslims sometimes kill one or both. The young woman's father or another male relative is the usual one to administer the execution—known as "cleaning up the filth" in Turkey. Sometimes, however, the woman's relatives accuse her lover of rape and kill him instead.[66] Because modern Israeli law does not allow these killings, Bedouin Arabs living in Israel sometimes kill the young woman by throwing her in a well to make her death appear to be an accident or suicide.[67]

Religions sometimes impose a celibacy rule on their clergy, prohibiting them from engaging in all sexual behavior. For example, Buddhist monks and nuns in Southeast Asia who engage in sexual behavior face automatic and permanent excommunication (called "defeat"): "As a man who has been beheaded cannot live with only a body, so a monk who has had sexual intercourse is not a monk anymore."[68] Nor may a monk talk to a woman in private without a third party present, spend a night in a house where a woman lives (whether others are present or not), or walk in the street with an otherwise unaccompanied woman. Nuns must avoid similar forms of closeness with men.[69] Although Roman Catholic priests and nuns also have a celibacy rule, in the twentieth and early twenty-first centuries numerous men accused priests in various countries (including the United States, Ireland, Germany, Austria, and Australia) of having had sexual relations with them when they were boys. Some of the priests resigned or committed suicide when the allegations surfaced, and others were transferred, expelled from the priesthood, or imprisoned.[70]

Too much intimacy between superiors and inferiors is often taboo. In traditional India, for instance, members of different castes cannot marry or engage in other intimacy. For a Brahmin (a member of the highest caste) to marry anyone of lower caste is nearly unthinkable ("almost outside the range of possibilities") and would result in permanent expulsion from the caste ("outcasteing").[71] A Brahmin who engages in any form of intimacy (such as eating food) with an Untouchable (a member of the lowest caste) also risks expulsion. So does a Brahmin widow who gives birth to a child, since it is conceivable that her lover was someone of lower caste: "Who knows who really fathered a Brahmin widow's illegitimate child?"[72]

Humans may likewise be too intimate with nonhumans. Such is the crime of bestiality (sexual intercourse with an animal). The Bible classifies bestiality as an "abomination" punishable by death, and Westerners have long condemned it as a violation of "the natural order of the universe."[73] Early Europeans and Americans considered it too disgusting even to mention ("a crime not to be named.")[74] In seventeenth- and eighteenth-century Sweden, where farm animals were considered part of the women's world that was closed to men, it was "improper" for a man even to enter a cowshed without good reason or to milk a cow or other animal (which required "contact with a female animal's intimate parts").[75] All the worse was sexual intercourse with an animal (usually a cow or mare, but possibly a pig, sheep, or dog)—a criminal offense that resulted in six hundred to seven hundred executions in the 1600s and 1700s (25 to 35 percent of all Swedish executions in those years) and numerous lesser punishments such as floggings and forced labor.[76] And because sexual intercourse with a human made a female animal unclean and unfit for further human contact (even as food or milk), they also executed the animal.[77]

People may be too intimate with themselves as well. The Church of medieval Europe called masturbation a "vice against nature."[78] Eighteenth- and nineteenth-century English authorities called it a "filthiness forbidden by God," "defilement by hand," "self-pollution," "self-abuse," and "onanism" (alluding to the "sin of Onan" in the Bible).[79] Physicians diagnosed it as "masturbatory insanity," and prescribed treatments such as a wire through the foreskin of the penis to interfere with erection and surgery to remove the clitoris.[80] And although hostility to masturbation has declined with modernization, it still carries "derogatory associations" in the Western world. The English slang term "wanker" for a male masturbator continues to be an "insult," for instance, as is "jack-off" in the United States.[81] Some also consider their own masturbation a form of immorality or mental illness. Even famous philosopher Ludwig Wittgenstein expressed concern in his journal about his involvement with himself: "Masturbated last night. Pangs of conscience. . . . How bad is it? I don't know."[82]

Yet in modern America masturbation is sometimes recommended as beneficial to mental health, happiness, and personal development.[83] The recent acceptance of masturbation reflects the increasing intimacy of people with themselves, including the growing frequency of living alone, spending time alone, and engaging in various activities alone (see "Postmodern Time" in chapter 8). For people already so close to themselves in other respects, sexual closeness with themselves is a relatively minor movement of relational time.

THE CRIME OF TOUCHING

Other touching is also deviant. For example, early Germanic legal codes required a man to pay compensation (in Roman silver coins called *denarii*) for touching any woman without her permission and, as one Frankish code illustrates, the required payment increased with the intimacy of the touch:

1. If any free man touches the hand or finger of a free woman, he shall be liable to pay 600 *denarii*. . . .
2. If he touches her arm, he shall be liable to pay 1,200 *denarii*. . . .
3. If he puts a hand above her elbow, he shall be liable to pay 1,400 *denarii*. . . .
4. If indeed he touches her breast, he shall be liable to pay 1,800 *denarii*.

Other codes required a single payment for all cases of "indecent groping" but doubled it for removing a woman's head covering ("bonnet-snatching"), disturbing her hair, or raising her dress above her knee ("pulling up clothes").[84]

The vertical location of touching is relevant as well. Relational distances are greater at higher elevations, among social superiors, so touching decreases as social status increases. At one time in Germany, for instance, a "gentleman" such as a military officer who touched a man of his own rank might be challenged to a duel with swords or pistols. A slap in the face made a duel virtually automatic, as did the statement, "Consider yourself slapped!"[85] Inferiors such as children more freely touch one another. In a study of an American daycare center, for example, sociologist M. P. Baumgartner found that children continually engage in physical contact, including "chronic petty or low grade violence" such as "hitting, kicking, or shoving," hair-pulling and other forms of coercion, and "pinching, biting, and punching."[86]

And upward touching is worse than downward touching.[87] For example, touching the queen of England is a "breach of protocol."[88] In traditional Hawaii even the shadow of a commoner could not touch a chief or his possessions, nor could a commoner walk on ground where a chief had recently walked.[89] In traditional India touching a Brahmin (whether intentionally or accidentally) is a serious offense by anyone, but especially an Untouchable. In some respects a Brahmin is untouchable to himself as well: He defiles himself if he touches his own mouth or saliva, for instance, and must therefore toss food into his mouth instead of putting it into his mouth by hand or biting it from a larger piece, must pour liquids into his mouth instead of sipping from a cup, and must smoke cigarettes through his hand so they do not touch his lips. He must also avoid contact with his own bodily fluids, such as his own blood and waste matter. To prevent his urine from splashing on himself, he must squat to urinate.[90]

Untouchables are too low to touch or be touched by anyone of higher caste. Food touched by an Untouchable is inedible by anyone of higher caste, and an Untouchable's social filth lingers on any object (such as a piece of cloth or a cooking pot) long after he or she touches it. A Brahmin must not hold a rope or other object at the same time as an Untouchable, nor stand on straw covering the floor of a cowshed at the same time as an Untouchable. To give an object to someone of higher caste, an Untouchable must place it on the ground to be picked up, so that they do not touch it at the same time.[91] To punish an Untouchable student, a teacher of higher caste must throw something at the offender instead of making physical contact. To prevent defilement of the ground on which they walk, Untouchables scavenging in the countryside must wear a pot suspended from their neck to spit, and drag a tree branch behind them to erase their footprints. Even their shadows are untouchable.[92] Although the Indian Untouchable is an extreme case, someone or something is untouchable everywhere.

THE CRIME OF LOOKING

Mere looking is another form of involvement that can be too intimate. Philosopher Alison Brown may exaggerate a bit when she suggests that the eyes "have more unspoken taboos associated with them" than any other part of the human body.[93]

But in any case, like taboos against touching, the nature of ocular taboos depends on the social elevation of those involved: Upward looking (at a superior) is worse than downward looking (at an inferior).

Looking at a superior is sometimes a serious crime. Commoners were once prohibited from looking at the king of Tonkin (part of Vietnam) in a public place, for example, and anyone who did so was killed on the spot. The sultan of Wadai (part of Chad) spoke from behind a curtain, and no one but intimates could look at his face. Looking at monarchs eating or drinking might also be punishable by death. On the Polynesian island of Tonga, "all the people turned their backs" when the king ate a meal. Dinner guests of the king of Persia ate in an adjoining room where "he could see them through a curtain on the door but they could not see him."[94] And before visiting the king of modern Spain, world-renowned painter Pablo Picasso had to learn how to back away from the king "without ever looking him in the eye."[95]

Other looking may also be too intimate. "Peeping Toms" are too intimate when they secretly look at women undressing or couples engaging in sexual relations behind closed doors.[96] Peeping is a crime in modern societies such as the United States, and some mental health experts consider it a symptom of a mental illness called "voyeurism" or "scopophilia."[97] In rural Andalusia (in southern Spain), anthropologist David Gilmore found that men sometimes form groups expressly to peep at women at night, though they risk arrest for doing so. Any other gazing at a woman (except by a close relative) is also too intimate. As Gilmore comments, in Andalusia the eye is "equivalent to the penis which penetrates, and at the same time to the vagina which is penetrated," and for this reason some staring is "akin to ocular rape"—and may provoke violence by any man closely associated with the woman.[98] In Muslim societies where women must cover their bodies and faces in public, looking at a woman is all the worse.[99]

Staring by Australian Aborigines may lead to violence between both women and men. One woman thus told an anthropologist that she attacked another woman entirely "because she was looking at" her. Even when they invite someone for a visit, Aborigines carefully "look away" when the visitor arrives—to prevent possible trouble.[100] Elsewhere people avoid looking at those with whom they have a particular relationship. Among the Piaroa Indians of Venezuela, for instance, brothers and sisters "refrain from looking one another in the eye when speaking with one another," and should "ignore one another's presence" if they happen to be physically close.[101]

Modern Japanese resent ocular intrusions by strangers and "go to great lengths to avoid eye contact" in public places. Those in criminal gangs (*yakuza*) are especially sensitive and have been known to attack anyone who looks at them too long or too closely. Even Japanese police officers avoid staring at anyone on the street and point their flashlights at people as little as possible.[102]

Some guards in American prisons punish inmates who look at them too intently—known as "eyeballing."[103] And when ethnic groups have differing levels of ocular intimacy, members of one group may inadvertently offend those of another by looking at them. In modern America, for instance, urban African Americans sometimes complain about what they regard as invasive looking by whites such as Italian Americans: "Why they gotta eyeball everybody?"[104] Mexican Americans likewise take offense at long stares ("bad looks"), especially by inferiors.[105] Such intrusions can lead to violence.[106]

SOCIAL CONTAMINATION

People separated by more vertical or cultural distance are also typically separated by more relational distance, and any increase of intimacy between them may cause trouble.[107] Castes (unequal groups with inherited membership) have a particularly high degree of relational separation ("segregation"), and higher castes commonly regard lower castes (especially those at the bottom) as morally inferior, dangerous, dirty, and otherwise disgusting, if not biologically inferior or even subhuman.[108] Mere friendliness between members of different castes may meet with disapproval, and greater closeness, such as sexual relations, may have violent consequences.

Japan has a lower caste known as the *burakumin*, whose ancestors are believed to have performed "unclean" work such as grave digging and butchering centuries ago. Many Japanese view all *burakumin* as "dirty, vulgar, smelly, untrustworthy, dangerous, treacherous, subhuman creatures" and think that male members of the caste have no testicles and only one rib. In earlier times *burakumin* were not permitted to eat, drink, or smoke near other Japanese, were required to walk on the edge of the road and remain in their hamlets at night, and could have no windows facing a road. Although their segregation has greatly decreased with modernization, some Japanese still oppose marriage or other forms of closeness with anyone descended from them.[109]

Jews were long a separate caste in Europe.[110] As early as the fourth century C.E., marriage between a Christian and a Jew was a criminal offense in Roman law—"the equivalent of adultery." Other laws later required considerable segregation of both Jews and Muslims. Beginning in the early thirteenth century, for example, Jews and

Muslims were required to wear distinctive clothing to prevent them from mingling invisibly with Christians. Sex was especially taboo. Some laws classified sexual intercourse between a Christian and a Jew as a form of bestiality, punishable by death. Both parties were often executed, possibly by burning at the stake or by drawing and quartering (pulling the limbs of the condemned apart by tying them to horses and spurring the animals in different directions).[111] Other punishments were also possible. In one fourteenth-century French town, for instance, a Jewish man convicted of having sexual intercourse with a Christian woman was castrated and his testicles displayed outside the royal palace. Jews punished sex and marriage with non-Jews as well.[112]

The degree of segregation between Christians and Jews increased for several centuries after the Middle Ages until their worlds were almost completely separate. Jews were confined to their own quarter (known as the "ghetto") in each city or town, and other regulations kept Christians and Jews apart in other ways. In the sixteenth century, for example, Pope Clement VIII announced rules prohibiting Christians from entering Jewish shops, houses, or synagogues; using Jewish physicians, midwives, or tutors; and borrowing money from Jews. Other rules prohibited Jews from visiting Christian prostitutes, talking to Christians after midnight, and teaching, employing, serving, or eating with Christians.[113] In one case in Barcelona, a Christian man even complained because a Jewish sewer ran beneath his neighborhood.[114] As late as the eighteenth century, the city of Berlin had a separate entrance gate for Jews—shared with cattle.[115]

Segregation between Christians and Jews declined in the eighteenth and nineteenth centuries but increased again in National Socialist (Nazi) Germany and its occupied territories in the 1930s and 40s. In 1935, for instance, the German government defined marriage or sexual intercourse between a Christian and Jew as a crime called "race defilement."[116] Jewish men were subject to prosecution and possibly execution for having sexual relations with Christian women. One Jewish man was imprisoned for kissing a Christian woman, another for having his stomach massaged by a Christian woman who was his physical therapist, and another for looking across the street at a fifteen-year-old Christian girl in the center of Frankfurt at 11 o'clock in the morning (which allegedly "had a clearly erotic basis"). But intimacy between Jewish men and Christian women was a more serious offense than intimacy between Christian men and Jewish women. In the former case the blame fell mainly on the Jewish man, while in the latter case it fell mainly on the Jewish woman. In one trial of a Christian man and a Jewish woman accused of having an intimate relationship, for example, the judge remarked that the woman was "a lascivious, morally depraved Jewess who used her unchecked sexual appetite and ruthlessness to acquire a strong influence over the defendant."[117]

The German government also announced various "anti-mixing ordinances" banning Jews from public places such as railway sleeping and dining cars, waiting rooms and restaurants in railway stations, and resorts, beaches, hospitals, and barbershops used by Germans. In addition, the ordinances prohibited "open friendliness" between Germans and Jews "as shown by conversation in the streets or visits to homes."[118] As a final separation, the Germans arrested, confined to concentration camps, and systematically killed nearly all the European Jews they could locate and capture—about two-thirds of the Jewish population (now known as the Holocaust or Shoah). German officer Heinrich Himmler, who planned and directed much of the extermination program, remarked that the Jews were "contaminating elements" who had to be removed for the sake of "cleanliness," and likened their destruction to the "de-lousing" of Europe.[119]

When racial segregation prevailed in the United States, whites and blacks regarded each other as morally if not biologically inferior.[120] Both especially discouraged sexual contact across the racial divide. Although whites tolerated white men who had sexual relations with black women, black men who had sexual relations with white women risked white violence. In turn, blacks discouraged intimacy with whites by black women. In one Southern town, for example, black men "organized a group that went around and beat up colored [black] women who had been most notorious in receiving white men, and drove some of them out of town."[121] During the same period, "anti-miscegenation laws" prohibited marriage between the races.[122] Other laws in the South (known as "Jim Crow laws") required separate schools, churches, hospitals, prisons, hotels, restaurants, swimming pools, public transportation, restrooms, drinking fountains, seating areas, cemeteries, and other facilities.[123] Decades after legal segregation, informal segregation still separated whites and blacks in some areas of life, and too much contact still caused conflict.

OVERINVOLVEMENT AS BAD MANNERS

Some intimacy is bad manners.[124] Rules of etiquette specify who may initiate a conversation with whom, when, where, and how, and what the subject may be. In modern life it is thus normally improper to initiate a conversation with a stranger walking in a public place—"inappropriate," if not "creepy" or frightening (though it might be acceptable to speak to strangers in other settings, such as in a bar or on an airplane).[125] Merely standing too close to another person may also be too intimate.[126] And because speaking distances sometimes differ across ethnic groups, members of one group may make members of another group uncomfortable when they have face-to-face encounters. For example, some Italian Americans complain that Puerto Rican Americans "stand painfully close" during conversations.[127]

It is likewise too intimate to say anything of a sexual or other personal nature to a casual acquaintance or stranger, or to "pry" into "delicate" subjects such as the marital or financial problems of another person.[128] The same applies to using someone's first name or other familiar form of address (such as "sweetheart," "honey," or "buddy"). The use of profanity should similarly be avoided, and interrupting a conversation or speaking too loudly or making other noise is criticized as "inconsiderate," "vulgar," or "uncouth." American college students complain about roommates who talk too loudly on the phone, for instance, or who play music too loudly when they are studying or trying to sleep.[129] Talking or laughing noisily in public or allowing children to do so elicits disapproval as well.[130] Still another form of trespass is listening to what one is not supposed to hear. One college student complained that her roommate listened to her phone conversations with her boyfriend ("eavesdropping"), for example, and (worse yet) sometimes commented on what she heard.[131] All such intrusions cause dislike and damage relationships. By contrast, we appreciate the "social skill" and "tact" of people who know how and when to keep their distance.[132]

Looking too closely at someone is still another form of discourtesy. Early American etiquette books thus instructed people never to stare at anyone, but always to display "civil inattention" toward anyone in a public place.[133] Nor should anyone look at anything that someone might not want others to see, such as a facial blemish or other physical imperfection: "The rule is imperative, that no one should see, or, if that is impossible, should seem to see, or to have seen, anything that another person would choose to have concealed."[134] Even in tribal societies where people have little privacy, they resent some intrusions. In one New Guinea tribe, for instance, a man "reacts violently to being observed by a woman, even his own wife, while defecating."[135] In a band of Bushmen in Botswana, where "daily life goes on in full view of the camp," it is improper to watch anyone having sexual relations: "Marital sex is carried on discreetly under a light blanket shared with the younger children around the family fire," and it is "bad manners for others to look."[136]

Too much involvement in oneself is also bad manners. In modern society, polite people do not touch themselves too intimately, put their fingers in their mouths, pick their teeth or noses, lick their fingers or hands, groom themselves, or even examine themselves too closely (except around those with whom they are already intimate). As one etiquette expert notes: "It is most unattractive to scratch one's head, or rub one's face or touch one's teeth, or to clean one's fingernails in public." A man should be especially careful to keep his distance from himself: "Men should never look in the mirror or comb their hair in public."[137]

Sociologist Erving Goffman observes that much behavior considered a symptom of mental illness is an extreme form of bad manners—a violation of "situational proprieties"—including various forms of overintimacy.[138] Too much self-involvement might be diagnosed as "narcissism" (a type of "neurosis"), for example, and talking to strangers on the street might be considered a form of "manic behavior" (a symptom of "manic-depressive" or "bipolar" disorder).[139]

Notice, then, that various forms of rudeness, such as staring, eavesdropping, asking overly personal questions, or picking one's teeth in public, belong to the same family as rape, burglary, masturbation, and military invasions. All are movements of relational time that cause conflict for the same reason: overinvolvement.

OVEREXPOSURE

Another form of intimacy is exposure: revealing our lives to someone else. It is always possible to reveal too much: *Conflict is a direct function of overexposure.*

Overexposure might pertain to anything normally unseen or unknown, including whatever someone would rather not see or know. One college student complained because a roommate sometimes "nonchalantly" appeared in a state of undress in front of her boyfriend, for example, and another was "extremely embarrassed and upset" because a roommate "regularly entertained" her boyfriend in an "openly sexual" fashion in their living room.[140]

Divulging a secret might also be a form of overexposure.[141] The Pueblo Indians of the American Southwest once executed those who revealed their secret rituals to outsiders: "A woman's woven belt was tied around the culprit's waist and the men pulled the belt until he was crushed to death—or 'until he was cut in two.' Then his head was cut off and tossed on top of a house."[142] Revealing a government secret in modern America is punishable by prison or (if treasonous) death. A professional who reveals information about a client (such as a medical patient) might face a lawsuit for "violation of trust."[143] Revealing a friend's secret might destroy the friendship.

NAKEDNESS AS RELATIONAL TIME

Nakedness is an overexposure of one's body. But what is too much exposure varies across social space. At one extreme are the Aran Islanders of Ireland who almost completely conceal their bodies virtually all the time, even from themselves. They "abhor" being seen undressed by anyone, including family members and medical professionals, and try to avoid seeing their own private parts as well. They do not undress to bathe, but wash only their "faces, necks, lower arms, hands, lower legs, and feet" (though they consider bare feet to be another embarrassing form of nakedness). Married couples and other family members change their clothing alone (possibly under bedcovers), and always wear underclothing when they sleep. Because swimming in a swimsuit exposes too much of the body, they do not learn to swim (though many are seafaring fishermen). And they regard as obscenity any reference to the uncovered body, to the elimination of waste, or to anything associated with sexuality, including pregnancy. They even try to prevent any exposure of the genitals, sexual behavior, or bodily functions of animals, including household pets, and punish animals for violations: "Dogs are whipped for licking their genitals and soon learn to indulge in this practice outdoors."[144]

At another extreme are simple tribes who wear little or no clothing at all. Yet they too may expose too much. The Mehinaku Indians of central Brazil wear only decorations and strings on their bodies, for example, but they disapprove of a man who displays an erection or a woman who displays her clitoris and inner labia in public. Although highly promiscuous, they also disapprove of public copulation.[145]

In modern society the public display of an unclothed body is a crime called "indecent exposure" or "public indecency." Some mental health specialists view such behavior as a symptom of a mental illness called "exhibitionism." In any case, what is criminal is exposing one's body to someone who would rather not see it. In modern England, for instance, the typical offender (known as a "flasher") exhibits himself in front of a female stranger, usually on a public street but sometimes in a park or in the countryside. In a survey of one hundred young English women, it was found that most had seen a flasher, and many more than once. Yet although their reaction often is "fear, shock, and disgust," few complain to the police.[146] Not unlike many victims of rape, they keep their involuntary intimacy to themselves.

Because being exposed to the nakedness of a friend or acquaintance is a smaller increase of intimacy than being exposed to a stranger's nakedness, the former causes less conflict than the latter (as does rape by a friend or acquaintance). For instance, anthropologist Barbara Yngvesson describes the case of a Swedish man who sometimes "ran naked" where he could readily be seen by his neighbors, but their only reaction was to gossip to each other that he was "abnormal" and seemed to have an "illness."[147] In a study of a middle-class suburb of New York City, sociologist M. P. Baumgartner learned about a man in a middle-class suburb of New York City who occasionally appeared completely undressed at the door of his next-door neighbors (saying he was returning some of their mail), threw pebbles at their window while dancing naked outside, and once defecated on the lawn in front of their daughter and her friends. But the neighbors only commented that someone "really ought to see about getting that poor man some help," and did nothing else.[148] Had he been a stranger, however, they undoubtedly would have called the police.

Public nakedness would seem to be mainly a modern crime. Sociologist Norbert Elias thus notes that in Europe before the sixteenth century the "greater closeness of individuals made the sight of the naked body, at least in the proper place, incomparably more commonplace." But as the closeness of communities declines with modernization, "the unconcern in showing oneself naked disappears, as does that in performing bodily functions before others."[149] The unconcern of others disappears as well, and nakedness becomes indecency.[150]

Appearing without clothing is sometimes even too intimate in a modern family. The mother of American poet Allen Ginsberg frequently appeared completely unclothed in front of his brother and him when they were growing up, for example, and his father berated her "for parading naked in front of the boys." Later when Ginsberg was a college student his mother's overexposure (which included spreading her legs on a bed) "distressed" him so much that he "stared ahead" or read a book to avoid looking at her. The problem ended when she was sent to a mental hospital.[151]

THE CRIME OF BEING NOTICED

Because downward intimacy is greater than upward intimacy, superiors may expose more of themselves to their inferiors than their inferiors may expose to them. In medieval and early modern Europe, men and women readily bathed in the presence of their servants and other inferiors of both genders, and some monarchs and aristocrats even thought nothing of eliminating waste in the presence of inferiors. But it was "a distasteful offense to show oneself exposed in any way before those of higher or equal rank."[152] In traditional India the "mere sight" of an Untouchable is similarly offensive to a Brahmin.[153]

In parts of the Muslim world (where women are treated as inferior to men), a woman must remain in her home nearly all the time and must allow no man beyond her family to see more than her hands and eyes. For instance, the Pashtun of Afghanistan and Pakistan permit women to appear in public only for special occasions (such as weddings or funerals) with the permission of a husband, father, or other male authority in their family. In public they must wear a large garment (*sadar*) "that covers them from head to foot like a shroud" and look "demurely away" and hide their faces "if a man chances to pass by."[154] At one time a Pashtun man would slice off the nose of any woman in his household who exposed too much, or possibly have a group of men stone her to death. But nowadays she only receives a beating.[155]

In modern Morocco an unveiled woman is said to be "nude" (*aryana*), and for any woman to appear unveiled in public is "an open act of exhibitionism" regarded by men as offensively provocative.[156] Women in modern Andalusia are also required to cover their bodies. In one Andalusian town in the late twentieth century, it was a criminal offense for a woman to expose her bare arms in public.[157]

Australian Aborigine brothers and sisters are highly segregated within their own family, and must be careful to keep their distance at all times. Fathers thus warn their sons (at the age of six or seven) that they must never bathe in a sister's presence, sleep in the same house or camp with her, eat food cooked by her, drink tea boiled by her, use her cup, smoke a cigarette rolled by her, discuss her, look at her or a photograph of her, or see or hear anything pertaining to her sexuality. They must never touch one another, and must always pass objects to each other through a third person. A brother must not even utter his sister's name. Because sisters are the inferiors, however, they have the greater burden to maintain distance between their brothers and themselves: "It is the women who constitute a danger to their brothers, and not the reverse."[158]

A sister must never expose herself to her brother in any way, or even be noticed by him. For her brother she should hardly exist at all. She should never allow herself to be too close to him or to do anything that might increase his awareness of her or anything about her. She must always stay at least four or five paces away from him (whether walking, sitting, or standing), and must never "stand in front of him when the wind is blowing in his direction"—in case he might smell her.[159] Most especially she must never allow anything concerning her "sexual, reproductive, and eliminatory functions" to come to his attention. And although it is sometimes permissible for a brother and sister to speak to one another from a distance, "it is best for them to communicate through a third person."[160]

A brother will physically attack his sister if she gets too close to him—a scenario known as *mirriri*. But since his sister is literally untouchable to him (like an Indian Untouchable), an offended brother must attack his sister from a distance by throwing a spear or other object.[161] Her closeness has the same effect when it is entirely accidental or someone else's fault. If a man chances upon his sister copulating with her husband or eliminating waste, for example, he will immediately attack her.[162]

One occasion for a *mirriri* attack (that has long been a mystery to anthropologists) is when a brother hears someone swearing obscenely at his sister, which commonly includes insults "about her sexual organs and appetite" (such as her "big vagina"). If a brother happens to hear any such language directed at his sister, he cries out in despair that he has been "speared in the ear" and immediately attacks her, usually by throwing spears.[163] One man said that the experience is "just the same as if [he] had been hit on the head with a club."[164]

But why is obscene language toward his sister so painful and offensive to her brother? And why does he attack her instead of the one who swears at her? The answer is her overexposure. The obscenity directed at his sister forces her brother to become aware of something that should never come to his attention: her sexual nature. Though not his sister's fault, the mere mention of her sexuality exposes it to her brother to an unbearable degree, much as if he had seen her naked or copulating. The "spear in the ear" is thus her overintimacy with her brother. So he attacks her.[165]

OVERINTIMATE ART

Modern artists sometimes depict intimate subjects in their art. Since the nineteenth century, in fact, European and American painters have portrayed people in increasingly private situations, and their audience has thereby become ever closer to their subjects.[166] But when art exposes too much, it causes trouble. Overintimate art provokes disgust and indignation, like a naked person in a public place. Viewers criticize it as "filthy" and "dirty," and legal officials prosecute it as "obscenity" and "pornography."[167]

In the early twentieth century, for instance, Austrians condemned the now famous painter Egon Schiele for his overly intimate subjects, including self-portraits depicting himself naked and masturbating. The police jailed him for showing his work to several young women at his home, and a judge burned one of his drawings in court.[168] During the same period one art critic spoke of Austrian Gustav Klimt's paintings (which included embracing couples) as "erotic pollution" and called the painter a "degenerate" and "criminal."[169] And because Italian painter Amedeo Modigliani included a nude woman's pubic hair in one of his works, the Paris police closed his first and only one-man show.[170]

In the late twentieth century, American painter Eric Fischl depicted such intimate subjects as an adolescent boy looking at his mother lying naked on a bed and a naked young woman looking at a naked old man.[171] Fischl once even described his work as a form of "overexposure" that makes the viewer "an unwilling witness" and "part of the intimacy," and he acknowledged its "disruptive" and "taboo" nature.[172] Late twentieth-century Norwegian painter Odd Nerdrum's intimate works have also been controversial, such as one self-portrait with an erection that was supposed to appear on a poster announcing an exhibition of his work in Stockholm. But its public display was prohibited by the Swedish authorities.[173]

In modern Europe and America, male nudity causes more conflict than female nudity: "The history of the male nude . . . is a history of repression and sublimation, and it is a history of the overcoming of a taboo."[174] A 1980 London exhibition of women's photographs of nude men "aroused enormous controversy," for instance, while in the same city at the same time any male photographer was "free to show pictures of the female nude and to share intimacies with his audience."[175] Films with male nudity are also more likely to be deemed obscene.[176] Any display of nude children is worse yet—a serious crime called "child pornography."

Intimate subjects in literary works have met resistance as well, including legal actions against publishers and booksellers.[177] In the late nineteenth century, an English court sent a seventy-year-old "distinguished publisher" to prison for printing translations of French novelist Émile Zola's books containing intimate material, for example, and the distribution of English novelist D. H. Lawrence's *Lady Chatterley's Lover* in 1928 led to seizures of the book and criminal prosecutions in England and the United States. In 1957, American customs officials confiscated a book by poet Allen Ginsberg that included his most celebrated poem ("Howl"), apparently because the poem contains references to male homosexuality, and the city of San Francisco prosecuted the publisher and a bookstore clerk who sold it to an undercover policeman.[178] The distribution of American novelist Henry Miller's *Tropic of Cancer* (which contains sexual content) in 1961 resulted in "hundreds of arrests" and other government actions.[179]

While opponents of censorship invoke the right of artists to freedom of expression, proponents of censorship demand prosecutions in the name of decency.[180] Many debate the difference between art and obscenity. But some art always exposes too much to someone.

OVEREXPOSURE AS BAD MANNERS

Other overexposure might be impolite. But here again what is offensively intimate differs from one place and time to another. Whereas medieval Europeans freely engaged in various bodily functions (including urinating and defecating) in public places, for instance, these and other forms of self-exposure steadily declined and gradually attracted condemnation as a form of bad manners.[181] In modern society it is now improper merely to spit, belch, doze, or clean one's ears or fingernails in public.[182] No one should emit odors either, whether of the body or the breath. And one should be circumspect when eating and drinking, always keeping one's mouth closed while chewing and sipping any liquids as quietly as possible.[183]

Modern etiquette also discourages any public display of strong emotions—another form of self-exposure that has declined with modernization: "Before the seventeenth and eighteenth centuries, extremes of jubilant laughter, passionate weeping, and violent rage were indulged with a freedom that in later centuries would not be permitted even to children."[184] By the nineteenth century etiquette demanded that everyone "conceal from the world his true feelings," and good manners came to mean that one must never "make a spectacle" of oneself.[185] Worse yet is obscene or profane language.

Nor should we overexpose ourselves by talking too much about our personal feelings, thoughts, health, activities, or plans. Featuring too many details about one's own life, especially intimate details, is a form of exhibitionism that belongs to the same family as exposing one's naked body in public. Constantly talking about oneself ("I this" and "I that") is particularly offensive when the speaker displays little or no interest in anyone else—a distinctive combination often criticized as "egocentrism" or "self-centeredness." Some Scottish islanders even discourage the use of the word "I" itself, and consider its frequent use by foreigners such as Americans as "immodest and gross."[186] Who cares what Americans think or do? They talk too much about themselves. They have no manners.

3 | Underintimacy

Any fluctuation of relational space is a movement of relational time. Whereas an increase of relational closeness is overintimacy, a decrease is underintimacy. We actively reduce our involvement in someone's life when we divorce a spouse or tell a lover we wish to end our relationship, and do so passively when we fail to contact someone as much as before or merely neglect to greet someone or inquire about their life: "How are you?" "How's your mother?" "How was your trip?" We also reduce closeness when we reveal less about our own life to someone with whom we were once more open.

A common way of handling deviant behavior is to reduce intimacy with the deviant.[1] In one West African tribe, for instance, any killer of a fellow clansman must leave the village—for a specific period of years if the death was unintentional, indefinitely if it was intentional.[2] In one East African tribe the usual way of handling a suspected witch is "to move away or make him move away."[3] Buddhist monks in Southeast Asia expel fellow monks who commit serious violations of their rules.[4] Judges exile criminals to prison. Guards isolate unruly prisoners. Employers fire incompetent employees. College students avoid annoying roommates.[5] Some people end contact with deviants forever by killing them, and others abandon everyone forever by killing themselves.

But whether active or passive, temporary or permanent, reductions of relational closeness cause trouble. And greater and faster rejections cause more:

Conflict is a direct function of underintimacy.

Although a gradual separation from an acquaintance might have little or no noticeable effect, a sudden and final termination of a close relationship (such as the abandonment of a spouse or lover) might detonate a social explosion. A man might even attack or kill a woman who tries to end their relationship.

Because intimacy is a zero-sum game, increasing closeness with one person decreases it with others and causes conflict in its own right. Whereas their marriage increases a couple's closeness to one another, for example, it decreases their closeness to others such as their parents and friends, and may therefore cause trouble that no one expected. Married people who increase their closeness to others likewise reduce the closeness of their marriage.[6] The birth of a child reduces both the closeness between the parents and their closeness to others. The remarriage of divorced or widowed people reduces their closeness to their children and to other relatives and friends. New friends reduce the closeness of old friends. All these movements of relational time cause resentment and other conflict.

UNDERINVOLVEMENT

Reducing contact with someone else is *underinvolvement*, and reducing the openness of one's own life to someone else is *underexposure*. Underinvolvement might be anything from a failure to converse to a divorce or declaration of independence. It might be a failure to honor a contract, return a favor, reciprocate a gift, or merely express gratitude.[7] All such actions have the same effect: *Conflict is a direct function of underinvolvement.*

ADULTERY AS RELATIONAL TIME

Adultery is sexual intercourse by a married person with someone other than a spouse (also called "cheating" or being "unfaithful"). Because of the zero-sum nature of intimacy, adultery reduces closeness to a spouse at the same time as it increases closeness with someone else.[8] And it is one of the surest causes of conflict in the social universe.[9]

Like rape, adultery is a quantum leap of relational time. But whereas rape imposes intimacy, adultery reduces intimacy. Rape is therefore worse in more distant relationships, where it imposes more closeness; and adultery is worse in closer marriages, where it reduces more closeness.

In many tribal societies adultery leads almost automatically to violence. Anthropologist Adamson Hoebel probably exaggerates when he says that every tribal society gives a husband the right to kill a wife caught committing adultery, and so might sociobiologists Martin Daly and Margo Wilson when they say that "the violent rages of cuckolds are a recognized risk everywhere." But adultery does cause a great deal of violence, from beatings to killings, in numerous societies.[10] In the Yanomamö tribe of Venezuela and Brazil, for instance, a husband might shoot an unfaithful wife with a barbed arrow, chop her with an ax, or cut off her ears.[11] A Cheyenne Indian might have his adulterous wife gang-raped by fellow tribesmen (known as putting her "on the prairie").[12] In the Jívaro tribe of Ecuador (known for shrinking the heads of their enemies), a man will slash the scalp of his wife's lover with a machete or kill one of her lover's relatives.[13] An Australian Aborigine man caught in a sexual relationship with another man's wife traditionally offered the husband "his rump to be jabbed with a spear."[14] Some tribes, such as the Soga of Uganda, punish adultery as a theft by the woman's lover.[15] Others require him to pay compensation to the husband.[16] In one New Guinea tribe adultery is so disturbing to men that many prefer to marry "sexually unattractive" women (such as those "disfigured by ringworm") who will have fewer opportunities to be unfaithful.[17]

One of the Ten Commandments addresses the same subject: "Thou shalt not commit adultery." In the ancient Indian code called the Laws of Manu, the punishment for adultery was especially severe when a man's lover was the wife of his spiritual teacher (*guru*): He had a choice of cutting off his own penis and testicles and carrying them in his hands until he fell to the ground and died, or killing himself by lying on a red-hot iron bed or by embracing a red-hot iron figure of a woman.[18] Early Germanic codes prescribed death for both parties.[19] In colonial New England a sexual relationship with a married or engaged woman was also punishable by death for both parties.[20] In parts of the modern Islamic world the penalty for adultery is still death for both—by stoning. In Afghanistan, for example, the guilty woman is buried up to her neck and the guilty man is tied to a wall, then pummeled to death with stones. Iran's penal code similarly specifies that "the stoning of an adulterer or adulteress shall be carried out while each is placed in a hole and covered with soil, he up to his waist and she up to a line above her breasts."[21]

Adultery and desertion together cause most wife-killings and a great deal of other violence in many societies, including the United States and other Western countries. Daly and Wilson thus report that "in every society for which we have been able to find a sample of spousal homicides, the story is basically the same: Most cases arise out of the husband's jealous, proprietary, violent response to his wife's (real or imagined) infidelity or desertion."[22] Adultery is the "most frequent reason" women become violent (toward both men and women) as well.[23] It also causes many suicides and divorces. As soon as American poet Robinson Jeffers' wife learned he was having an affair with another woman, for example, she lay down in a bathtub and shot herself in the heart (but the bullet hit a rib, and she survived).[24]

Conflict is chronic whenever two people seek a sexual relationship with a third.[25] It is therefore chronic in all polygynous families (those with more than one wife).[26] For instance, anthropologist Elizabeth Colson reports that polygyny in one Zambian tribe continually generates "jealousy and quarreling between wives who share one man," and adds that all the women "dislike" it "intensely."[27] The cause of violence between women in other Zambian tribes is likewise "almost always" competition for a man, and includes slapping, kicking, biting (occasionally mutilating ears and lips), and attacking with knives, axes, broken bottles, and boiling water (possibly with chili pepper rubbed on the rival's wounds to cause additional pain).[28] Other African women use a "love potion" or "love medicine" believed to undermine the sexual relationships of their rivals.[29] Australian Aborigine women fight over men with a three- to four-foot-long eucalyptus stick (called a *nulla nulla*).[30]

Too much closeness to something nonhuman can also cause trouble. Although Spanish painter Pablo Picasso had many conflicts with his wives and lovers about his involvement with other women, for example, his intense involvement in his art caused still more conflict.[31] Such was true of his work on one major painting called *Les Demoiselles d'Avignon*, which might have been all the more upsetting to his lover at the time because it depicted several young women: "Had they not taken Picasso away from her? Were they not responsible for his leaving her for days and nights on end?"[32] American painter Mark Rothko once even remarked that "marriage is an impossible situation for an artist."[33] But any competing involvement in anything weakens other relationships and causes conflict. For instance, one American woman's boyfriend complained that she loved her cat Norman "more than she loved him," and in a "drunken fury" stomped and kicked the cat to death.[34]

THE CRIME OF SAYING GOODBYE

A reduction of closeness between spouses might lead to the death of the marriage by abandonment or divorce—which commonly causes still more conflict.[35] But the seriousness of a marital death partly depends on the closeness of the couple, especially the closeness of the spouse left behind to the one who leaves. Leaving a closer spouse is worse.

Any inequality in a marriage is relevant as well. For example, a woman who leaves or divorces her patriarchal husband faces more trouble than a patriarchal husband who leaves or divorces his wife. One legal code of the highly patriarchal Burgundians of early Europe prescribed execution (in an unpleasant fashion) for any woman who left her husband: "Let her be smothered in mire." But a man who left his wife only had to make a payment to her and allow her to keep their children and household property.[36] A patriarch in a modern Muslim country might sadistically injure or kill his wife if she tries to end their marriage. In Pakistan and other parts of South Asia, he might throw acid in her face, mutilating and possibly blinding her for life.[37]

Leaving a man is dangerous in many societies. As Daly and Wilson note: "Men do not easily let women go. They search out women who have left them to plead and threaten and sometimes to kill."[38] Adultery often plays a role, but abandonment, divorce, or the threat of either is the immediate cause of most wife-killings.[39] In modern America, for instance, "the estranged wife, hunted down and murdered, is a common item in police files." As one man warned his wife: "I swear if you ever leave me, I'll follow you to the ends of the earth and kill you." Later when she did leave him, he killed her with a shotgun.[40] Another man who suspected his wife of infidelity or planning to leave him "followed her for days," and killed her when she asked for "more freedom."[41] Another told police he killed his wife because she said she no longer loved him.[42] Still another killed his five children and himself after his wife told him by phone that she was leaving him for another man. Although she later said he killed the children "to punish" her, if she had been available he probably would have killed her instead.[43] Ending or threatening to end a homosexual relationship may cause a similarly "passionate explosion."[44]

Other men rape the women who try to leave them. After one American woman told her husband she was divorcing him, for example, he grabbed her and tied her to a bed, stripped off her clothing, took photographs of her, and finally raped her.[45] Another woman said her husband threatened to make her pregnant to keep her from ending their marriage: "I told him if that happened I would get an abortion and still leave him. Then he slapped me and threw me around, tore my clothes off, and raped me."[46] After another woman began living alone and filed for a divorce, her husband asked her to come to his apartment "to discuss financial matters," but assaulted and raped her when she arrived. In still another case, a man abducted his estranged wife from a railroad station at gunpoint, took her to his home, tied her to a bed, and raped her several times during the following hours. But most spousal rapes occur after a lesser form of underintimacy: when a woman refuses to have sexual intercourse.[47]

Lost intimacy might also cause violence against someone unconnected to the loss. According to one American police officer, a man who loses someone close might rape a stranger: "Say a guy's grandmother has just gone into the hospital—he lives with Granny, and he's angry at her for leaving him and maybe for dying. He might go and rape an old woman because he's mad at Granny."[48] Or a rejected man might run amok, indiscriminately attacking strangers in a public place.[49] After losing his girlfriend and his job and being banished from his parents' home, one young man in Nebraska killed eight people and wounded a number of others in a shopping mall.[50] And after his girlfriend ended their relationship, a teenaged boy in Georgia randomly shot and wounded six students in his high school.[51] The loss of a close relationship has likewise led to the assassination of politicians (including American presidents).[52] Others with such losses have joined terrorist groups and engaged in mass killings.[53]

The termination of a close relationship sometimes attracts the intervention of third parties. Among the Kikuyu of Kenya, the clansmen of a man who evicts his wife "for no good cause" might try to change his mind by seizing him, tying ants' nests to his head, and disturbing the ants "until they bite furiously and the offender sweats with pain." The clansmen of a woman who leaves her husband might try to change her mind by giving her a whipping.[54] An Andalusian man who abandons his family might face a public shaming (known as *el vito*) until he relents or moves away. In one such case a group of men and boys gathered every night for several months outside the man's house and rang cowbells, blew horns, and harassed him in other ways until he died of a heart attack.[55] In southern Mexico, Zapotec Indian couples wishing to separate often meet opposition from their parents or (if they go to court) a judge, and town officials sometimes forcibly return women who leave their husbands and children.[56] In northern Mexico, Tarahumara Indian men and women who leave their families are punished with whippings and forced labor.[57] In modern America, a Pakistani American man strangled his daughter to death when she tried to end the marriage that he had arranged.[58]

Divorce was illegal in Catholic countries for centuries, and it is still opposed by the Catholic Church and various other religious groups.[59] Individuals such as relatives, friends, and children of the couple might oppose a divorce as well, possibly insisting that "a commitment is a commitment, no matter what," and that "the relationship must continue." Children might express anger toward a father who leaves, and display other hostility toward him when he visits—leading him to make fewer visits, which causes more hostility, fewer visits, and still more hostility: "The destructive cycle continues, and parent and children are forced farther and farther apart."[60]

Children sometimes express a grievance against their parents by "running away," but doing so causes more conflict. Tarahumara Indian children might run away after a beating or scolding by a parent, for example, but then must face punishment by legal officials when they are found.[61] Running away is defined as "juvenile delinquency" in modern America.[62] Parents who abandon or neglect children also attract legal attention: A failure to provide adequate care for a child is a crime called "child neglect," and a failure to provide adequate financial support for a child after a divorce or other marital separation is a crime called "nonsupport."[63] Abortion is a form of underintimacy that some call "murder."[64] It was a crime in the United States until 1973, and still causes controversy and occasional violence.[65]

Homicide ends not only the life of the victim but normally ends parts of other lives too, causing some of the most serious conflicts that ever occur, possibly including the killing of the killer.[66] A single killing sometimes gives rise to an exchange of killings over time, illustrated by the "blood feuds" found in some traditional societies and among urban gangs in modern societies such as the United States.[67] Or a killing might lead to a suicide. For instance, some American men kill themselves after killing their wives.[68]

Abandoned or rejected people might also kill themselves. According to sociologist Jack Douglas, the most common cause of suicide in modern America is "the loss of a loved one."[69] Typically the self-killer is an abandoned or rejected spouse or lover, such as one young man who left letters saying he was going to kill himself "because his bride of four months was not in love with him but with his elder brother and wanted a divorce so that she could marry the brother."[70] Because American men typically have fewer close relationships beyond their family than do their wives, they lose more intimacy when their marriage ends, and are ten times more likely than women to kill themselves afterward.[71]

Some abandoned or rejected homosexuals kill themselves as well. In a case in Belgium, for example, a popular singer and television personality known as Yasmine hanged herself from a tree after the woman she had married abandoned her for another woman.[72] And on the Valentine's Day after a California man named Rob told his partner Daniel that he wanted to end their relationship, he found Daniel hanging dead in their garage, along with the following note: "Rob, Happy Valentine's Day. I love you. Please take care of yourself and Ignatia [their dog]. I love you both very much. Daniel."[73]

The disintegration of societies also causes conflict, including warfare and other violence. A declaration of independence by a number of British colonies in North America caused the American Revolutionary War in the eighteenth century; the secession of the Southern states from the United States caused the American Civil War in the nineteenth century; declarations of independence by former European colonies in Africa and Asia caused wars and other violence in the twentieth century; and similar separation movements caused various conflicts that continued into the twenty-first century, such as those of Basques in Spain and France, Chechens in Russia, Kurds in Turkey, Tamils in Sri Lanka, and Muslims in the Philippines. All such movements belong to the same family as divorce, desertion, and running away.

UNDERINVOLVEMENT AS BAD MANNERS

Too little involvement might also be impolite. A failure to offer or return a greeting is a form of rudeness, for example, if not a display of outright hostility.[74] In the Hehe tribe of Tanzania, a failure to greet a neighbor might lead the slighted individual to try to harm or even kill the offender with sorcery or a curse.[75] The Tauade of New Guinea consider a failure to return a greeting a "humiliation" deserving of retaliation, possibly violent.[76] One modern American etiquette expert calls a failure to return a greeting a "cut," presumably because it inflicts a social wound: "A 'cut' is . . . a direct stare of blank refusal, and is not only insulting to its victim but embarrassing to every witness. Happily it is practically unknown in polite society."[77]

A failure to converse is similarly impolite. Everyone has an "obligation" to speak to acquaintances.[78] In some tribes an unsociable person might be killed as a witch.[79] In modern America, someone repeatedly guilty of "not talking" is said to lack "social graces" and might be covertly condemned as a "wet blanket," "cold fish," or "corpse."[80] Those in conversations are subject to what sociologist Erving Goffman calls "involvement obligations": They must give their "main focus of attention" to the conversation, appear to be "spontaneously involved in it," and never show any evidence of an "emigration of the self" by drumming their fingers on a table, displaying a "faraway look" in their eyes that might indicate "daydreaming," or otherwise seeming to be distracted by other "side involvements." The most fleeting failure to pay attention to what another person is saying, such as glancing away occasionally or not always listening with interest to what is being said, is a "discourtesy" that is not likely to escape notice. One American woman mentioned that she does not even like to paint her toenails while talking with her husband—because it requires "too much attention" and might offend him.[81]

A lack of involvement in a social situation might even be considered a symptom of mental illness. Some who habitually display too little involvement are diagnosed as "catatonic," or possibly "autistic."[82] The sickest dwell in deep holes in relational space, and ignore everyone.

UNDEREXPOSURE

Some offend others by exposing too much of themselves, but others expose too little. They fail to reveal enough about who they are and what they do, who and what they know, or what they think and feel. Early sociologist Georg Simmel observed that an obligation to expose one's life to others is especially strong in close relationships such as marriages and friendships.[83] And just as too little involvement causes conflict, so does too little exposure: *Conflict is a direct function of underexposure.*

SECRECY

Intimates who do not open their lives to one another are not really intimates. Especially inimical to intimacy is secrecy: not merely a failure to reveal the nature of one's activities but an active concealment of something. The discovery that an intimate has been keeping a secret is a sure cause of resentment and other conflict, even when the secret pertains to something in the past—merely because it was secret.[84] That is one reason adultery causes so much conflict: It is virtually always secret.

Tribal people know a great deal about everyone in their village or band. The Dou Donggo of eastern Indonesia expose almost everything about their lives to everyone else: "Going off to the bush to defecate is about the only activity for which [they] grant each other much privacy." They enjoy doing almost everything—"sleeping, eating, walking, bathing, praying, working"—in the presence of other people and "in as large and boisterous a group as possible." And anyone who tries to spend time alone or who is secretive about anything meets resistance if not hostility.[85] The Bushmen of Botswana view any effort to have a degree of "solitude" as a "bizarre form of behavior," and "pester" and "goad" those who do so until they return to the group.[86] The Igbo of Nigeria likewise expect everything about everyone in the same village to be highly "transparent": "Solitude is regarded as a mark of wickedness, of evil design," and "secretive" people are not only "held in contempt" but are "often the victims of unwarranted aggression and targets of sorcery accusations."[87] Eskimos believe that secrecy is supernaturally "dangerous": A secret violation of a taboo is thought to cause the sinner to suffer sickness and possibly death, or even an epidemic, famine, or other disaster harmful to the entire band.[88] Everyone must therefore be completely open about everything, including their sexual activities. Eskimos also believe sick people can recover only by confessing their past sins to a shaman.[89]

Because modern people are physically separate much of the time, any significant degree of intimacy requires active self-exposure by each party. Many modern couples expect "total openness" from each other: "Ideally there should now be no secrets between partners, everything should be told, all infidelities confessed, all fantasies divulged, even masturbation admitted."[90] Yet secrets remain in many otherwise close relationships. Sociologist Diane Vaughan believes that "we are all secret-keepers in our intimate relationships. We keep secrets from our partners about daily encounters, former lovers, true feelings about sex, friends, in-laws, finances, personal hopes, and worries about work, health, love, and life." Secrecy nevertheless causes trouble, and any increase of secrecy may mean a previously close relationship is nearing its end: "Uncoupling begins with a secret."[91]

Secrets also cause trouble in other relationships, including those of a professional nature. According to sociologist Robert Merton, for example, all scientists have an obligation to share their latest findings, theories, thoughts, and plans with fellow scientists, and those who fail to do so alienate their colleagues and damage their careers.[92] Although secrecy might be more acceptable in the business world, it still leads to serious conflicts in purely economic relationships, including lawsuits for "nondisclosure" and "fraud."[93]

And upward secrecy (by an inferior) is worse than downward secrecy (by a superior). Those with authority thus expect their subordinates to expose more to them than they might care to expose in return. Some religions also demand considerable self-exposure by their members. The Puritans of colonial New England required all new members to recount their previous personal history in great detail and to confess all their past sins before the congregation.[94] The Roman Catholic Church warns its members to confess all their serious sins to a priest, or they will go to hell.[95]

LYING

Although total openness may not be expected everywhere, everyone is expected to tell the truth. Lying distorts reality, disorients relationships, and counteracts closeness.[96] Allowing a falsehood to prevail without exposing it—lying by omission—is bad enough, but explicit lying is worse: It actively deceives people and poisons re-lationships.[97]

Those in close relationships tolerate nothing less than total honesty. Lovers who lie are not really lovers, and friends who lie are not really friends. To discover a lie is therefore not only to discover the nature of reality but the nature of a relation-ship: It is not as close as it seemed. Lying between intimates may cause a conflict as serious as whatever it distorts or conceals.[98] Although lying is probably a common part of conflict, it makes conflicts worse. And it magnifies transgressions such as adultery: "What hurts most is that you lied to me! How can I ever trust you again?"[99]

One of the Ten Commandments prohibits lying in legal cases, and possibly else-where: "Thou shalt not bear false witness against thy neighbor." Lying in a modern court is a crime called "perjury."[100] Upward lying is also worse than downward lying. But many superiors distrust inferiors anyway.[101] For example, historian Ken-neth Greenberg comments that during the days of American slavery "whites as-sumed that slaves lied all the time," and would not even allow them to testify in court. During the same period, however, calling a Southern gentleman a liar might lead to a duel with pistols, and possibly death: "The central insult that could turn a disagreement into a duel involved a direct or indirect attack on someone's word— the accusation that a man was a liar."[102] The same insult among other men might cause a fight.[103]

Early sociologist Charles Horton Cooley may have gone too far when he asserted that people everywhere follow a policy of "truth for friends and lies for enemies."[104] But whether justifiably or not, many people do not trust strangers, others beyond their family, or possibly anyone at all.[105] It is said, for instance, that Greek peasants distrust everyone and that they often lie. They even have an adage that "you can't live without lies."[106] And according to an old saying in rural Ireland, "You can't trust what an Irishman tells you." Apparently at least some of what Irishmen say is dismissed by other Irishmen as "blarney": mere words that should not be trusted.[107]

Yet nowhere is all lying acceptable.[108] Whereas Eskimos have no objection to lying to strangers, for example, in each band "lies and breaking one's word are con-sidered the most disgraceful habits for any man or woman, and in fact 'liar' is the worst accusation that can be made against anybody."[109] "Chronic lying" is "outra-geous" and possibly a capital offense: "The execution of liars is reported from Greenland to Alaska."[110] Lying damages closeness, so all close people must dislike if not despise liars.

Because people in a modern society such as the United States frequently have little personal knowledge of one another, modern life provides many opportunities for lying that are not available in a simpler society such as tribe. One subtle and possibly common form of modern lying is the presentation of a false self, such as falsely representing one's wealth, ancestry, or accomplishments.[111] Another is hypocrisy: falsely claiming to be virtuous and beyond reproach.[112] Still another is self-deception, or lying to oneself: denying one's true thoughts, feelings, and possibly even conduct to oneself. Whereas most lying separates people from others, then, self-deception separates them from themselves. Psychiatrist R. D. Laing also suggests that a "divided self"—partly "real" and partly "false"—is the heart of the mental illness called "schizophrenia."[113]

UNDEREXPOSURE AS BAD MANNERS

Too much silence about oneself is a form of secrecy, and good manners therefore demand a degree of self-exposure. Polite people reveal at least part of their lives to their associates, and resent those who do not. Those who conceal too much about their activities, thoughts, and feelings are said to be "too private," "tight-lipped," "close-mouthed," or "cagey." They are criticized as "distant" and "cold." We especially dislike those who take intimacy from us but do not give it in return—probing into our personal lives and asking what we think and how we feel about various subjects while revealing little or nothing about themselves. They are too close and too distant at the same time.

We all have our own personality, but how we behave must conform to the shape of social space. For example, those with whom we are closer expect us to reveal more about ourselves than we might reveal to others. Yet the boundaries of the self vary across the social universe. In a modern society such as the United States, different people from different groups (such as different ethnic groups) might expect different degrees of intimacy in different relationships, and the right amount of closeness in one group might be wrong in another. Hence, those regarded as too distant or too intimate might actually be conforming to the standards of their own group. For instance, some Americans might regard some Japanese as too distant—too secretive or insincere, or possibly just boring—because they might reveal less about their opinions and feelings than many Americans would normally reveal about theirs. But in Japan it is sometimes said that a man should not "blurt out his feelings" like a "frog" that "displays his whole inside" when "he opens his mouth."[114] Japanese might therefore view some Americans as shamefully exhibitionistic and vulgar (see also "Overexposure as Bad Manners" in chapter 2). Yet the same Japanese might sometimes behave in a manner many Americans would regard as too intrusive, such as by asking questions about their annual income, the cost of a possession, or the nature of their family life. In a multi-ethnic society such as modern America, differences in relational space across different groups would seem to be an unavoidable source of conflict in everyday life.

II | Vertical Time

4 | Overstratification

Social stratification is the vertical dimension of social space. Commonly known as inequality, it includes any difference in social status in any relationship, whether a difference in wealth, power, or performance.[1] Some societies (such as simple tribes) have little or no inequality, while others (such as ancient civilizations) have a great deal. And some relationships (such as friendships) typically have little, while others (such as patriarchal marriages) have more.

Vertical time is the dynamic dimension of vertical space. Vertical distances fluctuate in smaller and larger amounts, slowly and quickly. Life has its ups and downs, such as gains and losses of money, authority, or anything else that raises or lowers one person or group above or below another. Movements of vertical time also include various forms of good and bad fortune, such as inheritances, stock market crashes, accidents, diseases, and disasters.

Inequality is a zero-sum game: My gain is your loss, and your loss is my gain. If we are equals, you become my inferior if I rise and my superior if I fall. If you are my superior, I lose some of my inferiority if you fall and you lose some of your superiority if I rise. I might even become your equal or superior when I rise or when you fall. Any such change in anyone's social standing—upward or downward mobility—is a change in social stratification itself.

An increase of inequality is *overstratification*, and a decrease is *understratification*. Both cause conflict, and greater and faster movements cause more:

Conflict is a direct function of overstratification.

Notice that this principle does not say that inequality causes conflict. Instead it says that *increases* of inequality cause conflict. Only something dynamic—something that changes—can cause conflict or anything else.

An increase of inequality might be *oversuperiority* or *overinferiority*. The former occurs whenever anyone rises above someone else and the latter whenever anyone falls below someone else. Both cause conflict. First consider success.

OVERSUPERIORITY

Many sociologists assume that everyone desires and admires upward mobility—success. And many believe that a lack of upward mobility causes frustration and leads to crime, violence, and other problems.[2] But success has a dark side few sociologists have recognized: It causes hostility among those left behind, especially if they are falling at the same time: Did those who rose above others really deserve their success? Or did they gain their advantage at someone else's expense, such as by doing something improper or even evil? Success leads to suspicion, resentment, and accusations of wrongdoing, possibly entirely false: *Conflict is a direct function of oversuperiority.*

Those who acquire wealth or power or other social status often attract dislike. Some politicians and political movements define them as enemies and denounce them with epithets such as "fat cats" and "capitalist pigs." Karl Marx famously called for a "communist revolution" to "expropriate the expropriators"—the "ruling class" whose profits he considered a form of theft.[3] Successful corporations attract opposition as well, such as litigation to decrease their domination (known as "antitrust" lawsuits in the United States). Sociologist Arthur Stinchcombe suggests that the fluctuation of organizational stratification causes revolutions and other political violence.[4] And economist Reuven Brenner suggests that the fluctuation of international stratification—"when some nations suddenly outdo others"—causes wars.[5]

Because all competition has winners and losers, all competition causes conflict. Even competitive sports such as football and basketball cause conflict. The heart of every athletic contest is a movement of vertical time: Each contest pits individuals or teams against each other until a winner stands above a loser.[6] Every game is more than a game: It creates inequality.[7] Those associated with the athletes (such as schools, towns, and countries) and any other partisans ("fans") also rise or fall with each victory or loss. Winning athletes receive money and other rewards, and so do their coaches.[8] Losers lose their right to compete, and losing coaches lose their jobs. But too much athletic success attracts hostility. Many cheer for the "underdogs" to win, and dislike (possibly to the point of hatred) those who win too easily, too often, or by too much. In modern America, coaches attract criticism if they allow their teams to win by too much, sometimes known as "running up the score." One athletic association even passed a "score management" rule prohibiting high school football coaches from allowing their teams to win by fifty points or more.[9] One high school fired its basketball coach because he let his team win a game by a score of 100 to 0, and refused to apologize.[10]

Some resent those who do too well at anything, and possibly those who merely try to achieve more or otherwise try to improve their lives. Those who display too much pride and joy in their accomplishments also attract dislike. Successful people should never "crow" about their success but should act as though they actually did little or nothing at all, give credit to someone else, or say their success was only a matter of luck. Yet nothing fully excuses or protects those who do too well. Even intimates may resent their success. Rising too high damages friendships and dampens the love of brothers and sisters and possibly even parents. Too much success is unforgivable.

SUCCESS AS WITCHCRAFT

In many places and times people have been accused of black magic—witchcraft or sorcery—and possibly killed. Witches are said to be abnormal individuals with supernatural power harmful to others, while sorcerers are ordinary individuals who have learned magical techniques to advance their interests, sometimes by harming others.

Because witches are by nature evil, their neighbors consider them extremely dangerous—more so than anyone else. As one European resident of Africa remarked: "It is difficult to describe the deep and terrorizing fear of the witch that pervades all African society."[11] Moreover, because witches are inherently evil and cannot stop themselves from harming others, the only way to prevent them from doing more damage is to kill them, sometimes with a special method (such as burning) believed to destroy their power. Officials once executed thousands of alleged witches in the Western world, and they are still killed in other countries, especially in Africa.[12] Between 1970 and 1984, for instance, more than three thousand alleged witches were killed in Tanzania alone.[13] Because sorcerers are similar to ordinary criminals who can choose whether or not to continue their crimes, however, those accused of sorcery are less likely to be killed.[14] But of course those identified as witches have actually done nothing and can do nothing of a supernatural nature to harm anyone, and accused sorcerers have, at most, only tried. Why, then, do these accusations occur?

The typical witchcraft or sorcery case arises after someone suffers a misfortune such as an accident or illness, and the one accused is usually a social marginal such as a poor spinster or someone else on hard times.[15] But sometimes the accused witch or sorcerer is exactly the opposite: an individual who is relatively successful— *too* successful. For example, some East Africans say that people who use black magic are ambitious, jealous, and greedy individuals who are willing to use any means to become "powerful and wealthy."[16] They might therefore suspect any neighbor or other associate who does too well at anything.[17]

Anthropologist Audrey Richards reports that it is "dangerous" for any member of the Bemba tribe of Zambia to be too prosperous: "A man who is full when others are hungry is hardly considered to have achieved the good fortune by natural means. An occasional stroke of good luck is not resented, but to be permanently much more prosperous than the rest of the village would almost certainly lead to accusations of sorcery." Bemba believe a man can use black magic to "send out mysterious black birds (*mawa*) at night to steal the food of neighbors and convey it to their own granaries," for instance, and readily suspect that "if a man's crops are too fruitful he has used sorcery to steal the crops of his neighbors." Even a brief run of good fortune may attract suspicion: "To find one beehive with honey in the woods is luck, to find two is very good luck, [but] to find three is witchcraft."[18]

Accusations are especially frequent where Bemba are more likely to gain economic or other superiority over fellow tribesmen, such as in copper mines and urban areas. In the mines, for example, anyone promoted to a higher position eventually attracts suspicion: "How else did he gain the *bwana's* [boss's] favor?" And because they believe that sorcery is motivated by envy, a successful man fears not only being accused of sorcery but becoming the victim of sorcery himself. They are also quick to condemn any successful man for being "presumptuous" and "aping the chief." For various reasons, then, a Bemba man prefers only "a very modest competence" rather than conspicuous success, and if he does have some success will deny "that he is as well off as he is."[19]

The Kaguru of Tanzania similarly direct most of their accusations of black magic against "successful persons with many prosperous fields, much livestock, fine clothing, attractive wives, or many lovers."[20] So do the Shona of Zimbabwe: If a man "acquires wealth whilst those around him are so poor that they can hardly make a living, this not only shows that he is greedy and avaricious, but suggests that his wealth was obtained at the expense of his fellows." "Exceptionally talented" or otherwise "successful" individuals are also vulnerable.[21] In the American Southwest, Navajo Indians who "accumulate wealth too rapidly" attract accusations of witchcraft. Such cases were particularly common during the Great Depression, when most Navajo were suffering economically and anyone better off was more noticeable.[22]

In colonial Massachusetts "prospering and upwardly mobile people" were more vulnerable to witchcraft accusations, especially if they had enjoyed a "swift economic rise" above their neighbors.[23] In modern Japan rural villagers sometimes view a "rapid accumulation of wealth" as evidence that a family has been helped by the "spirit" of a fox or other animal: "It is believed, for example, that a fox brings money to his master's house" and that other spirits "bring silk cocoons and other things from neighboring houses into their master's house to make him rich."[24] And in at least one rural area of modern France, farmers may suspect witchcraft if a neighbor's fortunes have recently improved. Because they believe that witches gain whatever their victims lose, particularly relevant evidence of guilt is the rising of one neighbor when another is falling: "The witch grows richer, his health prospers, his cows are more and more productive, while the bewitched grows poorer, wastes away, and so on."[25] All such accusations may seem arbitrary and unjust, but all have a clear basis in reality: the rise of anyone above anyone else.

THE ENFORCEMENT OF EQUALITY

Simple tribes of hunter-gatherers subsist on whatever they can find, catch, or kill; own no land or other property that allows anyone to have more wealth than anyone else; and have no lasting surplus of any kind. Nor does anyone have authority over anyone else: They have no chiefs or officials, and they resist anyone who tries to exercise authority or coerce them in any way.[26] In a survey of forty-eight hunter-gatherer and other largely egalitarian tribes, anthropologist Christopher Boehm found that literally all such people actively oppose every form of domination by anyone over anyone else. He even speculates that the first rule of morality thousands of years ago was a prohibition against domination ("bullying behavior").[27] Anthropologist Pierre Clastres likewise comments that simple tribes have just one "law": "You are worth no more than anyone else; you are worth no less than anyone else."[28]

For example, the hunter-gatherer Bushmen of Botswana "fiercely" enforce equality within their bands, and anyone who attains or presumes superiority in any way faces various "leveling devices" such as "rough humor, back-handed compliments, put-downs, and damning with faint praise." As one Bushman explained:

> Say that a man has been hunting. He must not come home and announce like a braggart, "I have killed a big one in the bush!" He must first sit down in silence until I or someone else comes up to his fire and asks, "What did you see today?" He replies quietly, "Ah, I'm no good for hunting. I saw nothing at all . . . maybe just a tiny one." Then I smile to myself because I now know he has killed something big.[29]

Bushmen also expect everyone to share whatever they acquire: "To be stingy . . . is to hoard one's goods jealously and secretively, guarding them like a 'hyena.' The corrective for this, in the [Bushman] view, is to make the hoarder give 'till it hurts,' that is, to make him give generously and without stint until everyone can see that he is truly cleaned out." Nor do they defer to anyone, apologize for anything, or even say "please" or "thank you"—which might suggest a degree of inferiority to someone else.[30]

Eskimos likewise resent anyone who has too much success hunting or fishing, paddles his kayak faster than others, or outperforms anyone in any other way. In one tribe, for instance, "The more successful hunters were often surrounded by feelings of jealousy which were skillfully concealed and found expression in secretly performed sorcery. Fast kayakers were especially likely to be envied, and slower hunters used to throw spells on their kayaks."[31]

Simple farming tribes are highly egalitarian as well. The Buid of the Philippine highlands expect everyone to treat everyone else as an "autonomous equal," resist and condemn as "unnatural" anyone who tries "to establish superiority over others," and pointedly ignore or ridicule anyone who is "boastful."[32] New Guinea tribesmen try to maintain equality despite having leaders (known as "big-men") who have their positions partly because of their wealth. Although people encourage big-men to be their leaders, they nevertheless resist whatever leadership they try to exercise. Anthropologist Karen Brison comments, for example, that big-men "can do nothing right: They are expected to lead, but their attempts to do so inevitably meet opposition and criticism." Every big-man is the target of malicious gossip and rumors that he uses sorcery and other devious methods to get what he wants: "Almost anything a leader does creates resentment and slanderous rumors that frighten many prominent men into trying to get rid of their powers."[33] Big-men also fear the black magic of those who might wish to do them harm because of their prosperity, and "repeatedly" confided to anthropologist Michael Young that "they had at various times cut back their garden production or killed off their pigs to avoid being objects of sorcery attack."[34]

Anthropologist Christopher Hallpike describes one New Guinea tribe in which the men continually play a "negative-sum game" to prevent anyone from becoming superior to anyone else: "They are content to reduce what someone else has, by ridicule, rumor, theft, or violence, without actually gaining anything themselves," and "treat an enemy's loss as a gain to themselves." For example, in one case two men argued at length over ownership of a pandanus tree (valued for its large nuts, long leaves, and useful bark), until finally a Catholic missionary jokingly suggested cutting the tree down so that neither could have it. But to his amazement the men immediately embraced his idea as the "perfect solution" and together destroyed the tree, each "thoroughly satisfied" that the other could never own it.[35] Anthropologist Kenneth Read found that the men of another New Guinea tribe even refuse to have a winner when they play European football: "Each team aims to equal the goals scored by the other, and no team should win [and] establish its outright superiority. Games usually go on for days until the scores are considered to be equal."[36]

In some groups those who merely try to obtain something of value or who seek to improve their standard of living attract the hostility of their peers. In rural Malaysia, for instance, peasants resist not only whatever raises one man above another, but any effort at self-improvement: "The poor man who is tempted to break ranks must measure very carefully his short-term gain against the losses his angry neighbors may be able to impose." Any sign of ambition invites malicious gossip, ostracism, and possibly violence.[37]

Others use covert methods such as gossip, secret ridicule, and demeaning nicknames to lower anyone who rises too high or seeks to achieve too much. Like physical vandalism that damages property in the dark of night, these techniques are forms of social vandalism that can damage a person's social standing in the community.[38] Moralistic gossip is thus a secret trial in absentia that can significantly undermine a person's reputation and future, yet it is difficult if not impossible to prevent or undo.[39] Many Makah Indians of the Northwest Coast of North America pride themselves on being members of the "better" or higher-class families in their tribe, for instance, but everyone gossips that those who make such claims are really from lower-class families.[40] Andalusians in southern Spain engage in damaging gossip about anyone who does better or aspires to do better than others, including women who outdo other women in the competition for men. In one such case a beautiful young woman named Conchita was engaged to marry an "ambitious" young man with his own business and "prospects" of a successful future, while her friend María was doomed to marry a "worker" who was a "plain man" and "not so fine a catch." But María evened the scales somewhat by spreading a false story that Conchita was pregnant and that her coming marriage was a "shotgun affair" actually unwanted by her future husband. Embellished with other fabricated details (such as that Conchita's father had confronted her future husband for dishonoring his daughter), the rumor significantly damaged Conchita's reputation and dampened her happiness about her engagement (illustrating an old Andalusian saying that "the tongue has no teeth, yet bites deeper").[41]

Secret ridicule and nicknames have similar effects.[42] The Macah not only gossip about those who claim superiority over others, but use secret ridicule to "turn down" anyone who appears to be enjoying "greater prosperity," a position of "leadership in the tribe," or any other form of success.[43] Andalusians use sarcastic and unflattering nicknames for the same purpose, and also for anyone who displays too much ambition. "Middle-Class Joey" is their name for a poor laborer who inherited a few acres of good land, "Little Tony the Mayor" for a man who once said his son would someday be mayor of the town, and "the Little King" for a peasant working hard to improve his life. One prosperous man is called "Little Miss Candycane" because of his high-pitched voice, another "Always an Erection" because of his sexual appetite, and still another "Mule Shit" because of a diarrheic mule he once owned. Other successful and ambitious men have (for unknown reasons) such nicknames as "Chamber Pot," "Johnny Shits in the Road," and "Green Penis."[44] Like graffiti on something beautiful or a scratch on something smooth, a demeaning nickname tarnishes anyone who dares to shine too brightly.

THE CRIME OF DOING TOO WELL

Sociologists frequently assume that everyone wants to climb the social ladder, but they are wrong. So are those who think that everyone admires success. The reality is that many avoid doing anything that would improve their lives or place them above their peers, and discourage others from doing so as well. Nor is hostility to upward mobility limited to simple tribes and peasant communities such as those noted above; it is common in modern societies, too.

In the late 1920s and early 1930s, for example, a team of American researchers found that factory workers enforced an informal rule against working too hard:

"You should not turn out too much work. If you do, you are a 'rate-buster.'" Those who outperformed their workmates were subject to ostracism, ridicule, and a mild form of physical aggression called "binging" (a hard blow with a fist on the upper arm).[45] In modern Japan as well, working too hard "brings hatred."[46] According to anthropologist Max Gluckman, workers and students everywhere have a "golden mean" of industriousness "somewhere between underworking and overworking."[47]

Modern black American teenagers sometimes punish peers for "acting white," which includes working too hard and performing too well in school:

> Peer groups discourage their members from putting forth the time and effort required to do well in school and from adopting the attitudes and standard practices that enhance academic success. They oppose adopting appropriate academic attitudes and behaviors because they are considered "white." Peer group pressures against academic striving take many forms, including labeling (e.g., "brainiac" for students who receive good grades in their courses), exclusion from peer activities or ostracism, and physical assault.[48]

School-related behavior condemned as "white" includes "speaking standard English" (rather than the African American dialect), "spending a lot of time in the library studying," "working hard to get good grades in school," actually "getting good grades," and even "being on time" for classes. A black male student who works hard and does well, such as by enrolling in advanced courses or earning high grades, attracts ridicule as a "pervert" (homosexual) and typically has few (if any) friends.[49]

A serious and successful black male student can sometimes protect himself by "camouflaging" his "whiteness," such as by participating in sports (a "black" activity) or by behaving in a manner "suggesting he is a clown, comedian, or does not work very hard to earn the grades he receives." In the classroom he can similarly pretend not to know the answers to questions asked by teachers and try in other ways to make his skill and knowledge as inconspicuous as possible. But some social scientists have concluded that black students mostly prefer to perform below their abilities: "They have apparently decided consciously or unconsciously to avoid 'acting white.'"[50]

Beyond the school, any other behavior by low-income American blacks conducive to upward mobility may meet resistance from other blacks as well. Sociologist Elijah Anderson thus found that many urban blacks in Philadelphia follow a hedonistic and illicit way of life in a social arena they call "the street," and aggressively (possibly violently) discourage other blacks from behaving more respectably—which they condemn as "acting white" and "selling out" to the white establishment. Blacks trying to improve their lives therefore "have a great deal to overcome" in their own community.[51]

Upwardly mobile individuals also meet resistance in modern societies such as those of Scandinavia, the Netherlands, Australia, New Zealand, and parts of Asia. Scandinavians have what they sometimes call a "Jante Law" that prohibits anyone from claiming any form of superiority over anyone else. One Jante principle is "do not think you are special," and another is "do not think you are better than us."[52] The Dutch are likewise said to display a "deep resentment" of too much "success and ambition" and to "frown upon" those who "stand out in a crowd" because of their achievements.[53] The same applies to Australians and New Zealanders, who sometimes call their egalitarian ethic the "tall poppy syndrome" (meaning that they figuratively cut off the heads of those who rise too high).[54] Japanese say "the nail that sticks up gets hammered down."[55]

Jews have long been guilty of doing too well. And their high level of success in many areas of life partly explains the high degree of dislike, discrimination, and violence they have often attracted.[56] Late nineteenth-century philosopher Friedrich Nietzsche explained the widespread hostility to European Jews in his time entirely with their achievements in fields such as business, science, and the arts, which had "become so preponderant as to arouse mass envy and hatred" and had resulted in their "slaughter as scapegoats of every conceivable public and internal misfortune."[57] Historian Amos Elon comments that the upward mobility of Jews "was perhaps the fastest and greatest leap any minority has experienced in modern European history."[58] They were by far "the most upwardly mobile social group" in Germany: "The conspicuous success of the Jews in virtually all the professions and the arts excited the envy of the Germans, who inevitably felt themselves crowded out of their rightful opportunities on their home ground by an alien people."[59] The extent of Jewish achievement was so great that historian Yuri Slezkine even calls the twentieth century the "Jewish Century."[60]

According to early twentieth-century sociologist Werner Sombart, Jews largely invented capitalism and many of its mechanisms of finance and exchange, including various features of banking, securities, and the markets in which they are traded.[61] Central and Eastern European Jews once owned most of the businesses in many small towns and a large proportion of those in cities, and were also highly prominent in the professions such as medicine and law. In Hungary in the early twentieth century, for instance, they comprised about 5 percent of the population but "more than 50 percent of private medical doctors, lawyers, journalists, merchants, and businessmen."[62] And much as tribal and peasant people sometimes point to wealth or other success as evidence of witchcraft, European Christians have sometimes pointed to Jewish success as evidence of Jewish evil, often speaking of Jews as "thievish" and "crooked" businessmen and "parasites" or "bloodsuckers" who thrive on "the lifeblood of the poor" and continually "cheat" their customers.[63] Some Poles have claimed that the Talmud (which contains Jewish laws) requires all Jews to cheat Christians as much as possible.[64] More than cheaters, however, Jews have been characterized as evil incarnate— "enemies of the Cross of Christ"—even fiends and ghouls who kidnap, kill, and consume the blood of Christian children and engage in other unspeakable acts.[65]

The prominence of Jews in science, scholarship, and other intellectual realms has also caused resentment.[66] For instance, German scientists once formed an organization expressly devoted to discrediting what they called the "Jewish physics" of Albert Einstein, whose work had been receiving worldwide acclaim.[67] German leaders at the time reportedly "regarded this tousle-haired professor as the very embodiment of the German Jew, the totem of everything they hated about his kind." One even commented that "the Albert Einsteins" should all be sent to "a wild island where the only exit would be death" (a wish that soon effectively came true).[68]

Adolf Hitler's Nazi government introduced numerous anti-Jewish policies in the 1930s, including the boycotting of Jewish businesses, the banning of Jews from professions such as law and medicine, the firing of Jewish professors from German universities and research institutes, and the public burning of books by Jewish authors. Legal scholar Carl Schmitt urged German libraries to remove all books authored by Jews and said that German scholars should never cite contributions by Jews in their publications: "A Jewish author has for us no authority."[69] Eminent German philosopher Martin Heidegger complained that Jews occupied "a dominant position in cultural life beyond their proportional share of the overall population" and favored an end to what he called the "Judaization" (*Verjudung*) of the universities. As the rector of Freiburg University (and a member of the Nazi party), Heidegger is infamous for failing to support his equally eminent teacher Edmund Husserl when he was dismissed from the philosophy faculty and barred from the university (including its library) because of his Jewish ancestry.[70] Nazi official Joseph Goebbels proclaimed "the end of the age of Jewish intellectualism."[71]

Hitler and other German leaders falsely accused the Jews of various kinds of evil, such as conspiring to start both world wars for their own financial gain and planning to exterminate the entire German population if Germany could be defeated. In what they claimed was their own their own self-defense, they ultimately began a program to exterminate all the Jews of Europe (which they called the "Final Solution to the Jewish Problem"). They even viewed the genocidal program as their primary mission in World War II (which they called "the war against the Jews"). As they conquered each new area of Europe, their first concern was therefore always to capture the local Jews and either kill them where they lived or send them to concentration camps to be killed or used as slave laborers. Their larger plan was to kill all the Jews throughout the entire world: "Every last Jew, every Jewish child, had to die."[72]

The Nazi view of the Jews as a threat to German survival was a case of collective paranoia that possibly derived partly from the humiliating defeat of the Germans in World War I and their collapsing economy in the late 1920s and early 1930s.[73] But the Jews had also made the mistake of being too successful, and met a fate similar to that of the successful people killed as witches in simpler societies.[74] Moreover, their economic, intellectual, and other achievements continue to cause a great deal of anti-Semitism in the modern world. The prosperity and other achievements of the Jewish state of Israel, including its considerable military power, have likewise attracted hostility in the Middle East and elsewhere.

In the late twentieth and early twenty-first centuries, the United States became a major enemy to many people in various parts of the world, including Europe. And the accusations again arose partly if not primarily from too much success—another case of oversuperiority.[75] The United States had risen dramatically in the community of nations until it had attained a position of unprecedented global domination in the late twentieth century. Anti-Americanism correspondingly increased, reaching its highest level as the United States achieved superiority in nearly every sphere of human activity: economic, military, scientific, technological, and artistic (including popular culture such as music, fashion, and film).

Some explained American success with American evil and accused the United States of diverse crimes and a nefarious plan to rule and exploit the entire world. Anti-Americanism often included dislike and contempt not only for the American government and other instruments of American domination but for ordinary Americans as well, who were commonly considered vulgar, uncultured, ignorant, stupid, and otherwise inferior to Europeans or anyone else. Even when American behavior appeared to be admirable (such as when the United States provided economic, medical, and other help to other countries), American motives were said to be tainted by greed, selfishness, a lust for power, or other immoral tendencies. Virtually anything American was open to suspicion and subject to criticism and condemnation.[76]

The success of the United States also partly explains the emergence of a radical Muslim campaign of terrorism (which the Muslims considered a "holy war") intended to kill American and other Western civilians on airplanes and in other public places in the late twentieth and early twenty-first centuries.[77] After Muslim Arabs killed thousands in New York City's World Trade Center and in the Pentagon in Washington, D.C., in 2001 (known as the "9/11" terrorist attacks), for example, the leader of their organization (al-Qaeda) described the United States as the "satanic" leader of a "Crusade" against Islamic civilization, and the enemy of all Muslims.[78] Like the German campaign against the Jews half a century earlier, anti-American terrorism was to a significant degree a form of paranoid self-defense. But the rise of the United States to a position of global domination was not a delusion.[79] America's success had made it a witch among nations.

OVERINFERIORITY

Falling below others causes conflict as well. Some fall because of their own mistakes or failings, others because of the actions of someone else, and still others because of circumstances beyond anyone's control, such as economic declines, diseases, and accidents. Yet all such losses cause trouble, and the greater and faster the loss, the more trouble it causes: *Conflict is a direct function of overinferiority*.

Losers do not suffer losses gladly. No one forgives bosses who demote or fire them, peers who insult or humiliate them, or those who injure them, accidentally or otherwise. Even when their losses result entirely from their own incompetence, carelessness, or lack of effort, some losers still blame others. Tribal losers might blame a witch.[80] Modern losers might blame their society or a segment of their society, such as those who are rich and powerful, a particular race or ethnic group, or someone else.

And losers are dangerous. Sociologist Thomas Scheff suggests, for example, that losing nations are dangerous to other nations, and that both world wars of the twentieth century began at least partly because of earlier losses: World War I gave France a chance for revenge after losing a war to Germany in 1871, and World War II gave Germany a chance for revenge after losing World War I.[81] Whoever defeats anyone at anything should prepare for trouble.

SOCIAL CASTRATION

Honor is a form of social status based on force. A display of disrespect challenges a man of honor to defend himself in an appropriate fashion, or lose his honor.[82] And because honor is based on force, its defense requires force—violence: "The laundry of honor is only bleached with blood."[83] A defense of honor does not require victory, however, nor does it require physical power or skill. It requires only bravery: a willingness to risk injury or death.[84] Bravery assures that no man can be dishonored by anyone else.

Because violence has historically been the responsibility of men, honor has often been synonymous with masculinity itself. In Andalusia, for instance, the word for honor is "manliness" (*hombría* or *machismo*).[85] A man of honor is said to have "balls" (*cohones*), while a man who fails to defend his honor is said to have been "castrated" (*manso*).[86] Sicilians say that a brave man has "big testicles" (*coglioni grossi*), and a very brave man has "testicles reaching to the ground" (*coglioni fino a terra*). But a dishonored man has no testicles at all.[87]

Because a man can defend his honor only with force and bravery, only he can prevent his social castration. The Pashtun of Afghanistan and Pakistan thus say that only "the insulted person" can prove "his worth" by "recourse to force."[88] And a man of honor must answer every threat: "The honor of the affronted person is in jeopardy and requires 'satisfaction' if it is to return to its normal condition." Otherwise the loss is irreversible: "Honor is like glass. Once broken it cannot be mended."[89]

In Mexico and elsewhere in Latin America, a man of honor will tolerate no insult to himself or to a woman in his family, nor will he retreat from any threat to his honor.[90] As one young man explained: "If any so-and-so comes to me and says 'fuck your mother,' I answer 'fuck your mother a thousand times.' And if he gives one step forward and I take one step back, I lose prestige. . . . In a fight I never give up or say 'enough,' even though the other was killing me. I would try to go to my death smiling."[91] On the Micronesian island of Truk no man of honor ever backs down either, "even at the risk of death."[92] All true men prefer death to life as a coward.

"Codes of honor" specify when and how men should defend their honor, and all have similar rules.[93] One rule is that only an equal can threaten a man's honor.[94] A slave or other inferior cannot dishonor and thereby lower a free man or other superior, and it lowers a man even to notice an inferior's challenge.[95] For instance, the Berbers of Algeria consider it beneath a man to answer a black man's insult: "Let him bark until he grows weary of it."[96] Another rule requires a man always to defend his honor against the challenger himself and not against any of the challenger's associates, much less someone who might be especially weak or vulnerable (such as a woman or child).[97]

Social elites such as the nobility of feudal Europe and the warrior class (*samurai*) of feudal Japan had strict codes of honor, and apparently were ready to kill or die whenever their honor was challenged.[98] In the American South in the eighteenth and nineteenth centuries, an "affair of honor" between "gentlemen" such as plantation owners or politicians could quickly lead to a duel with pistols or swords.[99] Gentlemen in Germany and France, particularly military officers, had such duels as late as the early twentieth century.[100] The offended party normally requested an apology, and if no apology was given he demanded the "gentleman's satisfaction" of a duel. A refusal to give this satisfaction was dishonorable in itself.[101]

Although honor has declined in the modern West, it still survives in some social locations, particularly among young men at the bottom of society.[102] A "code of the street" regulates the defense of honor in low-income African American neighborhoods, for example, where a display of disrespect (known as "dissing") might lead to violence and death.[103] A related African American practice is a duel-like exchange of often witty insults (known by such names as "the dozens," "sounding," "rapping," or "ranking").[104] Each insult (or "put-down") provokes an insult in return, which in turn provokes another, and so on, until the exchange ends in a draw or escalates into violence or a threat of violence. Insulting someone's mother is a particularly serious and common provocation, as in the following example: "Man, tell your mama to stop coming around my house all the time. I'm tired of fucking her and I think you should know that it ain't no accident you look like me." Merely saying "your ma" or "your mother" is itself recognized as a challenge and might immediately lead to violence.[105]

Men of honor are known for their "touchiness," and might construe various incidents short of direct insults as challenges requiring a defense.[106] One must therefore be careful not do anything that could conceivably offend such a man, such as bump into him without a proper apology, stare at him without good reason, or push ahead of him in a line. As one former Los Angeles gang member remarked: "Where I lived, stepping on someone's shoe was a capital offense punishable by death."[107] For that matter, most American gang violence pertains to honor. Just as a young man will attack any peer who "disrespects" him, so his gang will attack any gang whose member "disrespects" his gang.[108]

The defense of honor is also a common cause of violence in American prisons.[109] Although the typical incident begins with an insult, prisoners occasionally seek to feminize and thereby dishonor a fellow prisoner by forcing or trying to force him into a passive homosexual role (known as a "punk"). They even speak of punks with feminine pronouns ("she" or "her"), and may fight to the death to avoid this fate. One prisoner commented that "if you are a man you must either kill or turn the tables on anyone who propositions you with threats of force." He described how he once defended his own honor: "The first prisoner—a middle-aged convict—who tried to fuck me I drew my knife on. I forced him to his knees, and with my knife at his throat made him perform fellatio on my flaccid penis in front of three of his partners."[110]

Nations have honor as well, and a challenge to national honor may cause a war.[111] As early twentieth-century historian Heinrich von Treitschke remarked: "If the flag of the state is insulted, it is the duty of the state to demand satisfaction, and if the satisfaction is not forthcoming, to declare war, however trivial the occasion may appear."[112] World War I began at least partly as a defense of national honor, and other nations joined the fighting for the same reason.[113] The American Civil War was likewise regarded as an affair of honor.[114] Honor is no less important on the field of battle itself. Those who fail to display bravery dishonor their nations, military units, and themselves. Some prefer death to surrender, and consider enemy soldiers who surrender to be cowards.[115]

A defense of honor is a defense of equality, and every challenge to honor requires violence, whether a fistfight between teenagers, a formal duel between aristocrats, a shooting between gangs, or a war between nations. Otherwise it is not a matter of honor. But insults and other assaults on a person's reputation also cause other forms of conflict. In ancient Greece an insult or other humiliation might lead to litigation.[116] In modern America a false statement that damages someone's reputation is legally actionable as "slander" or "defamation of character" (if spoken) or "libel" (if written). Yet when honor is at stake, litigation cannot replace a fist, knife, sword, or gun. The use of law only proves that a man is not really a man.

HARD TIMES

Poverty alone does not cause crime and violence. Poverty is a static condition, and a static condition cannot cause crime, violence, or any other kind of conflict. The poor are not inherently dangerous, nor is anyone else. But what *is* dangerous is downward mobility: *becoming* poor.

Nor do the poor steal merely because they are poor. What causes theft and related predatory crime such as burglary and robbery is not poverty but loss—what economist Reuven Brenner calls a "worsened position in the distribution of wealth." Predatory crime rises as people fall: "As the fraction of people who become relatively poorer increases, the crime rate increases."[117] In the United States during the first half of the twentieth-century, for example, burglary and robbery increased when the economic cycle worsened, and decreased when it improved.[118] So did embezzlement.[119]

Criminologist Donald Cressey interviewed more than a hundred embezzlers in prison and found that literally all had stolen money from their employers after suffering financial problems such as bad investments, gambling losses, or living beyond their means.[120] Shoplifting also increases during economic declines.[121]

Teenagers who perform poorly in school, sports, and other activities commit more crime ("juvenile delinquency"). Sociologist Albert Cohen suggests that youth gangs ("delinquent subcultures") arise mainly among "failures," especially boys who do poorly in school. Often their crimes are "non-utilitarian, malicious, and negativistic," such as vandalizing property, stealing things they do not need, or (in one unusual case) defecating on a teacher's desk. Such behavior is not random, however, nor is it merely "senseless," "anti-social," or "mean." The cause is a movement of vertical time: falling below their peers.[122]

Some losers attack those responsible for their losses. In at least twenty cases during the 1980s and 1990s, for instance, fired American postal workers killed or wounded their former supervisors (and often others) in a scenario so common it came to be known as "going postal."[123] One man killed his supervisor and her boyfriend at her home, then went to the post office and killed two other employees as they arrived for work. Another former postal employee killed four supervisors and wounded five other postal workers before killing himself.[124] In a similar case, an American university professor who had recently been denied tenure (a form of termination) shot and killed her department chairman and two other colleagues and wounded three others at a faculty meeting.[125]

Other losers disrupt and disturb their own families with such behavior as heavy drinking, using drugs, or abusing their wives and children. Anthropologist Katherine Newman thus describes a "reign of terror" that followed the employment problems of one young woman's father: "The more menial her father's jobs became, the more he drank. The more he drank, the more violent he became. He vented his rage and frustration on his wife and child, leaving 'bruises the size of oranges on [his wife's] face,' choke marks on the young woman's neck, and 'stains on the walls from the plates of food he threw in disgust.'"[126] One businessman shot and killed his wife, mother-in-law, three sons, and himself after losing his job and suffering losses in the stock market.[127] After another man lost his job and fell into debt, he killed his wife, five children, and himself.[128] Still other losers run amok and attack complete strangers, as occurred in the "McDonald's Massacre" of 1984 when a man who had lost his job went to a restaurant and killed twenty-one people.[129]

Losers are also politically dangerous. For example, political scientist James Davies observes that it is not the static condition of economic deprivation that causes revolutions or other political violence, but rather something dynamic: economic declines after periods of improvement (described by a curve in the shape of an inverted "J").[130] Lesser forms of political opposition (such as antigovernment protests and election defeats of incumbents) probably follow a similar pattern.

Losers are even dangerous to themselves. Sociologist Émile Durkheim long ago found that the chronically poor have one of the lowest suicide rates, and even proposed that a life of poverty is "a protection against suicide." But he also found that *becoming* poor does lead people to kill themselves: Suicide increases during economic declines such as stock market crashes, depressions, and recessions.[131] Sociologists Andrew Henry and James Short similarly report that in the first half of the twentieth century the American suicide rate rose during economic declines, and that those who had suffered the greatest and fastest losses were the most likely to end their lives.[132] Suicide so frequently results from financial problems in modern Japan that financial assistance has become a recognized form of suicide prevention.[133]

Some losers lose their sanity. Sociologist Edwin Lemert thus discovered that American men diagnosed as "paranoid" (because of their delusions of being targets of dangerous conspiracies) typically exhibited their symptoms after an "actual or threatened loss of status" or a "series of failures" such as demotions and terminations. He also found that after the men suffered setbacks in their careers some of their associates actually did begin to conspire against them in minor ways, such as by excluding them from workplace conversations, lunches, and other group activities.[134] Their paranoia had a basis in reality.

VIOLENCE AS VERTICAL TIME

Wealth includes any material condition of human existence such as food or shelter, a currency of exchange such as gold or money, a means of production such as land or slaves, or anything else of value.[135] The human body itself is a form of wealth, and the most fundamental means of production. The same applies to health, as acknowledged in the old saying that "my health is my wealth."[136] Healthy people are also a form of wealth for others—especially obvious in the case of slaves but equally true of relatives, friends, or others who provide help to anyone else.[137] Injury and sickness therefore belong to the same family as other fluctuations of wealth. A loss of health is a form of downward mobility, and the greatest decline is death.[138]

Homicide is prohibited by every code of law and morality, including the biblical commandment "thou shalt not kill." But the seriousness of homicide depends on who is killed. For example, killing a superior with more skills or responsibilities is more serious than killing someone with fewer skills and responsibilities. Killing a prominent citizen, such as a professional or business executive, is more serious than killing someone who is unemployed and poor, such as a homeless person with no responsibilities at all.[139] Killing a monarch or other political leader is all the worse.[140] And because any death is normally a loss for others besides the victim, killing someone with many relationships with others is more serious than killing someone with few relationships, or none at all.[141]

Some early legal codes listed specific amounts of compensation required for killing and injuring people with various skills and responsibilities. One Burgundian code required greater payments for killing slaves with greater skills: The payment for killing an unskilled slave was thirty *solidi* (a unit of currency) to the slave's owner, for instance, but the price rose to forty *solidi* for killing a slave who was a carpenter, fifty for killing a blacksmith, a hundred for killing a silversmith, and two hundred for killing a goldsmith.[142] In one Lombard code the payment for injuries was a precise proportion of the payment for killing a person of the victim's rank: The price for gouging out an eye or cutting off a nose or foot was one-half the death payment for someone of the victim's rank, for example; cutting off an ear was one-fourth the death payment; and cutting off a thumb was one-sixth the death payment. Lesser losses required lesser payments, such as sixteen *solidi* for cutting off an index finger, little finger, or big toe; eight for a ring finger; six for a second toe; five for a middle finger; three for a third or fourth toe; and two for a little toe.[143] The Brehon laws of ancient Ireland based the payment partly on the importance of the body part to the person who lost it. For instance, the loss of a fingernail by a harpist required a greater payment than the loss of a fingernail by someone else. The laws also specified the payments required of owners for damage done by their animals, such as marauding by pigs of various sizes (a measure of how much they eat), kicking by horses, biting by dogs, and stinging by bees.[144] Modern payments for deaths and injuries are reckoned according to their financial consequences as well.[145]

Another remedy for an injury is an equal injury to the one responsible—as in the Bible's "an eye for an eye, a tooth for a tooth, a hand for a hand, a foot for a foot" or the Koran's "life for life, eye for eye, nose for nose."[146] Some killings initiate exchanges of killings ("blood feuds") that continue for many years.[147] These exchanges typically occur when those involved are otherwise equal, so that each killing exactly reciprocates another.[148]

Whereas modern people distinguish between intentional injuries (such as violent attacks) and unintentional injuries (such as accidents), those in earlier and simpler societies may not, and their conceptions of who should be liable for injuries are sometimes broader than modern conceptions.[149] Among the Jalé of New Guinea, for example, the family of a man accidentally killed during a hunting trip expects a payment (in pigs) from the one who invited him to go hunting—because he would still be alive had he not been invited. And if a woman dies in childbirth, her relatives demand a payment from her husband—because he was responsible for her pregnancy: "She died by his penis."[150] When the Tlingit Indians of the Northwest Coast suffer an accident, they "blame the local people" where the accident occurred. In one case, for instance, the family of a chief who drowned when he drunkenly capsized his canoe demanded and received a payment of compensation from the village he visited before the accident.[151] The Kwakiutl Indians of the same region might attack and kill someone completely unconnected to their loss (a remedy similar to running amok). When several of a chief's relatives accidentally drowned during a canoe trip, for example, he exhorted his tribesmen to "let someone else wail!"—so they killed eight Indians of another tribe who happened to be camping near their village.[152]

Suicide and other self-injuries also cause conflict. Those who share a self-killer's life and benefit from it to some degree might even criticize the self-killer for victimizing *them*: "How could he do that to me?" "Why would he be so selfish?" The Igbo of southeastern Nigeria consider suicide an "abomination" and "offense against the Earth," and punish anyone who kills himself with ostracism— in death: His relatives will not touch his body or mourn him, and his corpse is thrown into a taboo area called the "evil forest" and left unburied.[153] In medieval England the Crown confiscated the property of any man who killed himself, and his body was barred from the church cemetery and buried at a crossroads with a stake through the heart.[154] Modern people might consider suicide a family disgrace, and try to keep it a secret or otherwise avoid talking about it. When philosopher Ludwig Wittgenstein's older brother Rudolf committed suicide, for instance, their father was so "ashamed" that he prohibited everyone in the family from ever mentioning his name again. Ludwig himself considered suicide a form of "cowardice."[155] Others might blame a suicide on someone else, including themselves—a "frequent" occurrence after suicides in modern America.[156] In some African tribes people might kill themselves (or threaten to do so) because they know a particular person will be blamed. The relatives of a woman who kills herself might thus blame her husband, as if he had killed her himself.[157] In early China a child or grandchild who caused the suicide of a parent or grandparent was beheaded.[158]

HEALTH AS WEALTH

Sickness is another form of downward mobility. It not only incapacitates and kills but frequently leads to a condition of social dependency similar to a child's, to confinement, and to avoidance by other people.[159] It also causes various kinds of conflict, including violence.

Many tribal people view sickness itself as a form of supernatural violence such as black magic or spiritual retribution, and look for someone to blame for every serious case. Whereas a minor sickness might cause only a vague suspicion, a fatal sickness might lead to the execution of a witch or sorcerer. The Azande of Sudan believe that literally every fatal illness and accident results from witchcraft: "All death to Azande is murder."[160] The Gebusi of New Guinea commonly blame sicknesses (especially fatal ones) on a particular form of sorcery: knotting some of the victim's excrement in a leaf, extending the length of the sickness by preserving the knotted leaf, and causing the victim to die by burning the leaf. Although few Gebusi actually engage in sorcery, they readily accuse fellow tribesmen of doing so to cause sickness and death in the tribe—and kill, butcher, cook, and eat the alleged offender in a communal feast.[161] The Kwanga of New Guinea likewise attribute "almost all deaths" to sorcery, but usually only gossip about the suspects and stigmatize them as murderers.[162]

Eskimos believe that every sickness results from the violation of a taboo by the victim and that recovery is possible only if the person confesses his or her sins to a shaman.[163] The Nuer of Sudan believe disease results from the violation of taboos, but do not think it is always the violator who suffers. A man's back problem might be blamed on his wife's adultery, for example, or his yaws (a disease with skin lesions) might be blamed on incest by one of his relatives.[164]

But conflict associated with illness need not involve a supernatural element. During slavery in the American South, for instance, slave owners sometimes blamed fatal sicknesses on poisoning by their slaves (known as "negro-poison")— almost certainly a false accusation in most if not all cases. As one Kentuckian noted at the time: "Every disease at all obscure and uncommon in its symptoms and fatal in its termination is immediately decided to be a case of negro-poison."[165] Modern Americans sometimes bring lawsuits against corporations (such as tobacco, liquor, and building materials companies) for causing various diseases (such as cancer and lung disorders) by selling unhealthful products or exposing people to unhealthful environments.

The nature of the blame for a disease or other misfortune depends on the scale of the loss. Whereas a single death might be blamed on a single individual (such as a witch or sorcerer), many deaths might be blamed on an entire group (such as another tribe or nation).[166] The Gebusi might thus blame a single fatal disease on a sorcerer in their own tribe, but blame epidemics that kill numerous people on "magical smoke" sent by weaker tribes who cannot defeat them in warfare.[167] The Shavante of Brazil likewise blame epidemics on black magic by weaker tribes, or possibly weaker factions in their own tribe—whom they attack and kill in retaliation.[168]

Collective blame also occurred during the historic epidemic of bubonic plague known as the "Black Death," which began in the fourteenth century and has been called "the greatest catastrophe that has befallen Western Europe in the last thousand years."[169] The epidemic killed at least one-third of Europe's population (as many as 100 million people), disrupted the economy, brought widespread famine, and otherwise radically reshaped Europe.[170] People fled their homes in panic with nowhere to go; entire communities disappeared; spouses were lost and replaced at an unprecedented rate; and wealth rapidly circulated by inheritance as the disease raced through the population.[171]

No one at the time knew that fleas carried by rats had spread the Black Death from China to Europe, but they soon developed another explanation of its origin: the Jews. In particular, a rumor arose that Jews were spreading the disease by poisoning Christian wells. Some said that a Spanish rabbi named Jacob was leading "an international Jewish conspiracy" with an "army of secret agents," and that "the Jews were contaminating the wells because they sought world domination."[172] Jewish leaders allegedly obtained the poison from Asia, prepared it from "spiders, owls, and other poisonous animals," or created it with "Jewish spells." In any case, partly because Jews had a lower death rate during the epidemic (possibly due to better hygiene and less contact with farm animals, where rats and fleas congregated) and partly because of confessions obtained from Jews by torture, the Jewish conspiracy theory gained widespread support.[173] The result was the most destructive violence ever inflicted on the Jews until the Germans killed six million in the twentieth century.[174]

Jewish communities were completely or nearly annihilated in numerous cities and towns in Germany, France, Austria, Switzerland, Holland, Belgium, Italy, Spain, and elsewhere. In Basel, Switzerland, for example, the entire Jewish community was herded into a large wooden house on an island in the Rhine River, the doors bolted, and the building set afire. The same process occurred in Strasbourg, France. In Brandenburg, Germany, Jews were "burned on a grill like meat." Elsewhere they were hunted down and "bludgeoned to death with pikes, axes, and scythes."[175] Although sometimes given a choice of conversion or death, many Jews chose to die in their burning homes (or killed themselves by other means) rather than accept baptism or face a worse death at the hands of enraged crowds. Those who agreed to be baptized were often killed anyway.[176]

Major outbreaks of the Black Death continued until the early eighteenth century, typically claiming the lives of one-third to one-half of each affected locality in a single year.[177] And with each new outbreak Christians blamed and killed any Jews they could find. The English had expelled their entire Jewish population in the thirteenth century and had no Jews to blame, but they developed their own theories of the epidemic's origin. When it struck in 1639, for instance, the English sometimes said the Scots had "poisoned the wells," and when it struck in 1665 they blamed the French for sending "bottles of infected air" to spread the disease.[178]

Many Western European Jews avoided the massacres by fleeing to Central and Eastern Europe, especially Poland (which was largely free of the epidemic and otherwise safe).[179] When few Jews remained anywhere in Western Europe, the blame shifted to "plague-makers" or "plague-spreaders" who allegedly infected the population with poisonous powders and ointments. After the Protestant Reformation in the sixteenth century, for example, Catholics sometimes said that Protestant Germany was "the home of the plague-makers." Italian Catholics in Naples and Milan blamed Lutherans, and Spanish Catholics blamed a seventeenth-century outbreak on Protestants from the Swiss city of Geneva.[180]

Both Catholics and Protestants also blamed the Black Death on social inferiors such as gravediggers, "vagabonds," and "vagrants." Suspects were tortured until they confessed, then burned alive. After the epidemic spread to one German town in 1607, for instance, officials burned nineteen people, including a number of gravediggers and their wives, the young son of one, and an elderly beggar. Prosecutions followed outbreaks of the disease until the late seventeenth century, and often involved unusually severe forms of capital punishment, such as pinching the flesh of convicted plague-spreaders with red-hot tongs and amputating their hands before burning them at the stake.[181]

The Black Death was a devastating movement of social time that decimated the population of Europe. Although it was not a case of crime or immorality, the epidemic was a good time for false accusations. And thousands were punished for something they did not do.[182]

5 | Understratification

Any form of inequality is a vertical distance, and any fluctuation of vertical distance is a movement of vertical time. An increase of inequality is overstratification, and a decrease is understratification. And just as too much inequality causes conflict, so does too little:

Conflict is a direct function of understratification.

Inequality decreases whenever a superior falls or an inferior rises. Superiors fall because of misfortunes or victimizations or their own incompetence or misconduct, and inferiors rise when for any reason their conditions of life improve or they challenge their superiors in any way. The fall of a superior is *undersuperiority*, and the rise of an inferior is *underinferiority*. The greater and faster any such decrease of inequality, the more conflict it causes.

UNDERSUPERIORITY

The fall of a superior might mean trouble for someone else, especially an inferior. Among the Tlingit Indians of the Northwest Coast, for instance, an aristocrat caught stealing might claim he was "bewitched" and could not help himself. Why else would he steal? Surely the guilty party was an inferior (such as a slave) who resented his wealth and power and wanted to ruin his life. Soon enough one of his slaves is identified as the witch and killed for causing the theft.[1] Modern superiors with problems might also blame inferiors, as when bosses blame their employees, officers blame their subordinates, or coaches blame their players. The greater and faster the fall, the greater the danger: *Conflict is a direct function of undersuperiority.*

MISFORTUNE AS WITCHCRAFT

Although all accusations of witchcraft are false, all make sociological sense. Some accused witches are guilty of rising too high above their peers, for example (see "Success as Witchcraft" in chapter 4), but more often the accusation occurs after a prosperous person suffers a misfortune such as an accident or sickness. When this happens the alleged witch is typically an inferior of the victim, who may then be killed by associates of the victim or possibly executed by a court of law. Yet the real witch is the movement of vertical time: the superior's fall.

Some tribal people and peasants see evidence of witchcraft in virtually any disturbing event. The Sukuma of Tanzania see the possibility of black magic in "almost anything stressful or unfortunate," including "sudden deaths of healthy people; miscarriages and infertility; the failure of rain when it falls so patchily and seems to avoid particular fields; deaths from snake-bite; the accidental burning down of a thatched roof house; thefts as well as road accidents."[2] The Shona of Zimbabwe even explain their own blunders with witchcraft: "Instead of blaming himself or analyzing his actions to learn from his past mistakes," a Shona man is quick to blame a witch—"the unseen enemy who is everywhere and is always ready to harm a good, honest, unsuspecting person."[3]

A suspicion of witchcraft normally arises when a person whose life has been going well suffers a sudden reversal such as an unexplained fire, the death of a horse or cow, or the sickness of a family member. Next he begins to wonder, "Who might envy me and wish to ruin my happiness?" The usual suspect is therefore someone whose life has not been going so well (such as a poor widow or someone else with economic difficulties), particularly a neighbor or other acquaintance who might have reason to take revenge against the victim.[4] Sorcery accusations have the same logic.[5]

In many societies people believe that success leads to envy and resentment and might in turn result in the use of black magic or other aggression, so they try to avoid seeming successful or possibly even being successful at all. In parts of Latin America where Indian peasants fear that any sign of superiority might provoke the attack of a witch, for instance, they try never to appear to be doing too well, such as by wearing shoes instead of going barefoot.[6] And if they suffer a misfortune after displaying any sign of prosperity, they are quick to suspect that a witch was responsible.[7] The Zapotec Indians of southern Mexico become especially suspicious when they suffer a loss after their fortunes "have risen" and a neighbor's "have sunk." In most cases they do not directly accuse the neighbor himself of witchcraft, however, but conclude that he must have hired a witch from another locality.[8]

When the Nyoro of Uganda suspect witchcraft caused a misfortune, they consult a shaman ("witch doctor"), who always decides that the witch was a less fortunate neighbor with reason to envy or dislike the victim. The alleged witch is then burned to death in dried banana leaves.[9] In some tribes the death of a child might lead to an accusation against a spinster or other childless woman assumed to be envious of the child's mother.[10] In polygynous tribes such as the Gusii of Kenya, the suspect is often a co-wife with no children of her own.[11]

Because modernization increases the fluctuation of wealth among tribal and peasant people, it sometimes increases the rate of witchcraft accusations as well.[12] In parts of East Africa, for example, migrant workers who suffer misfortunes after returning to their home villages might blame neighbors who could be envious of their new "riches."[13] The introduction of cotton as a cash crop increased witchcraft accusations in Tanzania: The typical accuser is a successful cotton farmer who suffers a loss, and the typical suspect is someone who might envy or resent the farmer's prosperity, such as a poor old woman without relatives to help her in times of need.[14]

Witchcraft accusations in the Western world also increased with modernization.[15] In sixteenth- and seventeenth-century England, for instance, every accused witch was someone poor enough to be envious of the victim, especially someone who might carry a grudge against the victim for something that happened in the past.[16] In one farming region of modern France, accusations of witchcraft still occasionally occur after a loss or series of losses by a farmer whose fortunes had been improving. Once again the accused witch is normally someone less fortunate who might be "displeased" by a neighbor's economic superiority. Because the farmers believe that witches gain whatever their victims lose, any recent improvement in the suspect's life provides all the more evidence of guilt.[17] But in every case a previously prosperous person's loss is what leads to the initial suspicion.

THE EVIL EYE

People might also suspect their neighbors of possessing a dangerous power called the "evil eye."[18] As in many witchcraft cases, the suspicion arises when a misfortune such as an accident or a sickness befalls someone whose life had been going well. The motivation for the evil eye is thought to be the envy of someone less fortunate as well.[19] But unlike cases of witchcraft, the harm done by the evil eye is believed to be unintended and unconscious. Those who possess the evil eye are nevertheless considered a constant danger to anyone who prospers in any realm of life.[20]

The evil eye is not dangerous to the high and mighty such as monarchs or aristocrats, however, but only to ordinary individuals who rise a bit too high above their peers. The usual suspect is someone largely similar to the victim who might still have reason to envy something the victim has recently accomplished or acquired.[21] Also subject to suspicion are those so poor they would presumably envy almost anyone. For this reason many beggars apparently receive much of their income from people who fear their evil glance.[22] It has even been speculated that one of the Ten Commandments—"thou shalt not covet thy neighbor's house . . . nor anything that is thy neighbor's"—was directed at the motivation behind the evil eye.[23]

Those who fear the evil eye commonly try to counteract its power by wearing protective amulets (such as a pendant depicting an eye), displaying ornaments (such as a horseshoe over their door), performing rituals (such as squeezing their testicles while spitting in the direction of someone suspected of possessing the evil eye), or using other techniques.[24] Fear of the evil eye is particularly strong on special occasions that might be likely to excite someone's envy, such as weddings, the completion of new houses, or the birth of children. It is believed that brides originally wore wedding veils to shield themselves from the evil eye, for example, and that housewarming parties were originally held to neutralize envy of the owner's new house.[25]

Those who fear the evil eye typically try to hide any good fortune they might enjoy, such as by dressing or living in a manner that makes them appear to have less wealth than is actually the case. But to be completely safe, one must truly have no superiority over anyone else. Some people therefore avoid doing anything that might raise them above their neighbors: "everything which has a chance of making one man and his family a bit more successful than the average." The safest are poor—as poor as everyone else.[26]

Yet because everyone eventually suffers an accident, a sickness, or other misfortune, evidence of the evil eye's power is always at hand. In one village in Tunisia, for instance, men who work as weavers of cloth can readily list particular accidents and other misfortunes they believe were suffered by fellow weavers who out-produced and out-earned their peers. And to protect themselves as much as possible, they limit their own production to "a golden mean that most weavers and their wives, even the poorly skilled, can attain." They also avoid anyone who works too hard, for fear of being inadvertently harmed by any evil glance the hard worker might attract.[27] The Shilluk of Sudan believe the victim of the evil eye is "always" a "shining mark," so they try not to "shine" at all—which means never appearing in public dressed in any clothing or with any possessions that might make them look prosperous and never doing anything else associated with wealth. Even so, when misfortune strikes they are still quick to blame a neighbor's envious glance.[28]

Romanian mothers consider their babies (especially attractive ones) to be vulnerable to the evil eye, and try to protect them by speaking of them in disparaging terms (such as "ugly thing" or "horror") when anyone is present who might envy their good fortune.[29] For the same reason Middle Eastern mothers might leave their children unwashed or even "filthy," dress them in tattered clothing, and publicly criticize them as "homely" or "dim-witted."[30]

The healthy also fear the envious glance of the sick and disabled, and the attractive fear those who are deformed or otherwise unattractive. In South India, "the person who is suffering from some physical defect such as blindness, deafness, lameness, or one who is a hunchback or an albino is greatly feared, as it is regarded as certain that such a person will be jealous of those blessed with health and soundness of body."[31] Sicilians fear anyone with a hunched back, hooked nose, long neck, or other feature considered ugly. Because the subordination of women is assumed to make women envious of men, men especially fear the evil eye of women. And because a beautiful woman has an advantage over other women, she too fears the evil eye of women. The veiling and seclusion of women in traditional Muslim societies might thus at least partly serve to protect both men and beautiful women from the evil eye of women.[32]

In most cases, however, people do not openly accuse anyone of possessing or casting the evil eye. More often they only gossip about those thought to have its power, and possibly ostracize them and avoid uttering their names, as if they no longer exist (a form of social death).[33] But violence is not unknown. Among the nomads of South Persia, for example, a person thought to have harmed someone with the evil eye might be subjected to a "severe beating or even lynching."[34] In one area of India, peasants have been known to treat a sickness attributed to the evil eye by knocking out the front teeth of the one believed responsible.[35] Some Greek peasants prescribe a more extreme remedy: "If it is a woman who has cast the eye, then destroy her breasts. If it is a man who has cast the eye, then crush his genitals."[36]

Yet the evil eye is not merely an irrational notion found among ignorant peasants in backward societies. It is a supernatural form of something found everywhere:

the danger of rising above one's peers. It also shows how the fall of a social superior can cause conflict, even when the fall is no one's fault at all.

THEFT AS VERTICAL TIME

All accusations of witchcraft and the evil eye are obviously false. No harm is ever really inflicted by the allegedly guilty party—usually a social inferior said to have victimized a superior. But of course some inferiors do victimize superiors. Such is true of most thieves, including burglars and robbers.[37] Theft always reduces some-one's wealth, and it typically reduces someone's superiority as well, if only to a small degree.[38] It causes conflict wherever economic inequality is found, and causes more conflict where inequality is greater.

Theft is the subject of a biblical commandment: "Thou shalt not steal."[39] But its seriousness depends both on how much is stolen and who steals from whom.[40] Just as stealing more is worse, so is stealing from a social superior. And the greater the superiority of the victim, the worse it is. Ancient India's Laws of Manu thus pun-ished lesser thefts with a fine multiplied by the amount stolen, but increased the punishment to amputation of the thief's hands or feet or even execution when the theft was greater and the victim's caste higher than the thief's.[41] The higher the caste of the thief, however, the less severe was the punishment, and those of the highest caste (Brahmins) were immune to almost all punishment.[42]

An early Frankish code listed the punishment for various thefts in great detail, such as the theft of various animals and other forms of property categorized to reflect their relative value, including horses ("a horse that pulls a cart," a colt, mare, pregnant mare, stallion), dogs (a hunting dog, herding dog, guard dog), birds (a hunting hawk, swan, goose, turtle dove), cattle (a bull, cow, cow with a calf), a pig, sheep, goat, beehive, tree, cow's bell, horse's hobble, a grafted twig from an apple tree, an eel net, a woman's girdle-belt, and assorted agricultural products. But the thief could always reduce the seriousness of the crime by returning or replacing whatever was stolen: Whereas a slave who committed a small theft was punished with 120 lashes of the whip and one who committed a larger theft with castration, for instance, the penalty declined to a fine in both cases if the property was returned or its full value paid to the victim.[43] The Burgundians sometimes subjected the thief to a special humiliation, such as making a man who stole a dog "kiss the posterior of that dog."[44]

Theft was the "most prevalent" crime in medieval Europe, and its punishment was extremely severe by modern standards, partly because the victim was so often greatly superior to the thief—who was likely to be a poor peasant or homeless wanderer.[45] In Germany the usual punishment for a cutpurse (similar to a pickpocket) was amputation of the thumb for a small theft, amputation of the hand for a larger theft, and hanging for any second offense. The Bamberg code punished larger thefts by amputating a hand or by blinding or hanging the thief. The Swabian code punished any theft from the Church with "breaking on the wheel": The executioner tied the offender to a wagon wheel in a spread-eagle position, broke each of his arm and leg bones with a blunt instrument, and then left him to die (which could take more than a day).[46]

In England until the eleventh century, a thief and his family might be enslaved.[47] In the twelfth century a thief caught in the act might be hanged. In Leicestershire in 1124, for instance, forty-four thieves were hanged in a single day. In the thirteenth century the courts punished a small theft ("petty larceny") with amputation of a thumb or ear, whipping, or exile for the first offense; amputation (such as loss of the second ear) for the second offense; and death for the third offense. If caught committing a major theft ("grand larceny"), a man might be beheaded, buried alive, thrown from a cliff into the sea, or tied to a stake at low tide to drown as the sea returned.[48]

By the fourteenth century almost three-fourths of all criminal cases in England pertained to theft.[49] Hanging was mandatory for horse thieves, burglars, robbers, and pirates, and optional for lesser thieves such as shoplifters and pickpockets.[50] For several centuries the "most popular" form of theft was "poaching": taking wild game, fish, firewood, stone, clay, medicinal herbs, or other natural resources from another's land without permission. Most of the victims were large landowners, while most of the offenders were poor peasants. And in the eighteenth century poaching joined the list of crimes punishable by hanging.[51]

Thieves who are equal or superior to their victims normally receive less severe punishments, if they are punished at all. Recall, for example, the leniency enjoyed by upper-caste thieves in India. In nineteenth-century America, a middle-class woman caught shoplifting was often defined as mentally ill—as might also occur today.[52] In the largely egalitarian Orokaiva tribe of New Guinea, the victim of a theft might inflict a further loss on himself as a way of "shaming" the thief. In one case, for example, a man who discovered that someone had stolen a watermelon from his garden immediately hacked the rest of his crop into small pieces and scattered them on a path where the thief "would pass and realize what he had done." After finding that one of his spears had been stolen from the veranda of his house, another man "took an ax and razed his house to the ground before the eyes of the whole village."[53]

In some social locations, however, theft causes little or no conflict at all. Those in close relationships such as families and friendships often share so much of everything that theft is nearly or literally impossible.[54] Theft is also difficult or impossible among simple hunter-gatherers who have little property and share whatever they have—a way of life Karl Marx and Friedrich Engels called "primitive communism."[55] According to anthropologist A. R. Radcliffe-Brown, for instance, the Andaman Islanders (near India) have "communism" and virtually no theft, and anthropologist Colin Turnbull mentions that theft is "almost nonexistent" among the Mbuti Pygmies of Zaire.[56] Such tribes are similar to fictional utopias where "nobody owns anything to rob."[57]

UNDERINFERIORITY

Upward mobility causes conflict when it introduces or increases inequality (see "Oversuperiority" in chapter 4), but also when it decreases inequality by reducing or eliminating the superiority of superiors. The more inferiors threaten the superiority of superiors and the faster they do so, the more conflict they cause: *Conflict is a direct function of underinferiority.*

The rise of an inferior nation might cause a war.[58] In his *History of the Peloponnesian War*, ancient Greek historian Thucydides argued that the rise of Athens in the fifth century B.C.E. caused a war with Sparta: "What made war inevitable was the growth of Athenian power and the fear this caused in Sparta."[59] Geographer Halford Mackinder argues that the major wars throughout history have resulted from fluctuations in international stratification: "The great wars of history—we have had a world war about every hundred years for the last four centuries—are the outcome, direct and indirect, of the unequal growth of nations."[60] Political scientists Abramo Organski and Jacek Kugler propose more precisely that the likelihood of war is a direct function of the speed at which an inferior nation rises to challenge the position of a superior nation.[61]

Organski and Kugler also note that "leapfrogging" by an inferior nation—becoming a former superior's superior—is all the more dangerous. From the late nineteenth to the late twentieth century, for example, every major war began when a less powerful nation rose or threatened to rise above a more powerful nation: "At the level of great powers, wars occur if the balance of power is not stable—if, and only if, one member of the pair is in the process of overtaking the other in power."[62] Leapfrogging or its threat preceded the Franco-Russian War in 1870, the Russo-Japanese War in 1904, World War I in 1914, and World War II in 1939. Twenty years before World War I, for instance, Great Britain was economically stronger than Germany; by 1905 the two nations were about equal; and by 1913 Germany had moved ahead. The war began the following year.

After losing World War I, Germany again caught up to Great Britain in the early 1920s and was economically superior by the beginning of World War II in 1939.[63] The same applies to changes in the stratification of military power: Germany challenged Great Britain as the leading naval power before World War I, and a revival of German military power preceded World War II. And after World War II, the Soviet Union's challenge to the military dominance of the United States threatened to cause a third world war.[64] World peace seemingly requires a stable stratification of nations, or no international stratification at all.[65]

REBELLION AS VERTICAL TIME

A rebellion challenges authority. It might be anything from the sassiness of a child to the insubordination of a soldier, a riot by prisoners, an uprising by slaves, a revolution by a social class, or a war for independence by an entire nation. It includes disrespect toward a parent, supervisor, police officer, judge, or anyone else with authority. It also includes any form of criticism of anyone with authority, including criticism of a government. Rebellions normally express grievances against those with authority and are therefore cases of what sociologist M. P. Baumgartner calls "social control from below," but they attract social control in return.[66]

The Ten Commandments effectively prohibit rebellion against a parent: "Thou shalt honor thy father and thy mother." According to another biblical passage, the proper penalty for striking a parent is death: "Whoever strikes his father or his mother shall be put to death." The same applies to cursing a parent. Still another passage says a "rebellious son" should be stoned to death.[67] Rebellion in early Chinese families was punishable by death as well. For scolding a parent or grandparent the penalty was strangulation; for striking a parent or grandparent it was beheading; for killing a parent or grandparent it was death by dismemberment (probably meaning the Chinese execution known as "death by a thousand cuts," or "slicing").[68] Because a slave was the equivalent of a master's "child," slaves suffered the same penalties for the same forms of rebellion.[69] The ten most serious offenses in Chinese law (called the "Ten Great Evils") included not only one called "rebellion" but "great lack of respect," "lack of filial piety," "acute family discord," and "insurrection."[70] A Chinese husband might also beat his rebellious wife.[71] In the Kaguru tribe of Tanzania, a rebellious wife might be killed as a witch.[72] Medieval English law defined killing a husband as "petty treason"—the same crime as the killing of a lord by a serf or vassal.[73]

A challenge to a legal official's authority is a crime in every legal system. In modern America, for example, resisting arrest is a crime, as is disobeying a police officer. Disrespect toward a police officer might also result in arrest, and has sometimes resulted in a beating or other violence.[74] Rioting against the police has been known to provoke indiscriminate violence toward anyone associated with the rioters—a form of collective liability.[75] Those who disobey or disrespect a judge might be held in "contempt of court" and fined or jailed. Prison guards are similarly sensitive to any challenge to their authority by prisoners. As one former inmate comments in his autobiography: "There is a way a convict can walk, just walk by, that's a challenge to a pig [guard]. A convict can give a pig a supreme insult just by standing and answering the pig without saying or doing anything you can put your finger on. There is a way of looking at them that they interpret as defiance." The usual punishment for rebellion by a prisoner is a beating, solitary confinement, or both.[76] Rebellion in a concentration camp is virtually if not literally always punishable by death, possibly after torture or other degradations.[77]

Rebellion against those with the most authority attracts the most punishment (see "The Geometry of Social Time" in chapter 8). Consider what happened in eighteenth-century France to a man who tried to assassinate Louis XV with a knife (but inflicted only a minor wound): The executioner first ignited sulfur on the hand that held the knife in the attack, then ripped pieces of flesh from his calves, thighs, arms, and breasts with hot pincers and poured molten wax, lead, and boiling oil on his wounds. Next his arms and legs were tied to horses and pulled in four directions until they came apart, leaving only the trunk of his body ("drawing and quartering"), and his remains were burned. His house was also razed to the ground; his father, wife, and daughter were banished from France; and his brothers and sisters were required to change their names, so that his family would effectively cease to exist.[78]

One man who tried to kill a ruler (*shah*) in nineteenth-century Persia (now Iran) received the following punishment: The executioner first inserted burning candles in his flesh, then shot him in the same place as he had shot the *shah*. Next he was stoned to death (probably while buried below the waist), and lastly his body was "ripped to shreds and blown from a mortar."[79] Rebellious slaves have normally received a whipping or flogging but sometimes mutilation such as amputation of their testicles or ears.[80] One nineteenth-century Persian slave accused of poisoning his master's family was "hung by the heels in the common marketplace and cut up in the same manner as a butcher does the carcass of a sheep. But unlike a sheep, he was denied the mercy of having his throat cut before being quartered."[81]

Collective rebellions often involve escalating violence by both sides, including collective punishment. Those who are defeated after rebelling against their rulers are sometimes massacred, possibly after special forms of humiliation and sadistic punishment, and their families and other associates might be punished as well. The following describes how one nineteenth-century Persian *shah* handled a local uprising:

> He ordered his soldiers to decapitate 600 rebels, hang two heads on each of 300 other captives, march these exemplary figures 120 miles in front of the horses, execute the second group, and then build minarets [towers] out of the bodies of the 900 men. He [next] ordered the city notables to appear and pay homage to his person. After this, he had their ears cut off, their eyes removed, and their bodies cast from the top of the castle. He then took 8,000 children as concubines and pages for his army. Finally, he "ordered his executioners to present to him seven thousand pairs of eyes of the despicable inhabitants."[82]

THE CRIME OF BEING UPPITY

Risers attract hostility even when they are not rebellious. For example, sociologist Allen Grimshaw argues that the upward mobility of American blacks in the late nineteenth and early twentieth centuries contributed to an increase of white violence against blacks.[83] Sociologist Susan Olzak found that white hostility during the same period was greatest toward American blacks (and newly arrived immigrants) when they had recently begun "to compete with those just above them in the status and job hierarchy" and to "achieve a higher standard of living."[84]

Historian Roberta Senechal de la Roche likewise suggests that "black progress" contributed to a highly publicized 1908 riot by whites against blacks in Springfield, Illinois:

> The violence in Springfield may . . . be understood partly as a reaction to a special form of deviant behavior—black progress—a visible violation of a previously inferior place in the social order. . . . Some Springfield blacks had violated their subordinate status by openly expressing higher aspirations and by actually achieving a modest measure of power and material success. . . . A significant number had managed to buy homes, and some had recently established successful businesses

downtown. During the riot, the deviant character of this black progress was demonstrated by the selection of black achievers as prime targets for attack.[85]

Springfield whites sacked and wrecked businesses and homes owned by prosperous blacks and killed two successful black men, one of whom had previously been warned that "he had too much property for a 'nigger,' and would be killed unless he and his family moved away."[86] During a similar riot in Atlanta two years earlier, whites were heard shouting, "Burn the place! It's too good for a nigger." And one black journalist observed that "the mob was not after the worst Negroes so much as they were after the best."[87]

In the first decades of the twentieth century, some American whites criticized blacks as "uppity" if they seemed to be doing too well. In a study of Mississippi race relations in the 1930s, for example, psychologist John Dollard found that whites were sometimes disturbed when blacks acquired large pieces of land, attained prestigious occupations, displayed special talents, or tried to "improve" their "socioeconomic position."[88] Black professionals and businessmen were especially likely to attract hostility. In one Mississippi case in 1925, whites forced a black physician and his fiancée off the road, beat them, and wounded them with gunfire. The National Association for the Advancement of Colored People investigated the incident and concluded that the physician's new automobile and house had provoked the attack. Dollard added that it was not merely "lower-class white people" in danger of losing their superiority over blacks who were bothered by rising blacks, but "middle-class" whites: "The only place they like to see [blacks] is in the fields working."[89]

Historian Neil McMillen mentions, however, that successful blacks could partly if not totally protect themselves by behaving in the manner of inferiors: "Although evidence of black success was in itself sometimes offensive, an accommodating demeanor might neutralize white resentment of a well-situated Afro-American's wealth, education, or occupation."[90] Apparently some blacks also tried to hide their success by such practices as living in houses more modest than they could afford, intentionally neglecting to paint their houses, or avoiding anything else that could suggest they were doing too well: "Prudent blacks did not smoke cigars in white company, wear dress clothes on weekdays, drive large or expensive cars, or otherwise carry an air of prosperity."[91] One black man chose not to buy more land because he "thought it dangerous to 'pop his head up too high,'" for instance, and another who owned more land than most blacks was "careful not to have the land all in one place but rather in parcels in different parts and counties, so that his prosperity would not be too obvious in any one region."[92]

But the crime of being uppity was not peculiar to the American South. Far from it. Social superiors in many times and places have prohibited inferiors from acquiring too much property, dressing in the style of their superiors, or otherwise comporting themselves in the manner of their superiors. The caste rules of traditional India thus prescribe who may own what land, wear what clothing, and engage in what activities. Untouchables may not own any land at all, for example, and stoneworkers (a higher but still inferior caste) may not own any "good" land.[93] Doing anything reserved for a higher caste ("upcasteing") is a serious offense, possibly punishable by death, particularly if the offender is an Untouchable.[94] In one incident when members of a lower caste in North India literally "dressed up" in clothing containing "sacred threads" worn only by the landlord caste, several members of the landlord caste tore the garments from the offenders, beat them, and fined them.[95]

In various parts of the world, "sumptuary laws" once regulated the clothing and other elements of appearance and lifestyle proper to each social rank. Early Chinese laws prohibited inferiors from owning, wearing, or using anything that distinguished superiors: "A man of higher status could use articles permitted to an inferior, . . . but a man of inferior status could never use articles that were the exclusive privilege of a superior." During the Han dynasty (206 B.C.E.–220 C.E.), for instance, commoners could wear only blue and green clothing, and in Ming times (1368-1643) male commoners could not wear yellow clothing, and female commoners could not wear yellow, blue-black, or scarlet. Other laws regulated who could wear a particular cloth or fur, particular decorations on hats and boots, and particular jewels and ornaments, and who could live in houses of various sizes and styles and travel by sedan chair, carriage, or horse. In Ming and Qing times (until 1912), any violation was punishable by fifty strokes of a bamboo rod. Family heads were also subject to punishment for failing to prevent violations by members of their households.[96]

Japan had sumptuary laws for centuries, including rules limiting the clothing (even undergarments), houses, food, and manner of entertainment of the merchant class to keep them visibly below the warrior (*samurai*) and ruling classes. Most punishments for violations were mild, but in at least one case officials confiscated an offending merchant's property, and in another they banished an offending merchant and his wife from the capital city. Other laws prohibited peasants (the lowest class) from wearing or using anything distinctive to townspeople. One such regulation specified that peasants could not wear hair combs made of anything better than wood or whalebone, and another that they could not wear cotton rain capes or use umbrellas instead of their usual capes and hats made of straw. Police stripped improper decorations or articles of clothing from offenders and incarcerated them. In the mid-eighteenth century, for instance, the punishment for wearing a tortoise shell comb was thirty days in jail.[97]

From the Middle Ages until the late eighteenth century, sumptuary laws prohibited people from "dressing beyond their station" in the Western world as well, including France, Italy, England, Germany, Spain, Switzerland, and the British colonies of New England.[98] Legal scholar Alan Hunt notes that "fashion" is sometimes a form "class struggle," and that sumptuary laws first appeared in Europe when fashion "became a vehicle" for upward mobility.[99] In France and Italy the laws were originally directed against members of the rising merchant class when they were beginning to challenge the position of the aristocracy in the thirteenth century. Other laws prohibited lower aristocrats from dressing in the manner of higher aristocrats.[100] One English law prohibited "anyone under the rank of a knight or lady [from] wearing any fur in their clothing," though (because animal pelts provide warmth in addition to decoration) a later law allowed the lowest class to wear some fur, but only that of "lambs, rabbits, cats, and foxes." Another English law prohibited those below the rank of lord from wearing gold cloth, purple silk, or sable, and those below the rank of knight from wearing velvet, satin, counterfeit silk, or ermine. Even the feet of inferiors had to look inferior: Only those with the rank of lord or higher could wear shoes with fashionably long toes—beyond two inches.[101]

EQUALITY AS BAD MANNERS

Inferiors must also behave like inferiors. Etiquette requires a proper display of deference toward superiors, including particular greetings (such as saluting or bowing) and modes of address (such as "sir" or "master").[102] And inferiors must not say or do anything that suggests equality with superiors. In the patriarchal families of Korea, for example, no one has a "right to judge" the male head of a household, nor should anyone say anything that implies such a judgment. Even to compliment a superior implies an evaluation and is therefore improper, and to criticize a superior is almost unthinkable.[103] An inferior should not ask a male superior what he "wants, thinks, or intends to do" either, but should only watch silently for "cues" to "figure out" the answer and accommodate him as much as possible.[104]

Etiquette demands greater displays of deference where inequality is greater, such as in societies with royalty, aristocrats, commoners, and slaves.[105] In traditional Hawaii, for instance, commoners prostrated themselves on the ground in the presence of chiefs.[106] In Imperial China commoners traveling by horseback yielded the right of way to members of the nobility and government officials: "When common people saw a noble or an official approaching, they had to dismount immediately and stand at the edge of the road to allow him and his attendants to pass." Officials of lower rank also deferred to those of higher rank: "Whether they were permitted to share the same road or whether one gave way by riding at the side or by holding his horse or carriage, or whether one took another road in order to avoid the meeting altogether depended upon the difference in the grades of the two persons in question." As late as the Qing dynasty (which ended in 1912), anyone failing to obey these rules was punished with fifty strokes of a bamboo rod.[107]

Strict codes of etiquette likewise prescribed how various ranks should behave in the presence of European monarchs, such as who should precede whom when entering a room occupied by the king or queen, who should bow how low, who could sit rather than stand, who could speak more or less loudly, and who must remain silent.[108] As the French Revolution began in the late eighteenth century, a decline of what had been considered proper manners signaled the decline of the monarchy itself. A close adviser to King Louis XVI thus warned the king that the prevalence of improper speech in his court showed that he was losing his authority: "Under Louis XIV one kept silent, under Louis XV one dared to whisper, and under you one talks quite loudly."[109] But matters soon got worse: The king was beheaded.

During slavery in the American South, etiquette required male slaves to touch their hats when meeting white people, to remove their hats and keep their eyes on the ground when conversing with whites, and to refrain from eating, drinking, or sitting in the presence of their masters.[110] After slavery racial etiquette continued to require a display of deference by blacks toward whites. In Mississippi in the 1930s, for example, black men were expected to address white men with titles such as "Mr. So-and-So" or "Sir," whereas white men addressed black men by their first names.[111] When speaking with whites, many blacks adopted a "white-folks manner" that was not only "polite" but "actively obliging and submssive." It is even said that some black men actively dramatized their inferiority by behaving in a childlike and seemingly incompetent manner. In any case, whites sometimes spoke of blacks who deviated from racial etiquette as "getting above themselves," "getting out of their place," or "getting uppity" (much as they might speak of blacks who were too successful or ambitious). Some considered a lack of deference by blacks not only impolite but "aggressive and even dangerous," and possibly deserving of aggression in return.[112]

When Germany invaded and occupied Poland in 1939, the German government imposed numerous restrictions and requirements on Poles and Jews, including rules of etiquette that displayed their inferiority. One rule required members of these groups to yield the sidewalk to German soldiers and police officers, and anyone failing to do so might be beaten or shot on the spot. One Polish woman thus learned that her father had been killed "for failing to step off the sidewalk at the approach of two drunken soldiers."[113]

Jewish men had to doff their hats and bow before German soldiers and police officers. In one case, for instance, a Jewish boy of about ten was running along a Warsaw sidewalk and "forgot to take his cap off to a German policeman coming toward him. The German stopped, drew his revolver without a word, put it to the boy's temple, and shot," then "calmly put the revolver back in its holster and went on his way."[114]

III | Cultural Time

6 Overdiversity

Culture is the expressive dimension of social life—from language, religion, and ideas to art, clothing, and table manners. Societies have their own patterns of culture, and so do ethnicities, social classes, genders, and smaller groups. Culture also distinguishes one person from another.

A cultural difference is a cultural distance: a degree of diversity.[1] Cultural space continually fluctuates, sometimes gradually, sometimes rapidly, and every fluctuation is a movement of *cultural time*. A movement of cultural time might be anything from a disagreement in a conversation to contact with a foreign tribe or the appearance of a new religion.

Cultural differences cause conflict. One Islamic legal scholar thus commented that "if you are not a Muslim, then you are guilty of not believing in God"—a serious offense in a Muslim nation.[2] When Islam is the dominant religion, in fact, other religions are normally prohibited or restricted. Some Muslims wage "holy war" (*jihad*) against non-Muslims largely because they are non-Muslims ("infidels").[3] Members of other religions might be similarly intolerant, illustrated by the many centuries of Christian hostility toward Jews ("anti-Semitism").

Culture is a zero-sum game: I cannot say that God both exists and does not exist, that Christianity and Judaism are both right, that any idea is both true and false, or that any custom is both good and bad. If your culture differs from mine, I can accept it or reject it. But I cannot do both. And I necessarily reject whatever I do not accept. The same applies to everyone.

Any increase of cultural distance is *overdiversity*, and any decrease is *underdiversity*. First consider conflict caused by the former:

Conflict is a direct function of overdiversity.

The greater a cultural difference and the faster it appears, the more conflict it causes. Hostility toward culturally different people might range from subtle and passive behavior such as reductions of friendliness or hospitality to more aggressive and collective behavior such as rioting or mass killing. Some diversity likewise leads to systematic and possibly coercive forms of avoidance such as segregation, exclusion, and expulsion.

All tribal societies in their traditional form are internally homogeneous, but they may experience drastic clashes of culture when they have contact with foreigners. By contrast, modern societies such as the United States or those of Europe have considerable internal diversity, partly from immigration and the incorporation of other cultures and partly from cultural innovation by their own members. And who says diversity says conflict.

Diversity increases when one tradition has contact with another or when something culturally new comes into being. The former is *overtraditionalism*, and the latter is *overinnovation*.

OVERTRADITIONALISM

Some of the most extreme clashes of culture occur when people invade and colonize another part of the world radically unlike their own. Because greater and faster increases of diversity cause greater conflicts, these clashes have contributed to many of the bloodiest episodes in human history: *Conflict is a direct function of overtraditionalism.*

SAVAGES

People who are culturally distant are often viewed as morally inferior—prone to various kinds of wrongdoing if not evil. Some tribes regard literally all foreigners as savages, if human at all.[4] American Indians such as the Illinois of the Great Plains and the Navajo of the Southwest call only members of their own tribe "human beings" or "people," while non-members are something else, such as "strangers" or "beasts."[5] The Chewong of Malaysia consider all non-Chewong to be less than "human" and always "bad"—"thieves and cheaters who will not stop at physical violence." They therefore "flee from the approach of any stranger," and may entirely abandon their villages to avoid contact. They even exhibited "general terror" when a female Norwegian anthropologist arrived to study them.[6]

Foreigners are also subject to false accusations and to unusual and sometimes highly unflattering conceptions of their way of life. The Xingu Indians of central Brazil thus believe that all non-Xingu are covered with vermin; reek with foul odors; defecate from the prow of their canoes into the water they drink; never bathe; eat rats, toads, pigs, and snakes; enjoy war; burn villages; kidnap children; rape their women; and kill their own kin.[7] When an American anthropologist arrived to study them, they asked in all seriousness whether it was true that Americans "eat babies."[8]

And to be different is dangerous. At one time, for example, the headhunting tribes of coastal Melanesia killed and ate "any stranger who was sighted unarmed or unprotected."[9] The headhunting Mundurucú Indians once attacked any foreign tribe in their part of central Brazil: "It might be said that enemy tribes caused the Mundurucú to go to war simply by existing, and the word for enemy meant merely any group that was not Mundurucú."[10] Some North American Indians tortured and killed any foreigners they captured, and the nature of the torture sometimes reached levels rarely if ever exceeded in human history, such as roasting and eating parts of their captives while they were still alive and forcing captives to eat parts of fellow captives or parts of themselves. Mohawks made one French woman eat part of the unborn baby they had torn from her womb, and an English woman had to eat her own fingers and ears.[11]

Killing foreigners is sometimes a religious virtue if not a religious obligation. For example, one passage in the Bible lists a number of groups God commanded the ancient Israelites to annihilate: "Thou shalt save alive nothing that breatheth, but thou shalt utterly destroy them, namely, the Hittites and the Amorites, the Canaanites and the Perizzites, the Hivites and the Jebusites—as the Lord thy God has commanded thee."[12] Muslims similarly regard "holy wars" against non-Muslims as pleasing to God.[13]

During the age of colonialism from the fifteenth to the nineteenth centuries, Europeans killed countless native people, drove them from their homes, and enslaved them. In the early nineteenth century, for instance, the British virtually exterminated the Aborigines of Tasmania: "Almost at once the Tasmanians were defined as enemies, actual or potential."[14] Any defense of Aborigine land was a criminal offense. And because the British did not regard the Aborigines as "civilized," they were granted no legal rights of any kind, including the right to defend themselves in court, where many were summarily convicted of murder and other crimes.[15] Their situation became increasingly difficult:

> As the white colony grew in numbers and confidence, the original Tasmanians found themselves treated more and more as predators or vermin. . . . Sometimes the black people were hunted just for fun, on foot or on horseback. Sometimes they were raped in passing, or abducted as mistresses or slaves. . . . We hear of children kidnapped as pets or servants, of a woman chained up like an animal in a shepherd's hut, of men castrated to keep them off their own women. In one foray seventy Aborigines were killed, the men shot, the women and children dragged from crevices in the rocks to have their brains dashed out. A man called Carrotts, desiring a native woman, decapitated her husband, hung his head around her neck, and drove her home to his shack.[16]

No one was prosecuted for the above actions, nor did the British ever prosecute anyone else for killing, assaulting, or otherwise victimizing Aborigines.[17]

Eventually the two hundred or so surviving Aborigines were moved to a nearby island, given Western clothing, and indoctrinated with Christianity. Forty-four were finally returned to the main island, where the last full-blooded Tasmanian Aborigine died in 1876. One British clergyman who lived in Tasmania noted that it was God's will that "when savage tribes came into collision with civilized races of men, the savages disappeared."[18]

Europeans also viewed American Indians as savages: "The savage was always inferior to civilized men. . . . Indian inferiority implied the rejection of his humanity and determined the limits permitted for his participation in the mixing of cultures. The savage was prey, cattle, pet, or vermin—he was never citizen."[19] When Hernando de Soto led a Spanish expedition to southeastern North America, for example, he was "much given to the sport of hunting Indians on horseback."[20] In the Southwest, Spaniards paid a bounty for Apache ears and shipped other Apaches (including women and children) to Cuba as slaves, though most did not survive the journey.[21]

The colonization of the Americas resulted in the total or nearly total destruction of many tribes and millions of individuals.[22] The Europeans massacred large numbers, but most died from epidemic diseases such as smallpox and measles unintentionally spread from Europe. Occasionally, however, Europeans deliberately tried to infect the Indians (an early form of "germ warfare"). "In 1763, for instance, Lord Jeffrey Amherst [Commander-in-Chief of the British forces in North America] ordered that blankets infected with smallpox be distributed among enemy tribes, and the order was acted on."[23] One British captain recorded in his journal that he and his men gave two unsuspecting Indian chiefs blankets and a handkerchief obtained from a smallpox hospital in the hope that the items would have "the desired effect," and soon the disease spread (possibly coincidentally) to various tribes along the Ohio River.[24] In any case, the British were always "strongly disinclined to take active measures against the spread of epidemic disease among the Indians," and the settlers celebrated its devastating impact on the Indians as a blessing of God.[25]

The Indians often killed British women and children (in addition to the men) when attacking their New England settlements, which might partly explain why the British viewed them as "savages," "cruell beasts," "murtherers and vagabonds," and "outlawes of humanity."[26] But the British did the same to the Indians, and justified their forcible acquisition of Indian land with a legal doctrine called "*vacuum domicilium*": Because the Indians only lived and hunted on their ancestral land but had not "subdued" it by farming, the land was legally "vacant" and subject to British appropriation and settlement.[27]

In the colony of Virginia, Powhatan Indians killed 347 of the 1,240 settlers (including some women and children) in one locality in a single day in 1622, and the British thereafter began a campaign of continuous vengeance against all Indians in that region. Shortly afterward, for instance, they invited the Pamunkey Indians to join them for "peace talks" over a meal, and killed two hundred with poisoned wine. In what is now the state of New York, the Dutch also engaged in the indiscriminate killing of all Indians, justified by the violence of other Indians. In 1643, for example, Dutch soldiers killed about one hundred Indian refugees and enslaved thirty others who had sought safety with them at their riverside encampments.[28] One witness reported seeing "infants torn from their mothers' breasts, . . . hacked to pieces in the presence of the parents, and the pieces thrown into the fire and in the water, and other sucklings being bound to small boards and then cut, stuck, and pierced and miserably massacred in a manner to move a heart of stone."[29] Other massacres of Indians occurred as the Europeans continued westward across North America.[30]

Conflict accompanies all migrations, whether of Europeans to the Americas, Jews to Europe, East Indians to Africa, West Indians to England, Chinese to

Indonesia, Indonesians to Holland, Koreans to Japan, Arabs to France, or Turks to Germany. Every new wave of immigration to the United States has thus brought its own wave of conflict, violent and otherwise. Whether Irish, Polish, Italian, Jewish, Chinese, Vietnamese, or Mexican, the newcomers invariably encountered a degree of hostility.[31] Most Africans migrated to the United States involuntarily as slaves, but their presence likewise resulted in considerable conflict that has continued into the present.

RACE AS CULTURE

What is race? Is it skin color? Facial features? Ancestry? Yes. Race is biological. And what is racism? It is hostility and favoritism based on race, including dislike and discrimination. But does race cause racism? No. Cultural differences cause racism.

Racial differences have long been associated with cultural differences, such as differences in language, religion, and customs. Moreover, racial differences have been associated with some of the greatest cultural differences in the world: differences in civilizations such as those between Europeans ("whites") and Africans or Asians.[32] Because contact between races has generally meant contact between different cultures, then, contact between races has caused conflict. What sociologists call "racial conflict" is mainly cultural conflict.

Strictly speaking, racial conflict does not even exist. World history contains no cases of continuing conflict based on physical differences alone, without corresponding cultural differences.[33] Racial characteristics such as skin and hair color have often indicated a particular cultural location, however, much as distinctive clothing might indicate a particular nationality or ethnicity. During the twentieth century, for example, most dark-skinned Americans of African ancestry shared what many called "black culture," meaning the culture of African Americans whose ancestors first came to the United States as slaves. Although originally the cultures of enslaved Africans were as diverse as their tribes of origin, a shared culture eventually evolved, featuring a distinctive dialect of the English language, a distinctive style of the Christian religion, and a distinctive taste in clothing, music, and other matters of a cultural nature. African Americans thus became an ethnicity.[34]

But black culture is not the culture of most dark-skinned people living outside of the United States in places such as Africa, Australia, or New Guinea. Nor is it the same as the culture of recent immigrants to the United States from Africa, the West Indies, or elsewhere. Some African Americans might even say that a person with dark skin from a country such as Nigeria or Ethiopia is not really "black" at all—meaning culturally black. And some African Americans might react critically to a dark-skinned person who "acts white" by displaying cultural characteristics associated with whites, or possibly disparage another African American as an "Oreo" (a dark cookie with a white filling)—meaning someone who is dark-skinned but culturally white.[35] In short, blackness in the United States is not merely a skin color but a cultural location.[36]

Most African Americans have more cultural closeness than do American whites. The reason is that whiteness in modern America is neither an ethnicity nor a clearly defined cultural location. Those called "white" have diverse ethnic backgrounds and share a culture with other whites only to a limited degree. But their cultural differences sometimes lead whites and blacks to view one another as inferior, if not immoral and dangerous. Both have often displayed various forms of racism, including avoidance (such as exclusion and segregation) and aggression (such as riots and other violence) based on race. Cultural differences cause conflict between American whites and blacks and other American ethnic groups as well, including other dark-skinned people (such as recent immigrants from Africa and the West Indies), Asian Americans (such as Chinese Americans and Korean Americans), and Hispanic Americans (such as Mexican Americans and Puerto Rican Americans). And racial conflict will continue as long as racial differences are associated with cultural differences.

Cultural differences have also caused centuries of conflict between Christians and Jews.[37] Christians massacred thousands of Jews before the modern era, for example, and some European countries completely expelled them (such as England in 1290 and Spain in 1492).[38] Some medieval Spaniards said that Jews spoiled the "purity" of Spanish "blood."[39] Others claimed that Jews were inherently "deceitful," "treacherous," "cowardly," "boastful," "arrogant," "wicked," and "cruel," and that they were "sodomites," "thieves," "robbers," and "murderers"—"evil incarnate."[40] Still others argued that "Jewish blood" made it difficult or impossible for Jews to become Christians: "Those who are racially Jews are also, or will be, religiously Jews."[41] But the purity of "Spanish blood" actually referred to the purity of Spanish culture, and the "racial" characteristics of Jews actually referred to their cultural characteristics (especially their religion, including their failure to accept the divinity of Jesus). In the twentieth century, German leaders similarly complained that Jews spoiled the "purity" of the "Nordic race."[42]

In the late twentieth and early twenty-first centuries, the arrival in Europe of immigrants from Africa, the Middle East, and other parts of Asia caused conflict with ethnic Europeans. And the greater the cultural differences between the Europeans and the immigrants, the greater has been the conflict. Sociologist Mark Cooney thus notes that conflict between ethnic Irish and immigrants to Ireland has been greater when the cultural differences between them have been greater. Muslim immigrants such as Nigerians, Pakistanis, Arabs, and Turks have reported more hostility than have immigrants from elsewhere in Europe (such as Poland and the Baltic countries), and all the more when they have worn traditional headscarves and other distinctive garments or spoken their native languages in public places. Dark skin alone has sometimes attracted hostility as well. For instance, immigrants from Nigeria have been especially likely to report being victimized by native Irish in public places. One Nigerian man said he was spat upon, for instance; another said bottles were thrown at him from a passing car; a woman said her breasts were fondled; several men said they were excluded from drinking establishments; and many others said they were called demeaning names such as "nigger" and "monkey."[43] Similar incidents have undoubtedly occurred in many parts of Europe.

Because ethnic culture is collective, shared by many, conflict caused by ethnic differences easily becomes collective and virtually continuous.[44] Yet such conflict is difficult to prevent. How can African Americans stop being African Americans, Jews stop being Jews, or Arabs stop being Arabs? Ethnic conflict will not disappear until ethnic diversity disappears.

THE CRIME OF BEING DIFFERENT

In eighteenth-century China, strangers such as wandering monks or beggars might be accused of stealing people's souls by performing magic on clippings of their hair—believed to be fatal for the victim. Crowds tortured and killed alleged soul stealers, who were typically identified by cultural differences: "Foreignness was nearly always a detonator of soul stealing panic. It was often noticed, at first contact, as a linguistic difference."[45] Traditional Kwanga of New Guinea suspect Christian converts of using sorcery, while Christian converts suspect traditional Kwanga of using sorcery.[46] Cultural differences might likewise lead the Kaguru of Tanzania to accuse someone of witchcraft. In one case, for instance, villagers suspected a visiting old woman of being a witch because she "wore her hair long and spoke loudly and aggressively in a manner unusual for Kaguru women among strangers."[47] The Buid of the Philippine highlands suspect all foreigners of being witches, including American anthropologists.[48]

Yet the cultural origin of conflict is commonly unrecognized. In modern societies such as the United States, for example, dislike and discrimination sometimes originate not only in ethnic differences but in cultural differences between different genders, generations, social classes, regions, and religions.[49] Men and women normally wear different clothing, hairstyles, and decorations such as jewelry and cosmetics; hold and carry themselves in different postures; and speak in different styles.[50] These differences contribute to sexism (such as men and women favoring members of their own gender as colleagues and friends). Some differences in human bodies are cultural as well. Insofar as people can shape their bodies by means of diet, exercise, or cosmetic surgery, they can choose their physical appearance much as they choose their clothing or hairstyle. But their choices have social consequences. Some criticize obese people as "fat hogs" or "slobs," for instance, and exclude them from employment, friendship, or other forms of social contact.[51]

Conflicts attributed to differences in "personality," "sophistication," or "taste" might also have ethnic or other cultural origins.[52] So might matters of etiquette such as table manners and proper dress. What is correct and proper in one cultural location (such as a particular ethnicity or social class) might be impolite or possibly vulgar in another. However much anyone might advocate the toleration and even appreciation of diversity, cultural differences will always cause tensions in human relations.[53]

OVERINNOVATION

Cultural diversity derives from innovations as well as incompatible traditions. New culture clashes with old culture. And the more culture deviates from the past and the faster it does so, the more conflict it causes: *Conflict is a direct function of overinnovation.*

Émile Durkheim observed that some of the greatest innovators in history have been considered criminals. One of his examples was the Greek philosopher Socrates, who was sentenced to death for disrespecting the gods and corrupting the youth of Athens—though he was later celebrated as a founder of Western philosophy. Another was Jesus of Nazareth.[54]

HERESY AS CULTURAL TIME

Heresy is a religious innovation that deviates from an established religion.[55] Many heretics have been considered criminals. According to the Christian Bible, Jesus was a rabbi who claimed to be the Messiah—Christ, the son of God. Most traditional Jews rejected his claim, and some are said to have convinced a Roman official to order his execution by crucifixion (a painful punishment reserved for non-citizens and slaves).[56] Yet soon his small Jewish sect evolved into the new religion of Christianity.

The followers of Jesus first met fierce opposition from both traditional Jews and polytheistic Romans. Christian missionaries attracted angry crowds, and the Romans arrested and punished Christians for refusing to worship Roman gods and for other alleged crimes. In 64 C.E., for example, the Roman emperor Nero falsely accused Christians of deliberately burning much of Rome, and executed many for arson and also for a crime called "hatred of the human race" ("*odio humani generis*").[57]

Christianity became a crime in itself. For several centuries the "normal charge" against a Christian was simply "being a Christian," and the usual punishment was execution, possibly by being thrown to wild beasts (such as lions or tigers) to be killed and devoured.[58] In 303 C.E. the Romans began a broader anti-Christian campaign (later known as the "Great Persecution") that included the destruction of Christian churches and houses containing Christian scriptures, the burning of Christian scriptures, the prohibition of meetings for Christian worship, the revocation of the legal rights of Christians, the arrest of Christian clergy, and the enslavement of all Christians (except soldiers) employed by the Roman government.[59] Christians were also falsely accused of various "abominations" such as incest and cannibalism, allegedly associated with their religion.[60] But ultimately the Romans themselves became Christians.

As Christianity spread and became more powerful, Christians became increasingly intolerant of deviations from their own doctrines. Although they executed heretics as early as 385 C.E., only in the early Middle Ages after Europe had become almost completely Christian was execution adopted as the usual punishment for challenging the teachings of the Church.[61] In 1022 King Robert the Pious of France introduced burning at the stake as a punishment for heretics.[62] Some heretics were also falsely charged with various forms of sexual immorality such as participation in orgies and other promiscuity: "Almost every sect from the beginning of Christian history has been accused of some kind of lewdness."[63]

In 1224 Holy Roman emperor Frederick II made burning at the stake the standard punishment for heretics, though amputation of the offender's tongue (the means of the crime) was occasionally allowed as a form of leniency. Heresy eventually became "one of the central preoccupations of Church and secular power alike," and "grew with the Middle Ages."[64] The great purge known as the Inquisition began in the thirteenth century, with secret trials for those suspected of deviating from

Church doctrines and, for those convicted, burning at the stake, denial of a Christian burial, confiscation of their property, and burning of their homes. Thousands were prosecuted and executed in many parts of Europe during the following centuries. The Spanish Inquisition alone (which began in the late fifteenth century) handled about fifty thousand cases between 1540 and 1700.[65]

Question whether Mary conceived Jesus without sexual intercourse, and die in the flames. Question whether Jesus rose from the dead, and die in the flames. Question any Christian belief, and die in the flames. Yet many heretical movements continued to appear.[66] In the early sixteenth century some grew into the larger movement known as the Reformation that ended in the seventeenth century with the division of Europe into Catholic and Protestant areas.[67] But both Catholics and Protestants continued to punish their own heretics. In Catholic Spain, for instance, any Protestant was subject to execution for the heresy of "Lutheranism" (a version of Protestantism advocated by German Reformation founder Martin Luther).[68] In Protestant Switzerland, eminent Spanish scientist Michael Servetus was burned at the stake over green wood (to make his death slower and more painful) with his heretical book tied to his arm.[69]

In seventeenth-century New England the Puritans expected purity in their version of Protestantism, illustrated by the prosecution, imprisonment, and ultimate banishment of Anne Hutchinson from the Massachusetts Bay Colony for a deviation called "antinomianism," which included various new ideas about God and salvation.[70] Two centuries later other Protestants in the United States aggressively opposed the new Church of Jesus Christ of Latter Day Saints, popularly known as the Mormons. In 1844, for example, armed Protestants killed the religion's founder Joseph Smith when he was jailed in Illinois. In Georgia in 1879 a group of Protestants told a Mormon missionary that "there is no law in Georgia for Mormons," and then killed him.[71] In Tennessee in 1884 masked Protestants attacked a Mormon gathering, killing four men and wounding one woman.[72] Similar incidents occurred in Alabama, Mississippi, Kentucky, North Carolina, and Florida.[73] Protestants also falsely accused Mormons of demanding sexual relations with young women prior to their baptism, requiring nudity during baptism, prostituting women, and planning to massacre non-Mormons.[74]

Asian religions have punished heretics as well. Early sociologist Max Weber noted, for example, that ancient Indian Hindus "fought, cursed, and hated" the "base and objectionable heresies" of Buddhism and Jainism. It was said that it is "better to meet a tiger than one of these heretics, because the tiger only destroys the body, but they destroy the soul." Buddhism and Jainism initially flourished despite considerable Hindu hostility, but Buddhism eventually migrated to other parts of Asia while Jainism survived only as a small and marginal religion in India.[75] In China, too, "despite the legend of unlimited toleration in the Chinese state, almost every decade of the nineteenth century [saw] all-out persecutions of heresies, including the torture of witnesses."[76]

Muslims have also punished heretics. A major deviation beginning in nineteenth-century Iran was the Baha'i Faith, which promoted ideas such as religious toleration and the equality of men and women that clashed with the teachings of traditional Islam. Modern Iranian authorities have subjected Baha'is to "unwarranted arrests, false imprisonment, beatings, torture, unjustified executions, confiscation and destruction of property owned by individuals and the Baha'i community, denial of employment, denial of government benefits, denial of civil rights and liberties, and denial of access to higher education."[77] Many Baha'is have therefore fled Iran for the United States and elsewhere.

All movements of religious time cause conflict. Try to improve your religion, and you will attract hostility. Establish or join a new religion, and you will attract hostility. Do anything religiously new, and you will attract hostility. The same is true of innovations in other domains of culture, including art and science.

OVERCREATIVITY IN ART

Art includes painting, poetry, singing, dancing, and the design of buildings, clothing, or anything else with an aesthetic dimension.[78] Although many in modern society speak with reverence of artistic creativity, deviations from normal art have often encountered resistance and hostility.[79] Modern painters later praised as great innovators or even geniuses commonly met rejection when their work first appeared, for example, and some suffered the same fate for the rest of their lives. They were too creative. The more creative they were, the more opposition they attracted.[80]

The newest paintings offend both the general public and members of the "art world": art critics, art historians, gallery owners, museum curators, collectors, and established artists.[81] People frequently find the most innovative paintings incompetent, ridiculous, or ugly. Gallery owners and exhibitors refuse to show them, and collectors refuse to buy them.[82] Leading critics condemned the early paintings of nineteenth-century French artist Paul Cézanne (later called the "father of twentieth-century art") as "meaningless" and "disgusting filth," for example, and called Cézanne himself "crazy as a savage" and "a hopeless failure."[83]

The most creative art reinvents art itself, and shocks almost everyone. Spanish painter Pablo Picasso (among the most celebrated artists of the twentieth century) shocked even his greatest admirers and closest associates with his 1907 painting *Les Demoiselles d'Avignon*, the first in a geometrical style later known as "cubism."[84] After seeing Picasso's radically new way of depicting the human form, prominent French painter Henri Matisse said that Picasso was "ridiculing modern painting," "swore he would make him sorry for what he had done," and "virtually never" spoke to him again.[85] Georges Braque (a French painter who soon became a cubist himself) was also "horrified" by the painting's "ugliness" and wondered "by what right" Picasso could distort the human form so "violently."[86] Word spread through Picasso's Paris neighborhood that he had "gone mad."[87] Decades later he still "constantly received insulting letters," was "denounced as degenerate and subversive," and occasionally was "forbidden to exhibit" his paintings at art shows.[88]

In the 1920s and 30s a new style called "surrealism" appeared, featuring dream-like images unlike anything depicted in paintings of the past. An example was Spanish painter Salvador Dalí's painting of two tigers leaping from a pomegranate toward a naked woman as an elephant with very long spindly legs walks in the background. Dalí declared that he had "assassinated" modern painting, and even some fellow surrealists criticized his work as too "violent" and "subversive" and "expelled" him from their group, leading him to say that his paintings were "too surrealist" for the surrealists.[89]

Whereas styles such as cubism and surrealism met opposition because they deviated too far from conventional depictions of reality, "abstract art" did so because it did not depict reality or any other subject that anyone could recognize.[90] Russian painter Wassily Kandinsky, credited with creating the first totally abstract painting in 1911, recalled that initially he "stood completely alone" and that his paintings were "rejected in the most vehement manner."[91] Some critics called him "crazy," and one joked that he had invented a new style called "idiotism."[92]

American abstract painter Jackson Pollock shocked the 1950s art world with paintings created by dripping streams of paint from a can instead of using brushes, an easel, and a palette—and was laughingly labeled "Jack the Dripper" (after the notorious serial killer "Jack the Ripper").[93] Experts ridiculed Pollock's technique and paintings, and refused to consider him an artist at all.[94] Influential critic Harold Rosenberg told him to his face that he painted like a "monkey."[95] But critic Clement Greenberg defended him partly by arguing that "all profoundly original art looks ugly at first."[96] And years later art historian Reginald Isaacs praised Pollock as "the preeminent figure in art history."[97]

New art displaces past art, which might be why critics view it as subversive and violent. Poet Guillaume Apollinaire asserted that the newest art "rapes the past" by violating the old with the new.[98] And English painter Francis Bacon (whose work drastically distorts the human form) said that the "violence of paint" can "shatter the old order."[99] One critic commented that looking at a Bacon painting was like "being hit in the crotch." Others judged him a "lunatic," a "charlatan," an "idiot," and possibly the victim of "a severe concussion of the brain," and called his paintings "disgusting," "repulsive," and "sick."[100] But a friendlier critic wrote that "like really important pictures of our time" Bacon's paintings "inaugurated a dimension that we could not have imagined, and still cannot wholly describe."[101] Another called him a "genius" and one of the greatest painters of the twentieth century.[102]

Innovators in other arts encounter opposition as well. Auguste Rodin (probably the most famous French sculptor) thus faced "enmity and mockery" throughout his life. Not only did one of his best-known works (*The Thinker*) attract "an avalanche of criticism" when it was first exhibited, but someone even shattered its plaster cast with "ax-blows."[103] Frank Lloyd Wright (viewed by many as the greatest American architect) "had to fight all his life" for acceptance, and Scottish architect Charles Rennie Mackintosh (often compared to Wright) also suffered "a lot of enemies, a lot of non-interest, and a lot of hostility."[104]

The greatest innovators in music sometimes suffer a similar fate. For example, eighteenth-century Austrian composer Wolfgang Amadeus Mozart found that his "inclination to innovate beyond the existing canon" was "extremely dangerous" for his career and made it difficult to earn a living. Many of his contemporaries (including Emperor Joseph II) regarded his music as incompetent and criticized him for his shortcomings.[105] Only later was he recognized as one of the greatest composers in history.

Modern art that finally brings the greatest fame at first meets the greatest rejection, while rapid recognition means a work of art is unlikely to be remembered in the history of art at all.[106] Some creative artists might therefore regard rejection as a sign of their success. After the critics in Berlin expressed universal dislike for a new piano concerto by German composer Richard Strauss, for instance, he remarked that although in his opinion the piece was "not bad," he had not realized "it was so good that it would be accorded the honor of unanimous rejection."[107] Francis Bacon similarly claimed that he was pleased when people called his paintings "ugly" or "really hated" them, since this might mean they were truly important.[108] And Picasso said that "anything new, anything worth doing, can't be recognized."[109] The same applies to all radically creative work.[110]

OVERCREATIVITY IN SCIENCE

Many think that scientists appreciate and celebrate the creativity of their colleagues. But in reality the newest scientific ideas often meet indifference and resistance, if not open opposition and hostility. Historian of science Frank Sulloway thus notes that the "bold thinkers" in science typically face "rejection, ridicule, and torment."[111] Even lesser innovators may find it difficult to attract financial support for their work, to publish their writings, to find employment, and to obtain tenure at a university.[112] Resistance to scientific innovation is so commonplace that physicist John Barrow sarcastically describes three stages in the life cycle of every new scientific idea later recognized as important: "Stage 1: It's a pile of shit and we don't want to hear about it. Stage 2: It's not wrong but it certainly has no relevance whatsoever. Stage 3: It's the greatest discovery ever made and we found it first."[113]

New science destroys old science. The most destructive is what historian of science Thomas Kuhn calls "revolutionary science": a new "paradigm" that radically reorients an entire field and replaces "normal science."[114] Examples include the theories of Nicholas Copernicus in astronomy, Isaac Newton and Albert Einstein in physics, and Charles Darwin in biology. All attracted fierce opposition.

If Copernicus had not died immediately after publishing his revolutionary theory of a sun-centered universe in 1543, he might have been burned as a heretic: "Not one person, except Copernicus, wanted to accept the Copernican idea that the Earth revolves around the sun."[115] Roman Catholic authorities viewed any endorsement or promulgation of his theory as a serious crime against the Church. But for many years few accepted the theory anyway: "During the half-century after Copernicus, no one was bold enough to champion his theory save a few eminent mathematicians . . . and a few incorrigible intellectual radicals like Bruno" (who was burned at the stake in 1600).[116] Eminent scientist Galileo Galilei embraced the theory fifty years after it appeared, but reversed his position after Church officials accused him of heresy and threatened him with torture. Later Galileo published evidence supporting the theory and was charged with heresy and sentenced to life imprisonment, reduced by the pope to house arrest for life after he again reversed his position.[117]

In the seventeenth century when Isaac Newton published his revolutionary ideas on subjects such as gravity, motion, and light, his closeness to leading scientists and his professorship at the University of Cambridge provided him with a degree of protection. But after his first paper (on light) met strong opposition, he complained that "a man must either resolve to put out nothing new, or become a slave to defend it."[118] Even so, in 1687 he published his book *Principia Mathematica*, which contained most of his major theories, including his "law of gravity" (possibly the best-known theory in the history of science).[119] Many of Newton's contemporaries scoffed at his idea that an object such as Earth could attract and influence the behavior of a distant object such as the moon. Leading scientist Christian Huygens dismissed the theory of gravitation as "absurd," for example, and it was not widely accepted until a century later.[120]

Newton vowed never to publish anything again, "isolated himself" from other scientists, and for the next fifty years refused even to answer any communications about his work.[121] But he still could not escape occasional ridicule and other hostility. For instance, a Cambridge student passing him on the street once shouted, "There goes the man that writt a book that neither he nor any body else understands!"[122] Few students attended his lectures, and it is said that he sometimes lectured to an empty room because of a university rule requiring all scheduled lectures to be given, regardless of attendance.[123]

In the nineteenth century Charles Darwin's theory that the environment shapes the characteristics of plants and animals (the "theory of natural selection") ignited a controversy that has continued into the present, mainly because the theory's central claim deviates from the biblical doctrine that God created everything on Earth in its final form over a six-day period. The Church of England condemned the theory as a "social crime"—"false, foul, French, atheistic, materialistic, and immoral."[124] Because Darwin had anticipated a negative reaction to the theory, he kept it completely secret for a number of years after developing it, and said he felt like he was "confessing a murder" when he finally revealed it to a close friend and colleague in 1844.[125] Fifteen years later he agreed to have the theory announced at a scientific meeting, and published it a year later in his book *On the Origin of Species by Means of Natural Selection.*[126]

One of Darwin's colleagues had predicted that he would face "considerable abuse" when the book appeared in 1859, and he was right. Reviewers were "dumbfounded that a squire of science should have turned to heresy," public speakers denounced him, and cartoons lampooned him.[127] Queen Victoria decided that the new theory disqualified Darwin for the knighthood she had planned to award him for his earlier work.[128] Some of his closest colleagues also expressed strong disapproval, including a former teacher who wrote to Darwin that he had read *On the Origin of Species* "with absolute sorrow" because it was so "utterly false and grievously mischievous" and "greatly shocked" his "moral taste."[129] A century passed before the theory was fully incorporated into modern biology and recognized as one of the greatest advances in the history of science.

Albert Einstein's "special theory of relativity" (which overturned earlier ideas such as absolute space and time) met only "icy silence" when it appeared in 1905.[130] Although he soon received some scattered recognition, "many people—physicists, philosophers, and laymen alike—denounced his ideas bitterly."[131] A decade later his "general theory of relativity" (a new theory of gravitation based on the curvature of space and viewed by many as his greatest achievement) met even greater hostility. It "outraged" and "horrified" many physicists and engineers and was also dismissed as "absolute nonsense" and "a big hoax."[132] An "anti-Einstein fever" spread across Germany, including public meetings in which experts denounced his theories and the publication of a critical book called *100 Authors Against Einstein*.[133] Nazi German scientists later condemned his theories as "Jewish" or "communist" physics, and Russian communist scientists condemned them as "bourgeois," "reactionary," and "counter-revolutionary."[134] But Einstein's worst crime was being too creative.[135]

Scientific conflict is a sign of scientific life. And the newest ideas make the most enemies. Like the art experts who attacked some of the greatest leaps of artistic time, science experts attack the greatest leaps of scientific time. Their highest praise is reserved for conventional ideas that do not disturb their universe, and that soon disappear from history.

INSANITY AS CULTURE

What is insanity? Why do we call anyone crazy, mad, or mentally ill? Insanity is a movement of social time. It is a movement of relational time when someone is inappropriately intimate with others, continually tries to converse with strangers, or refuses to converse at all. For instance, one psychiatrist said that one of her patients would not speak to her at all, masturbated through his pants pocket, and then unzipped his pants and masturbated openly in her presence.[136] Insanity is a movement of vertical time when someone randomly destroys property, steals unneeded objects, or repeatedly defies anyone with authority. The same psychiatrist thus mentioned that another patient often behaved disrespectfully and violently, and once stole a fountain pen he knew she cherished as a birthday present from her father.[137]

Insanity may also be a movement of cultural time: when someone's conceptions of reality are so unconventional that mental health experts would call them "delusional" or "hallucinatory" (classic symptoms of "psychotic disease," especially "schizophrenia").[138] Although considered an illness needing treatment, insanity of a cultural nature belongs to the same family as creative art and science—a kinship acknowledged by the modern notion of the "mad genius."[139]

Some of the greatest innovations seem insane when they first appear. One writer even says that "new political ideas, new aesthetic forms, or new scientific theories inevitably seem crazy."[140] As noted earlier, for example, one innovative painting by Pablo Picasso led people to speculate that he had "gone mad," and after seeing an exhibit of Picasso's work renowned psychiatrist Carl Jung diagnosed him as "schizophrenic."[141] The newest scientific theories might also seem "completely insane" when they first appear.[142] In fact, physicist Niels Bohr (a founder of "quantum theory") once famously commented that a prominent colleague's new ideas were "not crazy enough" to be truly important.[143]

But whereas innovations in art or science deviate from normal art or science, insanity deviates from common sense: how we understand reality in everyday life.[144] Insanity makes no sense at all.[145] Psychiatrist R. D. Laing similarly suggests that the primary test of insanity is "the degree of conjunction or disjunction between two persons, where one is sane by common consent."[146] For example, some might believe that space aliens are trying to kill them, that they are historic figures such as Napoleon or Jesus, or that they are God—whereas everyone else finds such claims not merely false but fantastic and therefore crazy.

Something is crazy in most if not all societies.[147] But common sense differs across societies, so what people consider insane differs as well. In some societies common sense says that witches cause disease and death, for instance, whereas elsewhere common sense says that witches do not exist. Or common sense might say that many gods or spirits inhabit the world, whereas elsewhere common sense says that only one god exists. In rural Ghana, everyone believes that witches, ghosts, fairies, and other spirits continually influence everyday reality and the lives of everyone, and to say otherwise is insane.[148] But elsewhere the same claims would be regarded as insane.

In Renaissance Germany some rulers were considered insane. One German princess thus said her husband was trying to poison her (though no evidence supported her belief), confessed she had killed her own children (though they were alive and well), and sometimes became violent for reasons no one could understand. Declared insane, she was confined to two rooms with bricked-up windows and doors for the rest of her life. A minor German duke in a Catholic area was treated for insanity because he accused some of his associates of being witches, said his father's Protestant physicians and druggists were trying to poison him, and insisted he was really the duke of France.[149]

Just as those diagnosed as mentally ill in modern society might think they are someone important such as Napoleon or Jesus, others say they are machines or something else not even human (known as a "delusional disorder"). Some report seeing things that are not actually present ("hallucinations") or believe someone or something is trying to kill them ("delusions of persecution," a symptom of "paranoid schizophrenia"). When their deviant conceptions of reality meet resistance, some become aggressive and violent, or possibly vegetative and mute ("catatonic").[150] We say they have "lost contact with reality" and "live in a world of their own." We encourage them to seek medical help such as drugs, psychotherapy, or hospitalization. The language is medical, but the treatment is actually a form of social control. When insanity is cultural, the goal of the treatment is to restore common sense.[151]

We can induce movements of social time with drugs such as alcohol, heroin, and hallucinogens. Some drugs lead to social withdrawal (a movement of relational time) or enhance or damage our performance in various activities (a movement of vertical time). Still others result in a movement of cultural time: Mind-altering drugs such as mescaline or lysergic acid diethylamide (LSD) induce radically new conceptions of reality that deviate from common sense and resemble symptoms of insanity. Some call these experiences "getting high" or "taking a trip."

Psychiatrists have occasionally even used mind-altering drugs to explore the nature of insanity, especially the psychotic condition called schizophrenia.[152] One described his experience after taking mescaline: "I scrutinized one hand and it appeared shrunken and claw-like. I realized that beneath the dried leathery skin was bone and dust alone—no flesh." A drink of water "tasted strange," and "I wondered if there might be something wrong with it. Poison crossed my mind."[153] Philosopher Alan Watts reported that LSD and other drugs caused him to have "the strange and seemingly unholy conviction that [he was] God"—"the very signature of insanity."[154] But in modern society drugs that violate common sense are closely regulated or prohibited.[155] Getting high is too much like going crazy.

7 | Underdiversity

Recall that a cultural difference is a cultural distance—a degree of diversity. Too much cultural distance is overdiversity, and too little is underdiversity. Both cause conflict. In the former case an increase of diversity itself causes conflict, while in the latter a rejection of diversity causes conflict. Heresy thus causes conflict because it introduces religious diversity, but the execution of heretics causes conflict because it rejects diversity—by eliminating the heretics. The greater and faster the rejection of diversity, the more conflict will occur:

Conflict is a direct function of underdiversity.

Recall too that culture is a zero-sum game. I cannot be both a believer and an atheist or a Christian and a Jew. I cannot say the world is both flat and round, or obey the customs of two cultures at once. If your culture is foreign or new, I can embrace it or reject it. But I cannot be neutral, and neither can you. We can agree to disagree, but our differences will remain. And mere toleration is not acceptance. As long as I do not accept your culture, I reject it.

A rejection of diversity resembles a rejection of intimacy or authority, except that culture is typically shared with others. If you reject someone's religion, for example, you reject the religion of anyone else with the same religion. People might passively reject something culturally different, such as when they ignore or otherwise fail to embrace a new religion or other innovation. But a rejection of something culturally different might also be more active and aggressive, such when a religion is repressed or its places of worship desecrated or destroyed.[1] A rejection of diversity might be as extensive as the expulsion of an entire ethnicity from a community or region, or even genocide.[2]

Because culture is normally collective, movements of cultural time sometimes cause collective conflict, possibly involving entire communities or societies and thousands or millions of people. Their cultural location might thereby place people in conflicts they did not initiate and cannot escape.[3] If a Christian insults the Prophet Mohammed, for example, Muslims might retaliate against any Christians they can find, illustrated in 2005 when thousands of Muslims rioted in various countries because a Danish newspaper had published cartoons disrespectful of Mohammed. And collective memories may be longer than individual memories. Five years later, a Somali Muslim man broke into the Danish cartoonist's house and tried to kill him with an ax.[4] In another case in 2010, Muslims from several countries were arrested for conspiring to kill a Swedish cartoonist who had depicted Mohammed as a dog several years earlier.[5] Members of religions and ethnicities might remember and pursue a grievance for many years, even centuries. We shall see, for instance, that some Christians still blame Jews for the crucifixion of Jesus. Jews are likely to remember the Holocaust for many years as well.

A rejection of diversity might also be bad manners.[6] One nineteenth-century American etiquette book thus instructed its readers never to disagree strongly with anyone in polite society: "If a gentleman advances an opinion which is different from ideas you are known to entertain, either appear not to have heard it, or differ with him as gently as possible. You will not say, 'Sir, you are mistaken!' 'Sir, you are wrong!' or that you 'happen to know better.'"[7] Religious disagreements were regarded as especially rude: "Religious controversy was to be shunned and the very topic of religious doctrine avoided."[8] In modern America, criticizing someone's religion is still regarded as rude or worse, and the same applies to the criticism of other matters of a cultural nature.

A rejection of old culture is *undertraditionalism*, and a rejection of new culture is *underinnovation*. Both cause conflict.

UNDERTRADITIONALISM

Countless traditions are dead. Religions have lost their worshippers, languages their speakers, and songs their singers. Other traditions struggle to survive. But old culture does not die quietly. Nor do its followers always tolerate rejection: *Conflict is a direct function of undertraditionalism.*

A rejection of traditional culture might even be a crime. In Turkey until 2008, for instance, "insulting Turkishness" was a crime.[9] Insulting a religion is sometimes a crime called "blasphemy." Medieval Christians believed that blasphemy was particularly serious because it angered God and might provoke divine retribution against an entire community, possibly resulting in many deaths and much suffering. In medieval Germany the punishment for blasphemy might be a fine, whipping, banishment, tearing out of the tongue, drowning, beheading, or burning.[10] Blasphemy is still punishable by death in parts of the Muslim world.

Refusing to practice a religion might be a crime as well. Before the ancient Romans adopted Christianity, for example, they executed any Christian who refused to worship the Roman gods. And because the Romans believed their gods punished any form of disrespect with disasters such as famines and earthquakes, they blamed and killed Christians whenever disasters occurred.[11] As the Christian theologian Tertullian commented at the time: "If the Tiber overflows or the Nile doesn't, if there is a drought or an earthquake, a famine or a pestilence, at once the cry goes up, 'The Christians to the lions!'"[12] As stated in the Ten Commandments, however, Christians are permitted to worship no god but their own: "Thou shalt have no other gods before me." Christians could therefore conform to Roman religion only by violating their own, and were guilty no matter what they did.

CONVERSION AS CULTURAL TIME

Religious conversion is the abandonment of one religion for another.[13] Any such abandonment is a form of cultural rejection that causes conflict. Because conversion replaces one religion with another, it is also a form of cultural treason. Medieval Christians who converted to Judaism or Islam might have their property confiscated and be burned at the stake.[14] German law still prohibited Christians from converting to Judaism in the nineteenth century.[15] During the same period some German Jews called converts to Christianity "traitors," and later during the Nazi era German Christians called converts to Judaism "traitors to the 'Aryan race'"— and for this they were "among the first to be persecuted and killed."[16] In Afghanistan in 2006, a Muslim court sentenced one man to death for converting to Christianity sixteen years earlier. The prosecutor noted that the man "would have been forgiven if he [had] changed back," but he "said he was a Christian and would always remain one. We are Muslims, and becoming a Christian is against our laws. He must get the death penalty."[17] Other Muslim countries have similar laws, and ban Christian missionaries as well.[18]

Some religious conversion is involuntary, possibly even forced under threat of death, and is therefore more akin to cultural rape than to treason. For example, Muslims have sometimes been known to give non-Muslims a choice of Islam or death: "The Koran or the sword!"[19] Spaniards colonizing the Americas in the sixteenth century forced Indians to become Catholics, warning them that any Indian refusing to accept Christianity would suffer "all the harm and damage" they could inflict—which included death or enslavement.[20] During Spaniard Hernando De Soto's expedition to southeastern North America, Indians who refused to accept Christianity were "put to the sword, thrown to the dogs, or burned alive" (though some had only "a hand or nose severed").[21] The English Puritans of colonial New England similarly "insisted" that all Indians "erase their values, renounce their way of life, and abandon their religious beliefs as a starting point in accepting Christianity."[22] Later, after relocating the tribes to reservations, the American authorities defined various elements of Indian culture as criminal offenses, including braided hair on men, face painting, customary clothing, and ecstatic dancing. They also forcibly took many Indian children from their homes and sent them to boarding schools for "de-Indianization." In Canada, where a policy of erasing Indian culture continued into the twentieth century, one official commented that a primary goal was to "to kill the Indian in the child."[23] But whether forced or voluntary, all conversion causes conflict.

Whereas Indians who refused to become Christians faced hostility from whites for not being civilized enough, those who became Christians faced hostility from traditional Indians for not being Indian enough. For example, some Algonquin and Iroquois Indians in northeastern North America subjected Indian converts in their tribes to torture, mutilation, and a painful death such as being slowly roasted or burned alive.[24] Indians in the American West who adopted white culture also met resistance from traditional Indians.[25] The Pueblo Indians of New Mexico punished young people for wearing non-Indian clothing and their parents for allowing them to do so: "Boys and girls who refused to take off their [white] dress have been forcibly stripped of their clothing, tied to a stake, and whipped. Parents who refused to make their children put on Indian dress have been tied by their thumbs, hung to posts, and flogged." Indians sending their children to American schools faced similar treatment.[26]

Traditional Indians considered Christian missionaries to be enemies of Indian culture, and treated them accordingly. In northeastern America (including parts of Canada), for instance, Indians captured, tortured, mutilated, and killed Jesuit missionaries seeking converts to their Catholic faith.[27] One missionary escaped with only a single finger on each hand, having lost the rest to torture, and another said that "there is not a day when we are not in danger of being massacred."[28]

Catholic missionaries also met opposition in Japan during its so-called Christian Century in the 1500s and 1600s. In 1597, for example, traditional Japanese captured, tortured, and executed twenty-six Spanish missionaries and Japanese converts, remembered in Catholic history as the "Twenty-Six Saints of Japan": First their noses and ears were slit, then they were dragged through the streets and crucified, their bodies left to rot on the crosses. In a related incident during the same period, Japanese burned fifty Catholics at the stake, and in another they beheaded sixty-one Portuguese merchants—apparently because some of the missionaries were Portuguese. Christianity ultimately became a crime punishable by death throughout Japan, and many Spanish and Portuguese missionaries and some three hundred thousand Japanese converts were tortured and killed.[29]

A common Japanese method for convincing people to abandon Catholicism was a torture called "suspension in the pit" (*ana-tsurushi*): Catholics were suspended by their feet over a pit of human excrement while tight ropes impeded the flow of blood to their brains (though their temples were slit to prevent premature death from cerebral bleeding), and could end their suffering (a sensation of bursting) only by renouncing their Catholicism with a hand signal.[30] The method was effective. In one case, for instance, the leader of the Jesuit mission to Japan renounced his Catholicism after five hours of suspension in the pit, adopted Zen Buddhism, took a Japanese name, and joined the campaign to eradicate Catholicism throughout the country. Those reverting to Catholicism after renouncing their faith were decapitated. The Christian Century formally ended in 1639 when all Japanese were prohibited from having contact with anyone from a Roman Catholic nation, later extended to anyone from the entire Western world. The policy continued for two centuries.[31]

Christian missionaries encountered resistance in China as well.[32] Initially banned from the Chinese interior in the early eighteenth century, they were allowed more freedom of movement only after Great Britain and France threatened China with military action. Other anti-Christian activity continued, however, including numerous false accusations against the missionaries and other Christians for various kinds of misconduct, especially sexual offenses. For example, it was said that Christians used sorcery to induce people to convert to Christianity; that Christian Sunday services concluded with copulation among everyone present; that the bride was required to have sexual intercourse with the pastor before every Christian marriage ceremony; that missionaries gave women drugs to make them lose interest in their husbands and seek sexual satisfaction from the missionaries; that the missionaries used sorcery to make women sexually promiscuous, removed the fetuses of pregnant women for alchemical and medicinal purposes, and kidnapped children; that Christian men drank the menstrual blood of women because they believed it made propagation possible; that Christians plugged and stretched the anuses of male and female infants to facilitate anal intercourse later in life; that they amputated the testicles of boys and the nipples of women; and that they plucked out the eyes of converts and mixed them with lead and mercury to make silver (which is why Christians were wealthy). They also claimed that the Romans crucified Jesus because he had seduced the wives and daughters of their officials and the concubines of the ruler; that Jesus planned to usurp the Roman throne; and that before dying he transformed himself into a pig and entered people's homes to engage in unnatural and illicit sex, easily accomplished because his grunt caused women's clothes to fall from their bodies and the women to submit to his insatiable sexual desires. One wall poster thus depicted Jesus as a pig with an erection.[33]

In the 1860s and 70s alone, Chinese crowds attacked Christian converts, missionaries, and other European Christians in thousands of incidents. In the "Tianjin Massacre" of 1870, for example, they attacked Catholic buildings, the French consulate, British and American chapels, and numerous Christian individuals, mutilating and killing thirty to forty Chinese converts and twenty-one foreigners: "Catholic sisters were stripped naked, their eyes gouged out, their breasts cut off, and their bodies violated before being burned alive. Catholic priests were subjected to equally horrible fates."[34]

GOING NATIVE

But foreigners do not always try to convert natives to their way of life. Some do exactly the opposite: They abandon their own culture and convert to that of the natives—known as "going native." Yet going native causes conflict for the same reason that the conversion of natives causes conflict: It abandons one culture for another. It is cultural treason.

Many whites in North America abandoned white culture and became cultural Indians ("white Indians"). One eighteenth-century Frenchman exclaimed (possibly with some exaggeration) that "thousands of Europeans are Indians, and we have no examples of even one of those Aborigines having from choice become European!" Most whites became Indians ("Indianized") after being captured by Indians, but some did so voluntarily, often after marrying an Indian. And some

African Americans became "black Indians," including one who later rose to be a chief of the Crow tribe.[35]

Traditional whites disliked all conversions to Indian culture, but especially when they occurred entirely by choice. The Puritans of New England (who sometimes spoke of Indians as "Satan's children" and their religion as "Devil worship") viewed the voluntary adoption of Indian culture as "particularly shocking" and "tantamount to a crime," and sentenced at least one man to death for becoming an Indian. White men who married Indian women and lived with their tribes were contemptuously known as "squaw men." Worse yet were "white renegades" who "plunged into the deepest pit of social degradation" and joined the Indians to fight against the whites.[36] Nor did whites accept the Indianization of those captured by Indians. All the worse were white women who committed the "disgrace" of marrying Indians.[37]

White Indians sometimes ran away from their tribes or otherwise voluntarily returned to white society, but if given the chance most refused to return.[38] When found and brought back (sometimes by force) to their white families, nearly all begged to be allowed to remain with their tribes. Typically, in fact, they "regarded their white saviors as barbarians and their deliverance as captivity."[39] In one case, for instance, an English minister's daughter from Massachusetts refused to leave the Mohawks who had captured her.[40] In another case a Texas woman who was captured as a young girl eventually married a Comanche chief and had children with him. When she was found almost twenty-five years later by Texas Rangers and returned to her white relatives, she tried to escape several times, refused to eat, and finally died a "broken" woman.[41] Many white Indians had to be closely guarded and tied hand and foot to keep them from returning to their tribes, though some still managed to escape. A few convinced their families to let them go back to their tribes, however, or to remain with them when they were found.[42]

Whereas traditional whites always expected white Indians to become culturally white again when back in white society, often they seemed not only unwilling but unable to be anything but Indian. Many answered only to an Indian name, spoke only an Indian language, and were otherwise so Indian that they continually astonished traditional whites.[43] Just as their clothing and hairstyles were Indian, so were their facial expressions, their gestures, their posture, and their walk. They even dreamed Indian dreams.[44] It can be difficult to reverse cultural time.

Sociologists call the adoption of another culture "cultural assimilation," especially when a minority adopts the culture of a majority. But assimilation is neither automatic nor inevitable. Cultural assimilation from one standpoint is cultural treason from another, and frequently causes dislike if not open conflict. Traditional blacks might criticize fellow blacks who adopt white culture (such as white speech and dress) for "acting white," for example, and immigrants might criticize fellow countrymen for discarding the traditions of the "old country."[45]

But too little assimilation might attract criticism from those in the majority. Immigrants therefore risk hostility from natives if they do not assimilate enough, and from fellow immigrants if they assimilate too much. For instance, sociologist Mark Cooney notes that immigrants to modern Ireland have sometimes encountered hostility from native Irish for not being Irish enough, and from fellow immigrants for being too Irish. In one of his examples, "a group of young Turkish men were chatting in their own tongue at a shopping center when an Irish man approached them and reprimanded them for not speaking English."[46] But in another case a Turkish man was reprimanded by a fellow Turk for *not* speaking Turkish: "When he went to his new friend's home, the friend would speak Turkish but he would reply in English. His friend was quite critical of him, complaining that he had 'changed' and was being a 'snob.'"[47]

In modern Germany, Turkish boys have been known to harass Turkish girls for "Westernizing," such as for failing to wear traditional Muslim headscarves to school or for using cosmetics (prohibited by traditional Muslims). Relatives of young women have also punished them for Westernizing. In one such case in Berlin, a young Turkish woman's brothers shot and killed her for abandoning Turkish customs and becoming too German: She had been dressing in a Western style (without a headscarf), learning to be an electrician at a technical school, and socializing with German men. A Turkish boy later explained why she was killed: "She deserved what she got. The whore lived like a German."[48] In a similar case in Canada, a Muslim man from Pakistan strangled his teenaged daughter to death for not wearing a headscarf.[49]

Westernization is all the worse in a Muslim country. Even wearing lipstick can be a capital offense. In the Iraqi city of Basra in 2007 and 2008, for example, Muslim vigilantes tortured, mutilated, and killed an average of one woman a week for appearing in public without a headscarf, using cosmetics, or engaging in other deviations from "Islamic teachings."[50]

GENDER AS CULTURE

Gender is the cultural dimension of sex: what makes males masculine and females feminine. Men and women normally differ not only in their clothing, jewelry, hairstyles, and cosmetics but in their speech, gestures, posture, and gait.[51] Although these differences might sometimes seem inborn and immutable, they are cultural. Biological men can be feminine, and biological women can be masculine.

It is also possible to convert from one gender to the other. But gender conversion causes conflict. Even the Bible prohibits dressing in the clothing of the opposite sex ("cross-dressing" or "transvestism"): "The woman shall not wear that which pertaineth unto a man, neither shall a man put on a woman's garment; for all that do so are an abomination unto the Lord thy God."[52] In the Norse law of early Scandinavia, cross-dressers were considered "outlaws" (literally outside the law), meaning anyone could harm them without legal consequences.[53] Cross-dressing was a crime throughout medieval and Renaissance Europe. In fifteenth-century France, for example, Joan of Arc was burned at the stake for dressing as a man.[54]

Legal scholar Wayne LaFave comments that cross-dressing was "offensive to a large segment" of American society in the 1950s. He also reports that the Detroit police arrested and expressed "contempt" for any male cross-dressers they encountered in a public place, subjected them to "ridicule," made them "dispose" of at least some of their female clothing at the police station, and held them in jail overnight.[55] Yet some ordinary citizens are more intolerant than the police. In one California case in 2008, for instance, a young man shot and killed another for coming to school "dressed in feminine attire."[56] And in 2009 a Colorado man dressed as a woman was beaten to death when another man discovered his real sex. The killer later referred to the victim as "it" (rather than "he" or "she") when describing the incident to the police.[57] Others consider men who wear women's clothing and cosmetics to be "weird," "perverted," or "mentally ill," and some cross-dressers view their own behavior as a mental illness.[58]

Many assume that all male cross-dressers are homosexual, but in modern societies such as the United States and England most are married and appear as women primarily (if not entirely) in the privacy of their own homes. Their behavior may still disturb their wives, however, especially when they first see their husbands in female clothing and cosmetics: "Initial reactions tend towards shock and disgust." Although the women usually continue their marriages, some limit the occasions on which they will allow their husbands to appear as women. One thus remarked that she could tolerate her husband's cross-dressing to a degree, but "wouldn't let him go to bed" in a women's nightgown. Another allowed her husband to wear a women's nightgown to bed for "a couple of nights," but was sorry she had allowed him to "make love" to her while wearing it: "I think that just shattered me. I couldn't even discuss it. . . . I ended up in the local psychiatric hospital."[59]

Cross-dressers are tolerated in some traditional societies if they begin their feminization as children. For example, some American Indian tribes largely accepted men who dressed as women and who otherwise acted like women, such as by doing women's work, dancing women's dances, participating in women's rituals, and observing women's taboos. Commonly called "berdaches" by anthropologists, they were usually raised as girls from an early age after their parents noticed their feminine proclivities, and apparently met little disapproval beyond a bit of friendly teasing. But since these men were never masculine in the first place, they did not actually convert from one gender to another.[60]

Although in modern societies feminine men and masculine women might attract hostility because they are assumed to be homosexual, in reality some are heterosexual, bisexual, or asexual. Yet gender deviations alone might provoke as much indignation as homosexuality, or possibly more.[61] The ancient Greeks tolerated some male homosexuality, for instance, but would not tolerate male femininity.[62] In eighteenth-century New England, homosexuality between a man and his servant or apprentice might be tolerated as well, but not if the man was feminine in his clothing, hairstyle, or anything else.[63] The Detroit police also displayed more hostility toward male cross-dressers than toward male homosexuals in male attire.[64] Because they abandon their own gender, the homosexuals in modern societies who generate the most dislike are feminine homosexual men (known as "queens" or "fairies") and masculine homosexual women (known as a "butches" or "dykes"). Masculine homosexual men and feminine homosexual women are less offensive.

Cultural differences between men and women decrease with modernization, but do not disappear. Feminine men and masculine women still challenge tradition, and attract disapproval from nearly everyone.

UNDERINNOVATION

Whereas a rejection of traditional culture is undertraditionalism, a rejection of new culture is underinnovation. And just as traditionalists defend their traditions, innovators defend their innovations: *Conflict is a direct function of underinnovation.*

Resistance to innovations begets resistance in return. The greater and faster the resistance, the more conflict is likely to occur. During the Protestant Reformation when Catholics condemned and killed Protestants who abandoned Catholicism for new forms of Christianity, for example, Protestants condemned and killed conservative Catholics. Resisting successful innovations is all the worse. Consider the longstanding hostility of Christians toward those who opposed Christianity from the beginning: the Jews. Although anti-Semitism has more than one cause, the original sin of the Jews was their rejection of Jesus.[65]

CONSERVATISM AS CULTURAL TIME

Most Jews refused to accept Jesus as their Messiah. They also rejected related Christian beliefs, such as that Jesus was born to a virgin, that he performed miracles such as walking on water and healing the sick, and that he rose from the dead after being crucified by the Romans. In the words of historian Gavin Langmuir, Jews have always been "the very incarnation of disbelief in Jesus."[66] But the Jews who rejected Jesus were not heretics. On the contrary, they were traditional and conservative. They were rejecting something radically new within their own religion: the claim that Jesus was the son of God.

The divinity of Jesus is a zero-sum game: He is either divine or not divine. To reject his divinity is to reject Christianity, and to accept his divinity is to reject Judaism. Judaism is therefore inherently anti-Christian, and Christianity is inherently anti-Jewish. The traditional Jews of ancient Israel not only rejected Jesus but, according to the Christian Bible, urged the Romans to crucify him.[67] So arose an ancient Christian epithet for Jews: "Christ-killers." Because to Christians no crime could be worse than killing Jesus, calling Jews his killers is the worst charge they can make. For centuries many Christians held all Jews liable for the death of Jesus, and some still do.[68]

After being expelled by the Romans from their homeland in the Middle East, some Jews migrated to Europe before its Christianization. Later they were "the only people who retained their religious faith" as the new religion of Christianity spread across the continent.[69] And as Christianity spread, so did anti-Semitism. Christianity's domination was greatest in early medieval Germany and declined from north to south, and anti-Semitism had the same geography: Germany was the most anti-Semitic region of Europe, followed by France, and the least anti-Semitic region was southern Spain, where Muslims still lived in large numbers.[70] Not until Christianity achieved nearly total domination of northern Europe in the eleventh century did "indisputable evidence of broad, popular anti-Judaism" appear, including numerous massacres.[71]

The first mass killings of European Jews occurred during the military expeditions known as the Crusades, organized to reclaim from Muslims the region

Christians call the "Holy Land": Jerusalem and the surrounding area where Jesus spent his life a thousand years earlier. As the First Crusade moved through Germany and France in 1096, soldiers and other Christians killed thousands of Jews in their home communities.[72] One writer noted at the time that the Christians explicitly defined the killings of Jews as revenge for the killing of Jesus: "As they passed through the towns where the Jews dwelled, they said to one another: 'Look now, we are going a long way. . .to avenge ourselves. . . when here in our very midst are the Jews, they whose forefathers murdered and crucified Him for no reason. Let us first avenge ourselves on them, and exterminate them from among the nations, . . . or let them adopt our faith.' "[73] Given a choice of conversion or death, many Jews chose death, sometimes killing themselves and their families to escape a worse death at the hands of Christian crowds.[74] Later Crusaders killed many more Jews, especially in Germany.[75]

The Jewish rejection of Jesus and their role in his death have been featured in countless other anti-Jewish incidents since the Middle Ages. Beginning in twelfth-century England and continuing for centuries in many parts of Europe, for example, Jews were sometimes accused of kidnapping and crucifying Christians (usually boys) in a ritual reenactment of the death of Jesus. The first known case occurred in 1144 in Norwich, England, when a group of townspeople claimed that local Jews had crucified a twelve-year-old Christian boy who had disappeared during Easter week.[76] Whenever Christian boys disappeared or died under ambiguous circumstances in England or elsewhere, Christians increasingly blamed Jews for kidnapping and killing them for their blood—a completely false accusation later known as the "blood libel."

One popular version of the blood libel was that each year Jews crucified and drained the blood of Christian boys to add to their unleavened bread (*matzah*) for the Jewish holiday of Passover. According to other versions, Jews crucified and drained blood from Christian boys to make sorcery potions and medicines.[77] In any case, Christian authorities prosecuted hundreds of blood-libel cases in courts across Europe, and convicted and executed thousands of Jews for committing this imaginary crime. After one such trial in 1171, for instance, a French court sentenced thirty-eight Jews to be burned at the stake, and after another in 1191 at least thirty were executed. Christian crowds might also bypass the courts and directly attack local Jews to avenge alleged killings of their children. In Germany in 1235, for example, one crowd "cruelly killed" all 34 Jews living in a small town for murdering and draining the blood from five Christian boys who had actually died in a Christmas fire.[78] Similar allegations and executions occurred for centuries.[79]

The Protestant Reformation in the sixteenth century did not significantly alter hostility to the Jews. German Reformation founder Martin Luther even called on Christians to destroy all the Jews of Europe because of their many crimes, especially the crucifixion of Jesus and the killing of children whose blood they had consumed and which "still shine[d] forth from their eyes and their skin."[80] Blood-libel accusations peaked in the late nineteenth century (with twenty-two trials in Europe between 1887 and 1891), and some still arose in the twentieth century (including a few in the United States). The blood libel is also found in modern Muslim countries, where the level of anti-Semitism sometimes resembles that of medieval Europe and Nazi Germany. In the early twenty-first century, for example, a government-sponsored newspaper in Egypt published a full-page article headlined "Jewish *matzah* made from Arab blood."[81]

Catholics often falsely accused Jews of another crime called "Host desecration": stealing and abusing a consecrated wafer (called "the Host"), considered to be the flesh of Jesus and consumed during Catholic rituals. In the typical case, one or more Jews were said to have reenacted the crucifixion of Jesus by piercing a holy wafer with a nail, needle, or knife until blood dripped from it—regarded by Catholics as the equivalent of torturing and injuring Jesus himself.[82] The usual evidence for the crime was either a mutilated wafer allegedly found in the possession of a Jew or the testimony of one or more Catholics who claimed to have seen blood or heard cries of pain coming from a wafer (called a "tortured Host").[83] In 1337, for instance, Catholics killed all the Jews in one Bavarian town for committing a Host desecration.[84] Numerous other Jews were killed over the centuries for the same reason, especially in Germany and Austria, where "thousands" died for engaging in this crime against Jesus that never actually occurred.[85]

Medieval Christian governments eventually expelled all Jews from a large part of Western Europe, including England and southern Italy in 1290, France in 1306 and 1394, much of Germany by 1350, Spain in 1492, and Portugal in 1497.[86] Most migrated to Central and Eastern Europe or the Turkish Empire. Centuries later many of their descendants returned to Western Europe, where the accusations began again.

Anti-Semitism reached its highest level in Nazi Germany and its conquered territories under the leadership of Adolf Hitler in the 1930s and 40s. The Nazis even rose to power partly on the basis of various false accusations (including the blood libel) against the Jews.[87] They blamed the Jews for Germany's defeat in World War I and for Germany's postwar economic depression, for example, and claimed they were conspiring to start another war and to exterminate the entire German population if Germany could be defeated. In his book *Mein Kampf* (*My Struggle*) published in the 1920s, Hitler called the Jews "a parasite on the body of other nations" and "the mortal enemy of Aryan humanity and all Christendom," and urged Christians to unite against them as their common enemy. He described his campaign against the Jews as the will of God: "I believe that I am acting in accordance with the will of the Almighty Creator: By defending myself against the Jew, I am fighting for the work of the Lord."[88]

With assistance from many local Christians in the countries they invaded, the Germans arrested millions of Jews across Europe, confiscated their property, imprisoned them, enslaved them, starved them, performed medical experiments on them, and executed more than six million of them. Millions were shot in the towns and villages where they lived, and millions more were transported elsewhere to be killed in gas chambers.[89] More than a decade after the mass killings (called the "Final Solution to the Jewish Problem" by the Germans), older Germans interviewed by a journalist still "as often as not" said the Jews had "brought the Final Solution on themselves." And they explained why: "Because they crucified our Lord Jesus Christ!"[90] But had Jesus lived in Europe, he too would have qualified as a Jew for their gas chambers.

BAD FAITH

Many medieval Jews converted to Christianity, frequently under threat of death or expulsion, but some (and some of their descendants) secretly continued to practice Judaism and to follow Jewish customs in the privacy of their homes. Secretly practicing one religion while outwardly practicing another is a form of cultural unfaithfulness akin to adultery, however, and it can be a dangerous practice. From a Christian standpoint secret Jews were guilty of bad faith, and sometimes attracted more hostility than Jews who had never converted in the first place.[91]

Practicing Judaism by a baptized Christian even came to be a criminal offense. In the thirteenth century, Pope Nicholas IV announced that any Christian baptism—voluntary or not—was irrevocable, and that any baptized Christian who practiced Judaism was guilty of heresy. In one case, for example, French authorities imprisoned a number of Jews for secretly practicing Judaism after they agreed to be baptized to save their lives during an anti-Jewish riot. In England during the same period, the archbishop of Canterbury complained that many Jewish converts had returned to Judaism "like dogs to their vomit," and urged King Edward I to prosecute them as criminals. But instead in 1290 he expelled the entire Jewish population from England—the first mass expulsion of Jews from a European country.[92]

King Ferdinand and Queen Isabella launched the Spanish Inquisition in 1478 expressly to find and punish "converts from Judaism who transgressed against Christianity by secretly adhering to Jewish beliefs and performing rites and ceremonies of the Jews." Their crime was called "Judaizing."[93] Known as *Conversos* (converts) or *Marranos* (swine), many of the alleged offenders were descendants of Jews who had been baptized as Christians under threat of death.[94] In 1492 the king and queen made any practice of Judaism, secret or not, a capital offense. All Spanish Jews then had a choice of conversion, expulsion, or death.

The Spanish Inquisition devoted particular attention to any involvement in Jewish traditions by Catholic monks, called "wolves in sheep's clothing" by King Ferdinand. Although many accusations of Judaizing were based wholly on hearsay or suspicion, others rested on such evidence as speaking or reading Hebrew (the ancient Jewish language), observing the Jewish Sabbath (from Friday evening to Saturday evening), following Jewish dietary laws (such as a prohibition against eating pork), or being circumcised (customary for all male Jewish infants).[95] But regardless of the nature of the evidence, in the Inquisition's first two decades virtually every convert investigated for Judaizing was convicted and burned at the stake. Later, however, those who apologized and reaffirmed their commitment to Christianity received a degree of leniency ("grace"), such as death by strangulation or "perpetual imprisonment."[96] In any case, two thousand to four thousand alleged Judaizers were burned at the stake during the first forty years of the Inquisition in Spain.[97]

As the Inquisition expanded to Portugal, Italy, and the Americas, its primary concern continued to be the discovery of Jewish converts to Christianity who practiced Judaism or followed other Jewish traditions. In Portugal from 1536 to 1732, for example, nine-tenths of the twenty thousand people convicted by the Inquisition's courts were alleged Judaizers.[98] But again those who reaffirmed their Christianity might receive a degree of leniency. In a series of Italian cases in 1555 in which the offenders were initially sentenced to strangulation or burning at the stake, for instance, the sentence was reduced to life as a galley slave for those who pledged their allegiance to the Christian faith.[99]

Most of the Christians accused of Judaizing denied their guilt even when subjected to extreme torture, and some scholars believe that most were probably innocent.[100] But in other cases the accused converts willingly acknowledged their adherence to Judaism and even declared its superiority to Christianity. In Spain one man was stoned to death by a crowd after he said that Judaism was "the best" religion, for example, and a woman was burned alive after proclaiming the "truth" of Judaism.[101] Such outright rejections of Christianity could not be tolerated.

THE CRIME OF BEING OLD-FASHIONED

Some ideas are too new, but others are too old. Just as innovators often attract opposition, so do those who oppose them. The modern artists acclaimed as the greatest innovators commonly attracted criticism in their early days, for example, but their critics later attracted criticism in return. Dutch abstract painter Piet Mondrian thus condemned those who first rejected his geometrical creations: "There is a certain way of clinging to tradition that is criminal. . . . One preempts the place of new life."[102] But abstract painting ultimately prevailed, and anyone opposing it was considered old-fashioned, if not ignorant and worthy of contempt.

Scientific conservatives risk a similar fate. A notable example was Albert Einstein, remembered by historians of science not only for his pioneering theories but also for his resistance to the revolutionary movement in physics known as "quantum theory."[103] He particularly objected to the idea in quantum theory that the behavior of atomic particles is inherently probabilistic, and favored instead the earlier view that everything in nature results from strict causation (a preference he expressed in his famous quip that "God does not play dice"). Einstein spent much of his later life trying to develop an alternative to quantum theory, but was "not taken seriously" by most physicists and was subjected to harsh criticism and even ostracism by such eminent colleagues as Wolfgang Pauli (who called him "reactionary") and J. Robert Oppenheimer (who called him "completely cuckoo"). Anyone who sided with Einstein met hostility as well.[104]

Yet what seems too old is sometimes too new: Fifty years after his death in 1955, some physicists had begun to consider the possibility that Einstein was right to question quantum theory. If so, history may yet show that he was again ahead of his time.[105]

Another movement in physics, known as "string theory," rose to prominence in the late twentieth century with the radically new idea that what had long been understood as the behavior of particles is actually the vibration of tiny strings of energy pervading the universe, and that separate particles do not even exist. Although string theory first met with indifference, resistance, and rejection, by the turn of the twenty-first century it dominated theoretical physics and was widely considered a revolutionary advance in the field.[106] And soon after their ideas won acceptance, many string theorists began to express hostility toward those who failed to join their movement. Anyone who did not embrace string theory was regarded as a "hold-out" or worse, and "most likely just too stupid and ignorant to understand it."[107] Physicist Lee Smolin recalls that string theorists sometimes attacked skeptics and critics in "remarkably unpleasant terms," excluded them from professional activities such as academic conferences, and obstructed their employment and promotion in universities.[108] It came to be "practically career suicide" for any young physicist to resist the string theory movement, and the movement itself increasingly resembled a "religious faith or political platform," with supporters more akin to "crusaders" than scientists.[109] What began as a new and daring scientific movement had thus evolved into a conservative establishment that tolerated no dissent.

Those who fail to accept something new are sometimes viewed as "uncool"— another word for old-fashioned. Such is the case in the modern youth culture of ever-changing fads and fashions in music, clothing, hairstyles, and other forms of expression. Young people continually adopt new styles as "cool" or "in," abandon others as "dead" or "out," and speak contemptuously of anyone associated with the past as "uncool," "unhip," or otherwise unacceptable. The uncool are socially unclean, modern untouchables who contaminate anyone else.[110]

Missionaries for each new style of rock music relegate to oblivion whatever was popular in the past (sometimes dismissing it as "dinosaur rock"), and look down upon if not ostracize all who disagree. After American musician and singer Kurt Cobain adopted a new style called "punk rock" in the early 1980s, for example, he avoided anyone who did not consider the new music superior to everything else: "I abandoned all my friends, 'cause they didn't like any of the music."[111] Later when Cobain and his band Nirvana became popular in the early 1990s with their version of punk known as "grunge," they claimed to have rendered "all that came before it entirely dated and old-fashioned," and declared victory over anyone who had opposed them: "We'd made them . . . bow down to our values and agree that we were right all along. We'd made them reject their own stupid standards and conform to our own. We'd made them kill their idols."[112]

Yet every victory in the youth culture is only temporary. Others eventually declared that punk itself was "dead," inferior to "rap" or "hip hop" (rhythmic speech with music), "techno" (electronic dance music), or something else. Styles of clothing and other elements of youth culture that are "in" today are "out" tomorrow as well, possibly to "come back" another day. Being cool is a constant struggle, and no one forgives anyone who falls behind. Peace is possible only when cultural time stands still.

8 Conclusion

The theory of moral time explains conflict: the clash of right and wrong. It explains why deviant behavior is deviant, and why some deviant behavior is worse—why it attracts more punishment or other social control. The theory also explains deviant behavior itself. It explains morality, including the prohibitions and obligations of law, ethics, and etiquette. It explains moral rights such as the right to privacy and property and freedom of expression. It explains why success and failure and sickness and death cause conflict. It explains why new religions and new styles of art and new scientific theories cause conflict. It explains accusations of witchcraft and allegations of conspiracies and attributions of other evils that never actually happened. It explains why conflict is inevitable, and why conflict causes more conflict.

The fundamental cause of conflict is the movement of social time: the fluctuation of social space. Social time moves in small and large steps, slowly and quickly, but never stops. And it is fateful: It causes every clash of right and wrong, from rudeness and dislike to litigation and violence. Conflict itself is a movement of social time, so conflict causes more conflict. Social time is moral time.

Social time includes movements of relational, vertical, and cultural time, and all cause conflict. A movement of social time might be a case of overcloseness or undercloseness, including overintimacy or underintimacy, overstratification or understratification, and overdiversity or underdiversity. Rape is thus a movement of relational time: a case of overintimacy. A display of disrespect toward an equal is a movement of vertical time: a case of overstratification. Heresy is a movement of cultural time: a case of overdiversity. All such movements of social time cause conflict. Greater movements cause greater conflicts, and lesser movements cause lesser conflicts. Even so, not all movements of social time are matters of right and wrong. Some are matters of achievement or good fortune such as economic gains or other forms of upward mobility, and some result from mistakes or misfortunes such as economic losses or accidents. Yet these too cause conflict.

The theory of moral time shows that morality is not arbitrary. Nor is morality merely a matter of religion or tradition, an expression of emotion, or an effort to prevent harm. It originates in something factual and has a social logic: It forbids the movement of social time.[1] Although morality does not forbid every movement of social time, everything it forbids is a movement of social time. And it forbids the same movements everywhere—overcloseness and undercloseness—whether too much or too little intimacy, inequality, or diversity.

Previous chapters introduced the following principles:

1. *Conflict is a direct function of overintimacy.*
2. *Conflict is a direct function of underintimacy.*
3. *Conflict is a direct function of overstratification.*
4. *Conflict is a direct function of understratification.*
5. *Conflict is a direct function of overdiversity.*
6. *Conflict is a direct function of underdiversity.*

These principles explain why people victimize and punish each other, why they regard others as dangerous, dislike them, or accuse them of wrongdoing that never even happened. They also explain the nature of right and wrong. But conflict about right and wrong is not the same everywhere, nor is morality.

THE GEOMETRY OF SOCIAL TIME

Every social location contains the seeds of its own conflicts. The reason is that social time varies across social space: The geometry of social space determines the nature of social time, and the movement of social time determines the nature of conflict.

When social relationships are close, the greatest movements of social time increase social distance, and when social relationships are distant, the greatest movements of social time increase social closeness. Close relationships therefore have more conflict caused by too much distance, and distant relationships have more conflict caused by too much closeness. Overcloseness conflicts are also more serious in distant relationships, and undercloseness conflicts are more serious in close relationships:

Overcloseness conflict is an inverse function of social closeness.

And:

Undercloseness conflict is a direct function of social closeness.

More specifically:

1. *Overintimacy conflict is an inverse function of intimacy.*
2. *Underintimacy conflict is a direct function of intimacy.*
3. *Overstratification conflict is an inverse function of stratification.*
4. *Understratification conflict is a direct function of stratification.*
5. *Overdiversity conflict is an inverse function of diversity.*
6. *Underdiversity conflict is a direct function of diversity.*

Increases of intimacy cause more conflict between strangers than between those already close, such as spouses, lovers, or friends. Rape is worse between strangers, for example, and so is every other trespass. In parts of the Muslim world where unrelated men and women are separated by a great deal of social distance, a woman must not even allow a male stranger to see her face or arms. But among closer people the most serious offenses are losses of closeness. For instance, the closest marriages have the most conflict when they weaken or come apart, such as when one spouse leaves the other for someone else.

Those who are equal oppose all forms of inequality more than those who are already unequal. Members of egalitarian tribes resent and resist anyone who rises above them in any way, for example, and young men in urban America might react violently if treated with disrespect by a peer. But reductions of inequality cause more conflict between those separated by more inequality in the first place. Rebellions therefore cause more conflict where inequality is greater, such as slave societies and patriarchies. The rise of American blacks likewise met more resistance from whites when racial inequality was greater.

Increases of diversity cause more conflict where culture is more homogeneous, such as in simple tribes. Heresy causes more conflict where religion is more homogeneous, illustrated by the high level of religious intolerance in medieval and Renaissance Europe, Puritan New England, and the Muslim Middle East. More diverse places tolerate more diversity, and they tolerate less intolerance. For example, religious intolerance causes more conflict in places such as modern America and Canada, where religious diversity is greater. Pejorative epithets (such as "nigger" for a black or "kike" for a Jew) are similarly more offensive where people are more diverse.

The same principles explain why moral rights vary across social space. The greater their social closeness, the more people will claim a right to closeness. The greater their intimacy, equality, and homogeneity, then, the more they will claim a right to intimacy, a right to equality, and a right to cultural purity. But the greater their social distance, the more they will claim a right to distance, including a right to privacy, a right to rise above others, and a right to be different. Moreover, because the geometry of social time changes across human history, these principles explain the evolution of conflict and morality.

The great transformation from the tribal to the modern age is largely an explosion of the social universe.[2] Tribes, villages, and families fall apart.[3] Strangers proliferate. Differences in wealth and other forms of inequality appear and expand. Traditions collide and disappear. Social time evolves accordingly, and so do moral rights: In my simple tribe I have a right to closeness to you, and you have a duty to be close to me. But in my modern society I have a right to distance from you, and you have a duty to leave me alone.

TRIBAL TIME

What is tribal about a tribe? Mainly it is *social closeness*. Within each camp or village, everyone is close to everyone else—relationally, vertically, and culturally. The greatest leaps of tribal time are therefore losses of closeness. And whatever is not close enough causes the most conflict. Tribal morality is a *morality of closeness*.

In the simplest tribes of hunter-gatherers, the earliest form of society in human history, social closeness reaches a level rarely seen in modern life.[4] Because most bands have fewer than twenty-five adults, everyone is relationally close to everyone else.[5] They are vertically close as well: No society has more equality. No castes or classes place anyone above anyone else. No one owns land or other major resources, and economic inequality is limited to small differences in personal possessions such as weapons and decorations. Husbands might have some authority over their wives, but most tribes still have less domestic inequality than any other societies in human history.[6] Because they have no state, no government official has authority over anyone else. Because they have no organizations, no one has supervisory authority over anyone else. They do not even have religious authorities such as priests or pastors. And no societies have more cultural closeness: Apart from gender differences, they are entirely homogeneous.

Simple hunter-gatherers thus have no significant relational, vertical, or cultural distance in their everyday lives. The same is largely true of more complex hunter-gatherers (who have property such as horses and canoes) and simpler tribes of herders and farmers (who have property such as livestock and crops). Because so much social closeness prevails, the primary cause of tribal conflict is undercloseness.

THE RIGHT TO INTIMACY

Tribal intimacy might be difficult for modern readers to imagine. For example, the first Europeans to visit North America were sometimes shocked by what seemed to them the promiscuity of the Indians. One French Jesuit missionary reported indignantly that the Ottawa Indians were "utterly abandoned" to "every sort of libertinism," including "debauches, indecent dances, and infamous acts"; another said that the Iroquois Indians engaged in sex "almost publicly and without shame"; and another noted that the Huron Indians were so "lascivious" it was "very rare" for a girl to remain a virgin beyond the age of seven.[7]

Arctic Eskimos are similarly "free concerning sexual matters." A "possibility" of "casual affairs" is a continuing feature of daily life, and men even occasionally exchange their wives (as long as the wives consent).[8] Some play a game called "putting out the lamp" in which married and unmarried people mill around a darkened igloo groping for a member of the opposite sex until a lamp is lit to reveal everyone's sexual partner for the night: the last one touched.[9] Boys and girls copulate "at a very early age, sometimes at ten or twelve," and adult men have sexual relations with young girls, including "little girls that are not yet nubile."[10] The Mehinaku Indians of central Brazil often pursue several extramarital relationships at once, and sometimes more than ten. Both married and single women copulate with anyone who gives them a small gift such as a fish or piece of soap, though a man might just take a woman by the wrist and pull her into the bushes.[11]

Marriage in these tribes is not a formal or otherwise ritualized event but simply begins whenever a man and woman start living together, and ends when one moves elsewhere. Although the turnover of partners is often high, the degree of separation between ex-partners is not necessarily what a modern reader might suppose. Eskimos almost always replace their first partner, for instance, but consider themselves married to all their ex-partners for the rest of their lives.[12]

Another form of tribal closeness is everyone's detailed knowledge of everyone else in their locality. The Mehinaku are not only well-informed about everyone living in their multifamily dwellings, for example, but also about virtually everyone in their village, partly because they can recognize the footprints of literally every adult.[13] The Gebusi of New Guinea likewise live in multifamily dwellings that are "never closed to anyone who might want to come in," making it "next to impossible to keep secrets for any length of time."[14]

Because tribal people are already so intimate, little conflict results from too much intimacy. Some modern forms of overintimacy can hardly even occur, and are unlikely to occur anyway. For instance, rape is so uncommon that anthropologists seldom even mention it.[15] In tribes where women and girls rarely resist the advances of men or boys, in fact, rape is almost impossible.[16] The same applies to various other forms of overintimacy defined as criminal in modern life. How can you trespass on someone's land when no one owns any land? How can you burglarize a house that anyone may enter? How can you invade anyone's privacy when privacy does not exist? In a world so close, it is difficult to be too close.

Moreover, people in simple tribes effectively enforce a *right to intimacy*, and a major cause of conflict is any loss of intimacy—underintimacy. Although Eskimos freely exchange their wives, for example, an Eskimo man might kill anyone who tries to steal his wife.[17] In the jungles of Malaysia, a Semai man abandoned by his wife might kill himself.[18] And despite what may seem a high degree of promiscuity to a modern observer, a major cause of violence in many tribes is adultery (especially if a woman reduces her intimacy with her husband while she has a sexual relationship with someone else).[19]

Tribal people also expect one another to share food and other resources (particularly with relatives), and to help anyone in need. Australian Aborigines "become angry" if "they are not given food by someone they consider to be related" and if "they are not supported in their wishes for help."[20] Bushmen in Botswana view "stinginess" as one of the "most serious" offenses, liken those who do not share their food to "hyenas," and "browbeat each other constantly to be more generous."[21]

And everyone in a simple tribe should be highly sociable. Bushmen "rarely spend time alone," and "to seek solitude is regarded as a bizarre form of behavior."[22] The Gebusi are "practically never alone" either, and find it "inconceivable" for anyone but a "very angry" person to be "aloof" or to seek "privacy."[23] People in some tribes even fear an unsociable person as dangerous, and possibly a witch.[24] A right to be alone is literally unknown, if not inconceivable.

THE RIGHT TO EQUALITY

Just as the sexuality of North American Indians shocked Europeans, so did their equality—especially their absence of authority. The Indians not only had no one with recognized authority of any kind, but pointedly ignored or actively opposed anyone who tried to tell them what to do. As one Jesuit missionary commented: "The savages cannot tolerate in any way those who wish to assume superiority over others."[25] Among the Mbuti Pygmies of the Congo as well: "Individual authority is unthinkable," and anyone who tries to give an "order" to anyone else meets contempt if not aggression in return.[26] They also reject and resist any other form of social superiority.

People in simple tribes thus enforce a *right to equality*. Eskimos have a "general rule" against the hoarding of any resources, for example, and deviations provoke "strong resentment" and possibly violence, such as when one man and his sons were killed for trying to monopolize a good hunting area. Everyone must also share whatever they acquire.[27] The Mehinaku (who are simple farmers) similarly "set limits on what anyone is able to accumulate."[28] Although everyone in a simple tribe might be poor, they are equally poor. No one starves. Destitution and begging did not appear in human history until a later stage of social evolution, when inequality became an established fact of life.[29]

Competition is likewise absent in simple tribes. No one should ever be "better" than anyone else, and merely to speak or carry oneself in a manner suggesting any degree of superiority attracts hostility. Bushmen view "arrogance" as one of the "most serious" offenses, for instance, and use various "leveling" mechanisms to burst anyone's "bubble of conceit" and to impose "humility" on anyone who seeks, achieves, or presumes prominence of any kind.[30] Upward mobility is taboo, and any stratification is overstratification.

Because no one in a simple tribe owns real estate, livestock, or other valuable property, conflict about its ownership, damage, or loss does not and cannot occur. And because they share almost everything, even theft is rare, absent, or impossible. All they can lose is their equality.

THE RIGHT TO PURITY

Simple tribes are also homogenous. Religion, ideas, music, clothing, and other elements of culture seldom vary. Australian Aborigines always "follow the tracks of their ancestors" in their religion, cosmology, arts, and otherwise, for example, and the body decorations worn by the Mehinaku have been "frozen" for all their known history.[31] More complex tribes are highly traditional as well. Among the Pashtun of northern Pakistan, for instance, any cultural deviation such as "shaving off one's beard or wearing a new style of hat" immediately provokes "ridicule and contempt." But cultural deviations rarely occur anyway: "Conformity accompanies a lack of innovation and creativity."[32]

Any significant diversity in a tribe results from foreign contact, and is never welcome. Some tribesmen attack any foreigner they encounter, and tolerate no one who adopts anything foreign that differs from their traditional culture. Recall the North American Indians who tortured and killed those who converted to Christianity, for example, and others who stripped and whipped young people who dressed like whites.

Whatever contaminates the cultural purity of a tribe causes conflict, and the only cultural sin is overdiversity. Anyone different is unworthy of their closeness, if not subhuman and worthy of death. They know nothing of freedom of expression, and readily tolerate intolerance. The only cultural right is a *right to purity*.

MODERN TIME

The history of all conflict is the history of social time. Simple tribes in their pristine form are small and compact, but they almost invariably come apart and die. Invaders kill and conquer them, infect and decimate them with diseases, and displace familiar faces with swarms of strangers. The newcomers introduce inequality of various kinds, foreign culture that clashes with their traditions, and markets that buy and sell whatever they produce, possess, or desire. Although some migrate and scatter, most intermingle with the foreigners and former enemies, cast off their traditional clothing, and forget their old languages, customs, and gods. Simple tribes dominated the world for most of human history, but finally lost their homes and way of life and shattered into social dust. In short, they modernized.

Modern life is nearly the opposite of tribal life. Whereas tribal space is small and tight, modern space is large and loose. Modern society still has tribal locations (such as ethnic subcultures, gangs, and families), but greater social distances separate nearly everyone else.[33] And whereas the greatest movements of tribal time are losses of social closeness, the greatest movements of modern time are losses of social distance.

Modern morality is therefore largely a *morality of distance*. Modern people defend their right to be left alone, to end relationships, to own property, to have an opportunity for achievement or whatever else they want, and to have their own religion, ideas, and other forms of culture. They expect others to mind their own business and to stay away from them. Whereas tribal virtue is largely a matter of preserving closeness, modern virtue is more a matter of maintaining distance. The distinctively modern cause of conflict is overcloseness.

THE RIGHT TO PRIVACY

Modernization expands relational space. Tribes, clans, and families disintegrate, leaving individuals to live their lives in a social landscape surrounded by strangers.[34] The average relational distance widens, and the lifespan of relationships shortens. What was stable becomes fluid, and what was collective becomes personal.[35] People abandon their families and friends for education and employment. Many have few if any close ties anyway, know few if any of their neighbors, belong to few if any groups, and have few if any continuing associates other than colleagues in the organizations where they spend their days, if they even leave their homes to work. Divorce increases; people marry later or never; and more live alone than ever before.[36]

Cities replace camps and villages, and people increasingly find themselves physically close but socially distant, a combination rarely seen in human history. Most obtain nearly all they need (such as food and clothing) from strangers. Economic relationships last only long enough to complete transactions, and many professionals are strangers to their clients. Many transactions occur without any direct contact at all, often electronically with unknown people in unknown places.

Whereas in simple tribes most relational conflicts result from too little closeness, in modern societies conflicts increasingly result from too much closeness, especially trespasses by strangers such as rape and burglary that are rare if not impossible in simple tribes. As communal closeness declines, law becomes ever more important as a form of social control.[37] Moral time becomes legal time. Numerous rules require everyone to keep their distance from everyone else. Criminal law formally applies to everyone, but in reality it mostly protects people from strangers. The same is true of civil law, such as contract and negligence law. And law deals more harshly with those who harm strangers. For example, American capital punishment is mainly reserved for killers of strangers.[38]

An American judge once commented that "the most comprehensive of rights and the right most valued by civilized men" is "the right to be let alone."[39] The right to be let alone has come to be known as the *right to privacy*—which implies the duty of everyone, including government officials, to stay out of the personal lives of other people. Nor should anyone expose anyone's personal affairs to anyone else. The right to privacy is a right to separation.

Modern people also expect the freedom to live where and how they please: to leave home if they wish, to end their relationships with intimates or anyone else, to choose their associates and forms of closeness (sexual or otherwise), and to go where they please.[40] Even modern etiquette requires a degree of relational distance from everyone else. Modern morality thus protects people from too much intimacy, a form of freedom unknown and unwanted in the close world of a simple tribe.

THE RIGHT TO OPPORTUNITY

Because tribal people have virtually no inequality, they have virtually no conflict caused by its loss, such as losses of property or power. But they do have conflict about losses of equality, such as when someone tries to hoard food or other resources, or achieves or presumes superiority over someone else. But with modernization inequality becomes commonplace. Competition is everywhere, and everyone has more or less of everything, whether property, income, authority, or anything else that places one above another.[41] A major cause of modern conflict is the appropriation or abuse of anything that belongs to anyone else, including theft or damage to property, accidental or otherwise. Other conflict results from the failure to compensate anyone else for goods and services, to reward anyone's achievements, or to obey anyone's authority.

Modern people also expect a chance to improve their lives—to climb the social ladder—to obtain more wealth, more power, better employment, better housing, or whatever else they desire. They demand a *right to opportunity,* which implies a right to compete with others and acquire more than others. A right to opportunity effectively implies a right to inequality.

Modern people commonly uphold an ideal of equality, but by this they do not mean a world like that of a simple tribe where no one can rise above anyone else. What they mean is equality of opportunity without regard to biological or social characteristics such as race, gender, ethnicity, or religion.[42] No one questions anyone's right to achieve more than anyone else. On the contrary, they demand a right to accumulate and enjoy more than others—to earn and inherit more money and other property than others and to have adequate protection of whatever they possess. Nor do they question the many forms of authority that subordinate some to others, such as citizens to government officials, employees to employers, and students to teachers. So again modern morality preserves and defends what tribal morality condemns.

THE RIGHT TO DIVERSITY

Whereas simple tribes are homogeneous, modern societies are diverse. Consider the mosaic of ethnicities, religions, and lifestyles found in modern America. American culture hardly exists in the sense of, say, Bushman or Eskimo culture or even Japanese or French culture. The United States is more a geographical and political location than a cultural location. And because Americans are so diverse, they might be more tolerant of diversity—and intolerant of intolerance—than anyone else in the world.

Modern people expect a right to freedom of expression such as freedom of religion and speech, including a right to criticize the religion or speech of others. Other modern rights (often called "civil rights") prohibit exclusion and other discrimination on the basis of religion, race, and ethnicity. Modern morality thus enforces a *right to diversity*—a right to be different. Some modern people even regard diversity as a social good, something to appreciate and celebrate.[43] Here too modern morality protects what tribal morality rejects, and rejects what tribal morality accepts.

POSTMODERN TIME

It might take centuries, decades, or years, but tribalism ultimately surrenders to modernism. Although the tribal right to social closeness continues in the small worlds of modern life such as families and ethnic enclaves, the modern right to social distance rules the wider world of strangers separated by chasms of social space such as different levels of wealth and power and different religions and other forms of cultural diversity.

Yet modernism also brings new forms of closeness. One of these is *self-closeness*. As modern people increasingly live alone, spend time alone, and engage in various activities alone, they become ever closer to themselves. For some, intimacy with themselves is their only intimacy from one day to the next, apart from whatever closeness they might maintain through modern media of communication such as phones and computers.

Another new form of closeness is *global closeness*. Social distance once corresponded to physical distance, but modern communication and transportation increasingly allow social closeness despite physical distance, even with those in different countries and on different continents. Whereas tribal people live in isolated localities and know little about anyone or anything else, modern technology shrinks the world as a whole and makes it increasingly familiar to everyone. Humanity comes to inhabit what media theorist Marshall McLuhan calls a "global village."[44] Morality evolves accordingly.

THE RIGHT TO HAPPINESS

Unlike the simple tribes that migrate nomadically from place to place, modern people increasingly migrate to themselves. Tribal people spend nearly all their time with others and have little closeness with themselves, and a tribal self hardly exists. But as tribal closeness weakens, people spend ever more time with themselves. Whereas tribal people devote most of their attention to one another, modern people devote ever more attention to themselves, even to a point of selfishness. Self-closeness replaces tribal closeness, and egoism replaces tribalism.[45]

And those closer to themselves have more conflicts with themselves. Some thus complain about their losses of closeness with themselves: "I've lost touch with myself"; "I don't know who I am"; "I don't know what I want." Others complain about their own thoughts and feelings, their behavior toward themselves or others, or their level of performance in their work or other activities. They expect to be happy, and complain when they are not: "I don't like myself"; "I worry too much"; "I'm depressed." But they do not view these problems as matters of right and wrong. Instead they pertain to health. Their complaints are matters of *therapeutic morality*, a morality that does not speak of conflict in a moral language but rather in a medical language and possibly as an illness needing treatment.[46]

The fundamental principle of therapeutic morality is a *right to happiness*—which implies not only that everyone deserves a feeling of well-being but also that all have a duty to pursue, protect, and preserve their own happiness, such as by seeking help whenever they are not happy.[47] Although some try to help themselves, others seek medication or other therapy from professionals. Often they reveal more of themselves, such as their hopes and fears and fantasies, to their therapist than to anyone else. Their relationship with their therapist might even become their closest relationship, apart from their relationship with themselves. But in therapy their self always remains the center of attention, and their closeness to themselves increases all the more.[48]

THE RIGHT TO RIGHTS

Whereas therapeutic morality results from the growing closeness of people to themselves, *global morality* results from the growing closeness of people to the world as a whole. As the world becomes a single society, with everyone connected to everyone else, movements of social time radiate ever more widely across the globe. People find themselves increasingly involved in conflicts far away, defending the rights of those who once had few if any rights resembling modern rights at all.

The fundamental global right is the *right to rights*: the right of everyone and everything to modern rights such as the right to life, liberty, security, privacy, food, shelter, medical care, freedom of religion, and freedom of expression—known as "human rights" in a global context.[49] Global citizens defend the rights of all victims of oppression, exploitation, warfare, genocide, and misfortunes such as floods, famines, and disease. Global morality even reaches farther—beyond humanity to "animal rights" for domestic and wild animals and "ecological rights" for other living and nonliving things.[50] Conservationist David Brower thus speaks of the rights of "creatures other than man"; philosopher Arne Naess argues that mountains, rivers, and other natural features of Earth are "living beings" with the same rights as human beings; and legal scholar Christopher Stone proposes the extension of legal rights to "the natural environment as a whole."[51] Global morality applies to everyone and everything.

THE GLOBAL SELF

Who then are these global citizens who defend a right to rights? Where on Earth did they originate? What is their social location?

They are the ones without a tribe, the most modern of modern people, close mostly to themselves. Although self-closeness and global closeness might seem drastically different or even complete opposites, they actually occur together: Those closest to themselves are likely to be global villagers as well, connected by modern technology to people and places everywhere. Because of the zero-sum nature of intimacy, people lacking closeness to other people in their daily lives are closer not only to themselves but to the world as a whole. Possibly egoistic to the point of selfishness, they are also closer to strangers, foreigners, animals, plants, and everything else in the world. And because social closeness breeds social altruism—help for those in need—global closeness breeds global altruism, a new and even revolutionary development in the history of humanity.[52]

Global altruism differs radically from the tribal altruism found among people with tribal closeness such as ethnic, village, and family closeness. Tribal closeness encapsulates tribal people within their groups, separating them from everyone and everything farther away. They live lives of collective isolation with little or no involvement in the world beyond their tribe if not their village or band. They care little or nothing about the suffering of anyone or anything in outer social space and have little or no charity for strangers or foreigners, whom they typically fear and avoid.[53] They help only those in their own tribe to whom they are already close, especially their own families. Collective closeness breeds collective selfishness.

Tribal closeness is even dangerous to outsiders.[54] Recall that some tribes attack and kill any foreigners they encounter, simply because they are foreigners. Some are not only hostile but sadistic. For example, anthropologist Jared Diamond notes that some New Guinea tribesmen derived pleasure from playing a "game" with captured foreigners, taking turns chopping off their arms and legs and watching them suffer.[55] And recall the extreme forms of torture American Indians inflicted on foreigners, including European women (see "Savages" in chapter 6).

Tribal closeness is dangerous to nonhumans as well. Anthropologist Jean Briggs describes the sadism of Eskimos toward their dogs: "I saw gleaming eyes and smiles of delight as dogs cowered and whined with bruises and bloody heads."[56] Some New Guinea tribesmen enjoyed inflicting pain on wild animals, such as by tying strings to live bats and lowering them near hot embers "for no other reason than amusement at the reactions of the tortured animals."[57] People in early Europe burned live cats, squirrels, and other small animals as part of their Easter and midsummer celebrations. During the midsummer festival in Paris, for instance, "it was the custom to burn a basket, barrel, or sack full of live cats," hung above the fire to maximize their suffering.[58]

Some modern people who inhabit tribal locations such as strong families, urban gangs, and ethnic subcultures still display collective selfishness and indifference if not hostility toward outsiders. As happens in simple tribes, their closeness isolates them from the rest of the world, and they have little or no involvement in anyone or anything beyond their own groups.[59] Occasionally their tribal closeness even contributes to collective violence such as lynching, rioting, and feuding—virtually always against outsiders—and on a larger scale it contributes to terrorism, warfare, and genocide.[60] The closest likewise care the least about modern rights such as the right to privacy and the right to diversity, much less global rights for humans and nonhumans across the world.[61]

Global morality is a distinctively modern morality, but something similar is sometimes seen in traditional societies among itinerant monks and mystics and among hermits and holy men who live alone in the wilderness. Like modern isolates connected electronically to the world as a whole, these individuals are closer to everyone and everything else and display a greater concern for all, human and nonhuman alike. In traditional India, for instance, Jainist monks who live a life of "wandering homelessness" are legendary for their compassion toward all living things, careful even to avoid stepping on an insect, lighting a fire that might burn a moth, or cutting their hair and harming a louse.[62] The same is true of nomadic Buddhist monks in traditional Japan, such as one who slept under netting to avoid accidentally killing mosquitoes and fleas but who left one leg exposed to make sure they "would not go hungry."[63] These wanderers and loners were known for their global morality long before globalization.

But global morality mainly appears in the most modern locations, among those both close to themselves and to the world as a whole. One example was Albert Einstein, a nonreligious German Jew who renounced his German citizenship and lived in various countries as a "citizen of the whole world."[64] He called himself a "lone traveler" who "never lost a sense of distance and a need for solitude," yet he had an "intimate bond to humanity" and a deep involvement in global justice. His own humanitarianism even puzzled Einstein: "My passionate sense of social justice and social responsibility has always contrasted oddly with my pronounced lack of need for direct contact with other human beings and communities."[65] Another example was philosopher Friedrich Nietzsche, who abandoned his German citizenship and lived alone in Switzerland and Italy. Famous for his declaration that "God is dead," he also bemoaned the moral condition of humanity, and once tearfully hugged a horse he saw being beaten on a public street.[66]

Global citizens often lack religion, but revere all life and nature.[67] Urban and urbane, they love animals and trees. Self-involved if not selfish, they are the friends of foreigners they will never meet. Their home is the world, and their morality has no boundaries.

Who am I? I am alone. I have no tribe, no traditions, and no gods. I confess I care only about myself. Yet I am close to everyone and everything. I know the prisoners in the torture cells and the hostages hidden in the cellars. I see the bones in the mass graves and the bodies bombed by the believers. I feel the suffering of the animals, hear the saws in the trees, and smell the poisons in the streams. Their losses are my losses, and their rights are my rights.

Yes, I am selfish. But my self is global. My time is global. And my conflict is everywhere.

Notes

CHAPTER 1

1. Deviant behavior is anything subject to social control, and social control is anything that defines and responds to deviant behavior. Black, *Behavior of Law*, 9.

2. See *idem*, "Crime as social control."

3. The agonistic style of social control pertains to a threat to someone's security. The defense might be anything from flight to a fight, assassination, warfare, or even genocide. For other styles of social control, see *idem*, *Behavior of Law*, 4–6; "Social control as a dependent variable," 6–9.

4. By "conflict" some sociologists mean a clash of interests between social classes or others involved in a competition or struggle. See, e.g., Marx and Engels, *Manifesto of the Communist Party*; Simmel, "Conflict"; Coser, *Functions of Social Conflict*; Dahrendorf, "Toward a theory of social conflict"; *Class and Class Conflict in Industrial Society*; "On the origin of inequality"; Collins, *Conflict Sociology*; Blumberg, "General theory of gender stratification"; R. Gould, *Collision of Wills*.

5. Apart from theories of why crime occurs, little scientific theory addresses why clashes of right and wrong occur. But see, e.g., Hume, *Treatise of Human Nature*, Book III; A. Smith, *Theory of Moral Sentiments*; Durkheim, *Rules of Sociological Method*, Chapter 3; Erikson, *Wayward Puritans*, Chapter 1; Scheff, *Microsociology*, Chapter 5; *Bloody Revenge*; Gould, *Collision of Wills*.

6. The mass media continually provide information ("news") about various forms of conflict, including crime, litigation, warfare, and other violence. Conflict might also be the most common subject of fiction and films.

7. Social scientists often say that social change causes conflict. But by "social change" they normally mean large-scale transformations such as industrialization, the spread of new technology,

urbanization, and political reorganization. See, e.g., Smelser, *Social Change in the Industrial Revolution*; Goode, *World Revolution and Family Patterns*; Moore, *Social Change*. We shall see, however, that the movement of social time occurs in every kind of social relationship in the social universe.

8. I elaborate several forms of social distance below. See also Black, *Behavior of Law*; "Epistemology of pure sociology"; "Dreams of pure sociology."

9. Unlike physical distances measured in inches or millimeters, social distances have no common denominator, making it difficult to compare one social distance to another. See *idem*, "Dreams of pure sociology," 349, 355.

10. Early sociologist Émile Durkheim proposed that the concept of time derives from the "rhythm of collective life," such as recurrent religious ceremonies, communal hunts, and other group activities: "What the category of time expresses is a time common to the group, a social time, so to speak." *Elementary Forms of Religious Life*, 23, note 6; see also 22–23, 488–492; Hubert, *Essay on Time*. Sociologists Pitirim Sorokin and Robert Merton similarly suggest that "social time" consists in "social periodicities"—sequences of social activities such as economic and religious events—and that the "duration" of social time consists in the duration of these activities. "Social time," 615, 619–620.

Most modern sociologists have limited their work on time to the human meaning and significance of physical time, such as the influence of clocks and calendars on social life. See, e.g., Gurvitch, *Spectrum of Social Time*; Elias, *Time*; Zerubavel, *Seven-Day Circle*. Philosopher Martin Heidegger examines the subjective nature of time, such as how people experience and can alter their experience of the speed at which time passes. *Being and Time*, Part I, Chapters 2–5; Safranski, *Martin Heidegger*, 192–195; see also Husserl, *On the Phenomenology of the Consciousness of Internal Time*.

11. Hume, *Treatise of Human Nature*, 33 (italics omitted).

12. Aristotle said that physical time is physical motion. *Physica*, Book IV, C; see also Bergson, *Creative Evolution*, 366; Aichelburg, "On the evolution of the concept of time"; Sorokin and Merton, "Social time," 615. And social time is social motion.

13. Minkowski, "Space and time"; see also Greene, *Elegant Universe*, 49–50, 66; A. Miller, *Einstein, Picasso*, 221–223; Isaacson, *Einstein*, 132–133.

14. Minkowski's conception came to be known in physics as "spacetime." See, e.g., Feuer, *Einstein*, Chapter 1; Coveney and Highfield, *Arrow of Time*, 82–83; Greene, *Elegant Universe*, 376–377. We might similarly view social space and social time together as social spacetime.

15. Sorli, "Mathematical time and physical time," 1; see also *idem*, "Time is change."

16. See, e.g., S. Gould, *Time's Arrow, Time's Cycle*; Coveney and Highfield, *Arrow of Time*.

17. Einstein's special theory of relativity predicts the slowing of physical time at higher speeds, and his general theory of relativity predicts the slowing of physical time near heavier objects. His general theory also implies that the shape of physical space is dynamic, constantly changing.

18. Social time is a new conception of human behavior. Theoretically speaking, it is the death of the act—which becomes a movement of social time. The same applies to social events of other kinds and to the social consequences of other events, such as upward and downward mobility, clashes of culture, and diseases and disasters. The idea of social time is itself a movement of social time: sociological time. Social time adds a dynamic element to pure sociology, the science of social life in the strictest sense. Pure sociology explains human behavior with its social geometry—its location and direction in social space and time. Social time is thus the dynamic geometry of social space. See, e.g., Black "Epistemology of pure sociology"; "Dreams of pure sociology"; "Purification of sociology"; "How law behaves," 44–46.

19. According to philosopher Henri Bergson, "Modern science must be defined pre-eminently by its aspiration to take time as an independent variable" (something that explains something else). *Creative Evolution*, 365–366 (italics omitted); see also 23–24, 357–375. The theory of moral time would seem to be an example of what Bergson advocates: Social time is an independent variable that explains conflict.

20. The theory of moral time also applies to conflict between humans and nonhuman animals and to conflict between nonhuman animals. For similarities in the handling of conflict by humans and nonhumans, see Black, "On the origin of morality," 114–116.

21. An "increase or decrease" of social closeness includes threats, plans, and attempts to alter social closeness, and it includes both passive and active alterations of social closeness.

22. Becker, *Outsiders*, 9; see also Durkheim, *Division of Labor in Society*, 81.

23. Social control responds to threatened, planned, and attempted deviant behavior as well.

24. Compare, e.g., Gottfredson and Hindelang, "Study of *The Behavior of Law*"; Black, "Common sense in the sociology of law."

25. Rape also involves violence: coercion and possibly the infliction of pain or injury.

26. An increase or decrease of intimacy might be unilateral (one-sided) or bilateral (two-sided). Whereas a rape is unilateral, for instance, a consensual sexual relationship is bilateral. Bilateral movements of social time sometimes cause conflict with third parties such as legal officials or associates of those involved. See "Filthy Involvements" in Chapter 2.

27. See, e.g., L. Williams, "Classic rape"; Estrich, *Real Rape*, Chapters 2–3; see also Black, *Behavior of Law*, 40–46.

28. The radiation of social time places people on different sides of conflicts. Whatever alters the social space of our family or friends alters our own social space, for example, and also that of anyone else who shares their lives. Compare Black, *Social Structure of Right and Wrong*, Chapter 7; M. Cooney, *Warriors and Peacemakers*; Phillips and Cooney, "Aiding peace, abetting violence." Our relational or cultural closeness may likewise make us vulnerable to others, as illustrated by riots and terrorist attacks against members of particular ethnicities or religions. See, e.g., Senechal de la Roche, "Collective violence as social control"; "Why is collective violence collective?"; Black, "Geometry of terrorism."

29. See, e.g., Merton, "Social structure and anomie"; W.B. Miller, "Lower class culture as a generating milieu of gang delinquency"; Cloward and Ohlin, *Delinquency and Opportunity*; Wolfgang and Ferracuti, *Subculture of Violence*; Hirschi, *Causes of Delinquency*; L. Cohen and Felson, "Social change and crime rate trends"; J. Blau and P. Blau, "Cost of inequality"; but compare Luckenbill, "Criminal homicide as a situated transaction"; Katz, *Seductions of Crime*, Chapter 1.

30. Also relevant to the occurrence, nature, and level of violence is the social geometry of the conflict, such as the relational and cultural distance between the parties and the social elevation of each. Different geometries give rise to such varied forms of violence as vengeance, lynching, feuding, terrorism, and genocide. See, e.g., Senechal de la Roche, "Collective violence as social control"; "Sociogenesis of lynching"; Black, "Elementary forms of conflict management"; "Geometry of terrorism"; "Violent structures"; Campbell, "Genocide as social control." The nature of all conflict varies with its social geometry. See, e.g, Black, *Social Structure of Right and Wrong*.

31. *USA Today*, "Santa gunman had lost job, wife before attack."

32. Imprisonment is partly a movement of vertical time as well: an imposition of authority and a deprivation of various kinds, such as a lowering of the prisoner's standard of living. All social control also lowers the deviant's respectability—another movement of vertical time. See Garfinkel,

"Conditions of successful degradation ceremonies"; Schwartz and Skolnick, "Two studies of legal stigma"; Black, *Behavior of Law*, 111–113.

33. The impact of punishment on the offender's life is also variable. Sending a corporate executive, lawyer, or other professional to prison deprives the offender of a rewarding position, for example, but sending an unemployed person to prison does not.

34. See, e.g., Lemert, "Concept of secondary deviation."

35. History keeps conflict alive. For example, historian Roberta Senechal de la Roche reports that in the 1980s African Americans in Springfield, Illinois, were still boycotting businesses whose previous owners had participated in a riot against African Americans more than fifty years earlier. *In Lincoln's Shadow*, 183.

36. Kopytoff, "Extension of conflict as a method of conflict resolution among the Suku of the Congo," 66–68. *Kembi* is an example of displaced liability, which locates accountability for an offense or injury in someone entirely unconnected to its occurrence. For other types of liability, see Black, "Compensation and the social structure of misfortune," 49–51.

37. Westermeyer, "Comparison of amok and other homicide in Laos," 703–707.

38. Ewing, "*Juramentado*." Running amok and *juramentado* normally conclude with the killing of the attacker (who undoubtedly expects that result from the beginning).

39. Levin and Fox, *Mass Murder*, 63; *Wikipedia*, "McDonald's Massacre." Other American examples of running amok include one in 1991 at a Texas restaurant (with twenty-four deaths), in 2007 at a Nebraska shopping mall (with eight deaths), and in 2007 at a Virginia university (with thirty-two deaths). All followed various reversals in the lives of the killers. *Wikipedia*, "George Hennard"; *Fox News*, "Nebraska mall shooter"; *Wikipedia*, "Virginia Tech massacre."

40. See, e.g., Fletcher, *What Cops Know*, 109; D. Russell, *Rape in Marriage*, 139.

41. See, e.g., Faludi, "Ghetto star"; see also Shakur, *Monster*.

42. See Durkheim, "Determination of moral facts."

43. See, e.g., A. Smith, *Theory of Moral Sentiments*. Legal scholar Patrick Devlin argues that the presence of "intolerance, indignation, and disgust" might justify a legal prohibition, such as a prohibition of homosexuality. *Enforcement of Morals*, 17.

44. Some say that only what is harmful should be illegal. See Mill, *On Liberty*; Hart, *Law, Liberty, and Morality*. Philosopher and novelist Ayn Rand argues that what is moral is whatever advances human self-preservation, while immorality is whatever undermines it. See, e.g., "Objectivist ethics." Biologist Richard Alexander suggests that morality advances the ability of humans to reproduce and survive as a species. *Biology of Moral Systems*.

45. By contrast, David Hume argues that "morality consists not in any relations that are the objects of science . . . [or] in any *matter of fact*, which can be discovered by the understanding." Instead, morality is a matter of human "passion." *Treatise of Human Nature*, 414, 422 (italics in original); see also generally Book III, Part I.

46. A dietary prohibition such as the Jewish or Muslim rule against eating pork or the Hindu rule against eating beef might seem arbitrary. But such prohibitions are cultural customs, and their violation is a rejection of these customs—a movement of cultural time. See, e.g., M. Douglas, *Purity and Danger*, Chapter 3. A traffic rule requiring people to drive on the right (or left) side of the road might seem arbitrary as well, but such a rule prevents injuries and deaths—movements of vertical and possibly relational time. See "Health as Wealth" in Chapter 4.

47. In the language of legal philosopher Hans Kelsen, the obligation to protect the shape of social space is the "*Grundnorm*." *Pure Theory of Law*, 8, 193–195.

48. Compare, e.g., Hohfeld, *Fundamental Legal Conceptions as Applied in Judicial Reasoning*, 38; Pinker, "Moral instinct."

49. See Bloom, "How do morals change?"

50. A legal fiction is a legal idea that contradicts reality.

51. E.g., L. Williams, "Classic rape"; Estrich, *Real Rape*, Chapters 2–3; see also "Rape as Relational Time" in chapter 2 of the present volume.

52. See M. Cooney, *Is Killing Wrong?*, Chapter 3.

53. See Lundsgaarde, *Murder in Space City*; M. Cooney, *idem*, Chapter 8.

54. See M. Cooney, *idem*, Chapter 3.

55. Because the ideal of equality before the law ignores the movement of social time, its application would arguably be a form of injustice. The same applies to the rule of law or any other application of social control that ignores the movement of social time.

We also know that law varies with the social geometry of the cases: their location and direction in social space. See, e.g., Black, *Behavior of Law*; "Geometry of law"; "Legal relativity"; M. Cooney, *Is Killing Wrong?* The theory of moral time partly explains why law varies with the social geometry of the cases. As noted earlier, for example, stranger rapes attract more law than intimate rapes because stranger rapes entail a greater movement of social time.

56. See Black, "Epistemology of pure sociology," 862–863. Whereas accountability for conduct alone (apart from motivation) is strict liability, accountability for motivation alone (apart from conduct) is subjective liability. See *idem*, "Compensation and the social structure of misfortune," 49–51. Because the contents of a person's mind are unobservable, it is impossible to defend oneself or anyone else against an attribution of a bad motive—except to point out that it is impossible to know the truth of the attribution. See *idem*, "Epistemology of pure sociology," 863–864, note 166.

57. See, e.g., Markovits, *Uncouth Nation*.

58. The Western philosophy of virtue traces to thinkers in ancient Greece, especially Aristotle. See *Aristotle's Eudemian Ethics*; *Nicomachean Ethics*. Philosopher William Frankena similarly distinguishes the "morality of traits of character" that defines ideal conduct (such as loyalty and honesty) from the "morality of principles" that prohibits conduct (such as killing and stealing). *Ethics*, 53–54; see also A. Smith, *Theory of Moral Sentiments*, Part VI; Anscombe, "Modern moral philosophy"; Fuller, *Morality of Law*, 5–6; Black, "On the origin of morality," 109, note 4; McCloskey, "Hobbes, Rawls, Nussbaum." Some tribal people apparently place primary emphasis on virtues rather than prohibitions. See, e.g., Gillin, "Crime and punishment among the Barama River Carib," 334; Hoebel, *Political Organization and Law-Ways of the Comanche Indians*, 6; Overing, "Styles of manhood," 89.

59. See, e.g., Pinker, "Moral instinct." The "Scout Law" of the Boy Scouts of America lists most of these virtues as the traits of an ideal Boy Scout. The founder of the Boy Scouts, Robert Baden-Powell, even called the organization a "character factory." Quoted in Hunter, *Death of Character*, 58.

60. See Christie, "Restorative justice," 370–372.

61. Unlike everyday virtue that maintains the shape of social space, we sometimes celebrate the heroic virtue of those who introduce new ideas or seek to change the course of human history. But in their own time such people are commonly condemned as heretics or rebels. See, e.g., Rand, *Virtue of Selfishness*, ix–xv; *Fountainhead*, xi–xiii; see also "Overinnovation" in chapter 7 of the present volume.

62. See Gluckman, "Moral crises," 23; see also Aristotle, *Aristotle's Eudemian Ethics*; *Nicomachean Ethics*.

63. The concept of "false accusation" sometimes refers to a case in which an innocent person is accused of wrongdoing that was actually committed by someone else. But here the term refers only to an accusation of wrongdoing that never occurred at all.

64. Conflict itself breeds false accusations. People might thus characterize their enemies as worse than they really are. An example from World War I was a claim made by some Germans that "Belgian women amused themselves by putting out the eyes of wounded German soldiers and forcing buttons ripped from their uniforms into the empty sockets." Quoted in Elon, *Pity of It All*, 319. False accusations might in turn lead to higher levels of violence against the enemy, such as massacres of prisoners or civilians.

65. See Herf, *Jewish Enemy*, 1–2.

66. Other deviations (such as bestiality, failing to be sociable, or being culturally different) might also lead to an accusation of witchcraft. See "Filthy Involvements" in chapter 2, "Underinvolvement as Bad Manners" in chapter 3, and "The Crime of Being Different" in chapter 6 of the present volume.

67. See, e.g., Pape, *Dying to Win*, 220–228, 241–259. Other factors are also relevant to Muslim terrorism, including cultural differences between Western and Islamic societies and military actions by the United States and other Western nations against Islamic societies. See Black, "Geometry of terrorism."

CHAPTER 2

1. Every distance is a difference, and a relational distance is a difference in existence: a degree of separation between one life and another. See Black, *Behavior of Law*, 40–46; "Dreams of pure sociology," 348, note 13.

2. See *idem*, "Epistemology of pure sociology," 835, note 37.

3. *Idem*, "Dreams of pure sociology," 349.

4. Amos, "Falling in love costs you friends."

5. See P. Blau and Schwartz, *Crosscutting Social Circles*, 13–14.

6. Dollard, *Caste and Class in a Southern Town*, 169; see also Simmel, *Sociology of Georg Simmel*, 321; Goffman, *Relations in Public*, 40–41.

7. Lindholm, *Generosity and Jealousy*, 220. In one fictional depiction of a patriarchal family in modern Turkey, the father "wouldn't permit anyone to close the doors to their rooms. Privacy meant suspicious activity; everything had to be visible, in the open. The only place where you could lock the door was the bathroom, and even there someone would knock on the door if you lingered inside for too long." The children also had to "talk in whispers" to avoid disturbing their father. Shafak, *The Bastard of Istanbul*, 307–308.

More generally, intimacy varies inversely with social stratification: the more inequality, the less intimacy. Spouses in patriarchal marriages normally share less of their lives than do spouses in more equal marriages (such as those often seen in modern societies such as the United States), for example, and friendships are more likely and closer between equals than between those who are unequal.

8. Compare M. Douglas, *Purity and Danger*; Milner, *Status and Sacredness*, 110–112.

9. See Pollock and Maitland, *History of English Law*, Volume 2: 525–526; Goffman, "Mental symptoms and public order," 147; *Relations in Public*, Chapter 2; Lyman and Scott, "Territoriality"; L. Lofland, *World of Strangers*.

10. See, e.g., Frazer, *Golden Bough*, Volume 1: 150; see also 151–160; Knauft, "Melanesian warfare," 256.

11. Rasmussen, *Netsilik Eskimos*, 202.

12. See, e.g., Pape, *Dying to Win*.

13. Violence is the use of force, and may include the infliction of an injury—a movement of vertical time. See "Violence as Vertical Time" in chapter 4.

14. See, e.g., Argentine National Commission on the Disappeared, *Nunca Más*, 20–51; E. Peters, *Torture*.

15. Holmstrom and Burgess, *Victim of Rape*, 246–247; L. Williams, "Classic rape"; Estrich, *Real Rape*, Chapters 2–3; LaFree, *Rape and Criminal Justice*, 222; see also Hanawalt, *Crime and Conflict in English Communities*, 104–110.

16. Marrying the victim might nullify the crime, however. Pollock and Maitland, *History of English Law*, Volume 2: 490–491; see also Lipsett-Rivera, "Slap in the face of honor," 194–195.

17. Ruggiero, *Violence in Early Renaissance Venice*, 165–167, 169–170.

18. *Idem*, 168.

19. D'Emilio and Freedman, *Intimate Matters*, 31.

20. See D. Russell, *Rape in Marriage*, Chapters 22, 24, Appendix II.

21. The rape of a superior imposes an inferior's will on a superior and is therefore partly a movement of vertical time. See chapter 5, "Understratification."

22. Drew, *Burgundian Code*, 44, 46; see also *Laws of the Salian Franks*, 155.

23. Spindel, *Crime and Society in North Carolina*, 108–109, 135.

24. See, e.g., Partington. "Incidence of the death penalty for rape in Virginia"; Wolfgang and Riedel, "Rape, race, and the death penalty in Georgia"; Dorr, *White Women, Rape, and the Power of Race in Virginia*, 5. In South Africa during racial segregation (known as "apartheid"), the execution of nonwhites for raping whites was "the general rule," but never occurred when whites raped nonwhites. Welsh, "Capital punishment in South Africa," 416.

25. See, e.g., Senechal de la Roche, "Sociogenesis of lynching."

26. *Idem, In Lincoln's Shadow*. Also apparently contributing to the Springfield riot was an incident five weeks earlier in which a white man was stabbed to death by a black man after the white man had chased the black man from a bedroom in his house, where the black man was presumably planning to rape his sixteen-year-old daughter. *Idem*, 18–20, 118, 142–143.

27. Epstein, *Sex Laws and Customs in Judaism*, 180.

28. See, e.g., Drew, *Lombard Laws*, 92; *Laws of the Salian Franks*, 155, 162.

29. Barton, *Ifugao Law*, 81–82.

30. LeVine, "Gusii sex offenses," 976–977.

31. Meggitt, *Blood Is Their Argument*, 14, 70, 192, note 14.

32. Ch'ü, *Law and Society in Traditional China*, 199.

33. Meijer, "Homosexual offenses in Ch'ing law," 126.

34. Jane Richardson, *Law and Status among the Kiowa Indians*, 35.

35. But the woman's husband was allowed to rescue her if he wished. R. Harper, *Code of Hammurabi*, Section X.

36. Zeid, "Honour and shame among the Bedouins of Egypt," 256.

37. See, e.g., Sahibzada, "Politics of rape in Pakistan."

38. Gilmartin, "Violence against women in China," 214; see also Brownmiller, *Against Our Will*, 74.

39. See, e.g., Brownmiller, *idem*, 78–87; Haglunds, *Enemies of the People*, 216; compare Patterson, *Slavery and Social Death*.

40. Pomeroy, *Goddesses, Whores, Wives, and Slaves*, 86.

41. Quoted in Brownmiller, *Against Our Will*, 407; Holmstrom and Burgess, *Victim of Rape*, 102.

42. See, e.g., Holmstrom and Burgess, *idem*, 31–33, 60. Rarely is the victim's word enough to convict an accused rapist. *Idem*, 244–245; see also Hanawalt, *Crime and Conflict in English Communities*, 59–61; J. M. Beattie, *Crime and the Courts in England*, 124–132. In Seattle in 1974 and Kansas City in 1975, 635 rape complaints produced a total of 10 convictions. LeGrand, Reich, and Chappell, *Forcible Rape*, 48, cited in Holmstrom and Burgess, *idem*, 258. Accused rapists receive some of the immunity provided by intimacy in other cases. See Black, *Behavior of Law*, 40–46.

43. See, e.g., Brownmiller, *Against Our Will*, 402. Some rape is at least partly a punishment of the victim or her associates. In fourteenth-century England, for instance, men might gang rape a woman as revenge against her husband. Hanawalt, *idem*, 109–110. Some rape in modern America is also a punishment. See, e.g., Finkelhor and Yllo, "Forced sex in marriage"; Cleaver, *Soul on Ice*, 14. Soldiers sometimes rape women in the course of defeating an enemy, illustrated by the mass rape of Chinese women by Japanese soldiers during their invasion of Nanking in 1937 and that of Bengali women by West Pakistani soldiers during the Bengali uprising of 1971. Chang, *Rape of Nanking*, 89–99; Brownmiller, *idem*, Chapter 3.

44. See, e.g., Baumgartner, "Law and social status in colonial New Haven," 157–158.

45. Herman, *Father-Daughter Incest*, 50. In a survey of 250 societies, anthropologist George Murdock found the incest taboo to be universal between males and females in nuclear families (parents and children or brothers and sisters). *Social Structure*, 284–285; see also J. Brown, "Comparative study of deviations from sexual mores," 146.

46. Herman, *idem*, 51; see, e.g., Durkheim, *Incest*; Murdock, *idem*, Chapter 9; Ellis, "Origins and development of the incest taboo," 123–143; Girard, *Violence and the Sacred*, Chapter 8; Herman, *idem*, Chapter 4.

47. Hart, *Law, Liberty, and Morality*, 50.

48. Powers, *Crime and Punishment in Early Massachusetts*, 261, 307; Hinckeldey, "History of crime and punishment," 107–108.

49. See, e.g., van der Meer, "Tribades on trial," 438.

50. Devlin, *Enforcement of Morals*, 1.

51. Ariès, "Thoughts on the history of homosexuality," 69.

52. See, e.g., Humphreys, *Tearoom Trade*.

53. van der Meer, "Tribades on trial," 424–425, 437–439; see also Hekma, "Homosexual behavior in the nineteenth-century Dutch army."

54. Comstock, *Violence against Lesbians and Gay Men*, 36, 145.

55. Denton-Edmundson, "Students, officials respond to bias-motivated assault."

56. G. Hughes, *Swearing*, 230–232; see also 229.

57. *Fox News*, "Lesbian's 'extreme' gang rape investigated in California."

58. See generally D. Greenberg, *Construction of Homosexuality*, Chapter 2; see also Lévi-Strauss, *Tristes Tropiques*, 307.

59. Herdt, "Ritualized homosexual behavior in the male cults of Melanesia," 50, 56; Allen, "Homosexuality, male power, and political organization in North Vanuatu"; Schwimmer, "Male couples in New Guinea"; Serpenti, "Ritual meaning of homosexuality and pedophilia among the Kimam-Papuans of South Irian Jaya"; Van Baal, "Dialectics of sex in Marind-Anim culture."

60. Herdt, *Ritualized Homosexuality in Melanesia*; Herdt and Stoller, *Intimate Communications*, 57–58, 285; see also Herdt, *Guardians of the Flutes*, 238, Chapters 7–8; "Semen transactions in Sambia culture." Anal intercourse between a man and a boy is also common in southwest New Guinea. Herdt, "Ritualized homosexual behavior in the male cults of Melanesia," 77, note 25. During one tribe's initiation into manhood, a designated man is "supposed to have regular homosexual intercourse with the boy to make him strong with the semen that is inserted into his body," and others often participate, so that "sometimes seven or more men have anal intercourse with the boy during the same night." Serpenti, *idem*, 304, 306.

61. Dover, *Greek Homosexuality*, 91–109; Gagarin, *Early Greek Law*, 67–68.

62. Veyne, "Homosexuality in ancient Rome," 26–31.

63. Meijer, "Homosexual offenses in Ch'ing law," 130; see also 124, 127.

64. See, e.g., *Fox News*, "Gay couple convicted in Malawi."

65. Muir, "Iraqi gay men face 'lives of hell.'"

66. van Eck, *Purified by Blood*, 37, 48, Chapter 2.

67. Ginat, *Blood Disputes among Bedouin and Rural Arabs in Israel*, Chapter 5.

68. Wijayaratna, *Buddhist Monastic Life*, 91–92; see also Chapter 6.

69. *Idem*, 96, 99–100.

70. See *Wikipedia*, "Roman Catholic sex abuse cases."

71. E. Harper, "Ritual pollution as an integrator of caste and religion," 171.

72. *Idem*, 171–172; see also Mandelbaum, *Society in India*, Volume 1: 201–202; Milner, *Status and Sacredness*, 39–41, 60–61.

73. See, e.g., Beirne, "Rethinking bestiality," 321.

74. *Idem*, 320.

75. Liliequist, "Peasants against nature," 416. Many societies even have masculine and feminine spaces. See Spain, *Gendered Spaces*. Some tribal societies have separate walking paths for men and women. See, e.g., Herdt, "Semen transactions in Sambia culture," 171.

76. The Buid of the Philippine highlands allow domestic animals (such as pigs and chickens) into their homes, but prohibit sex with them or even speaking to them. Gibson, "Symbolic representations of tranquility and aggression among the Buid," 73–74. The Kaguru of Tanzania consider bestiality to be evidence that someone might be a witch who must be killed. Beidelman, "Witchcraft in Ukaguru," 67, note 1. Eskimos tolerate sexual intercourse with dead seals or caribou by men and with dogs by both men and women, but view such behavior as somewhat "ridiculous." Rasmussen, *Netsilik Eskimos*, 197–198.

77. Liliequist, "Peasants against nature," 394–395, 400. The killing of female animals after human sexual contact is not unlike the fate of some human victims of rape. In fact, sociologist Piers Beirne argues that bestiality *is* a form of rape. "Rethinking bestiality," 326; see also *Confronting Animal Abuse*: Chapter 3.

78. MacDonald, "Frightful consequences of onanism," 430; Boswell, *Christianity, Social Tolerance, and Homosexuality*, 323; see also Wijayaratna, *Buddhist Monastic Life*, 95.

79. L. Hall, "Forbidden by God, despised by men"; see also Hare, "Masturbatory insanity," 19, note 3; MacDonald, *idem*, 423, note 1; Laqueur, *Solitary Sex*, 13–14. The following is the first part of the title as it originally appeared on the title page of an anonymously authored book that was popular in eighteenth-century England: *ONANIA; OR, THE Heinous Sin OF Self Pollution, AND All its Frightful Consequences, in both SEXES, Consider'd. WITH Spiritual and Physical Advice to those, who have already injur'd themselves by this Abominable Practice.*

80. Hare, *idem*, 10–11, 22, notes 23–26.

81. L. Hall, "Forbidden by God, despised by men," 386–387; but see Laqueur, *Solitary Sex*, Chapter 2.

82. Quoted in Monk, *Ludwig Wittgenstein*, 380.

83. E.g., Woods, *Masturbation, Tantra and Self Love*.

84. Drew, *Laws of the Salian Franks*, 188; Schild, "History of criminal law and procedure," 48.

85. McAleer, *Dueling*, 47.

86. Baumgartner, "War and peace in early childhood," 5, 27–28. But one orthodox Jewish school in the United States has a rule that "boys and girls must not touch one another, even accidentally." Feldman, "Orthodox paradox," 4.

87. In modern life, however, touching a child can lead to prosecution for "child molesting" (especially when a stranger is involved), while touching an adult (including an inferior such as an employee) can lead to a complaint about "sexual harassment." See, e.g., Makin, "Abusers who breach trust get shorter sentences."

88. Dixon, "Protocol is abandoned as Michelle Obama cosies up to Queen."

89. Sahlins, *Social Stratification in Polynesia*, 20–21.

90. Lingat, *Classical Law of India*, 41; Milner, *Status and Sacredness*, 111; Douglas, *Purity and Danger*, 32–33; E. Harper, "Ritual pollution as an integrator of caste and religion," 169. Squatting also prevents a man's genitals from being seen by others (which would violate another taboo). E. Harper, *idem*.

91. See Dumont, *Homo Hierarchicus*, 138–139; M. Douglas, *idem*, 34; Orenstein, *Gaon*, 151; see also Milner, *idem*, 110–112.

92. Orenstein, *idem*, 150–151; Dumont, *idem*, 138–139.

93. A. Brown, *Subjects of Deceit*, 92.

94. Frazer, *Golden Bough*, Volume 1: 161–165; see also Babb, "Glancing."

95. John Richardson, *Life of Picasso: The Triumphant Years*, 51.

96. The label "Peeping Tom" derives from the medieval English legend of Lady Godiva, whose husband would agree with her request to cancel a burdensome tax on the people of Coventry only if she would ride naked on a horse through the town. She accepted his offer, but first warned the townspeople to stay inside and avoid looking at her during her ride. All obeyed except a tailor named Tom, who bored a hole in his shutters and looked at her as she passed. It is said that he was instantly struck blind. In any case, he came to be known as "Peeping Tom."

97. See generally R. Spencer Smith, "Voyeurism."

98. Gilmore, *Aggression and Community*, 161–162, 165.

99. See Duvignaud, *Change at Shebika*, 228; Mernissi, *Beyond the Veil*, 83. Stripping a person may be a form of punishment. Some American Indians would strip a male captive and tie him to a pole to be tormented by women and children, or they might make him run naked between lines of people who beat him as he passed (known as "running the gauntlet"). See, e.g., Axtell, "White Indians of colonial America," 77; Demos *Unredeemed Captive*, 81. Medieval Italians sometimes made adulterers run naked through the streets while being beaten (known as *correre la terra*, or "running the land"). Trexler, "*Correre la terra*," 888. The leader of a modern American religious sect called the Divine Light might discipline members of the sect by having them "publicly stripped" in front of other members. Jacobs, *Divine Disenchantment*, 94.

100. Burbank, *Fighting Women*, 85.

101. Kaplan, *Piaroa*, 86.

102. Bayley, *Forces of Order*, 45. Unlike American or other Western police, however, Japanese police readily speak to people in public places, such as by using loudspeakers on their patrol cars to admonish people parking illegally or crossing a street against a signal. *Idem.*

103. Abbott, *In the Belly of the Beast*, 66–67.

104. Suttles, *Social Order of the Slum*, 67; see also Anderson, *Streetwise*, 220.

105. Goffman, *Relations in Public*, 45–46.

106. See Katz, *Seductions of Crime*, 110–112.

107. Relational distance varies directly with cultural distance (such as ethnic and religious differences).

108. See M. Weber, *Sociology of Religion*, 108–109.

109. Hane, *Peasants, Rebels and Outcastes*, 139–143, 148–149; Alldritt, "Buddhism and the *burakumin*."

110. See, e.g., M. Weber, *Sociology of Religion*, 108–109; Arendt, "Antisemitism," 73–75.

111. Some scholars believe that "drawing" in "drawing and quartering" refers to the process of dragging the condemned to the place of execution, while others believe it refers to the process of emasculating and disemboweling the condemned (followed by the burning of his genitals and entrails). In any case, when crimes were punishable by drawing and quartering, women were normally executed by the more lenient punishment of being burned at the stake.

112. Nirenberg, *Communities of Violence*, 130–144; Beirne, "Rethinking bestiality," 321.

113. M. Cohen, *Under Crescent and Cross*, 194; Davidson, "Inquisition and the Italian Jews," 27.

114. Nirenberg, *Communities of Violence*, 127.

115. Elon, *Pity of It All*, 1–4.

116. Hilberg, *Destruction of the European Jews*, Volume 1: 42–48; see also Müller, *Hitler's Justice*, 93, 96–97.

117. Müller, *idem*, 102–115.

118. Hilberg, *Destruction of the European Jews*, Volume 1: 47–49.

119. Quoted in Arendt, "History of the great crime," 457.

120. See, e.g., Bay, *White Image in the Black Mind*.

121. Dollard, *Caste and Class in a Southern Town*, 155.

122. See Williamson, *New People*, 97–98.

123. See Woodward, *Strange Career of Jim Crow*.

124. See Goffman, *Behavior in Public Places*, Chapters 8–9; see also Simmel, *Sociology of Georg Simmel*, 321.

125. Goffman, *idem*, 140; see also Chapter 8; Cavan, *Liquor License*.

126. See, e.g., J. Murray, *George Washington's Rules of Civility*; E. Hall, *Hidden Dimension*, Chapters 10–12; Kasson, *Rudeness and Civility*, 13.

127. Suttles, *Social Order of the Slum*, 66.

128. See, e.g., Eder, "Structure of gossip"; Zerubavel, *Elephant in the Room*, 29.

129. Emerson, "Responding to roommate troubles," 488, 494, 498.

130. See Goffman, *Behavior in Public Places*, 88.

131. Emerson, "Responding to roommate troubles," 495.

132. See Zerubavel, *Elephant in the Room*, 29–31.

133. Quoted in Goffman, *Behavior in Public Places*, 84.

134. Quoted in Kasson, *Rudeness and Civility*, 126–127; see also Goffman, *Behavior in Public Places*, 83–88.

135. Van Baal, "Dialectics of sex in Marind-Anim culture," 151.

136. Lee, *!Kung San*, 461.

137. Quoted in Goffman, *Behavior in Public Places*, 66. Grooming and other contact with one's body in the presence of other people is not only overinvolvement but overexposure: exhibiting something usually concealed.

138. Goffman, *Behavior in Public Places*, Chapter 14.

139. *Idem*, 147–148; "Alienation from interaction," 122; "Insanity of place," 359, 389.

140. Emerson, "Responding to roommate troubles," 493, 499.

141. See Simmel, *Sociology of Georg Simmel*, 330–338, Chapter 4; see also Bok, *Secrets*.

142. Hoebel, "Keresan Pueblo law," 113.

143. See, e.g., Scheppele, *Legal Secrets*, 222–226.

144. Messenger, "Sex and repression in an Irish folk community," 18–19, 29.

145. Gregor, *Mehinaku*, 137–138, 155; *Anxious Pleasures*, 102; see also Turnbull, *Wayward Servants*, 202–205.

146. About 5 percent contacted the police. S. McNeill, "Flashing," 99–100.

147. Yngvesson, "Responses to grievance behavior," 360–361; "Atlantic fishermen," 67–69.

148. Baumgartner, *Moral Order of a Suburb*, 74–75.

149. Elias, *Civilizing Process*, 164–165 (punctuation edited).

150. Overexposure can also be an act of aggression. For example, women in some tribal societies display their private parts as a way of insulting a man. See, e.g., Evans-Pritchard, *Witchcraft, Oracles and Magic among the Azande*; Lambert, *Kikuyu Social and Political Institutions*, 56, 99; Beidelman, "Witchcraft in Ukaguru," 67. Medieval European armies had men (called "ribalds") drop their pants and shout obscenities at the enemy as a "collective insult." Trexler, "*Correre la terra*," 848–849, especially note 8. In the early twentieth century, a Canadian religious sect called the Doukhobors engaged in mass nudity to protest government policies. Woodcock and Avakumovic, *Doukhobors*, Chapter 13. And in the 1960s, American young people occasionally disrobed to protest policies of their government. See, e.g., J. Rubin, *Do It!*, 140–141.

151. Miles, *Ginsberg*, 21, 76, 81.

152. Elias, *Civilizing Process*, 139; see also 138, 164.

153. Lingat, *Classical Law of India*, 40.

154. Men effectively own public space in traditional Muslim societies, and for a woman merely to appear in public is a form of "trespass." Mernissi, *Beyond the Veil*, 85.

155. Lindholm, *Generosity and Jealousy*, 219.

156. Mernissi, *Beyond the Veil*, 85–86.

157. Gilmore, *Aggression and Community*, 161.

158. Makarius, "Incest and redemption in Arnhem Land," 152; see also Burbank, *Fighting Women*, 152.

159. A medieval Jewish rule requiring the separation of unmarried men and women was similar to the Aborigine taboo against a brother smelling his sister: "Even to smell the perfume upon her is prohibited." Feldman, "Orthodox paradox," 4.

160. Hiatt, *Kinship and Conflict*, 114–115; "Spear in the ear"; Maddock, "Structural interpretation of the *mirriri*," 171; Burbank, "*Mirriri* as ritualized aggression," 50–52.

161. See, e.g., Maddock, *idem*; Burbank, *idem*, 50.

162. Warner, *Black Civilization*, 65; Burbank, *idem*, 51; *Fighting Women*, 152.

163. Burbank, *Fighting Women*, 51, 112–118; Hiatt, *Kinship and Conflict*, 117; see also Warner, *idem*, xx, 66; Burbank, "*Mirriri* as ritualized aggression," 50–51.

Modern Aborigines say that "blackfellow law" requires a brother to attack his sister when he is "speared in the ear" (though "whitefellow law" prohibits it). Maddock, "Structural interpretation of the *mirriri*," 168; see also Makarius, "Incest and redemption in Arnhem Land."

164. W. Lloyd Warner, quoted in Hiatt, *idem*, 113.

165. Aborigine men sometimes attack apparently blameless women in other situations. One or more men might thus attack and possibly kill a woman when men quarrel about her ownership since, as they say, "she is really the cause of all the trouble." Hiatt, *idem*, 118–119, note 3; see also 100, 139–140.

166. The relational closeness of artists to their subjects has also increased, illustrated to an extreme when their subjects are themselves. At the same time, the social status of their subjects has declined. For example, painters have increasingly depicted ordinary people instead of those with great authority, wealth, or supernatural power such as monarchs, aristocrats, military commanders, or gods. And they have reduced the cultural distance of the subjects by increasingly depicting members of their own society instead of historical or mythological figures. Their audiences have thereby become closer to the subjects on several dimensions: relationally, vertically, and culturally. See Black, "Dreams of pure sociology," 348, especially note 14.

167. Although the display of an overintimate subject is a form of overexposure, its consumption is a form of overinvolvement.

168. Simon Wilson, *Egon Schiele*, 8–9; see also Joanna Scott, *Arrogance*, 196–197, 265–267. Critics later recognized Schiele as one of the most important artists of the twentieth century (which is also true of the other artists mentioned below).

169. Quoted in Comini, *Gustav Klimt*, 6.

170. Hobhouse, *Bride Stripped Bare*, 139.

171. Reproduced in Jencks, *Post-Modernism*, 88; Kuspit, *Fischl*, 73.

172. Quoted in Kuspit, *idem*, 36, 39, 42, 54, 57.

173. Reproduced and discussed in Eggen, "Odd one."

174. Weiermair, *Hidden Image*, 27; see also Ellenzweig, "The homoerotic photograph."

175. Kent and Morreau, "Preface," 1; see also Kent, "Scratching and biting savagery."

176. See, e.g., de Grazia and Newman, *Banned Films*, 121–125, 297–303.

177. See generally de Grazia, *Girls Lean Back Everywhere*.

178. Miles, *Ginsberg*, 227, 232.

179. de Grazia, *Girls Lean Back Everywhere*, xi, 93, 370.

180. See e.g., Hunter, *Culture Wars*, Chapter 9.

181. Elias, *Civilizing Process*, 129–143; see also Chapter 2.

182. See Goffman, *Behavior in Public Places*, 68–69.

183. See Canetti, *Crowds and Power*, 223.

184. Kasson, *Rudeness and Civility*, 147.

185. Quoted in *idem*, 148.

186. Goffman, "Alienation from interaction," 122, 124–125, note 6; *Relations in Public*, 55–56.

CHAPTER 3

1. See Baumgartner, "Social control in suburbia," 85–86; *Moral Order of a Suburb*, Chapter 3; Black, *Social Structure of Right and Wrong*, xvi; Hirschman, *Exit, Voice, and Loyalty*; Haglunds, *Enemies of the People*, Chapter 8; for illustrations, see, e.g., Woodburn, "Minimal politics," 252; Merry, *Getting Justice and Getting Even*, 40, 48, 50; Just, "Going through the emotions," 301–302.

2. Ejidike, "Human rights in the cultural traditions and social practice of the Igbo," 76; Achebe, *Things Fall Apart*, 74. The killer might also commit suicide or give the victim's family a wife "to bear children in the name of the victim." Ejidike, *idem*.

3. Beidelman, "Witchcraft in Ukaguru," 73.

4. Wijayaratna, *Buddhist Monastic Life*, 143–145.

5. Emerson, "Responding to roommate troubles," 502–503.

6. See Baumgartner, "Violent networks," 20.

7. See, e.g., Gouldner, "Norm of reciprocity"; Mauss, *Gift*; Kiefer, *Tausug*, 65–69; Macaulay, "Non-contractual relations in business."

8. Adultery also violates the right of each spouse to sexual exclusivity. See van Sommers, *Jealousy*.

9. Anthropologist Suzanne Frayser found that adultery was condemned in all of the fifty-four societies she studied. *Varieties of Sexual Experience*, 210–211, 215; see also Baumgartner, "Violent networks," 210–211. In a survey of 250 societies, anthropologist George Murdock found only one group (the Todas of India) with an apparent "indifference to adultery" and another (the Kaingang of Brazil) so "promiscuous" that they did not consider adultery a serious form of deviant behavior. *Social Structure*, 264.

10. Hoebel, *Law of Primitive Man*, 286; Daly and Wilson, *Homicide*, 195; see also Hiatt, *Kinship and Conflict*, 101, 107. Apparently Hoebel was unaware that some tribal people virtually or literally never engage in violence against members of their own group, and would surely be horrified if a man were to kill his wife because of adultery or anything else. See, e.g., Howell and Willis, *Societies at Peace*; Fry, *Human Potential for Peace*.

Hoebel also notes that the right of a wife to kill a husband caught in the act of adultery is "rare" in tribal societies. *Idem*, 286.

11. Chagnon, *Yanomamö*, 82–83.

12. Llewellyn and Hoebel, *Cheyenne Way*, 202–203; see also Reid, *Law of Blood*, 115–116.

13. Harner, *Jívaro*, 175.

14. Strehlow, *Aranda und Loritja-Stämme in Zentral-Australien*, 9 ff., cited by Hoebel, *Law of Primitive Man*, 303.

15. Fallers, *Law without Precedent*, 101, 111; see also Hoebel, "Keresan Pueblo law," 103; Radcliffe-Brown, *Andaman Islanders*, 50. When anthropologist Lloyd Fallers asked a Soga chief why the Soga prosecute an adulterous woman's lover but not the woman herself, the chief replied, "If someone were to steal your shoes, would you accuse the shoes?" *Idem*, 101.

16. See, e.g., Hallpike, *Bloodshed and Vengeance in the Papuan Mountains*, 132.

17. Young, *Fighting with Food*, 54.

18. Bühler, *Laws of Manu*, 451–452; Lingat, *Classical Law of India*, 55.

19. However, a man who had a sexual relationship with his married slave could make adequate amends by freeing the woman and her husband. See, e.g., Drew, *Burgundian Code*, 68; *Lombard Laws*, 93; see also 208.

20. Haskins, *Law and Authority in Early Massachusetts*, 149; Baumgartner, "Law and social status in colonial New Haven," 158.

21. Robinson, "Casting stones," 37.

22. Daly and Wilson, *Homicide*, 202; see also Wolfgang, *Patterns in Criminal Homicide*, Chapter 1; Lundsgaarde, *Murder in Space City*, 56–74; M. Cooney, Law, Morality, and Conscience, 60–62.

23. Burbank, "Female aggression in cross-cultural perspective," 92–93.

24. She shot herself in a bathtub to make it easier to clean up her blood. Karman, *Robinson Jeffers*, 132–133.

25. An American "reality television" series (that presents people in unscripted situations) once had a show called *Temptation Island*, which separated couples by placing the man with unattached women and the woman with unattached men entirely to elicit conflicts in the couples for the enjoyment of the audience. Godard, "Reel life," 91.

26. See, e.g, Burbank, "Female aggression in cross-cultural perspective," 87; *Fighting Women*, 111–113; Baumgartner, "Violent networks," 211.

27. Colson, *Marriage and the Family among the Plateau Tonga of Northern Rhodesia*, 123; see also 128–130, 132. Polyandrous households (those with more than one husband) are very rare—an "ethnological curiosity." Murdock, *Social Structure*, 25.

28. Schuster, "Women's aggression," 324–325.

29. Keller, "Marriage and medicine"; Schuster, *idem*, 325.

30. Burbank, *Fighting Women*, 57–60, 74, 130.

31. See, e.g., Huffington, *Picasso*.

32. John Richardson, *Life of Picasso*, Volume 2: 20. Picasso's lover would also have known that he liked to paint naked.

Picasso himself recognized the zero-sum nature of intimacy: "To choose one person is always, in a measure, to kill someone else." Quoted in Gilot and Lake, *Life with Picasso*, 101.

33. Quoted in Breslin, *Mark Rothko*, 219.

34. Maull, "Hung jury declared in cat killer trial." Also akin to adultery is the sin of idolatry, which is included in the Ten Commandments: "Thou shalt have no other gods before me." See Margalit, "After strange gods," 30.

35. See Baumgartner, "Violent networks," 210–211; Retzinger, *Violent Emotions*, Chapter 2; Scheff and Retzinger, *Emotions and Violence*, Chapters 1–2; Scheff, *Bloody Revenge*, 1–35.

36. Drew, *Burgundian Code*, 45–46.

37. See, e.g., Kristof, "Terrorism that's personal"; Popham, "Pakistan horrified by feudal husband's acid attack on beauty." An unmarried woman who rejects a man might suffer the same fate.

38. Daly and Wilson, *Homicide*, 219.

39. See, e.g., Barnard, Vera, Vera, and Newman, "Till death do us part," 274, 277–279; Margo Wilson and Daly, "Spousal homicide risk and estrangement."

40. Daly and Wilson, *Homicide*, 219.

41. Barnard et al., "Till death do us part," 279.

42. Lundsgaarde, *Murder in Space City*, 61.

43. *Fox News*, "Woman says husband killed 5 children to punish her."

44. Pollak, "Male homosexuality—or happiness in the ghetto," 51.

45. D. Russell, *Rape in Marriage*, 363–364.

46. Quoted in *idem*, 244.

47. D. Russell, *idem*, 364, 371; see also generally Chapters 4–6.

48. Fletcher, *What Cops Know*, 109.

49. See, e.g., Westermeyer, "Comparison of amok and other homicide in Laos."

50. *Fox News*, "Nebraska mall shooter broke up with girlfriend, lost job before massacre."

51. The shooter's "grades had fallen recently" as well. *CNN*, "Teen suspect in Georgia school shooting may face adult charge."

52. Ridgeway, *Dynamics of Small Groups*, 26–28.

53. Sageman, *Understanding Terror Networks*, 116, 126–135. A loss of intimacy might also lead to a nonviolent crime. For example, check forgery typically occurs "at a critical point in a process of social isolation," such as after a divorce, separation, or other form of "family alienation and repudiation." Lemert, "An isolation and closure theory of naïve check forgery," 101, 103. A loss of previous involvements might likewise lead someone to join a religious sect. Lofland and Stark, "Becoming a world-saver," 870.

54. Lambert, *Kikuyu Social and Political Institutions*, 113.

55. Pitt-Rivers, *People of the Sierra*, 171–172, cited in Gilmore, *Aggression and Community*, 49.

56. Nader, *Harmony Ideology*, 204, 209.

57. Fried, "Relation of ideal norms to actual behavior," 291.

58. Schoetz, "Daughter rejects marriage, ends up dead." The daughter's rejection of the marriage challenged her father's authority and was therefore a form of rebellion as well. See Dorell, "'Honor killings' in USA raise concerns"; "Social Castration" in chapter 4 and "Rebellion" in chapter 5 of the present volume.

59. See, e.g., Ariès, "Indissoluble marriage."

60. Vaughan, *Uncoupling*, 219, 229.

61. Fried, "Relation of ideal norms to actual behavior," 291.

62. Merry, *Getting Justice and Getting Even*, 54–59.

63. In ancient Rome abandoning unwanted children (especially newborns) was an accepted practice. Boswell, *Kindness of Strangers*, 128–137.

64. See, e.g., Nader, *Harmony Ideology*, 213–216.

65. See, e.g., Hunter, *Before the Shooting Begins*. Separation from a nonhuman (such as an animal or nonliving object) may also cause conflict. For instance, painter Mark Rothko called his paintings his "children," and became upset if one of them did not have a proper "home" where it would receive adequate care and attention. In one case when he learned that a painting of his was going to be sold by the owner (which he considered an act of "infidelity"), he went to the owner's home and slashed the painting with a knife. Breslin, *Mark Rothko*, 305–306.

66. See M. Cooney, *Is Killing Wrong?*; see also "Violence as Vertical Time" in chapter 4 of the present volume.

67. See Black, "Violent structures," 153–154. In one unusual case, an Israeli man attacked several army officers with a knife after they told him that his son had been killed in action. Chernofsky, "Comforting the bereaved," 4.

68. See, e.g., S. Stack, "Homicide followed by suicide."

69. J. Douglas, *Social Meanings of Suicide*, 328. See also "Violence as Vertical Time" in chapter 4.

70. Dublin and Bunzel, *To Be or Not to Be*, 294, quoted in J. Douglas, *idem*, 311.

71. Kposowa, "Marital status and suicide," 257–260; "Divorce and suicide risk;" see also Manning, Suicide as Social Control, Chapter 3. Divorced men also lose intimacy with their children, who usually remain with their mother. Court-ordered financial support for an ex-wife (including child support) may be costly (if not financially ruinous) for an ex-husband as well. In any case, whereas divorced and separated men are more than twice as likely than married men to commit suicide, divorced and separated women have the same suicide rate as married women. *Idem*, "Marital status and suicide," 257–260. See also Durkheim, *Suicide*, 259–276.

72. Bradshaw, "Flemish TV personality Yasmine takes her own life."

73. D. Kelly and Quinones, "Engineer led solitary life marred by tragedy."

74. See Goffman, *Behavior in Public Places*, 114–116.

75. Winans and Edgerton, "Hehe magical justice," 747, 749, 761–764.

76. Hallpike, *Bloodshed and Vengeance in the Papuan Mountains*, 247–249.

77. Quoted in Goffman, *Behavior in Public Places*, 115.

78. Foucault, "Minimalist self," 4; see also Goffman, *Behavior in Public Places*, 3–4, 104–110, 193–196.

79. E.g., Monica Wilson, "Witch-beliefs and social structure," 104; Waller, "Witchcraft and colonial law," 257.

80. Goffman, "Alienation from interaction," 129.

81. *Idem*, 114–117, 127–128; *Behavior in Public Places*, 70, 110, 194; see also Chapters 3–5.

82. *Idem, Behavior in Public Places*, especially Chapters 14–15.

83. Simmel, *Sociology of Georg Simmel*, 323.

84. See Ariès, "Love in married life," 136.

85. Just, "Going through the emotions," 294, 310, note 3.

86. Lee, *!Kung San*, 461.

87. Uchendu, "Igbo world," 231–232, 261.

88. Hoebel, *Law of Primitive Man*, 71; see also Hepworth and Turner, "On the universality of confession," 70–73.

89. See, e.g., Rasmussen, *Netsilik Eskimos*, 197–199.

90. Béjin, "Extra-marital union today," 163.

91. Vaughan, *Uncoupling*, 3; see also Chapter 1. Because closeness requires exposure, those with something to hide (such as professional criminals or ex-mental patients) may avoid close relationships entirely. Goffman, *Stigma*, 99–100; Lemert, "Behavior of the systematic check forger," 112. And just as sharing secrets is a form of closeness, divulging secrets to others is a form of separation. See Åkerström, *Betrayal and Betrayers*.

92. Merton, "Normative structure of science," 270, 273–274.

93. See, e.g., Scheppele, *Legal Secrets*, Chapters 6–7.

94. Haskins, *Law and Authority in Early Massachusetts*, 86.

95. See B. Turner, "Confession and social structure," 41–46, 51–57; Hepworth and Turner, "Introduction," 11–12; Brundage, *Medieval Canon Law*, 24–26.

96. See Simmel, *Sociology of Georg Simmel*, 312.

97. See Bok, *Lying*, 13.

98. See Simmel, *Sociology of Georg Simmel*, 313; Barnes, *Pack of Lies*, 79–82.

99. See Barnes, *idem*, 20.

100. Some regard lying as a natural part of conflict. In the Islamic courts of Morocco, for instance, "witnesses are not sworn before testifying, even in criminal proceedings, nor is any punishment for perjury recognized—the common assumption being that in the face of such proceedings one may well be expected to make statements that do not bear on the truth." Rosen, *Anthropology of Justice*, 32. But lying may be no less frequent in modern legal systems such as that of the United States. See, e.g., Wishman, *Confessions of a Criminal Lawyer*, 36–37, 232, 239–240.

101. See Black, "Strategy of pure sociology," 165–167.

102. K. Greenberg, *Honor and Slavery*, 8, 11, 39–40.

103. See, e.g., Gorn, "'Gouge and bite, pull hair and scratch.'"

104. C. Cooley, *Human Nature and the Social Order*, 388.

105. See Barnes, *Pack of Lies*, 72–75, 80–81.

106. du Boulay, *Portrait of a Greek Mountain Village*, 191; see also 192–200.

107. Messenger, "Types and causes of disputes in an Irish community," 30, note 4; "Sex and repression in an Irish folk community," 11–13, 31.

108. Barnes, *Pack of Lies*, 138.

109. Rasmussen, *Netsilik Eskimos*, 200.

110. Hoebel, *Law of Primitive Man*, 90.

111. See Goffman, *Presentation of Self in Everyday Life*; *Stigma*; "Expression games."

112. See Arendt, *On Revolution*, 94–105.

113. Laing, *Divided Self*, Chapters 6, 10–11.

114. Benedict, *Chrysanthemum and the Sword*, 216.

CHAPTER 4

1. See Black, "Dreams of pure sociology," 349, note 20.

2. E.g., Merton, "Social structure and anomie"; Henry and Short, *Suicide and Homicide*, Chapters 3–4; Cloward and Ohlin, *Delinquency and Opportunity*; Messner and Rosenfeld, *Crime and the American Dream*.

3. E.g., Marx and Engels, *Manifesto of the Communist Party*.

4. Stinchcombe, "Social structure and organizations," 171–180.

5. Brenner, *Betting on Ideas*, 3; see also 5–10.

6. A level of performance in a sport is a form of "functional status." See Black, "Dreams of pure sociology," 349, note 20.

7. Anthropologist Claude Lévi-Strauss notes that every sports contest has a "disjunctive effect": It ends with "the establishment of a difference between individual players or teams where originally there was no indication of inequality.... They are distinguished into winners and losers." He even suggests that to win a sports contest is "symbolically 'to kill' one's opponent." *Savage Mind*, 32.

8. On the social significance of success in sports, see, e.g., Azoy, *Buzkashi*, 17–34; Gregor, *Anxious Pleasures*, 96, 98; Poliakoff, *Combat Sports*, 19, 105; Nandy, *Tao of Cricket*, 103–120.

9. Courchesne, "Rule tackles blowouts in high school football."

10. *USA Today*, "Coach of 100-point win fired."

11. Gelfand, *Witch Doctor*, 52.

12. See, e.g., Midelfort, *Witch Hunting in Southwestern Germany*; Jensen, *Path of the Devil*.

13. Wijsen and Tanner, "*I Am Just a Sukuma*," 135.

14. See, e.g., Evans-Pritchard, *Witchcraft, Oracles and Magic among the Azande*, Chapter 8; Middleton and Winter, *Witchcraft and Sorcery in East Africa*; Marwick, "Introduction," 12–13; Obeyesekere, "Sorcery, premeditated murder, and the canalization of aggression in Sri Lanka."

15. See "Misfortune as Witchcraft" in chapter 5 of the present volume.

16. Waller, "Witchcraft and colonial law," 256–257.

17. Anthropologist Max Gluckman similarly notes that in some tribes a man who "outdoes his fellows too much" may be suspected of witchcraft or sorcery. *Politics, Law and Ritual in Tribal Society*, 88; see also "Moral crises," 22–23.

18. Richards, *Land, Labour, and Diet in Northern Rhodesia*, 207, 215. Gluckman, "Moral crises," 23, citing Richards, *idem*; Gluckman, *Politics, Law and Ritual in Tribal Society*, 88, citing an

unidentified report by Richards. The reference to "witchcraft" in the last quote should probably be to "sorcery" (the use of a magical technique by an ordinary person).

19. Richards, "Modern movement of witch-finders," 176; *Land, Labour, and Diet in Northern Rhodesia*, 215, note 1; Gluckman, *Politics, Law and Ritual in Tribal Society*, 88. Accusations of witchcraft nevertheless ultimately decline with modernization. See Marwick, "Decline of witch-beliefs in differentiated societies."

20. Beidelman, "Witchcraft in Ukaguru," 74.

21. Gelfand, *Witch Doctor*, 51; Crawford, *Witchcraft and Sorcery in Rhodesia*, 68; see also Monica Wilson, "Witch-beliefs and social structure," 253–254.

22. A prosperous Navajo man is all the more vulnerable to a witchcraft accusation if he is "stingy with his relatives or fails to dispense generous hospitality"—forms of underintimacy. Kluckhohn, *Navajo Witchcraft*, 110–111, 119–120. The Gisu of Uganda have a similar pattern: "The successful man must be particularly careful to be generous in fulfilling his obligations lest he provoke the envy and jealousy of others or be suspected of having used witchcraft to attain his position." La Fontaine, "Witchcraft in Bugisu," 217.

23. Boyer and Nissenbaum, *Salem Possessed*, 199; see also 208, Chapters 1, 4, 8.

24. Yoshida, "Spirit possession and village conflict," 87. Rural Japanese believe that families inherit the power of animal spirits and that "spirit holders" have "a mystical power" to use their spirits "to possess others and cause them to become ill or to experience misfortune." *Idem.*

25. Favret-Saada, *Deadly Words*, 207, punctuation edited.

26. See, e.g., Leacock and Lee, "Introduction," 7. Woodburn, "Egalitarian societies." Here I refer specifically to simple hunter-gatherers rather than to more complex hunter-gatherers (who sometimes have considerable inequality, including slavery). See Knauft, "Violence and sociality in human evolution."

27. Boehm, "Egalitarian behavior and reverse dominance hierarchy," 228–232; "Conflict and the evolution of social control," 82, 85, 95–97; see also *Hierarchy in the Forest*.

28. Clastres, *Society against the State*, 186 (italics omitted). See also Black, *Sociological Justice*, 82.

29. Lee, *!Kung San*, 244, 458; see also 246.

30. *Idem*, 458; see also "Eating Christmas in the Kalahari," 63; Tavuchis, *Mea Culpa*, 149, note 29.

31. Balikci, *Netsilik Eskimo*, 175.

32. Gibson, "Symbolic representations of tranquility and aggression among the Buid," 64, 66.

33. Brison, *Just Talk*, 207–208, punctuation edited.

34. Young, *Fighting with Food*, 90.

35. Hallpike, *Bloodshed and Vengeance in the Papuan Mountains*, 249.

36. Read, "Leadership and consensus in New Guinea society," 429 (punctuation edited).

37. J. Scott, *Weapons of the Weak*, 262–263.

38. Brenner, *History—The Human Gamble*, 18.

39. Black, "Elementary forms of conflict management," 86; "Epistemology of pure sociology," 855, note 129; see also Gluckman, "Gossip and scandal"; Paine, "What is gossip about?"; "Gossip and transaction"; P. Wilson, "Filcher of good names"; Merry, "Rethinking gossip and scandal."

40. Colson, *Makah Indians*, 205; Gluckman, "Gossip and scandal."

41. David Gilmore comments that gossip in Andalusia serves as the "vengeance of the envious." *Aggression and Community*, 53–56; see also Chapter 4.

42. *Idem*, 79, 90; see also Chapter 5; Pitt-Rivers, "Moral foundations of the family," 83–90.

43. Colson, *Makah Indians*, 218–219.

44. Gilmore, *Aggression and Community*, 81–83.

45. They also had an informal rule against not working hard enough (being a "chiseler"). Roethlisberger and Dickson, *Management and the Worker*, 421–422, 522–523; see also 416–423, 517, 519, 524–576.

46. Like American workers, Japanese also expect everyone to work as hard as everyone else. Lebra, "Nonconfrontational strategies for management of interpersonal conflicts," 43.

47. Gluckman, "Moral crises," 23.

48. Fordham and Ogbu, "Black students' school success," 183; see also Fryer, "Acting white."

49. Fordham and Ogbu, *idem*, 186; Fryer, *idem*. Successful Hispanic American students also have fewer friends. Fryer, *idem*.

50. E.g., Fordham and Ogbu, *idem*, 187, 191, 194, 202.

51. Anderson, *Code of the Street*, 65; see also 53–64.

52. *Wikipedia*, "Jante Law." The concept of "Jante Law" derives from Aksel Sandermose's 1933 novel called *A Fugitive Crosses His Tracks* that describes life in a small Danish town called Jante at the beginning of the twentieth century. The Law has ten principles, known as the "Ten Laws of Jante":

1. Do not think you are special.
2. Do not think you have the same importance as us.
3. Do not think you are smarter than us.
4. Do not think you are better than us.
5. Do not think you know more than us.
6. Do not think you are more important than us.
7. Do not think you are good at anything.
8. Do not laugh at us.
9. Do not think that anyone cares about you.
10. Do not think you can teach us anything.

Another fictional depiction of enforced equality appears in Kurt Vonnegut's short story called "Harrison Bergeron."

53. Dorsman, "Hirsi Ali's fall."

54. *Wikipedia*, "Tall poppy syndrome." The "tall poppy" metaphor derives from a legend about a Roman tyrant who cut off the heads of the tallest poppies in his garden as a signal to kill all the prominent people in a recently captured city.

55. See, e.g., L. Lewis, "Nail that stuck up has been 'hammered down.'"

56. Because Jesus and his first followers were Jews, the founding of Christianity might be considered an historic Jewish accomplishment in itself.

57. Nietzsche, *Human, All-Too-Human*, 62 (italics omitted). The term "anti-Semitism" (coined in the nineteenth century) refers not only to hostility toward those who practice the Jewish religion (Judaism) but toward those of Jewish ancestry, including converts to Christianity and individuals who practice no religion at all.

58. Elon, *Pity of It All*, 206; see also generally Chapters 6–8.

59. *Idem*, 206; Bailey, *Germans*, 176; see also Elon, *Pity of It All*, 5-6, Chapter 8; Golczewski, "Rural anti-Semitism in Galicia," 101; Slezkine, *Jewish Century*, 47–52, 118–127.

60. Slezkine, *idem*.

61. Sombart, *Jews and Modern Capitalism*, especially Chapter 6; compare, e.g., Weber, *Protestant Ethic and the Spirit of Capitalism*.

62. T. Frank, *Double Exile*, 26–28.

63. Beauvois, "Polish-Jewish relations in the territories annexed by the Russian Empire," 88–90. Sombart suggests that the conception of Jewish businessmen as "cheats" arose at least partly from their greater involvement in competitive business practices (such as aggressive marketing and the maximization of profits) when these practices were not widely accepted among Christians. *Jews and Modern Capitalism*, Chapter 7.

64. Golczewski, "Rural anti-Semitism in Galicia," 102.

65. See, e.g. Goldhagen, *Hitler's Willing Executioners*, 411–412; Dundes, *Blood Libel Legend*; Elon, *Pity of It All*, 22–26; "Conservatism as Cultural Time" in chapter 7 of the present volume.

66. The intellectual and artistic achievements of some modern Jews have also attracted hostility because they challenged established ideas and styles of art. Examples are the political ideas of Karl Marx, the psychological theories of Sigmund Freud, the theoretical physics of Albert Einstein, the philosophy of Ludwig Wittgenstein, the fiction of Franz Kafka, the paintings of Gustav Klimt, and the music of Gustav Mahler. See, e.g., Janik and Toulmin, *Wittgenstein's Vienna*; Slezkine, *Jewish Century*; "Overcreativity in Art" and "Overcreativity in Science" in chapter 6 of the present volume.

67. See, e.g., White and Gribbin, *Einstein*, 148–150; Grunfeld, *Prophets without Honour*, Chapter 5; Isaacson, *Einstein*, 284–289.

68. Grunfeld, *idem*, 149.

69. Quoted in Lilla, "Enemy of liberalism," 38.

70. Safranski, *Martin Heidegger*, 253–257; Elon, *Pity of It All*, 390. Heidegger "broke off all contacts" with Husserl and other Jewish scholars and students, and at the urging of his publishers withdrew the dedication to Husserl on the flyleaf of his best-known book, *Being and Time*. Safranski, *idem*, 257–258.

71. Elon, *idem*, 395.

72. Herf, "Jewish war"; *Jewish Enemy*; Goldhagen, *Hitler's Willing Executioners*, 412–414; Mann, *Dark Side of Democracy*, Chapters 7–10; see also Campbell "Genocide as social control," 155. Because German leaders accused the Jews of planning to exterminate the German population, sociologist Michael Mann calls the German extermination of the Jews a "preemptive strike." *Idem*, 184, 199.

During the same period the Germans launched a campaign in the Middle East and North Africa to encourage Muslims to join forces with them to exterminate the seven hundred thousand Jews in those regions. See Herf, *Nazi Propaganda for the Arab World*. Arabs themselves have also advanced and endorsed conceptions of the Jews similar to those promulgated by the Germans. See, e.g., *idem*, 255–260.

73. By "paranoid" I refer not to a symptom of mental illness but rather to an obviously false claim that someone or something is extremely dangerous—a form of false accusation. Historian Jeffrey Herf calls the Nazi view of the Jews "paranoid" as well, but he attributes its origin entirely to Adolf Hitler. *Jewish Enemy*, 1–2. Historian Daniel Jonah Goldhagen comments that on the subject of Jews the Germans lacked a capacity for "reality-testing" and that their claims about Jews were "absolutely fantastical, the sorts of beliefs that ordinarily only madmen have of others." *Idem*, 412. But whether collective or individual, paranoia may have a basis in reality: a movement of

social time, such as a decline in social standing (a movement of vertical time) or a rejection by others (a movement of relational time). See, e.g., Lemert, "Paranoia and the dynamics of exclusion"; see also "Hard Times" in the present chapter.

74. Another source of Christian anti-Semitism has been the refusal of Jews to accept the divinity of Jesus, coupled with their minority status and other differences between Christians and Jews. Over the centuries, for example, the distinctive economic functions of Jews (such as commercial activities and money lending) separated them from most Christians (who were mainly involved in food production). Since their expulsion by the Romans from their homeland in the Middle East until the modern era, many Jews have also been somewhat nomadic (whether because of their mode of livelihood or because they experienced difficulties of various kinds), making them strangers to many Christians. Even when they were settled in a community, considerable segregation separated Christians and Jews. Although this segregation was enforced by both Christians and Jews, Jews have often been criticized for their "clannishness": "The Jewish community was regarded as a closed shop: 'Jews always stick together,' runs the old saw." Bailey, *Germans*, 176. Still another source of anti-Semitism in the modern period (especially among German Nazis and other nationalists and fascists) was the disproportionate number of Jews involved in left-wing political movements, including communism (sometimes called "Judeo-Bolshevism" by the Nazis). See, e.g., Sombart, *Jews and Modern Capitalism*, Chapters 13–14; Elon, *Pity of It All*, Chapter 1; Slezkine, *Jewish Century*, Chapters 1, 3; "Conservatism as Cultural Time" and "Bad Faith" in chapter 7 of the present volume.

75. Some blamed American Jews for the evils of the American government, which they claimed was controlled by Jews. See, e.g., Rubin and Rubin, *Hating America*, 94–95, 137; see also Markovits, *Uncouth Nation*, Chapter 5.

76. See generally Rubin and Rubin, *idem*; Markovits, *idem*.

77. See also Black, "Terrorism as social control"; "Geometry of terrorism."

78. See, e.g., Osama bin Laden and Abu Mussab al-Zarqawi, quoted in Pape, *Dying to Win*, 120–122; see also Osama bin Laden, quoted in Jacquard, *In the Name of Osama bin Laden*, 258–259; Judt, "America and the war," 4.

79. Also relevant to the hostility of Muslims to the West was the historical decline of Islamic civilization. The United States and the Western world rose in the global system of social stratification as the Muslim world fell from its powerful position five centuries earlier.

80. Gelfand, *Witch Doctor*, 51; see also "Misfortune as Witchcraft" in chapter 5 of the present volume.

81. Scheff, *Microsociology*, 77–79; see also *Bloody Revenge*, Chapters 4–5; Lindner, *Making Enemies*.

82. See Black, "Elementary forms of conflict management," 45; see also Pitt-Rivers, "Honour and social status," 30, 57–58; Goffman, "Where the action is," 239–258.

83. An old French saying quoted in Pitt-Rivers, *idem*, 25; see also Wolfgang and Ferracuti, *Subculture of Violence*, 282.

84. See, e.g., Pitt-Rivers, "Honour and social status"; Peristiany, *Honour and Shame*; Gilmore, *Honor and Shame and the Unity of the Mediterranean*; Stewart, *Honor*; Ikegami, *Taming of the Samurai*, 197–201; M. Cooney, *Warriors and Peacemakers*, 107–119; R. Gould, *Collision of Wills*, 172.

85. Some women also have honor. In modern America, for instance, young African American women in urban areas sometimes become involved in violent honor conflicts with other women. See Anderson, *Code of the Street*, 63; Bing, "Homegirls."

86. Pitt-Rivers, "Honour and social status," 45.

87. Blok, "Rams and billy-goats," 429, 432–433, 437, note 4.

88. Barth, *Political Leadership among Swat Pathans*, 82–83.

89. Pitt-Rivers, "Honour and social status," 26, 45; "Moral foundations of the family," 83; Gilmore, *Aggression and Community*, 135. The quotation is a Spanish proverb.

90. Honor commonly requires the domination and protection of women (known as "family honor"). Because a woman's misconduct (including any improper involvement with men or improper mode of dress in public) dishonors her father, husband, and other men in her family, they may punish her transgression, possibly with death. Family honor also requires the defense of its women, such as any woman insulted or embarrassed by someone outside the family. See, e.g., Gilmore, *idem*, 131–133; *Honor and Shame and the Unity of the Mediterranean*; "Introduction," 8–16; van Eck, *Purified by Blood*; Dorell, "'Honor killings' in USA raise concerns."

91. O. Lewis, *Children of Sánchez*, 38 (punctuation and capitalization edited).

92. M. Marshall, *Weekend Warriors*, 56; see also Chapter 5.

93. See, e.g., J. Williams, *Dueling in the Old South*, 87–104.

94. See Berger, Berger, and Kellner, *Homeless Mind*, 86; Gorn, "'Gouge and bite, pull hair and scratch,'" 41–42; Stowe, *Intimacy and Power in the Old South*, 13–14, 20–23.

95. See Patterson, *Slavery and Social Death*, 81–97.

96. Bourdieu, "Sentiment of honour in Kabyle society," 199–200, 207.

97. Codes of honor also require that a violent confrontation begin with equal conditions for the participants, such as identical weapons and a fair warning before their use. See, e.g., J. Williams, *Dueling in the Old South*.

98. See, e.g., Ikegami, *Taming of the Samurai*, 197–201; Kaeuper, *Violence in Medieval Society*; see also M. Cooney, "Decline of elite homicide."

99. See J. Williams, *Dueling in the Old South*; Stowe, *Intimacy and Power in the Old South*, Chapter 1.

100. See, e.g., McAleer, *Dueling*; Nye, *Masculinity and Male Codes of Honor in Modern France*.

101. See, e.g., J. Williams, *Dueling in the Old South*, 46, 48–49.

102. See Berger, Berger, and Kellner, *Homeless Mind*, 83–96; see also Dollard, "The dozens," 15; Daly and Wilson, *Homicide*, Chapter 6; M. Cooney, *Warriors and Peacemakers*, 113–119.

103. Anderson, *Code of the Street*, Chapters 2–3.

104. See, e.g., Dollard, "The dozens"; Abrahams, "Playing the dozens"; Kochman, *Rappin' and Stylin' Out*, 256–264; Labov, "Rules for ritual insults"; see also Ayoub and Barnett, "Ritualized verbal insult in white high school culture."

105. Violence is more likely to erupt when an audience is present (especially when it includes females) and when the participants are strangers, near-strangers, or members of an "out-group." But an insult that cuts deeply enough (such as one about someone's mother) may also lead to violence between those who are socially close. See Kochman, *idem*, 261; H. Brown, "Street talk," 205–206; Abrahams, *idem*, 219, note 3; Dollard, *idem*, 13, 15, 17.

106. See, e.g., M. Cooney, *Warriors and Peacemakers*, 111–119; Anderson, *Code of the Street*, 78.

107. Shakur, *Monster*, 102; see also Anderson, *Place on the Corner*, 5–6.

108. See generally Shakur, *idem*.

109. See, e.g., A. Cohen, "Prison violence."

110. Abbott, *In the Belly of the Beast*, 93–94 (punctuation edited).

111. See O'Neill, *Honor, Symbols, and War*, especially Chapters 6–10; Lebow, *Tragic Vision of Politics*, 271–274.

112. Quoted in O'Neill, *idem*, 143.

113. Offer, "Going to war in 1914."

114. See, e.g., Linderman, *Embattled Courage*, 11–12.

115. E.g., Chang, *Rape of Nanking*, 42–46; see also Einwohner, "Opportunity, honor, and action in the Warsaw Ghetto Uprising of 1943."

116. D. Cohen, *Law, Violence, and Community in Classical Athens*, 143; see also 94, note 14; Chapters 6–7.

117. Brenner, *History—The Human Gamble*, 14, 17; see also 13–16; *Betting on Ideas*, 43–45; 206, note 32.

118. Henry and Short, *Suicide and Homicide*, Appendix 5.

119. *Idem*, 152.

120. Cressey, *Other People's Money*, Chapter 2.

121. Urbina and Hamill, "As economy dips, arrests for shoplifting soar."

122. A. Cohen, *Delinquent Boys*, 25–28, 117, 121; see also Chapters 4–5.

123. See *Wikipedia*, "Going postal."

124. R. Davis, "Tragic trend played out at two sites"; see also Suplee, "Berserk!"

125. *USA Today*, "Survivor: Alabama university shooter fired suddenly."

126. Newman, *Falling from Grace*, 138–139.

127. Winton, Larrubia, and Yoshino, "Father kills family and himself."

128. Winton, Blankstein, and Bloomekatz, "Los Angeles man kills his 5 children, wife, self."

129. Levin and Fox, *Mass Murder*, 63; *Wikipedia*, "McDonald's Massacre."

130. Davies, "Toward a theory of revolution"; see also Brinton, *Anatomy of Revolution*, 28–39; Gurr, *Why Men Rebel*, 37–58; compare, e.g., de Tocqueville, *Old Regime and the French Revolution*, 169–179; Elias, *Power and Civility*, 300–303. A fall in wealth or other social status after a rise (featured in Davies' J-curve theory of rebellion) probably causes some everyday crime as well.

131. Durkheim, *Suicide*, 241–242, 245.

132. Henry and Short, *Suicide and Homicide*, Chapter 2.

133. Hosaka, "For suicidal Japanese, help is finally at hand." When faced with Japan's defeat in the last year of World War II, numerous Japanese servicemen sacrificed their lives in so-called *kamikaze* ("divine wind") attacks by crashing airplanes and small submarines into ships of the United States and its allies. See Ohnuki-Tierney, *Kamikaze, Cherry Blossoms, and Nationalisms*.

134. Lemert, "Paranoia and the dynamics of exclusion," 201–212; see also Goffman, "Insanity of place," 360–361.

135. See Black, *Behavior of Law*, 11.

136. Physical attractiveness is also a form of wealth.

137. The Piaroa of Venezuela (who live in large multifamily houses) measure a man's wealth by the number of people in his house, which ranges from fifteen or sixteen to more than a hundred: "A rich Piaroa lives with a great many people," while "a poor Piaroa lives in a small house with only a few people." Kaplan, *Piaroa*, 29–30; see also Granovetter, "Strength of weak ties"; C. Stack, *All Our Kin*.

138. Claude Lévi-Strauss likens death to losing a game: "It is only the living who win in the great biological and social game which is constantly taking place between the living and the dead." *Savage Mind*, 32.

139. See Black, *Behavior of Law*, 21–28; M. Cooney, *Is Killing Wrong?*, Chapter 3. See also "The Crime of Saying Goodbye" in chapter 3 of the present volume.

140. See, e.g., Foucault, *Discipline and Punish*, Chapters 1–2; see also "Rebellion as Vertical Time" in chapter 5 of the present volume.

141. See Black, *Behavior of Law*, 48–54; M. Cooney, *Is Killing Wrong?*, Chapter 5.

142. Drew, *Burgundian Code*, 19, 30–31.

143. *Idem, Lombard Laws*, 239–240, note 7; 61–71.

144. Ginnell, *Brehon Laws*, 196–198.

145. See Black, *Behavior of Law*, 26–27.

146. See, e.g., Hoebel, *Law of Primitive Man*, 84–89; Reid, *Law of Blood*, Chapters 9–10. Early Chinese courts punished commoners and slaves with five punishments: death, castration, amputation of one foot, amputation of the nose, or tattooing of the face. Ch'ü, *Law and Society in Traditional China*, 174. Medieval German courts sometimes directed the punishment to the part of the body involved in the offense (known as a "matching" punishment), such as amputation of the penis or castration for rape, amputation of the hand for forging a document, and amputation of the tongue for perjury, slander, blasphemy, or other offensive speech. Schild, *History of Criminal Law and Procedure*, 106, 145–148.

147. See, e.g., Hasluck, *Unwritten Law of Albania*; E. Peters, "Some structural aspects of the feud among the camel-herding Bedouin of Cyrenaica"; Boehm, *Blood Revenge*; Stephen Wilson, *Feuding, Conflict and Banditry in Nineteenth-Century Corsica*.

148. See Black, "Violent structures," 153–154.

149. See Black, "Compensation and the social structure of misfortune," 49–51.

150. Koch, *War and Peace in Jalémó*, 86–88.

151. Emmons, *Tlingit Indians*, 48, 51; field notes of Frederica de Laguna and Catherine McClellan, quoted in *idem*, 48.

152. Codere, *Fighting with Property*, 102, 117 (punctuation edited); see also "Luck as Social Time" in chapter 1 of the present volume.

153. Ejidike, "Human rights in the cultural traditions and social practice of the Igbo of southeastern Nigeria," 77; see also Achebe, *Things Fall Apart*, 117.

154. Pollock and Maitland, *History of English Law*, Volume 2: 359, 488; Hanawalt, *Crime and Conflict in English Communities*, 101–103.

155. Waugh, *House of Wittgenstein*, 22–23, 35. Wittgenstein's brother Konrad also committed suicide, and his brother Hans disappeared while traveling abroad and was presumed to have done so (possibly by drowning).

156. J. Douglas, *Social Meanings of Suicide*, 311.

157. Jeffreys, "Samsonic suicide or suicide of revenge among Africans," 120–121; Koch, *War and Peace in Jalémó*, 75–76; 255, note 5; Emmons, *Tlingit Indians*, 51. In some African tribes, those who commit suicide (or threaten to do so) believe their ghost will later take vengeance on the one who provoked them. Jeffreys, *idem*, 119. But some suicide is self-punishment. J. Douglas, *idem*, Chapter 7; Black, "Social control of the self," 65–66; J. Manning, Suicide as Social Control, Chapter 2. Others kill themselves to attain a better existence in an afterlife. Killing their children allows the children to go with them—a form of altruism. See also "The Crime of Saying Goodbye" in chapter 3 of the present volume.

158. Ch'ü, *Law and Society in Traditional China*, 49–51; see also MacCormack, *Spirit of Traditional Chinese Law*, 81–84, 93; 142–143.

159. Parsons, "Illness and the role of the physician"; *Social System*, 436–439; Parsons and Fox, "Illness, therapy and the modern urban American family."

160. Any Azande sick man is "sure that witches are gnawing his vitals and that if he fails to discover their identity he will die." Evans-Pritchard, *Witchcraft, Oracles and Magic among the Azande*, 267–268; see also 541.

161. Knauft, *Good Company and Violence*, 96–103, 123–125, 405, note 9; see also Chapter 11. Although the Gebusi regard most fatal diseases (and some lesser ones) as the result of sorcery, they kill an alleged sorcerer in only about half the cases (typically an older man known for trying to dominate others in their highly egalitarian society—a form of oversuperiority). *Idem*, 109–110, 123–126.

162. Brison, *Just Talk*, 47; see also Chapter 3. The Piaroa of Venezuela likewise consider every death from sickness or injury a result of sorcery, but always blame someone in another locality. Kaplan, *Piaroa*, 27, note 1; 150–151.

163. The shaman sometimes prescribes a penance to atone for the sin, such as sexual intercourse with the shaman (if the patient is a woman). Hoebel, *Law of Primitive Man*, 70–73; see also Balikci, *Netsilik Eskimo*, 226–228.

164. Evans-Pritchard, *Nuer Religion*, 183–185.

165. Quoted in Wyatt-Brown, *Southern Honor*, 424.

166. Macfarlane, *Witchcraft in Tudor and Stuart England*, 198, note 4; K. Thomas, *Religion and the Decline of Magic*, 559; see also Girard, "Generative scapegoating."

167. Knauft, *Good Company and Violence*, 106–108, 225.

168. Maybury-Lewis, *Akwē-Shavante Society*, 275; see also 176, 219, 274, 276.

169. Cohn, *Pursuit of the Millennium*, 131; see also Nohl, *Black Death*, 7; W. McNeill, *Plagues and Peoples*, 149.

170. See W. McNeill, *idem*, 162–163.

171. See Nohl, *Black Death*, Chapters 1,9.

172. J. Kelly, *Great Mortality*, 232.

173. Nohl, *Black Death*, 114–115; see also Brenner, *History—The Human Gamble*, 146–147, 158–160.

174. See, e.g., J. Kelly, *Great Mortality*, Chapter 10, especially 255–257; Nohl, *idem*, Chapter 8; Cohn, *Pursuit of the Millennium*, 138–139; see also Girard, *Scapegoat*, Chapters 1–2.

175. J. Kelly, *idem*, 255–257.

176. Nohl, *Black Death*, 115–119; Cohn, *Pursuit of the Millennium*, 139.

177. W. McNeill, *Plagues and Peoples*, 151.

178. K. Thomas, *Religion and the Decline of Magic*, 559.

179. Nohl, *Black Death*, 125–126; W. McNeill, *Plagues and Peoples*, 161.

180. W. McNeill, *idem*, 106–113.

181. *Idem*, 108–113.

182. Accusations of witchcraft also increased during outbreaks of the Black Death. Jensen, *Path of the Devil*, Chapter 5. See "Injustice" in chapter 1 of the present volume.

CHAPTER 5

1. Oberg, "Crime and punishment in Tlingit society," 149, 155. Some inferiors voluntarily take the blame for superiors. In Imperial China a poor man might confess to a crime committed by a wealthier man and suffer the penalty—including execution—in return for a payment to his family. van der Sprenkel, *Legal Institutions in Manchu China*, 71. In traditional Thailand an inferior might

confess to a crime (without compensation) in place of his "patron" who normally stands ready to help him in times of need. Engel, *Code and Custom in a Thai Provincial Court*, 74. In modern America a lower-ranking Mafia member might become a "fall guy" who confesses to a crime and serves prison time for a higher-ranking member. See Black and Baumgartner, "Toward a theory of the third party," 106.

2. Wijsen and Tanner, *"I Am Just a Sukuma,"* 65–66 (punctuation edited).

3. Gelfand, *Witch Doctor*, 51.

4. See, e.g., Kluckhohn, *Navajo Witchcraft*, 104; Macfarlane, *Witchcraft in Tudor and Stuart England*, 151, 205–206; K. Thomas, "Relevance of social anthropology to the historical study of English witchcraft," 64; Midelfort, *Witch Hunting in Southwestern Germany*, 184–185.

5. Recall that whereas witches are believed to be abnormal individuals whose nature is to harm others, sorcerers are ordinary people who use magical techniques to advance their interests, which might involve harming others. See "Success as Witchcraft" in chapter 4 of the present volume.

6. E. Wolf, "Types of Latin American peasantry," 450, 459–460.

7. See, e.g., Tumin, *Caste in a Peasant Society*, 89; E. Wolf, *idem*, 450.

8. Selby, *Zapotec Deviance*, 106, 108, 112, 116.

9. Beattie, "Sorcery in Bunyoro," 30–32, 46; see also Baxter, "Absence makes the heart grow fonder," 165; Senechal de la Roche, "Why is collective violence collective?"

10. See, e.g., Knauft, *Good Company and Violence*, 94; see also Lepowsky, "Gender in an egalitarian society," 203.

11. Le Vine, "Witchcraft and sorcery in a Gusii community," 241–242.

12. See, e.g., Middleton and Winter, "Introduction," 20; M. Douglas, "Thirty years after *Witchcraft, Oracles and Magic*," xix–xx; see also "Success as Witchcraft" in chapter 4 of the present volume.

13. See Middleton and Winter, *idem*, 21.

14. Wijsen and Tanner, *"I Am Just a Sukuma,"* 136–138.

15. See, e.g., Macfarlane, *Witchcraft in Tudor and Stuart England*; Midelfort, *Witch Hunting in Southwestern Germany*; Boyer and Nissenbaum, *Salem Possessed*; Demos, *Entertaining Satan*.

16. Macfarlane, *idem*, 150–151, 172–176. Accused English witches were not usually the "poorest in the village," however, but only "moderately poor." *Idem*, 151.

17. In the French cases the classic accusation results from both the downward mobility of the alleged victim and the upward mobility of the alleged witch. Favret-Saada, *Deadly Words*, Chapter 9, 139, 203, 216; see also "Success as Witchcraft" in chapter 4 of the present volume.

18. See, e.g., Maloney, "Introduction," xii–xiii; *Evil Eye*; Roberts, "Belief in the evil eye," 234; Dundes, *Evil Eye*.

19. However, no one blames the evil eye for large-scale disasters such as epidemics or famines. Garrison and Arensberg, "Evil eye," 292–293, 298, 322.

20. Schoeck, "Evil eye"; Maloney, "Introduction," vii–x; Di Stasi, *Mal Occhio (Evil Eye)*, 49–52; Dundes, "Wet and dry, the evil eye," 263–270.

21. Pocock, "Evil eye—envy and greed among the Patidar of central Gujerat," 204; see, e.g., Barth, *Nomads of South Persia*, 145; Herzfeld, "Honour and shame," 343; but see also Spooner, "Evil eye in the Middle East," 313.

22. Maloney, "Don't say 'pretty baby,'" 108; Spooner, "Evil eye in the Middle East," 315.

23. See Roberts, "Belief in the evil eye," 223–224.

24. Maloney, *Evil Eye*; Dundes, *Evil Eye*; Pitrè, *"Jettatura* and the evil eye," 137–138; 141, note 7.

25. Schoeck, "Evil eye," 196; Donaldson, "Evil eye in Iran," 71–72; see also Babb, "Glancing," 393.

26. Schoeck, *idem*, 199.

27. Teitelbaum, "Leer and the loom," 68–73.

28. Oyler, "Shilluk's belief in the evil eye," 80–83.

29. Murgoci, "Evil eye in Roumania," 125.

30. Spooner, "Evil eye in the Middle East," 316; Donaldson, "Evil eye in Iran," 71; see also Harfouche, "Evil eye and infant health in Lebanon," 88–91.

31. Woodburne, "Evil eye in South Indian folklore," 56.

32. Pitrè, "*Jettatura* and the evil eye," 132.

33. *Idem*, 138, 141, note 12; Dundes, "Wet and dry, the evil eye," 294; Haglunds, *Enemies of the People*, 216.

34. Barth, *Nomads of South Persia*, 145.

35. Woodburne, "Evil eye in South Indian folklore," 64.

36. Dionisopoulos-Mass, "Evil eye and bewitchment," 46.

37. See Jerome Hall, *Theft, Law, and Society*, 98–109; Hobsbawm, *Primitive Rebels*, Chapter 2.

38. Theft sometimes includes a trespass (such as a burglary), force (such as an armed robbery), or the appropriation of something to which the victim is especially close (such as a favorite article of clothing or family heirloom). Most theft is predatory (for gain), but some is moralistic (for justice), such as when it collects a bad debt or compensates for someone's wrongdoing. Some is even a form of recreation (for sport or excitement). See Black, "Crime as social control," 37; Tucker, "Employee theft as social control"; "Everyday forms of employee resistance"; Turnbull, *Wayward Servants*, 199; Dentan, *Semei*, 56–57; Bolton, "Aggression and hypoglycemia among the Qolla," 233; Katz, *Seductions of Crime*, Chapter 2.

The Crow Indians of the Great Plains referred to horse theft from whites as "capturing" horses, and considered it "a kind of retaliation or summary justice" for the "trespass committed through their country from one end to the other by mercenary white men who [were] destroying the game and [taking] all the beaver and other rich and valuable furs out of their country, without paying them an equivalent or, in fact, anything at all for it." Catlin, *Letters and Notes on the Manners, Customs, and Condition of the North American Indians*, 46 (punctuation edited). Reciprocal raiding of livestock (sometimes found in herding societies) is also moralistic. See, e.g., L. Sweet, "Camel raiding of North Arabian Bedouin"; Tanner, "Cattle theft in Musoma," 41; Ekvall, *Fields on the Hoof*, 52–53; Schneider, "Of vigilance and virgins," 4; Ruffini, "Disputing over livestock in Sardinia," 229, 241.

39. Theft includes the unauthorized use of property, including intellectual or other cultural property, illustrated by copyright, patent, and trademark infringements and the use of written material without properly crediting its author ("plagiarism").

40. See Black, *Behavior of Law*, Chapters 2–6.

41. Bühler, *Laws of Manu*, 309–313.

42. See, e.g., Gough, "Caste in a Tanjore village," 48; Lingat, *Classical Law of India*, 67, 219.

43. Drew, *Laws of the Salian Franks*, 201–217; see also 36.

44. *Idem*, *Burgundian Code*, 84.

45. Hanawalt, *Crime and Conflict in English Communities*, 75.

46. Schild, "History of criminal law and procedure," 103–104.

47. Pollock and Maitland, *History of English Law*, Volume 1: 56.

48. *Idem*, Volume 2: 496–498.

49. Hanawalt, *Crime and Conflict in English Communities*, 66; Beattie, *Crime and the Courts in England*, 140.

50. See, e.g., Rediker, *Villains of All Nations*; Beattie, *Crime and the Courts in England*, Chapter 4.

51. James Scott, "Everyday forms of resistance," 9; see also *Weapons of the Weak*, xvi; Hay, "Poaching and the game laws on Cannock Chase"; Howkins, "Economic crime and class law"; Colburn, *Everyday Forms of Peasant Resistance*.

52. See, e.g., Abelson, *When Ladies Go A-Thieving*.

53. An Orokaiva man's handling of a grievance with self-destruction might range from "merely fasting or running away from home for a while, to delivering himself up to an enemy tribe or hanging himself from a tree." F. Williams, *Orokaiva Society*, 332–333. Anthropologist Francis Williams refers to self-destructive social control as "the revenge of being injured," and anthropologist Marie Reay calls it "the masochistic sanction of self-injury." *Idem*, 332; Reay, "Social control amongst the Orokaiva," 116–117.

54. Intimacy also reduces the seriousness of theft. See Black, *Behavior of Law*, 40–44. For example, in Imperial Chinese law a theft between non-relatives was subject to more punishment than a theft between relatives, and within a family "the punishment varied in inverse ratio to the closeness of the relationship." Ch'ü, *Law and Society in Traditional China*, 67. And whereas the Chinese normally tattooed the word "thief" on the forearm, face, or neck of the thief as part of the punishment, they did not do so if the offender was a relative of the victim. *Idem*, 68, 96–97, 296. The Indian Laws of Manu also reduced the punishment for a theft between people with a preexisting relationship. Bühler, *Laws of Manu*, 312. The written law of modern societies does not mention the relationship between the thief and the victim, but those whose victims are closer to them receive less severity as well. See, e.g., Vera Institute of Justice, *Felony Arrests*, Chapters 3–5.

55. E.g., Engels, *Origin of the Family, Private Property, and the State*, 34; see also Lee, *!Kung San*, 460; Blurton Jones, "Selfish origin for human food sharing"; "Tolerated theft."

56. Radcliffe-Brown, *Andaman Islanders*, 42–43, 50; Turnbull, *Forest People*, 120; see also 20. Anthropologist Nicholas Blurton Jones suggests that simple hunter-gatherers do not actually lack theft but rather "tolerate" theft. "Selfish origin for human food gathering"; "Tolerated theft." Some American employers tolerate minor stealing by employees as part of their wages. Liebow, *Tally's Corner*, 37.

57. Le Guin, *Dispossessed*, 149; see also 139.

58. See Howard, *Causes of Wars*, 1; Brenner, *Betting on Ideas*, Chapter 1.

59. Quoted in Howard, *idem*, 9.

60. Mackinder, *Democratic Ideals and Reality*, 1–2; see also Howard, *idem*, 16.

61. Organski and Kugler, *War Ledger*, 54–55.

62. *Idem*, 50.

63. *Idem*, 58–59, 61; see also generally 33–63.

64. Howard, *Causes of Wars*, 19–21.

65. A challenge to a nation's honor (also a movement of vertical time) might cause a war as well, and so might an invasion or other trespass (a movement of relational time) or a clash of culture (a movement of cultural time).

66. Baumgartner, "Social control from below," especially 336–338. Baumgartner notes that it is sometimes difficult to detect social control from below, including "covert retaliation" (such as pilfering), "non-cooperation" (such as intentionally low productivity), and personal "distress" (such as the feigning of sickness). *Idem*, 308–316, 324–334; see also James Scott, *Weapons of the Weak*; Tucker, "Everyday forms of employee resistance."

67. Exodus 21:15, 17; Deuteronomy 21:18–21.

68. The Chinese believed that the condition of a dead body continued in the afterlife, so mutilating the body of a criminal was both an unusually severe and eternal punishment. The most severe execution was "death by slicing": cutting the offender's entire body with a small knife (sometimes performed even when the offender had already died—because of its eternal consequences). See McKnight, "Sung justice"; Ch'ü, *Law and Society in Traditional China*, 46.

69. Ch'ü, *idem*, 43–44, 192–194.

70. Waley-Cohen, *Exile in Mid-Qing China*, 102.

71. See Gilmartin, "Violence against women in contemporary China," 209.

72. Beidelman, "Witchcraft in Ukaguru," 74.

73. Pollock and Maitland, *History of English Law*, Volume 2: 436. Killing a monarch was "grand treason." *Idem*.

74. See, e.g., Piliavin and Briar, "Police encounters with juveniles"; Chevigny, *Police Power*, 51–83; Black, "Social organization of arrest," 95–100; *Manners and Customs of the Police*, 36, 169–172.

75. See, e.g., Hayden, *Rebellion in Newark*; Bergesen, "Official violence during the Watts, Newark, and Detroit race riots," 153; Black, *Manners and Customs of the Police*, 37–38; Collins, *Violence*, Chapter 3.

76. Abbott, *In the Belly of the Beast*, 66–67 (italics omitted).

77. E.g., Bardach and Gleeson, *Man Is Wolf to Man*.

78. *Wikipedia*, "Robert-François Damiens"; see also Foucault, *Discipline and Punish*, 3–5.

79. Rejali, *Torture and Modernity*, 33.

80. See, e.g., Mullin, *Flight and Rebellion*, 62; Kolchin, *Unfree Labor*, 285; Spindel, *Crime and Society in North Carolina*, 134–135.

81. Quoted in Rejali, *Torture and Modernity*, 23–24.

82. Rejali, *idem*, 27–28 (including quotation from a chronicle of the event). Only the *shah* had the power to order the punishment of exoculation (blinding by destroying the eyeballs). And because piercing the eyeballs is more painful than gouging them out, he sometimes ordered piercing for more serious offenses. *Idem*, 20, 27.

83. Grimshaw, "Factors contributing to color violence in the United States and Great Britain"; see also R. Brown, *Strain of Violence*, 205–211.

84. Olzak, *Dynamics of Ethnic Competition and Conflict*, 3, 216 (italics omitted); see also "Competition model of ethnic collective action," 17–20.

85. Senechal de la Roche, *In Lincoln's Shadow*, 151, 195.

86. *Idem*, 131–141. The white crowd that attacked black-owned businesses also attacked a number of Jewish-owned businesses. *Idem*, 33–34.

87. Quoted in *idem*, 195; see also 196; R. Brown, *Strain of Violence*, 206–207.

88. Dollard, *Caste and Class in a Southern Town*, 298–300.

89. McMillen, *Dark Journey*, 30; Dollard, *idem*, 299.

90. McMillen, *idem*.

91. *Idem*, 24–25; see also 26–27; Dollard, *Caste and Class in a Southern Town*, 299.

92. Dollard, *idem*, 300 (punctuation edited).

93. Beals, *Gopalpur*, 39; Mandelbaum, *Society in India*, Volume 2: 477.

94. Mandelbaum, *idem*, Volume 2: 474; see also Chapter 25; Bharati, "India," 238.

95. Rowe, "New Chauhans," 76.

96. Ch'ü, *Law and Society in Traditional China*, 137, 150–151.

97. Shively, "Sumptuary regulation and status in early Tokugawa Japan," 124, 128, 133–134, 153–154. Just as people of lower rank were expected to consume and behave in a manner proper to their position, those of higher rank were expected to live up to their position. As one eighteenth-century Japanese writer commented: "In clothing and houses, provisions for banquets, and articles of gifts, some are extravagant and others are too frugal. Both of these are at variance with the rules of propriety. The superior and inferior should observe their proper station, and they should not go either to excess or be deficient." Quoted in *idem*, 152 (italics omitted); see also 153.

98. Hinckeldey, *Criminal Justice Through the Ages*, 290–296; Hughes, "Sumptuary laws and social relations in Renaissance Italy"; Hunt, *Governance of the Consuming Passions*, Chapter 2.

99. Hunt, *idem*, 169–170, 356.

100. Hughes, "Sumptuary laws and social relations in Renaissance Italy," 99; Hunt, *idem*, 150–156; Heller, "Anxiety, hierarchy, and appearance in thirteenth-century sumptuary laws."

101. Hunt, *idem*, 299–300, 307.

102. See Goffman, "Nature of deference and demeanor"; *Behavior in Public Places*; *Relations in Public*; Collins, "Situational stratification," especially 29–41.

103. Browder, "Social life of Koreans studying overseas."

104. Lim and Choi, "Interpersonal relationships in Korea," 132.

105. See Black, *Behavior of Law*, 33–36.

106. Sahlins, *Social Stratification in Polynesia*, 20–21.

107. Ch'ü, *Law and Society in Traditional China*, 149–150 (punctuation edited).

108. See Elias, *Court Society*, Chapter 5.

109. *Idem*, 87, 94.

110. Doyle, *Etiquette of Race Relations*, 13–14, 19–20.

111. Whites were also expected to conform to racial etiquette. For example, Dollard notes that when he arrived in Mississippi to begin his study of race relations, one white man gave him the following advice: "Never, he said, address a Negro man or woman as 'Mr.' or 'Mrs.', and do not refer to them thus in talking to a white person; don't shake hands with a Negro; . . . don't tip your hat to a Negro, man or woman, but call him or her by the first name whenever you know it." *Caste and Class in a Southern Town*, 343. While racial etiquette (including the etiquette of slavery) features racial stratification, it does so partly through the regulation of intimacy. As noted above, for instance, black slaves were expected to avoid eye contact with whites (and instead look at the ground) when conversing with a white, and they could not use a familiar form of address (such as a first name) when speaking with a white. Shaking hands was too intimate as well.

112. *Idem*, 174–180, 185, 257–258, 304, 343–349; see also 302–303.

113. Opdyke, *In My Hands*, 257.

114. Szpilman, *The Pianist*, 49, 128–129 (punctuation edited).

CHAPTER 6

1. See Black, *Behavior of Law*, 73–78.

2. Quoted in *Fox News*, "Report: Non-Muslims deserve to be punished."

3. See, e.g., D. Williams, "Egypt forces Copts to hide as Muslims hit Swiss minaret ban"; Jurgensmeyer, *Terror in the Mind of God*, Chapters 4, 8–9; D. Cook, "Suicide attacks or 'martyrdom operations' in contemporary *jihad* literature."

4. See Sumner, *Folkways*, 28–29.

5. Kennedy, *Jesuit and Savage in New France*, 159; *Wikipedia*, "Navajo people"; see also Neeley, *Last Comanche Chief*, 2. The names by which we know these tribes (such as "Illinois" or "Navajo") were typically coined by outsiders, however, and have various meanings in other languages.

6. Howell, "'To be angry is not to be human, but to be fearful is,'" 50–55. The Mehinaku Indians of central Brazil similarly welcome fellow Mehinaku with "hospitality and decorum" but subject foreign traders to "abuse" such as derisive laughter and ridicule. Gregor, *Mehinaku*, 306.

7. Gregor, "Uneasy peace," 116–117.

8. *Idem, Anxious Pleasures*, 12–13.

9. Knauft, "Melanesian warfare," 256 (punctuation edited).

10. Murphy, "Intergroup hostility and social cohesion," 1026.

11. Knowles, "Torture of captives by the Indians of eastern North America," 188–189, 192–193; Heard, *White into Red*, 67, 114.

12. Deuteronomy 20:16–17 (punctuation edited; italics and pronunciation marks omitted); see also D. Wilson, *Darwin's Cathedral*, 133–136.

13. See, e.g., Jurgensmeyer, *Terror in the Mind of God*, Chapters 4, 8–9.

14. Morris, "Final solution, down under," 65.

15. Ryan, *Aboriginal Tasmanians*, 88.

16. Morris, "Final solution, down under," 65.

17. The British had a program (called "black catching") in which they paid a bounty for each Tasmanian captured and delivered alive (five pounds for an adult and two pounds for a child), which probably reduced the killing to some degree. Quammen, *Song of the Dodo*, 360.

18. Ryan, *Aboriginal Tasmanians*, 65–70, 88.

19. Jennings, *Invasion of America*, 59.

20. Quoted in D. Weber, *Spanish Frontier in North America*, 51.

21. D. Weber, *idem*, 232.

22. Scholars estimate the pre-colonial Indian population in the Americas to have been about a hundred million. Two hundred years after the Spaniards arrived in the late fifteenth century, many tribes had entirely disappeared, and some Indian territories had lost more than 90 percent of their inhabitants. See, e.g., W. McNeill, *Plagues and Peoples*, 180–181; Thornton, *American Indian Holocaust and Survival*.

23. W. McNeill, *idem*, 222.

24. Quoted in Thornton, *American Indian Holocaust and Survival*, 79.

25. Chalk and Jonassohn, *History and Sociology of Genocide*, 177; see also Nash, *Red, White, and Black*, 80; W. McNeill, *Plagues and Peoples*, 183–184.

26. Quoted in Jennings, *Invasion of America*, 78–81 (capitalization omitted). Indians did not kill Indian women and children. Nash, *idem*, 151.

27. Jennings, *idem*, 82, Chapter 13; see also 135–138. After Israel's founding in 1948, Israeli law defined the territory of nomadic Bedouins in the Negev desert as "dead land" subject to ownership and settlement by others. See Shamir, "Suspended in space."

28. Steele, *Warpaths*, 46–47, 116.

29. Quoted in Jennings, *Invasion of America*, 164–165 (punctuation edited).

30. See, e.g., Thornton, *American Indian Holocaust and Survival*, 104–133; Chalk and Jonassohn, *History and Sociology of Genocide*, 196–203.

31. See, e.g., Gilje, *Road to Mobocracy*, Chapter 5.

32. See, e.g., S. Cook, *Colonial Encounters in the Age of High Imperialism*; Huntington, *Clash of Civilizations and the Remaking of World Order*.

33. Even when a racial difference involves no cultural difference, racial conflict might still occur. People might incorrectly assume that someone with a particular racial appearance has a cultural location unlike their own, for example, and thereafter avoid or behave in a hostile fashion toward the individual concerned (a case of mistaken cultural identity).

34. In addition to an identifiable pattern of culture, an ethnic group might have other distinctive social characteristics, such as a particular family system or style of sociability. See, e.g., "The Crime of Looking" in chapter 2 and "Underexposure as Bad Manners" in chapter 3. Ethnic groups sometimes also harbor grievances against one another, possibly because of incidents in the distant past.

35. See, e.g., Fordham and Ogbu, "Black students' school success."

36. Writer Norman Mailer calls whites who adopt black culture "white Negroes," and sociologist Gary Marx calls blacks with white cultural characteristics "Negro whites" and "black whites." See Mailer, "The white Negro"; G. Marx, "The white Negro and the Negro white."

37. The Jewish ethnic group historically included such cultural characteristics as a distinctive religion (Judaism), language (Hebrew, Yiddish, or Ladino), and dietary restrictions (including the prohibition of pork and shellfish). But many modern Jews practice little or no religion, speak only the language of the place where they live, and obey no dietary laws.

38. See, e.g., Roth, *Conversos, Inquisition, and the Expulsion of the Jews from Spain*, Chapter 8; Langmuir, *History, Religion, and Antisemitism; Toward a Definition of Antisemitism*.

39. See, e.g., MacKay, "Popular movements and pogroms in fifteenth-century Castile," 52.

40. Netanyahu, *Origins of the Inquisition in Fifteenth Century Spain*, 984.

41. *Idem*, 983 (italics omitted); see also Kamen, *Inquisition and Society in Spain*, 41; Haliczer, *Inquisition and Society in Early Modern Europe*.

42. For more details on anti-Semitism, see "The Crime of Doing Too Well" in chapter 4; "Conservatism as Cultural Time" and "Bad Faith" in chapter 7.

43. M. Cooney, "Ethnic conflict without ethnic groups," 480–482.

44. See Senechal de la Roche, "Collective violence as social control," 115–122.

45. P. Kuhn, *Soulstealers*, 114; see also 41.

46. Brison, *Just Talk*, 6–9.

47. Beidelman, "Witchcraft in Ukaguru," 78; see also 68, 74; La Fontaine, "Witchcraft in Bugisu," 217.

48. Gibson, *Sacrifice and Sharing in the Philippine Highlands*, 5.

49. See, e.g., Bourdieu, *Distinction*; Fussell, *Class*.

50. See, e.g., O'Barr, *Linguistic Evidence*, 61–75.

51. See Stearns, *Fat History*. The shape of the body sometimes varies with social class. In modern societies such as the United States, for instance, obesity is more common in the lower than in the higher classes. See Fussell, *Class*, 51–54.

52. See, e.g., Morrill, *Executive Way*, 68–69, 156.

53. See, e.g., Hunter, *Culture Wars*, 215–219; *Before the Shooting Begins*, 196–211.

54. Durkheim, *Rules of Sociological Method*, 67, 70–72; *Moral Education*, 53, 90–91.

55. See Simmel, *Conflict*, 47–48.

56. Some scholars question whether Jesus actually claimed to be the Messiah. The role of the Jews in the execution of Jesus, if any, is debated as well. For relevant biblical passages, see Matthew 26–27, Mark 14–15, Luke 22–23, John 18–19.

57. de Ste. Croix, "Why were the Christians persecuted?"

58. *Idem*, 7–8, 13, 18.

59. *Idem*, "Aspects of the Great Persecution," 75–77.

60. *Idem*, "Why were the Christians persecuted?," 20–21.

61. Because heresy was said to destroy the heretic's soul for eternity, some Christians considered the execution of a heretic to be an "ultimate kindness" to those who might have lost their souls under the heretic's influence ("just as the amputation of a putrid member may save a body"). Bainton, *Hunted Heretic*, 77–78.

62. A crowd of peasants apparently would have burned the heretics anyway. Other crowds sometimes burned heretics instead of waiting for their execution by courts of law. Jeffrey Russell, *Dissent and Reform in the Early Middle Ages*, 31, 81; see also 249 ff.

63. *Idem*, 27–34, 103–104, 213.

64. Leff, *Heresy in the Later Middle Ages*, Volume 1: 36–47.

65. Haliczer, *Inquisition and Society in Early Modern Europe*. In Spain and elsewhere, Inquisition officials often accused Jewish converts or their descendants of secretly practicing Judaism. *Idem*, "First holocaust," 1–2; see "Conservatism as Cultural Time" and "Bad Faith" in chapter 7 of the present volume.

66. See, e.g., Cohn, *Pursuit of the Millennium*.

67. See, e.g., Swanson, *Religion and Regime*.

68. Contreras, "Impact of Protestantism in Spain," 59.

69. Bainton, *Hunted Heretic*, Chapters 9–11, especially 211–212.

70. See, e.g., Erikson, *Wayward Puritans*, 71–92.

71. Driggs, "'There is no law in Georgia for Mormons.'"

72. Wingfield, "Tennessee's Mormon massacre."

73. Driggs, "'There is no law in Georgia for Mormons,'" 746.

74. See, e.g., Wingfield, "Tennessee's Mormon massacre"; Driggs, *idem*. In 1857 a group of Mormons in Utah did in fact kill more than one hundred non-Mormons in a wagon train from Arkansas. Brooks, *Mountain Meadows Massacre*.

75. M. Weber, *Religion of India*, 193, Chapters 6–9; see also Zwilling and Sweet, "'Like a city ablaze,'" 361, note 12.

76. M. Weber, *Religion of China*, 214 (punctuation edited).

77. *Wikipedia*, "Persecution of Baha'is." Muslims also had earlier heretics. See, for example, Elif Shafak's novel called *The Forty Rules of Love*, which depicts the teaching and ultimate assassination of Shams of Tabriz, a now legendary Persian mystic (known as a Sufi or Dervish) who was considered a heretic by some thirteenth-century Muslims.

78. See Black, "Strategy of pure sociology," 168–169.

79. Creativity in art and other domains often occurs in episodes and possibly cycles rather than on a continuous basis. See, e.g., Gray, "Paradoxes in Western creativity." It appears that creativity is a direct function of other movements of social time (including other creativity). See also Black, "Pure sociology and the geometry of discovery."

80. See, e.g., Black, "Strategy of pure sociology," 165–169; "Dreams of pure sociology," 349–351; compare Collins, *Sociology of Philosophies*, 68–69.

81. See, e.g., Wolfe, *Painted Word*, 67–68; Becker, *Art Worlds*, especially Chapters 1, 5; R. Hughes, *Shock of the New*.

82. Modern art also causes conflict when it is too intimate, such as when it displays too much human nakedness. See "Overintimate Art" in chapter 2.

83. "Father of 20th-Century Art" is the subtitle of art historian Michel Hoog's book called *Cézanne*; quotations at 146.

84. See, e.g., R. Hughes, *Shock of the New*, 21.

85. Cabanne, *Pablo Picasso*, 119; see also John Richardson, *Life of Picasso*, Volume 2: 43, 45.

86. R. Hughes, *Shock of the New*, 24; Cabanne, *idem*, 119.

87. Cabanne, *idem*, 120.

88. Lord, *Picasso and Dora*, 25. Cabanne notes that "for almost 40 years" in France, Picasso "had been made to feel an outlaw of art, subjected to sarcasm, wrath, and insult." *Idem*, 332.

89. Dalí, *Secret Life of Salvador Dalí*, 287, 314, 394; *Diary of a Genius*, 10 (capitalization omitted). The painting mentioned in the text is entitled *Dream Caused by the Flight of a Bee around a Pomegranate, a Second before Waking Up*. It was completed in 1944.

Viewers (including other surrealists) also objected to the overly intimate subjects in some of Dalí's paintings (such as depictions of a male erection and human feces). *Idem, Diary of a Genius*, 10–11; see "Overintimate Art" in chapter 2 of the present volume.

90. See, e.g., Mailer, *Portrait of Picasso as a Young Man*, 305, 307.

91. Kandinsky, letter of September 5, 1938, quoted in Lindsay and Vergo, *Kandinsky*, Volume 2: 863, note 7.

92. Kandinsky, "Interview with Karl Nierendorf," 807–808.

93. See Wolfe, *Painted Word*, 67.

94. Edward F. Cook, quoted in Potter, *To a Violent Grave*, 88.

95. Nicholas Carone, quoted in *idem*, 182.

96. Clement Greenberg, quoted in *idem*, 80.

97. Reginald Isaacs, quoted in *idem*, 277–278.

98. Cabanne, *Pablo Picasso*, 119; see also Lucie-Smith, *Movements in Art since 1945*, 53–54.

99. Sylvester, *Brutality of Fact*, 81; see also 182; Archimbaud, *Francis Bacon*, 152; John Russell, *Francis Bacon*, 76; Golding, "Simply himself," 8. Bacon's parents were English, but he grew up in Ireland.

100. Nigel Gosling, quoted in Sinclair, *Francis Bacon*, 207; Sinclair, *idem*, 298; Kimmelman, "Unnerving art," 74.

101. Lawrence Gowing, quoted in Farson, *Gilded Gutter Life of Francis Bacon*, 10–11.

102. Sinclair, *Francis Bacon*, 250; see also 219, 287.

103. Rilke, *Rodin*, 27, 91; Pinet, *Rodin*, 82.

104. Tafel, *Years with Frank Lloyd Wright*, 51; Mary Newbery Sturrock, quoted in Moffat, *Remembering Charles Rennie Mackintosh*, 72. A central theme of Ayn Rand's novel *The Fountainhead* is the rejection suffered by an unusually creative American architect named Howard Roark. Late in the story Roark makes the following statement: "The great creators—the thinkers, the artists, the scientists, the inventors—stood alone against the men of their time. Every great new thought was opposed. Every great invention was denounced." 710.

105. Elias, *Mozart*, 130; see also 129.

106. The same fate did not necessarily apply to the art of earlier societies (such as ancient Greece or Renaissance Italy) later recognized as important.

107. The piano concerto, entitled *Panathenäenzug (Pan-Athenian Procession)*, was written for the left hand and commissioned and played by Paul Wittgenstein (an older brother of the philosopher Ludwig), a professional pianist who had lost his right hand in the First World War. One critic called Wittgenstein's performance "an absolute failure" that went "beyond the limits of our

endurance." In Vienna two months later, however, his performance of the same work received an "ecstatic" review by a leading critic and was more generally a "critical and public success." Waugh, *House of Wittgenstein*, 158.

108. Sinclair, *Francis Bacon*, 250; see also Peppiatt, *Francis Bacon*, 108–109.

109. Gilot and Lake, *Life with Picasso*, 197. Poet Rainer Maria Rilke also noted that "every recognition (with very rare, unmistakable exceptions) should make one mistrustful of one's own work. Basically, if it is good, one can't live to see it recognized; otherwise, it's just half good." Rilke, *Letters on Cézanne*, 58 (punctuation edited).

110. Because the recognition of creative work commonly undermines the conditions that made the work possible (such as social isolation and tranquility), a lack of recognition might be an advantage for creative people who wish to remain creative. See Black, "Dreams of pure sociology," 359. Poet Robinson Jeffers makes a similar point in his poem called "Let them alone":

> If God has been good enough to give you a poet
> Then listen to him. But for God's sake let him alone until he is dead; no prizes, no
>   ceremony,
> They kill the man. A poet is one who listens
> To nature and his own heart; and if the noise of the world grows up around him, and
>   if he is tough enough,
> He can shake off his enemies but not his friends.

Jeffers' own ability to write poetry appreciated by others apparently declined after he became a celebrity and lost his solitude on the coast of northern California. Karman, *Robinson Jeffers*, 124–134.

111. Sulloway, *Born to Rebel, 368*; see also Barber, "Resistance by scientists to scientific discovery"; Eysenck, *Genius*, 288; Black, "Epistemology of pure sociology," 846.

112. See, e.g., Magueijo, *Faster Than the Speed of Light*; Smolin, *Trouble with Physics*, Chapters 18–19.

113. Quoted in Magueijo, *idem*, 258.

114. T. Kuhn, *Structure of Scientific Revolutions*; see also I. Cohen, *Revolution in Science*; Black, "Epistemology of pure sociology," 864–870.

115. Zukav, *Dancing Wu Li Masters*, 191; see also T. Kuhn, *Copernican Revolution*, 199.

116. Burtt, *Metaphysical Foundations of Modern Science*, 56; see also T. Kuhn, *idem*, 186, 199.

117. Mason, *History of the Sciences*, 159–164; Redondi, *Galileo*, 260–261.

118. Quoted in Andrade, *Sir Isaac Newton*, 64–65.

119. The full title of the book is *Philosophiae Naturalis Principia Mathematica* (*Mathematical Principles of Natural Philosophy*).

120. Westfall, *Never at Rest*, 472; I. Cohen, *Revolution in Science*, 172. Some also accused Newton of stealing or failing to acknowledge their ideas. Robert Hooke claimed that Newton stole his theory of gravitation, for example, and Gottfried Wilhelm Leibniz claimed to have invented calculus before Newton. Westfall, *idem*, 446, 452, 471–472, 511–512, Chapter 14; see also Merton, "Priorities in scientific discovery."

121. Westfall, *idem*, 279–280, 335.

122. Quoted in *idem*, 468.

123. *Idem*, 209.

124. Desmond and Moore, *Darwin*, xviii.

125. Quoted in Gruber, *Darwin on Man*, 26, note 10. The confidant was Joseph Hooker.

126. Darwin agreed to make his theory public after learning that Alfred Russel Wallace had independently developed a nearly identical theory. Both theories were read at the same scientific meeting. Darwin later recalled that the only published reaction to the papers (written by a Dublin professor) was that "all that was new in them was false, and what was true was old." *Autobiography of Charles Darwin*, 122; see also 120–121; Shermer, *In Darwin's Shadow*, Chapters 4–5; Desmond and Moore, *Darwin*, 467–470.

127. Thomas Huxley, quoted in I. Cohen, *Revolution in Science*, 284.

128. Desmond and Moore, *Darwin*, 488, 492.

129. Adam Sedgwick, quoted in Gruber, *Darwin on Man*, 88.

130. Quoted in I. Cohen, *Revolution in Science*, 406.

131. Hoffmann, *Albert Einstein*, 85.

132. Whitrow, *Einstein*, 42–43; see also Bernstein, *Einstein*, 72; H. Levy, quoted in Whitrow, *idem*, 43; Paul Weyland, quoted in Isaacson, *Einstein*, 284.

133. Hoffmann, *Albert Einstein*, 168; Regis, *Who Got Einstein's Office?*, 21; White and Gribbin, *Einstein*, 148–150.

134. Hoffmann, *idem*, 143; Isaacson, *Einstein*, 284–289; Pais, *Einstein Lived Here*, 159. Einstein's Jewish ancestry made him all the more unpopular in Germany, and by the early 1930s most leading German scientists opposed him. The Bavarian Academy of Science expelled him, and the Prussian Academy of Science planned to expel him before he voluntarily resigned. The German government revoked his citizenship, confiscated his house and bank account, and publicly burned his writings. Frank, *Einstein*, 167, 232, 237–238; Hoffmann, *idem*, 168. Had Einstein returned to Germany from a visit to the United States, he probably would have been deported, sent to a concentration camp, or killed.

One exception to those who opposed Einstein was eminent physicist Max Planck, who praised Einstein's contributions before the Prussian Academy of Science in 1933. Hitler reprimanded Planck for doing so, and said that only his advanced age had "saved him from being sent to a concentration camp." Hoffmann, *idem*, 168–169.

135. Innovative scientists who receive or are destined to receive major recognition for their work also attract hostility from their colleagues for being too successful—a form of overstratification. See "The Crime of Doing Too Well" in chapter 4.

136. Farber, "Schizophrenia and the mad psychotherapist," 98–99.

137. *Idem*, 93–98; see also "Theft as Vertical Time" in chapter 5 of the present volume. Stealing the cherished birthday present was also a relational crime: If successful, it would have deprived the psychiatrist of something to which she was very close.

138. See, e.g., Laing, *Politics of Experience*, 132; see also 108; *Divided Self*, 189; Foucault, *Madness and Civilization*; Dick, "Drugs, hallucinations, and the quest for reality." Even when a mental illness results from a brain malfunction or chemical imbalance, its symptoms are movements of social time. Mental illness might also result from movements of social time, such as losses of intimacy and social standing. See, e.g., Lemert, "Paranoia and the dynamics of exclusion."

139. See, e.g., Simonton, *Genius, Creativity, and Leadership*, 55–57.

140. Smith, "Structural hierarchy in science, art, and history," 44.

141. John Richardson, *Life of Picasso: The Triumphant Years*, 485; A. Miller, *Einstein, Picasso*, 243.

142. Heisenberg, *Across the Frontiers*, 159.

143. Bohr's remark pertained to a lecture on particle physics presented by Wolfgang Pauli in 1958. After the lecture, Pauli turned to Bohr and said, "You probably think these ideas are crazy." Bohr replied, "I do, but unfortunately they are not crazy enough." Quoted in Pais, *Niels Bohr's Times*, 29.

144. See Geertz, "Common sense as a cultural system"; see also Garfinkel, *Studies in Ethnomethodology*; Black, "Common sense in the sociology of law," 18. The most innovative science also deviates from common sense when it first appears. Historical examples noted earlier include the theory that Earth revolves around the sun (Copernicus), that humans evolved from lower organisms (Darwin), and that space and time are variable rather than constant (Einstein). See Crick, *What Mad Pursuit*, 63.

145. See Foucault, *Madness and Civilization*, 21.

146. Laing, *Divided Self*, 36 (punctuation edited).

147. See Horwitz, *Social Control of Mental Illness*; see also Field, *Search for Security*, 315.

148. See Field, *idem*, especially 43–88, 315–352.

149. Midelfort, *Mad Princes of Renaissance Germany*, 58–60, 98–124.

150. See Laing, *Divided Self*.

151. See, e.g., Goffman, *Asylums*; Black, *Behavior of Law*, 4–6; Horwitz, *Social Control of Mental Illness*.

152. See, e.g., Mogar, "Psychedelic states and schizophrenia"; Osmond, "On being mad," especially 22–23.

153. Osmond, *idem*, 25–26 (punctuation edited).

154. Watts, *Joyous Cosmology*, 63.

155. Mind-altering drugs may also be part of a cultural tradition in which they do not cause conflict. See, e.g., Harner, *Hallucinogens and Shamanism*; "Common themes in South American Indian yagé experiences"; Naranjo, "Psychological aspects of the yagé experience."

CHAPTER 7

1. Damaging or destroying something with cultural significance is sometimes called a "crime against culture." See, e.g., Barthel-Bouchier, "Crimes against culture."

2. See Campbell, "Genocide as social control"; "Contradictory behavior during genocides." The expulsion of an ethnic group is known as "ethnic cleansing" or "ethnic purification."

3. See Black, *Social Structure of Right and Wrong*, Chapter 7.

4. See, e.g., *Wikipedia*, "*Jyllands-Posten* Muhammad cartoons controversy"; *USA Today*, "Police in Denmark stop attack on controversial cartoonist."

5. Sharrock, "Seven Muslims arrested over 'plot to kill cartoonist.'" The Swedish cartoonist had published his cartoon of Mohammed several years earlier. Muslims prohibit all depictions of Mohammed, whether disrespectful or not.

6. See Fuchs, *Against Essentialism*, 327–328.

7. McCabe, *National Encyclopaedia of Business and Social Forms*, 419, quoted in Kasson, *Rudeness and Civility*, 158.

8. Kasson, *idem*, 158.

9. McConaloque, "EU criticizes Turkish law on 'insulting Turkishness.'" In 2008 the wording of the law was changed from a prohibition against "insulting Turkishness" to a prohibition against "insulting the Turkish nation." *Wikipedia*, "Article 301 (Turkish Penal Code)."

10. Hinckeldey, "History of crime and punishment," 110; see also Levy, *Blasphemy*.

11. de Ste. Croix, "Aspects of the Great Persecution," 75–77.

12. Quoted in de Ste. Croix, "Why were the Christians persecuted?," 26 (punctuation edited); see also 24–25.

13. Religious conversion is a form of underdiversity because the convert abandons a religion (known as apostasy), but the adoption of a different religion is a form of overdiversity.

14. Nirenberg, *Communities of Violence*, 127–128; see also Roth, *Conversos, Inquisition, and the Expulsion of the Jews from Spain*, 204.

15. Elon, *Pity of It All*, 85.

16. *Idem*, 81, 125; *Wikipedia*, "Mischling." Because some traditional Jews did not believe conversion to Christianity would protect them from anti-Semitism, they said the converts were not merely "traitors" but "stupid traitors." Elon, *idem*, 81; see also T. Frank, *Double Exile*, 45–50.

17. D. Cooney, "Christian convert faces death penalty in Afghanistan."

18. See, e.g., Winter, "Slaughter of foreigners in Yemen."

19. See, e.g, M. Cohen, *Under Crescent and Cross*, 169.

20. Quoted in D. Weber, *Spanish Frontier in North America*, 22; see also 15.

21. D. Weber, *idem*, 51.

22. Nash, *Red, White, and Black*, 106; see also Eccles, *Canadian Frontier*, 10. French Catholic missionaries in Canada initially planned to "eradicate everything" Indian and "impose a completely European scale of values," but later they became more tolerant and tried only to convert the Indians to Christianity. Eccles, *idem*, 48; Jennings, *Invasion of America*, 57; Demos, *Unredeemed Captive*, 120–122.

23. Hagan, *Indian Police and Judges*, 70, 84, 107–108, 122, 171–172; Heard, *White into Red*, 154; Farley, "Canada to apologize for abuse of native students." The Canadian prime minister apologized in 2008. Also in Australia between 1910 and 1970, as many as one hundred thousand Aborigine children were "taken forcibly or under duress from their families by police or welfare officers" and removed to new homes. The object was to replace their "Aboriginality" with the culture of white Australians. The Australian prime minister likewise apologized in 2008. European Network for Indigenous Australian Rights, "Stolen generations."

24. French Jesuit missionaries considered Indian converts killed by traditional Indians to be "martyrs" deserving of honor, and recorded their suffering down "to the last appalling detail" as "supreme proofs" of their success as missionaries. Demos, *Unredeemed Captive*, 130–131. Christian missionary activity and conversion in the Igbo tribe of Nigeria also caused considerable conflict, including the burning of churches and killing of converts. Ohadike, "Igbo culture and history," 251–253; Achebe, *Things Fall Apart*, Chapters 16–19. Conflict erupted in the Kikuyu tribe of Kenya when Christian converts tried to end the Kikuyu custom of female circumcision. Edgerton, *Mau Mau*, 42.

25. See, e.g., Heard, *White into Red*, 154–157.

26. Letter from W. P. McClure (Federal Indian Agent at Albuquerque) to Commissioner of Indian Affairs, December 4, 1889, quoted in Hoebel, "Keresan Pueblo law," 94 (punctuation edited).

27. See, e.g., Jennings, *Invasion of America*, 56; Demos, *Unredeemed Captive*, 130–131.

28. Kennedy, *Jesuit and Savage in New France*, 128; quotation from *idem*, 129; see also 87–88; Eccles, *Canadian Frontier*, 51. Christian missionaries normally require converts to renounce their non-Christian beliefs and practices. Protestant missionaries in New Guinea thus told the converts

"it was either Christ or the spirits"—which sometimes provoked considerable hostility. In one case in 1968, for instance, traditional tribesmen killed and ate two missionaries after one of them convinced some converts to burn their tribal "fetishes" in a bonfire. H. Manning, *To Perish for Their Saving*, 64–68; see also Chapters 15–16.

29. Elison, *Deus Destroyed*, 131–132, 136–140, 188, 193–194, 397, note 16.

30. Another torture was the "wooden horse": The Japanese placed Catholics on horse-like wooden seats with stone weights attached to their ankles, and tried to prevent them from "merely dying" until they renounced their faith. *Idem*, 205, 448, note 60.

31. *Idem*, 186–187, 190, 205.

32. See, e.g., Liao, *Antiforeignism and Modernization in China*, 41; see also Gernet, *China and the Christian Impact*, 181–192; P. Cohen, *China and Christianity*, 21; Chapters 8, 10.

33. P. Cohen, *idem*, 31, 45–55, 58, 91, 237–242, illustrations at 140 ff.

34. *Idem*, 3, 275–276, 230–231, 233 (punctuation edited). Similar violence against Christian missionaries and converts has occurred in modern India. In 2008, for instance, one Hindu official called the presence of Christian missionaries in the country a "cultural invasion" and "an attack on our culture." Over several months Hindus killed numerous Christians, burned their homes and churches, and forced thousands to flee their communities, often giving them a choice of Hinduism or death. *USA Today*, "Christians in India face attacks."

35. Hallowell, "American Indians, white and black," 520, 522–523. Historian Norman Heard estimates that "hundreds of white captives became almost completely Indianized." *White into Red*, 5.

36. Hallowell, *idem*, 524–526.

37. Heard, *White into Red*, 99.

38. *Idem.*

39. Axtell, "White Indians of colonial America," 62.

40. Demos, *Unredeemed Captive.*

41. Neeley, *Last Comanche Chief*, especially Chapters 1, 3.

42. See, e.g., Axtell, "White Indians of colonial America," 61–63; Heard, *White into Red*, 119–124, 138–139.

43. Axtell, *idem*, 64.

44. Ackerknecht, "'White Indians,'" 27, 31–32.

45. Fordham and Ogbu, "Black students' school success"; see also "The Crime of Doing Too Well" in chapter 4 of the present volume.

46. M. Cooney, "Ethnic conflict without ethnic groups," 482.

47. *Idem*, "Cultural conflict in contemporary Ireland."

48. Biehl, "'The whore lived like a German.'"

49. Wattie, "Dad charged after daughter killed in clash over *hijab*."

50. Damon, "Violations of 'Islamic' teachings' take deadly toll on Iraqi women." In modern Iran men are likewise discouraged from adopting Western hairstyles and other fashions. See Harrison, "Iran ban on 'Western' hairstyles."

51. During secret rituals conducted by some Australian Aborigines, men even speak a separate language unknown to women. See, e.g., Hamilton, "Complex strategical situation," 77–82.

52. Deuteronomy 22:5.

53. Bullough and Bullough, *Cross Dressing, Sex, and Gender*, 45–46; see also William Miller, *Bloodtaking and Peacemaking*, 354–355, note 35.

54. Bullough and Bullough, *idem*, 57, 75, 95–96. The authorities originally prosecuted Joan of Arc for heresy, but could not reach agreement on any final disposition except to execute her for the crime of cross-dressing.

55. LaFave, *Arrest*, 466–469.

56. *Fox News*, "Teen shot in junior high classroom taken off life support."

57. Correll, "Colorado transgender woman's slaying tried as hate crime."

58. Woodhouse, *Fantastic Women*, 23, Chapter 4.

59. *Idem*, Chapter 3, especially 56, 97, 101, 104; Bullough and Bullough, *Cross Dressing, Sex, and Gender*, 207–213, 292–293.

60. D. Greenberg, *Construction of Homosexuality*, 40–73. For similar roles in other societies, see J. Sweet, "Male homosexuality and spiritism in the African diaspora"; Zwilling and Sweet, "'Like a city ablaze.'"

61. See D. Greenberg, *idem*, 26–40; Talley, "Gender and male same-sex erotic behavior in British North America," 405–407; see also "Filthy Involvements" in chapter 2 of the present volume.

62. See, e.g., Dover, *Greek Homosexuality*.

63. Talley, "Gender and male same-sex erotic behavior in British North America," 404.

64. LaFave, *Arrest*, 469.

65. See, e.g., Arendt, "Antisemitism," 68–69; Langmuir, *History, Religion, and Antisemitism*, 20, 109–111; see also "The Crime of Doing Too Well" in chapter 4 and "Race as Culture" in chapter 6 of the present volume.

66. Langmuir, *idem*, 284; see also B. Lewis, *Cultures in Conflict*, 33–34.

67. See the discussion and biblical references in "Heresy as Cultural Time" in chapter 6.

68. Langmuir, "Toward a definition of antisemitism," 333, 347. For their role in the death of Jesus, Jews are sometimes said to be collectively and for all time guilty of the sin of deicide: God-killing. See, e.g., *Wikipedia*, "Jewish deicide." When Albert Einstein was the only Jewish student in his class at a Catholic primary school in late nineteenth-century Germany, one of his teachers "brought a long nail to the lesson and told the students that with just such nails Christ had been nailed to the cross by the Jews." Einstein, quoted in Fölsing, *Albert Einstein*, 16. Another German Jew tells of being called a "Christ-killer" by his childhood playmates: "When I was playing outside with the non-Jews they would say, 'You killed Christ, didn't you?' They always nagged me, but we played together." Sciutto, "Holocaust survivor remembers pain of war." Such incidents appear to have been common in Germany and elsewhere.

69. Elon, *Pity of It All*, 21.

70. Langmuir, "Anti-Judaism as the necessary preparation for antisemitism"; "Transformation of anti-Judaism," 65; "Medieval antisemitism"; Dundes, *Blood Libel Legend*.

71. Langmuir, "Anti-Judaism as the necessary preparation for antisemitism," 59.

72. See *idem*, "Transformation of anti-Judaism," 93–99; "Medieval antisemitism," 304–305.

73. Quoted in B. Lewis, *Cultures in Conflict*, 30–31.

74. Langmuir, "Transformation of anti-Judaism," 97; *History, Religion, and Antisemitism*, 292–293; M. Cohen, *Under Crescent and Cross*, 174–175. Medieval Jews given a choice of conversion or death by Muslims were more likely to choose conversion than were Jews given the same choice by Christians, possibly because Islam is religiously closer to Judaism. Like Judaism but unlike Christianity, for example, Islam is "unambiguously monotheistic." Islam also includes customs (such as male circumcision and the avoidance of pork) required by the Jewish but not the Christian religion. M. Cohen, *idem*, 169.

Some Jewish converts were highly critical of traditional Jews. In medieval Spain they were even described as "the worst enemies of Jews." Roth, *Conversos, Inquisition, and the Expulsion of the Jews from Spain*, 188; see also Szép, *Smell of Humans*, 22.

75. Langmuir, *Toward a Definition of Antisemitism*, 276.

76. *Idem*, "Thomas of Monmouth," 213, 225, 234; Dundes, *Blood Libel Legend*, vii.

77. One such medicine was supposedly used to treat the circumcision wound on Jewish boys. See, e.g., Dundes, "Ritual murder or blood libel legend," 337–338; Langmuir, "Historiographic crucifixion"; *Encyclopaedia Judaica*, "Blood libel."

78. Dundes, *idem*; Langmuir, *Toward a Definition of Antisemitism*, 264.

79. Landau, "Ritual murder accusations in nineteenth-century Egypt"; Langmuir, "Medieval antisemitism," 308–309; Dundes, "Ritual murder or blood libel legend," 339–340; *Encyclopaedia Judaica*, "Blood libel."

80. Langmuir, *idem*, 309–310, quoting Luther's pamphlet called *The Jews and Their Lies*, reissued in Germany in 1935.

81. Dundes, "Ritual murder or blood libel legend," 339–340; *Blood Libel Legend*, vii; Duker, "Twentieth-century blood libels in the United States." According to the entry on "Blood libel" in the *Encyclopaedia Judaica*, the Egyptian headline appeared in the newspaper *Al-Ahram* in October 2000. The entry also states that during the same period Arab television programs (on the Al-Jazeera and the Al-Manar networks) sometimes "evoke[d] the blood libel" and more generally portrayed Jews as "bloodthirsty and frighteningly ferocious."

Mohammed is said to have resented the Jews for rejecting him as a prophet, and some believe this rejection partly explains the long history of anti-Semitism in the Muslim world. In 1066, for instance, Spanish Muslims massacred the entire Jewish population of Granada. M. Cohen, *Under Crescent and Cross*, 165–166.

82. See, e.g., Shepard, "Present state of the ritual crime in Spain," 163; Rappaport, "Ritual murder accusation," 333; Schultz, "Blood libel," 288; Langmuir, *History, Religion, and Antisemitism*, 300. In post-Reformation Poland, Catholics also accused Protestants of Host desecration. Rappaport, *idem*, 309.

83. Langmuir, "Medieval antisemitism," 308.

84. Rappaport, "Ritual murder accusation," 316–317.

85. Langmuir, "Medieval antisemitism," 308; Dundes, "Ritual murder or blood libel legend," 357.

86. Langmuir, *idem*, 303.

87. *Encyclopaedia Judaica*, "Blood libel."

88. Hitler, *Mein Kampf*, Volume 1: 56, 65 (italics omitted); Volume 2: 305–308, 561–565; see also "The Crime of Doing Too Well" in chapter 4 of the present volume.

89. See, e.g., Goldhagen, *Hitler's Willing Executioners*; Szép, *Smell of Humans*; Gross, *Neighbors*; Mann, *Dark Side of Democracy*, Chapters 7–10.

90. Bailey, *Germans*, 158. Bailey does not say how many people he interviewed. He also notes that during the same period more Austrians than Germans blamed the Jews' rejection of Jesus for their genocide. As one Austrian commented: "After all, for what happened to the Jews, the Jews have only themselves to blame." *Idem*. Alluding to the fact that Austria is overwhelmingly Catholic whereas Germany is only part Catholic, another Austrian (who was part Jewish) remarked that "a Catholic country *must* be anti-Semitic." *Idem*, 159 (italics in original).

91. See Bromley, "Deprogramming as a mode of exit from new religious movements"; Jacobs, *Divine Disenchantment*.

92. Roth, *Conversos, Inquisition, and the Expulsion of the Jews from Spain*, 207. Jews were not allowed back into England until more than 350 years later.

93. The number of Jewish converts who continued to practice Judaism or to follow other Jewish traditions in Spain was once believed to be large. But historian Benzion Netanyahu presents evidence that the number of secret Jews among the baptized Jews was a minority, possibly a very small minority. Netanyahu, *Marranos of Spain*.

94. Netanyahu, *Origins of the Inquisition in Fifteenth Century Spain*, 3; see also 142–167; Kamen, *Inquisition and Society in Spain*; Haliczer, *Inquisition and Society in Early Modern Europe*. It is believed that about 60 percent of Spain's Jews converted to Christianity during the fifteenth century. Elon, *Pity of It All*, 81. Netanyahu traces the origin of the word *Marrano* to the Hebrew word for convert (*mumar*), and suggests that its affinity to the Spanish word for swine (with its derogatory connotations) may have been entirely accidental. *Marranos of Spain*, 59, note 153.

95. Roth, *Conversos, Inquisition, and the Expulsion of the Jews from Spain*, 232, Chapter 7.

96. Cantor, *Sacred Chain*, 188; Roth, *idem*, 221–222, Chapter 7; Netanyahu, *Origins of the Inquisition in Fifteenth Century Spain*, xiv.

97. Cantor, idem, 188; see also Kamen, *Inquisition and Society in Spain*, 41; Haliczer, *Inquisition and Society in Early Modern Europe*; Roth, *idem*, 204; Netanyahu, *idem*.

98. Davidson, "Inquisition and the Italian Jews"; Haliczer, "First holocaust," 12–16.

99. B. Lewis, *Cultures in Conflict*, 38; see also Davidson, *idem*, 21.

100. Netanyahu, *Marranos of Spain*.

101. *Idem, Origins of the Inquisition in Fifteenth Century Spain*; Roth, *Conversos, Inquisition, and the Expulsion of the Jews from Spain*, Chapter 7, especially 237–238, 242. The Inquisition later prosecuted Muslim converts to Christianity for secretly reverting to Islam. B. Lewis, *Cultures in Conflict*, 47. After the Spaniards conquered Mexico, they sometimes executed Aztec converts for reverting to their traditional religion. W. McNeill, *Plagues and Peoples*, 184; Klor de Alva, "Colonizing souls"; Moreno de los Arcos, "New Spain's Inquisition for Indians from the sixteenth to the nineteenth century."

102. Mondrian, "Natural reality and abstract reality," 107.

103. Ironically, Einstein's 1905 conception of light as composed of discrete packets of energy ("light quanta") contributed significantly to the development of quantum theory, and was the primary reason he received the 1921 Nobel Prize in Physics.

104. Smolin, "The other Einstein," 80; Fölsing, *Albert Einstein*, 589; Regis, *Who Got Einstein's Office?*, 24; Isaacson, *Einstein*, 320–325.

105. See, e.g., Smolin, *idem*, 80–83.

106. See, e.g., *idem, Trouble with Physics*, Chapter 1, 111, 114.

107. *Idem*, 276, 283; Woit, *Not Even Wrong*, 202.

108. Smolin, *idem*, 276, Chapter 16.

109. *Idem*, xx, 276, 284.

110. Compare Milner, *Freaks, Geeks, and Cool Kids*.

111. Quoted in Arnold, *On the Road to Nirvana*, 197. Punk rock has a raw and aggressive style and often contains lyrics that express irreverence, cynicism, and hostility toward modern society.

112. Arnold, *idem*, 276, 300. The grunge version of punk included a personal appearance sometimes described as "anti-style" (such as unkempt hair, a plain flannel shirt, and dirty blue jeans), similar to the appearance of many homeless men in American cities. See generally Arnold, *idem*; McNeil and McCain, *Please Kill Me*.

CHAPTER 8

1. Social time is a fundamental feature of all social life. Movements of social time attract super-natural power, for example, including the intervention of gods and the application of black magic, particularly when something is difficult or impossible to accomplish (such as the prevention of death or the achievement of eternal life). Compare, e.g., Durkheim, *Elementary Forms of Religious Life*; Malinowski, *Magic, Science and Religion*; Swanson, *Birth of the Gods*; but see Senechal de la Roche, "Behavior of the dead." While a supernatural being (such as Satan) might be said to cause sin, other supernatural beings (such as God) are said to punish sin (such as by making sinners sick, sending them to Hell, or harming their group). In Heaven, however, social time stands still.

2. In his book called *The Great Transformation*, historian and sociologist Karl Polanyi argues that the rise of the market economy caused the "collapse" of "nineteenth-century civilization," and that the impact of colonialism on non-Western tribes was similar to the market economy's impact on the Western world: Both damaged traditional culture and weakened tribal solidarity. *Idem*, 3, 164–168.

3. For a description of the impact of British colonialism on the Igbo tribe of Nigeria, see Chinua Achebe's novel called *Things Fall Apart*.

4. For differences between simple and complex hunter-gatherers, see Knauft, "Violence and sociality in human evolution."

5. Families in nomadic tribes sometimes move from one band to another (especially when conflict occurs), but the families themselves remain close. See, e.g., Woodburn, "Minimal politics"; Fry, *Human Potential for Peace*, Chapter 16.

6. See, e.g., Blumberg, "General theory of gender stratification." Unlike most hunter-gatherers, Australian Aborigines are patriarchal. See, e.g., Meggitt, *Desert People*, Chapter 7. So are Arctic Eskimos. See, e.g., Balikci, *Netsilik Eskimo*, 109; Briggs, *Never in Anger*, 107–108.

7. Quoted in Kennedy, *Jesuit and Savage in New France*, 121–122.

8. Balikci, *Netsilik Eskimo*, 140–143, 161; see also Rasmussen, *Netsilik Eskimos*, 195–196; Burch, "Marriage and divorce among the North Alaskan Eskimos," 180–181.

9. Hoebel, *Law of Primitive Man*, 83.

10. Rasmussen, *Netsilik Eskimos*, 197.

11. Gregor, *Mehinaku*, 133–136, Chapter 9; *Anxious Pleasures*, 32.

12. Burch, "Marriage and divorce among the North Alaskan Eskimos," 186–187. Cherokee Indians sometimes change partners "as frequently as three or four times a year." Reid, *Law of Blood*, 117. The Buid of the Philippine highlands average about five marriages during a lifetime, and ten marriages is "by no means uncommon." Gibson, *Sacrifice and Sharing in the Philippine Highlands*, 78.

13. Gregor, *Mehinaku*, 72–74.

14. Knauft, *Good Company and Violence*, 64.

15. For example, the Jívaro of Ecuador have no concept of rape at all, and "could recall no case of a woman violently resisting sexual intercourse"; the Goodenough Islanders of New Guinea have no "term" for rape either, and would view any accusation of rape with suspicion; rape is "completely unknown" among the Vinatinai Islanders of New Guinea; and it does not seem to occur among the Mbuti Pygmies of Zaire. Harner, *Jívaro*, 176; Young, *Fighting with Food*, 115; Lepowsky, "Gender in an egalitarian society," 194; Turnbull, *Wayward Servants*, 121; see also Lee, *!Kung San*, 454; Good, *Into the Heart*, 158, 199; D. Marshall, "Sexual behavior on Mangaia," 129, 152.

16. Something is too intimate in every relationship. But even incest does not always cause a serious conflict. The Mehinaku claim to condemn incest, for example, but in at least one case they

largely tolerated a man who openly maintained a sexual relationship with his daughter for "many years." Whether the relationship caused a serious conflict with other members of the man's family (such as his wife or daughter), however, was apparently not ascertained. Gregor, *Anxious Pleasures*, 61–65.

17. Balikci, *Netsilik Eskimo*, 161; see also Rasmussen, *Across Arctic America*, 246, 250; Hoebel, *Law of Primitive Man*, 83.

18. Robarchek, "Hobbesian and Rousseauan images of man," 41.

19. See, e.g., Lee, *!Kung San*, 376–392. A Bushman woman in Botswana noted when adultery is most dangerous for a woman: "If her heart feels passion only for her lover and is cold toward her husband, that is very bad. Her husband will know and will want to kill her and the lover. A woman has to want her husband and her lover equally; that is when it is good." Quoted in Shostak, *Nisa*, 287–288, cited in Fry, *Human Potential for Peace*, 212.

20. Myers, "The logic and meaning of anger among Pintupi Aborigines," 598.

21. Lee, *!Kung San*, 458; see also Turnbull, *Forest People*, 134; *Wayward Servants*, 158.

22. Lee, *idem*, 461.

23. Knauft, *Good Company and Violence*, 64.

24. E.g., Monica Wilson, "Witch-beliefs and social structure," 104; Gregor, *Mehinaku*, 188.

25. Quoted in Kennedy, *Jesuit and Savage in New France*, 158; see also Walter Miller, "Two concepts of authority." Not all American Indians had simple forms of social organization, nor were all highly egalitarian. For example, the horticultural Natchez of the lower Mississippi Valley had a chief who "ruled despotically" and presided over a hierarchy of lesser officials with similar powers. Kennedy, *idem*, 166.

26. Turnbull, *Wayward Servants*, 181, 212; see also Boehm, "Egalitarian behavior and reverse dominance hierarchy."

27. Balikci, *Netsilik Eskimo*, 176; see also 178–179.

28. Gregor, *Mehinaku*, 118; see also Lepowsky, "Gender in an egalitarian society," 181, 188.

29. See Polanyi, *Great Transformation*, 94–95, 108–109, 171–172.

30. Lee, *!Kung San*, 458; see also 244, 246.

31. Hamilton, "Descended from father, belonging to country," 103–104; Gregor, *Anxious Pleasures*, 47.

32. Lindholm, *Generosity and Jealousy*, 204. But something only slightly new (such as a small variation in a design or decoration) might spread quickly through a tribe by mutual imitation and cause no conflict at all. See, e.g., Radcliffe-Brown, *Andaman Islanders*, 122.

33. Modern children often form tribe-like groups that are intimate among themselves, largely equal, and culturally homogenous. In some respects their conflict therefore resembles conflict in a simple tribe. See Baumgartner, "War and peace in early childhood"; compare, e.g., Piaget, *Moral Judgment of the Child*.

34. See, e.g., Goode, *World Revolution and Family Patterns*.

35. Black, *Behavior of Law*, 134–135; see also Baumgartner, *Moral Order of a Suburb*.

36. See, e.g., Putnam, *Bowling Alone*; McPherson, Smith-Lovin, and Brashears, "Social isolation in America"; L. Cohen and Felson, "Social change and crime rate trends." Divorce increased in modern societies such as the United States in the twentieth and twenty-first centuries, but this does not necessarily mean that the closeness of marital relationships declined. It fact, modern marriages would appear to be closer than those of the past. For instance, modern husbands and wives frequently spend more time together and share more of their lives than do more traditional

and patriarchal couples. Many modern couples also have fewer close ties to other people than did couples of the past, and for this reason they are closer to one another as well.

37. By "law" I mean governmental social control. Because simple tribes have no government on a permanent basis, they have no law. See Black, *Behavior of Law*, 2, 86–92, Chapter 7.

38. *Idem*, 40–48; see also "Epistemology of pure sociology," 842–844; Macaulay, "Non-contractual relations in business"; Engel, "Oven bird's song"; S. Gross and Mauro, "Patterns of death," 58–59.

39. Justice Harry A. Blackmun, Dissenting Opinion, *Bowers v. Hardwick*, 478 U.S. 186 (1986); see also Warren and Brandeis, "Right of privacy"; Devlin, *Enforcement of Morals*, 18–19.

40. Staying away, moving away, or otherwise reducing contact is a common mode of social control in many modern settings. See, e.g., Hirschman, *Exit, Voice, and Loyalty*; Baumgartner, *Moral Order of a Suburb*.

41. But modern societies have far less inequality than many societies of the past, including ancient civilizations such as early Babylonia and Greece and the feudal societies of Europe and Asia.

42. "Equality" might also refer to the equal value or equal rights of humans, such as their equal right to life or liberty, or equal treatment in matters such as law enforcement and employment.

43. A "multiculturalism" movement in late twentieth-century America promoted the value of diversity in various areas of life. See, e.g., Hunter, *Culture Wars*, 215–219; *Before the Shooting Begins*, 196–211.

44. McLuhan, *Understanding Media*, 47; Held and McGrew, *Global Transformations Reader*. For a study of conflict management among people who communicate only by computer, see Godard, Moral Order of Cyberspace.

45. See Durkheim, *Suicide*, Chapters 2–3; Lasch, *Culture of Narcissism*.

46. See Black, *Behavior of Law*, 4–6; "Epistemology of pure sociology," 835–836, note 37; see also Goffman, *Asylums*; Black and Baumgartner, "Toward a theory of the third party," 119–121; Durkheim, *idem*, 210–216; Horwitz, *Creating Mental Illness*; L. Davis, "Encyclopedia of insanity"; J. Davis, After Psychology. The movement called psychoanalysis (founded by Sigmund Freud) has promoted therapeutic morality since the turn of the twentieth century. See, e.g., Rieff, *Freud*; *Triumph of the Therapeutic*.

47. Sociologist Philip Rieff similarly comments that psychotherapy encourages "an intensely private sense of well-being." *Triumph of the Therapeutic*, 261.

48. See Black, "Social control of the self," 66; "Epistemology of pure sociology," 835–836, note 37; see also Horwitz, *Social Control of Mental Illness*; "Therapy and social solidarity," 238–244; *Creating Mental Illness*; Tucker, *Therapeutic Corporation*, 20, 127–128; "Therapy, organizations, and the state"; "New Age religion and the cult of the self"; J. Davis, After Psychology. Involuntary therapy differs considerably from the self-initiated therapy discussed in the text. See, e.g., Goffman, *Asylums*; Szasz, *Myth of Mental Illness*; *Law, Liberty, and Psychiatry*; Horwitz, "Therapy and social solidarity," 211–217; Foucault, *Abnormal*.

49. See the United Nations "Declaration of Human Rights," published in 1948.

50. See, e.g., Regan, *Case for Animal Rights*; Singer, *Animal Liberation*; Sessions, *Deep Ecology for the 21st Century*; Beirne, *Confronting Animal Abuse*.

51. David Brower, quoted in Sessions, *idem*, xi; Arne Naess, "Equality, sameness, and rights," 224; Stone, "Should trees have standing?," 456; see also Naess, "Self-realization"; Stone, "Habeas corpus for animals? Why not?"; Bergesen, "Deep ecology and moral community," 194;

"Eco-alienation," 125. Naess elsewhere suggests that human beings should expand "their narrow concept of self to embrace the entire planetary ecosystem." Grimes, "Arne Naess." Global morality also pertains to the protection of manmade places and objects such as old buildings, burial grounds, and religious icons with historical or other human significance. See, e.g., J. Lofland, *Demolishing a Historic Hotel*; Barthel-Bouchier, "Crimes against culture."

52. See Black and Baumgartner, "On self-help in modern society"; Black, "Social control as a dependent variable," 21–22; *Social Structure of Right and Wrong*, Chapter 7; compare Michalski, "Financial altruism or unilateral resource exchanges?"

53. See, e.g., Gelfand, *Witch Doctor*, 52; Ejidike, "Human rights in the cultural traditions and social practice of the Igbo of south-eastern Nigeria," 78.

54. See Black, *Social Structure of Right and Wrong*, 156–157, note 10.

55. Diamond, "New Guineans and their natural world," 264.

56. Briggs, *Never in Anger*, 46; see also Turnbull, *Forest People*, 101.

57. Diamond, "New Guineans and their natural world," 263–264.

58. Frazer, *Golden Bough*, Volume 2: 282–283; see also Van Vechten, *Tiger in the House*, 93–96. People extend more protection and support to closer animals such as household pets and livestock. In the Western world, the first laws against cruelty to animals (in the seventeenth century) pertained exclusively to such domestic animals as dogs, horses, and cows. Beirne, *Confronting Animal Abuse*, Chapters 1–2. Tribal people sometimes develop close and supportive relationships with domestic animals as well. See, e.g., Evans-Pritchard, *Nuer*, Chapter 1.

59. See Granovetter, "Strength of weak ties"; Baumgartner, *Moral Order of a Slum*, Chapters 3–4.

60. See Senechal de la Roche, "Collective violence as social control"; "Sociogenesis of lynching"; "Modern lynchings"; Black, "Violent structures," 153–154; "Terrorism as social control," 13; Campbell, "Genocide as social control"; "Contradictory behavior during genocides."

61. People with stronger ties are more likely to oppose abortion and uphold the unborn child's right to its parents' support, while those with fewer strong ties are more likely to uphold a mother's right to have an abortion and to view the prohibition of abortion as an intrusion on her privacy and personal freedom. Compare, e.g., Hunter, *Culture Wars*; *Before the Shooting Begins*.

62. M. Weber, *Religion of India*, 197, 199.

63. Stevens, *Zen Masters*, 119.

64. Max Born, quoted in Isaacson, *Einstein*, 95; see also Lise Meitner, quoted in Perutz, "Passion for science," 42.

65. Isaacson, *Einstein*, 551; see also 274, 393; Einstein, quoted in Hoffmann, *Albert Einstein*, 253.

66. See, e.g., Chamberlain, *Nietzsche in Turin*, 208–209.

67. Global citizens sometimes have a distinctive conception of religion. Einstein considered his "awe" of the "mysterious" yet orderly nature of the universe to be "religious" in nature, for example. Quoted in Isaacson, *Einstein*, 387. The poet Robinson Jeffers viewed the entire universe as "one being" that he was "compelled to love" as the "one God." "Letter to Sister Mary James Power." In one of his poems (called "Hurt hawks"), he also speaks of "the wild God of the world."

References

Aaronson, Bernard, and Humphrey Osmond (editors) 1970 *Psychedelics: The Uses and Implications of Hallucinogenic Drugs.* Garden City, NY: Anchor.

Abbott, Jack Henry 1981 *In the Belly of the Beast: Letters from Prison.* New York: Vintage, 1982.

Abelson, Elaine S. 1989 *When Ladies Go A-Thieving: Middle-Class Shoplifters in the Victorian Department Store.* New York: Oxford University Press.

Abrahams, Roger D. 1962 "Playing the dozens." *Journal of American Folklore* 75: 209–220.

Abramsky, Chimen; Maciej Jachimczyk; and Antony Polonsky (editors) 1986 *The Jews in Poland.* Oxford, England: Basil Blackwell.

Achebe, Chinua 2009 *Things Fall Apart.* Critical Edition: Authoritative Text, Contexts and Criticism, edited by Francis Abiola Irele. New York: W. W. Norton (original edition, 1958).

Ackerknecht, Erwin H. 1944 "'White Indians': psychological and physiological peculiarities of white children abducted and reared by North American Indians." *Bulletin of the History of Medicine* 15: 15–36.

Aichelburg, Peter C. 2005 "On the evolution of the concept of time and its implications for modern cosmology." Paper prepared for a conference entitled "Science and Religion: Global Perspectives," Philadelphia. Online (June 4–8): http://72.14.207.104/search?q=cache:8c_xchRSX8QJ:www.metanexus.net/conference2005/pdf/aichelburg.pdf+aichelburg+time&hl=en.

Åkerström, Malin 1991 *Betrayal and Betrayers: The Sociology of Treachery*. New Brunswick: NJ: Transaction.

Alexander, Richard D. 1987 *The Biology of Moral Systems*. New Brunswick, NJ: Aldine Transaction.

Alldritt, Leslie D. 2003 "Buddhism and the *burakumin*: oppression or liberation?" Pages 183–206 in *Action Dharma: New Studies in Engaged Buddhism*, edited by Christopher Queen, Charles Prebish, and Damien Keown. London: Routledge/Curzon.

Allen, Michael R. 1984 "Homosexuality, male power, and political organization in North Vanuatu: a comparative analysis." Pages 83–126 in Herdt 1984b.

Amos, Jonathan 2010 "Falling in love costs you friends." *BBC News*. Online (September 15): http://www.bbc.co.uk/news/science-environment-11321282.

Anderson, Elijah 1978 *A Place on the Corner*. Chicago: University of Chicago Press.

——— 1990 *Streetwise: Race, Class, and Change in an Urban Community*. Chicago: University of Chicago Press.

——— 1999 *Code of the Street: Decency, Violence, and the Moral Life of the Inner City*. New York: W. W. Norton.

Andrade, E. N. da C. 1954 *Sir Isaac Newton*. Garden City, NY: Anchor.

Anonymous 1716 *Onania; or, The Heinous Sin of Self-Pollution, And All Its Frightful Consequences, in Both Sexes Consider'd, &c.* London (publisher unknown).

Anscombe, G. E. M. 1958 "Modern moral philosophy." *Philosophy* 33: 1–19.

Archimbaud, Michel 1992 *Francis Bacon: In Conversation with Michel Archimbaud*. London: Phaidon, 1993.

Arendt, Hannah circa 1938–39 "Antisemitism." Pages 46–121 in Arendt 2007.

——— 1952 "The history of the great crime: a review of *Bréviaire de la haine: Le IIIe Reichet les juits*" (*Breviary of Hate: The Third Reich and the Jews*), by Léon Poliakov. Pages 453–461 in Arendt 2007.

——— 1963 *On Revolution*. New York: Viking, 1965.

——— 2007 *The Jewish Writings*, edited by Jerome Kohn and Ron H. Feldman. New York: Schocken.

Argentine National Commission on the Disappeared 1984 *Nunca Más: Report of the Argentine Commission on the Disappeared*. New York: Farrar, Straus, Giroux, 1986.

Ariès, Philippe 1982a "The indissoluble marriage." Pages 140–157 in Ariès and Béjin 1982.

——— 1982b "Love in married life." Pages 130–139 in Ariès and Béjin 1982.

——— 1982c "Thoughts on the history of homosexuality." Pages 62–75 in Ariès and Béjin 1982.

Ariès, Philippe, and André Béjin (editors) 1982 *Western Sexuality: Practice and Precept in Past and Present Times*. New York: Basil Blackwell, 1985.

Aristotle 1930 *Physica*. Oxford, England: Clarendon. Written in the fourth century B.C.E.

——— 1982 *Aristotle's Eudemian Ethics: Books I, II, and VIII*. Oxford, England: Clarendon. Written in the fourth century B.C.E.

——— 1985 *Nicomachean Ethics*. Indianapolis, IN: Hackett. Written in the fourth century B.C.E.

Arnold, Gina 1995 *On the Road to Nirvana*. London: Pan (corrected edition; first published 1993).

Axtell, James 1975 "The white Indians of colonial America." *William and Mary Quarterly* 32: 55–88.

Ayoub, Millicent R., and Stephen A. Barnett 1965 "Ritualized verbal insult in white high school culture." *Journal of American Folklore* 78: 337–344.

Azoy, G. Whitney 1982 *Buzkashi: Game and Power in Afghanistan*. Philadelphia: University of Pennsylvania Press.

Babb, Lawrence A. 1981 "Glancing: visual interaction in Hinduism." *Journal of Anthropological Research* 37: 387–401.

Bailey, George 1972 *Germans: The Biography of an Obsession*. New York: World.

Bainton, Roland, H. 1953 *Hunted Heretic: The Life and Death of Michael Servetus, 1511–1553*. Boston: Beacon.

Balikci, Asen 1970 *The Netsilik Eskimo*. Garden City, NY: Natural History Press.

Barber, Bernard 1961 "Resistance by scientists to scientific discovery." *Science* 134: 596–602.

Bardach, Janusz, and Kathleen Gleeson 1998 *Man Is Wolf to Man: Surviving the Gulag*. Berkeley: University of California Press.

Barnard, George W.; Hernan Vera; Maria I. Vera; and Gustave Newman 1982 "Till death do us part: a study of spouse murder." *Bulletin of the American Association of Psychiatry and Law* 10: 271–280.

Barnes, J. A. 1994 *A Pack of Lies: Towards a Sociology of Lying*. Cambridge: Cambridge University Press.

Barth, Fredrik 1959 *Political Leadership among Swat Pathans*. London: Athlone.

——— 1961 *Nomads of South Persia: The Basseri Tribe of the Khamseh Confederacy*. Boston: Little, Brown.

Barthel-Bouchier, Diane 2007 "Crimes against culture." Unpublished paper, Department of Sociology, Stony Brook University, Stony Brook, NY.

Barton, Roy Franklin 1919 *Ifugao Law*. Berkeley: University of California Press.

Baumgartner, M. P. 1978 "Law and social status in colonial New Haven, 1639–1665." Pages 153–178 in *Research in Law and Sociology: An Annual Compilation of Research*, Volume 1, edited by Rita J. Simon. Greenwich, CT: JAI.

——— 1984a "Social control from below." Pages 303–345 in Black 1984c.

——— 1984b "Social control in suburbia." Pages 79–103 in Black 1984d.

——— 1988 *The Moral Order of a Suburb*. New York: Oxford University Press.

——— 1992a "Violent networks: the origins and management of domestic conflict." Pages 209–231 in *Violence and Aggression: The Social Interactionist Perspective*, edited by Richard B. Felson and James Tedeschi. Washington, DC: American Psychological Association.

——— 1992b "War and peace in early childhood." Pages 1–38 in Volume 1: "Law and Conflict Management," edited by James Tucker. *Virginia Review of Sociology: A Research Annual*. Greenwich, CT: JAI.

Baxter, P. T. W. 1972 "Absence makes the heart grow fonder: some suggestions why witchcraft accusations are rare among East African pastoralists." Pages 163–191 in Gluckman 1972a.

Bay, Mia 2000 *The White Image in the Black Mind: African-American Ideas about White People, 1830–1925*. New York: Oxford University Press.

Bayley, David H. 1976 *Forces of Order: Police Behavior in Japan and the United States*. Berkeley: University of California Press.

Beals, Alan R. 1962 *Gopalpur: A South Indian Village*. New York: Holt, Rinehart & Winston.

Beattie, J. M. 1986 *Crime and the Courts in England: 1660–1800*. Princeton, NJ: Princeton University Press.

Beattie, John 1963 "Sorcery in Bunyoro." Pages 27–55 in Middleton and Winter 1963b.

Beauvois, Daniel 1986 "Polish-Jewish relations in the territories annexed by the Russian Empire in the first half of the nineteenth century." Pages 78–90 in Abramsky, Jachimczyk, and Polonsky 1986.

Becker, Howard S. 1963 *Outsiders: Studies in the Sociology of Deviance*. New York: Free Press.

——— 1982 *Art Worlds*. Berkeley: University of California Press.

Beidelman, T. O. 1963 "Witchcraft in Ukaguru." Pages 57–98 in Middleton and Winter 1963b.

Beirne, Piers 1997 "Rethinking bestiality: towards a concept of interspecies sexual assault." *Theoretical Criminology* 1: 317–340.

——— 2009 *Confronting Animal Abuse: Law, Criminology, and Human-Animal Relationships*. Lanham, MD: Rowman & Littlefield.

Béjin, André 1982 "The extra-marital union today." Pages 158–167 in Ariès and Béjin 1982.

Benedict, Ruth 1946 *The Chrysanthemum and the Sword: Patterns of Japanese Culture*. New York: New American Library, 1974.

Berger, Peter; Brigitte Berger; and Hansfried Kellner 1973 *The Homeless Mind: Modernization and Consciousness*. New York: Random House.

Bergesen, Albert 1980 "Official violence during the Watts, Newark, and Detroit race riots of the 1960s." Pages 138–174 in *A Political Analysis of Deviance*, edited by Pat Lauderdale. Minneapolis: University of Minnesota Press.

——— 1995a "Deep ecology and moral community." Pages 193–213 in *Rethinking Materialism*, edited by Robert Wuthnow. Grand Rapids, MI: Eerdmans.

———1995b "Eco-alienation." *Humboldt Journal of Social Relations* 21: 111–126.

Bergson, Henri 1907 *Creative Evolution*. New York: Random House, 1944.

Bernstein, Jeremy 1973 *Einstein*. New York: Viking.

Bharati, Agehananda 1983 "India: South Asian perspectives on aggression." Pages 237–260 in *Aggression in Global Perspective*, edited by Arnold P. Goldstein and Marshall H. Segall. New York: Pergamon.

Biehl, Jody K. 2005 "'The whore lived like a German': the death of a Muslim woman." *Der Spiegel.* Online (March 2): http://service.spiegel.de/cache/international/0,1518,344374,00.html.

Bing, Léon 2001 "Homegirls." *Rolling Stone* (April 12): 75–86.

Black, Donald 1971 "The social organization of arrest." Pages 85–108 in Black 1980.

———1979a "Common sense in the sociology of law." *American Sociological Review* 44: 18–27.

———1979b "A strategy of pure sociology." Pages 158–170 in Black 1998.

———1980 *The Manners and Customs of the Police*. New York: Academic Press.

———1984a "Crime as social control." Pages 27–46 in Black 1998.

———1984b "Social control as a dependent variable." Pages 1–26 in Black 1998.

——— (editor) 1984c *Toward a General Theory of Social Control*. Volume 1: *Fundamentals*. Orlando, FL: Academic Press.

——— (editor) 1984d *Toward a General Theory of Social Control*. Volume 2: *Selected Problems*. Orlando, FL: Academic Press.

———1987 "Compensation and the social structure of misfortune." Pages 47–64 in Black 1998.

———1989 *Sociological Justice*. New York: Oxford University Press.

———1990 "The elementary forms of conflict management." Pages 74–94 in Black 1998.

———1992 "Social control of the self." Pages 65–73 in Black 1998.

———1995 "The epistemology of pure sociology." *Law & Social Inquiry* 20: 829–870.

———1998 *The Social Structure of Right and Wrong.* San Diego, CA: Academic Press (revised edition; first edition, 1993).

———2000a "Dreams of pure sociology." *Sociological Theory* 18: 345–367.

———2000b "On the origin of morality." *Journal of Consciousness Studies* 7: 107–119.

———2000c "The purification of sociology." *Contemporary Sociology* 29: 704–709.

———2002a "The geometry of law: an interview with Donald Black." *International Journal of the Sociology of Law* 30: 101–129.

———2002b "Pure sociology and the geometry of discovery." Pages 668–674 in "A Continuities Symposium on Donald Black's *The Behavior of Law*," edited by Allan V. Horwitz. *Contemporary Sociology* 31.

———2002c "Terrorism as social control." Pages 9–18 in *Terrorism and Counter-Terrorism: Criminological Perspectives*, edited by Mathieu Deflem. Amsterdam: Elsevier, 2004.

———2004a "The geometry of terrorism." Pages 14–25 in "Theories of Terrorism," a symposium edited by Roberta Senechal de la Roche. *Sociological Theory* 22.

———2004b "Violent structures." Pages 145–158 in Zahn, Brownstein, and Jackson 2004.

———2007 "Legal relativity." Pages 1292–1294 in *Encyclopedia of Law and Society: American and Global Perspectives*, Volume 3, edited by David S. Clark. Thousand Oaks, CA: Sage.

———2010a *The Behavior of Law.* Bingley, England: Emerald (special edition; first edition, 1976).

———2010b "How law behaves: an interview with Donald Black." *International Journal of Law, Crime and Justice* 38: 37–47.

Black, Donald, and M. P. Baumgartner 1980 "On self-help in modern society." Pages 193–208 in Black 1980.

———1983 "Toward a theory of the third party." Pages 95–124 in Black 1998.

Blau, Judith R., and Peter M. Blau 1982 "The cost of inequality: metropolitan structure and violent crime." *American Sociological Review* 47: 114–129.

Blau, Peter M., and Joseph E. Schwartz 1984 *Crosscutting Social Circles: Testing a Macrostructural Theory of Intergroup Relations*. Orlando, FL: Academic Press.

Blok, Anton 1981 "Rams and billy-goats: a key to the Mediterranean code of honour." *Man* 16: 427–440.

Bloom, Paul 2010 "How do morals change?" *Nature*. Online (March 25): http://www.nature.com/nature/journal/v464/n7288/full/464490a.html.

Blumberg, Rae Lesser 1984 "A general theory of gender stratification." Pages 23–101 in *Sociological Theory*, edited by Randall Collins. San Francisco, CA: Jossey-Boss.

Blurton Jones, Nicholas G. 1984 "A selfish origin for human food sharing: tolerated theft." *Ethology and Sociobiology* 5: 1–3.

——— 1987 "Tolerated theft: suggestions about the ecology and evolution of sharing, hoarding and scrounging." *Social Science Information* 26: 31–54.

Boehm, Christopher 1984 *Blood Revenge: The Enactment and Management of Conflict in Montenegro and Other Tribal Societies*. Philadelphia: University of Pennsylvania Press, 1986.

——— 1993 "Egalitarian behavior and reverse dominance hierarchy." *Current Anthropology* 34: 227–240.

——— 1999 *Hierarchy in the Forest: The Evolution of Egalitarian Behavior*. Cambridge, MA: Harvard University Press.

——— 2000 "Conflict and the evolution of social control." *Journal of Consciousness Studies* 7: 79–101.

Bok, Sissela 1978 *Lying: Moral Choice in Public and Private Life*. New York: Pantheon.

——— 1982 *Secrets: On the Ethics of Concealment and Revelation*. New York: Pantheon.

Bolton, Ralph 1973 "Aggression and hypoglycemia among the Qolla: a study in psychobiological anthropology." *Ethnology* 12: 227–257.

Boswell, John 1980 *Christianity, Social Tolerance, and Homosexuality: Gay People in Western Europe from the Beginning of the Christian Era to the Fourteenth Century*. Chicago: University of Chicago Press.

——— 1988 *The Kindness of Strangers: The Abandonment of Children in Western Europe from Late Antiquity to the Renaissance*. New York: Pantheon.

Bourdieu, Pierre 1966 "The sentiment of honour in Kabyle society." Pages 191–241 in Peristiany 1966.

——— 1979 *Distinction: A Social Critique of the Judgement of Taste*. Cambridge, MA: Harvard University Press, 1984.

Boyer, Paul, and Stephen Nissenbaum 1974 *Salem Possessed: The Social Origins of Witchcraft*. Cambridge, MA: Harvard University Press.

Bradshaw, Lisa 2009 "Flemish TV personality Yasmine takes her own life." *Flanders Today*. Online (July 1): http://www.flanderstoday.eu/content/flemish-tv-personality-yasmine-takes-her-own-life.

Brenner, Reuven 1983 *History—The Human Gamble*. Chicago: University of Chicago Press.

——— 1985 *Betting on Ideas: Wars, Inventions, Inflation*. Chicago: University of Chicago Press.

Breslin, James E. B. 1993 *Mark Rothko: A Biography*. Chicago: University of Chicago Press.

Briggs, Jean L. 1970 *Never in Anger: Portrait of an Eskimo Family*. Cambridge, MA: Harvard University Press.

Brinton, Crane 1965 *The Anatomy of Revolution*. New York: Vintage (revised and expanded edition; first edition, 1938).

Brison, Karen J. 1992 *Just Talk: Gossip, Meetings, and Power in a Papua New Guinea Village*. Berkeley: University of California Press.

Bromley, David G. 1988 "Deprogramming as a mode of exit from new religious movements: the case of the Unification movement." Pages 185–204 in *Falling from the Faith: Causes and Consequences of Religious Apostasy*, edited by David G. Bromley. Newbury Park, CA: Sage.

Brooks, Juanita 1962 *The Mountain Meadows Massacre*. Norman: University of Oklahoma Press (new edition; first edition, 1950).

Browder, Chris 1999 "The social life of Koreans studying overseas: collectivism as manifested in Korean society at the University of Buffalo." *GeoCities*. Online: http://www.geocities.com/c_browder/ethnography.htm.

Brown, Alison Leigh 1998 *Subjects of Deceit: A Phenomenology of Lying*. Albany: State University of New York Press.

Brown, Julia S. 1952 "A comparative study of deviations from sexual mores." *American Sociological Review* 17: 135–146.

Brown, H. Rap 1969 "Street talk." Pages 205–208 in Kochman 1972.

Brown, Richard Maxwell 1975 *Strain of Violence: Historical Studies of American Violence and Vigilantism.* Oxford: Oxford University Press.

Brownmiller, Susan 1975 *Against Our Will: Men, Women and Rape.* New York: Bantam.

Brundage, James A. 1995 *Medieval Canon Law.* London: Longman.

Bühler, Georg (translator) 1886 *The Laws of Manu.* New York: Dover, 1969.

Bullough, Vern L., and Bonnie Bullough 1993 *Cross Dressing, Sex, and Gender.* Philadelphia: University of Pennsylvania Press.

Burbank, Victoria Katherine 1985 "The *mirriri* as ritualized aggression." *Oceania* 56: 47–55.

——— 1987 "Female aggression in cross-cultural perspective." *Behavior Science Research* 21: 70–100.

——— 1994 *Fighting Women: Anger and Aggression in Aboriginal Australia.* Berkeley: University of California Press.

Burch, Ernest S., Jr. 1970 "Marriage and divorce among the North Alaskan Eskimos." Pages 171–204 in *Divorce and After,* edited by Paul Bohannan. Garden City, NY: Anchor.

Burtt, Edwin Arthur 1954 *The Metaphysical Foundations of Modern Science.* Garden City, NY: Doubleday (revised edition; first published 1952).

Cabanne, Pierre 1975 *Pablo Picasso: His Life and Times.* New York: William Morrow, 1977.

Campbell, Bradley 2009 "Genocide as social control." *Sociological Theory* 27: 150–172.

——— 2010 "Contradictory behavior during genocides." *Sociological Forum* 25: 296–314.

Canetti, Elias 1960 *Crowds and Power.* New York: Viking, 1963.

Cantor, Norman F. 1994 *The Sacred Chain: A History of the Jews.* New York: HarperCollins.

Catlin, George 1844 *Letters and Notes on the Manners, Customs, and Condition of the North American Indians.* New York: Dover, 1973. Two volumes.

Cavan, Sherri 1966 *Liquor License: An Ethnography of Bar Behavior.* Chicago: Aldine.

Chagnon, Napoleon 1977 *Yanomamö: The Fierce People.* Holt, Rinehart & Winston (second edition; first edition, 1968).

Chalk, Frank, and Kurt Jonassohn 1990 *The History and Sociology of Genocide: Analyses and Case Studies.* New Haven, CT: Yale University Press.

Chamberlain, Lesley 1996 *Nietzsche in Turin: An Intimate Biography.* New York: Picador USA.

Chang, Iris 1997 *The Rape of Nanking: The Forgotten Holocaust of World War II.* New York: Basic Books.

Chernofsky, Erica 2006 "Comforting the bereaved." *Jerusalem Post.* Online (October 1): http://www.jpost.com/servlet/Satellite?cid=1159193352771&pagename=JPost/JPArticle/ShowFull.

Chevigny, Paul 1969 *Police Power: Police Abuses in New York City.* New York: Vintage.

Christie, Nils 2007 "Restorative justice: answers to deficits in modernity?" Pages 368–378 in *Crime, Social Control, and Human Rights: From Moral Panics to States of Denial. Essays in Honour of Stanley Cohen*, edited by David Downes, Paul Rock, Christine Chinkin, and Conor Gearly. Devon, England: Willan.

Ch'ü, T'ung-Tsu 1961 *Law and Society in Traditional China.* Paris: Mouton.

Clastres, Pierre 1974 *Society against the State: Essays in Political Anthropology.* New York: Zone, 1989.

Cleaver, Eldridge 1968 *Soul on Ice.* New York: McGraw-Hill.

Cloward, Richard A., and Lloyd E. Ohlin 1960 *Delinquency and Opportunity: A Theory of Delinquent Gangs.* New York: Free Press.

CNN 1999 "Teen suspect in Georgia school shooting may face adult charge." Online (May 20): http://www.cnn.com/US/9905/20/conyers.school.shooting.05/.

Codere, Helen 1950 *Fighting with Property: A Study of Kwakiutl Potlatching and Warfare, 1792–1930.* Seattle: University of Washington Press.

Cohen, Albert K. 1955 *Delinquent Boys: The Culture of the Gang.* New York: Free Press.

——— 1976 "Prison violence: a sociological perspective." Pages 3–22 in *Prison Violence*, edited by Albert K. Cohen, George F. Cole, and Robert G. Bailey. Lexington, MA: D. C. Heath.

Cohen, David 1995 *Law, Violence, and Community in Classical Athens.* Cambridge: Cambridge University Press.

Cohen, I. Bernard 1985 *Revolution in Science*. Cambridge, MA: Harvard University Press.

Cohen, Lawrence E., and Marcus Felson 1979 "Social change and crime rate trends: a routine activity approach." *American Sociological Review* 44: 588–608.

Cohen, Mark R. 1994 *Under Crescent and Cross: The Jews in the Middle Ages*. Princeton, NJ: Princeton University Press.

Cohen, Paul A. 1963 *China and Christianity: The Missionary Movement and the Growth of Chinese Antiforeignism, 1860–1870*. Cambridge, MA: Harvard University Press.

Cohn, Norman 1970 *The Pursuit of the Millennium: Revolutionary Millenarians and Mystical Anarchists of the Middle Ages*. New York: Oxford University Press (revised and expanded edition; first published 1957).

Colburn, Forrest D. (editor) 1989 *Everyday Forms of Peasant Resistance*. Armonk, NY: M. E. Sharpe.

Collins, Randall 1975 *Conflict Sociology: Toward an Explanatory Science*. New York: Academic Press.

—— 1998 *The Sociology of Philosophies: A Global Theory of Intellectual Change*. Cambridge, MA: Harvard University Press.

—— 2000 "Situational stratification: a micro-macro theory of inequality." *Sociological Theory* 18: 17–43.

—— 2008 *Violence: A Micro-sociological Theory*. Princeton, NJ: Princeton University Press.

Colson, Elizabeth 1953 *The Makah Indians: An Indian Tribe in Modern American Society*. Manchester: Manchester University Press.

—— 1958 *Marriage and the Family among the Plateau Tonga of Northern Rhodesia*. Manchester: Manchester University Press.

Comini, Alessandra 1975 *Gustav Klimt*. London: Thames & Hudson.

Comstock, Gary David 1991 *Violence against Lesbians and Gay Men*. New York: Columbia University Press.

Contreras, Jaime 1987 "The impact of Protestantism in Spain, 1520–1600." Pages 47–63 in Haliczer, 1987b.

Cook, David 2002 "Suicide attacks or 'martyrdom operations' in contemporary *jihad* literature." *Nova Religio: The Journal of Alternative and Emergent Religions* 6: 7–44.

Cook, Scott B. 1996 *Colonial Encounters in the Age of High Imperialism*. New York: HarperCollins.

Cooley, Charles Horton 1922 *Human Nature and the Social Order*. New York: Schocken, 1964 (revised edition; first edition, 1902).

Cooney, Daniel 2006 "Christian convert faces death penalty in Afghanistan." *Guardian Unlimited*. Online (March 20): http://www.guardian.co.uk/international/story/0,1734776,00.html.

Cooney, Mark 1991 Law, Morality, and Conscience: The Social Control of Homicide in Modern America. Unpublished doctoral dissertation, Department of Sociology, University of Virginia, Charlottesville.

—— 1997 "The decline of elite homicide." *Criminology* 35: 381–407.

—— 1998 *Warriors and Peacemakers: How Third Parties Shape Violence*. New York: New York University Press.

—— 2008 "Cultural conflict in contemporary Ireland." Unpublished version of M. Cooney 2009a.

—— 2009a "Ethnic conflict without ethnic groups: a study in pure sociology." *British Journal of Sociology* 60: 473–492.

—— 2009b *Is Killing Wrong? A Study in Pure Sociology*. Charlottesville: University of Virginia Press.

Correll, Dee Dee 2009 "Colorado transgender woman's slaying tried as hate crime." *Los Angeles Times*. Online (April 19): http://articles.latimes.com/2009/apr/19/nation/na-transgender19.

Coser, Lewis 1956 *The Functions of Social Conflict*. New York: Free Press.

Courchesne, Shawn 2006 "Rule tackles blowouts in high school football." *Hartford Courant*. Online (May 25): http://www.courant.com/news/local/hc-srule0525.artmay25,0,6520354.story?coll=hc-headlines-local.

Coveney, Peter, and Roger Highfield 1990 *The Arrow of Time: A Voyage Through Science to Solve Time's Greatest Mystery*. New York: Fawcett Columbine.

Crawford, J. R. 1967 *Witchcraft and Sorcery in Rhodesia*. London: Oxford University Press.

Cressey, Donald R. 1953 *Other People's Money: A Study in the Social Psychology of Embezzlement*. Glencoe, IL: Free Press.

Crick, Francis 1988 *What Mad Pursuit: A Personal View of Scientific Discovery*. New York: Basic Books.

Dahrendorf, Ralf 1956 "Toward a theory of social conflict." *Journal of Conflict Resolution* 2: 170–183.

—— 1959 *Class and Class Conflict in Industrial Society*. Stanford, CA: Stanford University Press (revised edition; first edition, 1957).

—— 1968 "On the origin of inequality among men." Pages 151–178 in *Essays in the Theory of Society*. Stanford, CA: Stanford University Press.

Dalí, Salvador 1942 *The Secret Life of Salvador Dalí*. New York: Dover, 1993.

—— 1964 *Diary of a Genius*. New York: Prentice Hall, 1986.

Daly, Martin, and Margo Wilson 1988 *Homicide*. New York: Aldine de Gruyter.

Damon, Arwa 2008 "Violations of 'Islamic teachings' take deadly toll on Iraqi women." *CNN*. Online (February 8): http://www.cnn.com/2008/WORLD/meast/02/08/iraq.women/.

Darwin, Charles 1887 *The Autobiography of Charles Darwin: 1809–1882*, edited by Nora Barlow. New York: W. W. Norton, 1958.

Davidson, Nicolas 1987 "The Inquisition and the Italian Jews." Pages 19–46 in Haliczer 1987b.

Davies, James E. 1962 "Toward a theory of revolution." *American Sociological Review* 27: 5–19.

Davis, Joseph E. 2010 After Psychology: Self and Suffering in the Age of Prozac. Unpublished book manuscript, Department of Sociology, University of Virginia, Charlottesville.

Davis, L. J. 1997 "The encyclopedia of insanity: a psychiatric handbook lists a madness for everyone." *Harper's Magazine* (February): 61–66.

Davis, Robert 1993 "Tragic trend played out at two sites." *USA Today* (May 7–9): 1A–2A.

de Grazia, Edward 1992 *Girls Lean Back Everywhere: The Law of Obscenity and the Assault on Genius*. New York: Random House.

de Grazia, Edward, and Roger K. Newman 1982 *Banned Films: Movies, Censors and the First Amendment*. New York: Bowker.

D'Emilio, John, and Estelle B. Freedman 1988 *Intimate Matters: A History of Sexuality in America*. New York: Harper & Row.

Demos, John 1982 *Entertaining Satan: Witchcraft and the Culture of Early New England*. New York: Oxford University Press.

—— 1994 *The Unredeemed Captive: A Family Story from Early America*. New York: Alfred A. Knopf.

Dentan, Robert Knox 1968 *The Semei: A Nonviolent People of Malaya*. New York: Holt, Rinehart & Winston.

Denton-Edmundson, Matthew 2009 "Students, officials respond to bias-motivated assault." *Cavalier Daily*. Online (April 14): http://www.cavalierdaily.com/news/2009/apr/14/students-officials-respond-to-bias-motivated-assau/.

Desmond, Adrian, and James Moore 1991 *Darwin*. New York: Warner, 1992.

de Ste. Croix, G. E. M. 1954 "Aspects of the Great Persecution." *Harvard Theological Review* 47: 75–113.

—— 1963 "Why were the Christians persecuted?" *Past & Present* 26: 6–38.

de Tocqueville, Alexis 1856 *The Old Regime and the French Revolution*. Garden City, NY: Anchor, 1955.

Devlin, Patrick 1965 *The Enforcement of Morals*. London: Oxford University Press.

Diamond, Jared 1993 "New Guineans and their natural world." Pages 251–271 in *The Biophilia Hypothesis*, edited by Stephen R. Kellert and Edward O. Wilson. Washington, DC: Island.

Dick, Philip K. 1964 "Drugs, hallucinations, and the quest for reality." Pages 167–174 in *The Shifting Realities of Philip K. Dick: Selected Literary and Philosophical Writings*, edited by Lawrence Sutin. New York: Vintage, 1995.

Dionisopoulos-Mass, Regina 1976 "The evil eye and bewitchment in a peasant village." Pages 42–62 in Maloney 1976b.

Di Stasi, Lawrence 1981 *Mal Occhio (Evil Eye): The Underside of Vision*. San Francisco: North Point.

Dixon, Laura 2009 "Protocol is abandoned as Michelle Obama cosies up to Queen." *Times of London*. Online (April 2): http://www.timesonline.co.uk/tol/news/politics/G20/article6018322.ece.

Dollard, John 1939 "The dozens: dialectic of insult." *American Imago* 1: 3–25.

—— 1957 *Caste and Class in a Southern Town*. Garden City, NY: Doubleday Anchor (third edition; first edition, 1937).

Donaldson, Bess Allen 1938 "The evil eye in Iran." Pages 66–77 in Dundes 1981a.

Dorell, Oren 2009 "'Honor killings' in USA raise concerns." *USA Today*. Online (November 30): http://www.usatoday.com/news/nation/2009-11-29-honor-killings-in-the-US_N.htm.

Dorr, Lisa Lindquist 2004 *White Women, Rape, and the Power of Race in Virginia, 1900–1960*. Chapel Hill: University of North Carolina Press.

Dorsman, Pieter 2006 "Hirsi Ali's fall." *Peaktalk: Politics and Markets*. Online (May 15): http://www.peaktalk.com/archives/002210.php.

Douglas, Jack D. 1967 *The Social Meanings of Suicide*. Princeton, NJ: Princeton University Press.

Douglas, Mary 1966 *Purity and Danger: An Analysis of Concepts of Pollution and Taboo*. London: Routledge & Kegan Paul.

—— 1970a "Thirty years after *Witchcraft, Oracles and Magic*." Pages xiii–xxxviii in M. Douglas 1970b.

—— (editor) 1970b *Witchcraft Confessions and Accusations*. London: Tavistock.

Dover, K. J. 1989 *Greek Homosexuality*. Cambridge, MA: Harvard University Press (revised edition; first edition, 1978).

Doyle, Bertram Wilbur 1937 *The Etiquette of Race Relations in the South: A Study in Social Control*. Chicago: University of Chicago Press.

Drew, Katherine Fischer (editor) 1949 *The Burgundian Code: Book of Constitutions or Law of Gundobad*. Philadelphia: University of Pennsylvania Press.

—— 1973 *The Lombard Laws*. Philadelphia: University of Pennsylvania Press.

—— 1991 *The Laws of the Salian Franks*. Philadelphia: University of Pennsylvania Press.

Driggs, Ken 1989 "'There is no law in Georgia for Mormons': the Joseph Standing murder case of 1879." *Georgia Historical Quarterly* 73: 745–772.

Dublin, Louis I., and Bessie Bunzel 1933 *To Be or Not to Be: A Study of Suicide*. New York: Harrison Smith & Robert Haas.

du Boulay, Juliet 1974 *Portrait of a Greek Mountain Village*. Oxford: Oxford University Press.

Duker, Abraham G. 1980 "Twentieth-century blood libels in the United States." Pages 233–260 in Dundes 1991.

Dumont, Louis 1980 *Homo Hierarchicus: The Caste System and Its Implications*. Chicago: University of Chicago Press (revised English edition; first published 1966).

Dundes, Alan (editor) 1981a *The Evil Eye: A Casebook*. Madison: University of Wisconsin Press, 1992.

——1981b "Wet and dry, the evil eye: an essay in Indo-European and Semitic worldview." Pages 257–312 in Dundes 1981a.

—— 1989 "The ritual murder or blood libel legend: a study of anti-Semitic victimization through projective inversion." Pages 336–376 in Dundes 1991.

——(editor) 1991 *The Blood Libel Legend: A Casebook in Anti-Semitic Folklore*. Madison: University of Wisconsin Press.

Durkheim, Émile 1893 *The Division of Labor in Society*. New York: Free Press, 1964.

——1895 *The Rules of Sociological Method*. New York: Free Press, 1964.

——1897a *Incest: The Nature and Origin of the Taboo*. New York: Lyle Stuart, 1963.

——1897b *Suicide: A Study in Sociology*. New York: Free Press, 1951.

——1906 "The determination of moral facts." Pages 35–62 in *Sociology and Philosophy*. Glencoe, IL: Free Press, 1953.

——1912 *The Elementary Forms of Religious Life*. New York: Free Press, 1995.

——1925 *Moral Education: A Study in the Theory and Application of the Sociology of Education*. New York: Free Press, 1961.

Duvignaud, Jean 1968 *Change at Shebika: Report from a North African Village*. New York: Pantheon, 1970.

Eccles, W. J. 1969 *The Canadian Frontier, 1534–1760*. New York: Holt, Rinehart, & Winston.

Eder, Donna 1991 "The structure of gossip: opportunities and constraints on collective expression among adolescents." *American Sociological Review* 56: 494–508.

Edgerton, Robert B. 1989 *Mau Mau: An African Crucible*. New York: Ballantine.

Eggen, Torgrim 1998 "The Odd one." Interview with Odd Nerdrum. *The Egg-Files*. Online: http://www.torgrimeggen.no/Reportasje/nerdrum.htm.

Einwohner, Rachel L. 2003 "Opportunity, honor, and action in the Warsaw Ghetto Uprising of 1943." *American Journal of Sociology* 109: 650–675.

Ejidike, Okey Martin 1999 "Human rights in the cultural traditions and social practice of the Igbo of south-eastern Nigeria." *Journal of African Law* 43: 71–98.

Ekvall, Robert B. 1968 *Fields on the Hoof: Nexus of Tibetan Nomadic Pastoralism*. New York: Holt, Rinehart & Winston.

Elias, Norbert 1939a *The Civilizing Process: The Development of Manners*. New York: Urizen, 1978.

—— 1939b *Power and Civility: The Civilizing Process*. New York: Pantheon, 1982.

—— 1969 *The Court Society*. New York: Pantheon, 1983.

—— 1987 *Time: An Essay*. Oxford, England: Blackwell, 1992.

—— 1991 *Mozart: Portrait of a Genius*. Berkeley: University of California Press, 1993.

Elison, George 1973 *Deus Destroyed: The Image of Christianity in Early Modern Japan*. Cambridge, MA: Harvard University Press.

Ellenzweig, Allen 1992 *The Homoerotic Photograph: Male Images from Durieu/Delacroix to Mapplethorpe*. New York: Columbia University Press.

Ellis, Albert 1963 "The origins and development of the incest taboo." Pages 121–174 in English translation of Durkheim 1897a.

Elon, Amos 2002 *The Pity of It All: A Portrait of the German-Jewish Epoch, 1743–1933*. New York: Metropolitan.

Emerson, Robert M. 2008 "Responding to roommate troubles: reconsidering informal dyadic control." *Law and Society Review* 42: 483–512.

Emmons, George Thornton 1991 *The Tlingit Indians*, edited with additions by Frederica de Laguna. Seattle: University of Washington Press (original manuscript completed in 1927).

Encyclopaedia Judaica 2008 "Blood libel." Reprinted in *Jewish Virtual Library*. Online: http://www.jewishvirtuallibrary.org/jsource/judaica/ejud_0002_0003_0_03147.html.

Engel, David M. 1978 *Code and Custom in a Thai Provincial Court: The Interaction of Formal and Informal Systems of Justice*. Tucson: University of Arizona Press.

—— 1984 "The oven bird's song: insiders, outsiders, and personal injuries in an American community." *Law and Society Review* 18: 551–582.

Engels, Friedrich 1891 *The Origin of the Family, Private Property, and the State: In the Light of the Researches of Lewis H. Morgan*. New York: International Publishers, 1942 (fourth edition; first edition, 1884).

Epstein, Joseph M. 1948 *Sex Laws and Customs in Judaism*. New York: Bloch.

Erikson, Kai. T. 1966 *Wayward Puritans: A Study in the Sociology of Deviance*. New York: John Wiley.

Estrich, Susan 1987 *Real Rape*. Cambridge, MA: Harvard University Press.

European Network for Indigenous Australian Rights 2009 "The stolen generations." ENIAR.org. Online: http://www.eniar.org/stolengenerations.html.

Evans-Pritchard, E. E. 1937 *Witchcraft, Oracles and Magic among the Azande*. Oxford: Oxford University Press.

—— 1940 *The Nuer: A Description of the Modes of Livelihood and Political Institutions of a Nilotic People*. London: Oxford University Press.

—— 1956 *Nuer Religion*. Oxford, England: Clarendon.

Ewing, J. Franklin 1955 "*Juramentado*: institutionalized suicide among the Moros of the Philippines." *Anthropological Quarterly* 28: 148–155.

Eysenck, H. J. 1995 *Genius: The Natural History of Creativity*. Cambridge: Cambridge University Press.

Fallers, Lloyd A. 1969 *Law without Precedent: Legal Ideas in Action in the Courts of Colonial Busoga*. Chicago: University of Chicago Press.

Faludi, Susan 1999 "Ghetto star: 'Monster' Kody Scott and the culture of ornament." *LA Weekly*. Online (October 6): http://www.laweekly.com/news/news/ghetto-star/6277/?page=1.

Farber, Leslie H. 1966 "Schizophrenia and the mad psychotherapist." Pages 89–118 in *R. D. Laing and Anti-Psychiatry*, edited by Robert Boyers. New York: Harper & Row, 1971.

Farley, Maggie 2008 "Canada to apologize for abuse of Native students." *Los Angeles Times*. Online (June 10): http://articles.latimes.com/2008/jun/10/world/fg-apology10.

Farson, Daniel 1993 *The Gilded Gutter Life of Francis Bacon.* New York: Pantheon.

Favret-Saada, Jeanne 1977 *Deadly Words: Witchcraft in the Bocage.* Cambridge. Cambridge University Press, 1980.

Feldman, Noah 2007 "Orthodox paradox." *New York Times.* Online (July 22): http://www.nytimes.com/2007/07/22/magazine/22yeshiva-t.html?pagewanted=1&ei=5087%0A&em&en=4f9d372ba8aa7e8a&ex=1185336000.

Feuer, Lewis S. 1982 *Einstein and the Generations of Science.* New Brunswick, NJ: Transaction (second edition; first published 1974).

Field, M. J. 1960 *Search for Security: An Ethno-Psychiatric Study of Rural Ghana.* New York: W. W. Norton.

Finkelhor, David, and Kersti Yllo 1982 "Forced sex in marriage: a preliminary report." *Crime and Delinquency* 34: 459–.478

Fletcher, Connie 1991 *What Cops Know: Cops Talk about What They Do, How They Do It, and What It Does to Them.* New York: Villard.

Fölsing, Albrecht 1997 *Albert Einstein: A Biography.* New York: Viking.

Fordham, Signithia, and John U. Ogbu 1986 "Black students' school success: coping with the burden of 'acting white.'" *Urban Review* 18: 176–206.

Foucault, Michel 1961 *Madness and Civilization: A History of Insanity in the Age of Reason.* New York: Pantheon, 1965.

——— 1975 *Discipline and Punish: The Birth of the Prison.* New York: Pantheon, 1977.

——— 1983 "The minimalist self." Pages 3–16 in *Politics, Philosophy, Culture: Interviews and Other Writings, 1977–1984,* edited by Lawrence D. Kritzman. New York: Routledge, 1988.

——— 2003 *Abnormal: Lectures at the Collége de France, 1974–1975.* New York: Picador.

Fox News 2007 "Nebraska mall shooter broke up with girlfriend, lost job before massacre." Online (December 6): http://www.foxnews.com/story/0,2933,315441,00.html.

——— 2008a "Teen shot in junior high classroom taken off life support; classmate charged." Online (February 16): http://www.foxnews.com/story/0,2933,330866,00.html.

—— 2008b "Report: Non-Muslims deserve to be punished." Online (April 1): http://www.foxnews.com/story/0,2933,344409,00.html.

—— 2008c "Lesbian's 'extreme' gang rape investigated in California." Online (December 23): http://www.foxnews.com/story/0,2933,471308,00.html.

—— 2009 "Woman says husband killed 5 children to punish her." Online (April 6): http://www.foxnews.com/story/0,2933,512875,00.html.

—— 2010 "Gay couple convicted in Malawi, face 13-year jail term in case sparking global criticism." Online (May 18): http://www.foxnews.com/world/2010/05/18/malawi-judge-finds-gay-couple-guilty-unnatural-acts-gross-indecency-286954383/.

Frank, Philipp 1947 *Einstein: His Life and Times*. New York: Alfred A. Knopf.

Frank, Tibor 2009 *Double Exile: Migrations of Jewish-Hungarian Professionals Through Germany to the United States, 1919–1945*. Bern, Switzerland: Peter Lang.

Frankena, William F. 1963 *Ethics*. Englewood Cliffs, NJ: Prentice-Hall.

Frayser, Suzanne G. 1985 *Varieties of Sexual Experience: An Anthropological Perspective on Human Sexuality*. New Haven, CT: HRAF.

Frazer, James G. 1890 *The Golden Bough: A Study in Comparative Religion*. New York: Avenel, 1981. Two volumes.

Fried, Jacob 1953 "The relation of ideal norms to actual behavior in Tarahumara society." *Southwestern Journal of Anthropology* 9: 286–295.

Fry, Douglas P. 2006 *The Human Potential for Peace: An Anthropological Challenge to Assumptions about War and Violence*. New York: Oxford University Press.

Fryer, Roland G. 2006 "Acting white." *Education Next* 6. Online: http://educationnext.org/actingwhite/.

Fuchs, Stephan 2001 *Against Essentialism: A Theory of Culture and Society*. Cambridge, MA: Harvard University Press.

Fuller, Lon L. 1964 *The Morality of Law*. New Haven, CT: Yale University Press.

Fussell, Paul 1983 *Class: A Guide Through the American Status System*. New York: Simon & Shuster.

Gagarin, Michael 1986 *Early Greek Law*. Berkeley: University of California Press.

Garfinkel, Harold 1956 "Conditions of successful degradation ceremonies." *American Journal of Sociology* 61: 420–424.

—— 1967 *Studies in Ethnomethodology*. Englewood Cliffs, NJ: Prentice-Hall.

Garrison, Vivian, and Conrad M. Arensberg 1976 "The evil eye: envy or risk or seizure? paranoia or patronal dependency?" Pages 286–328 in Maloney 1976b.

Geertz, Clifford 1975 "Common sense as a cultural system." *Antioch Review* 33: 5–26.

Gelfand, Michael 1964 *Witch Doctor: Traditional Medicine Man of Rhodesia*. London: Harvill.

Gernet, Jacques 1982 *China and the Christian Impact: A Conflict of Cultures*. Cambridge: Cambridge University Press, 1985.

Gibson, Thomas P. 1986 *Sacrifice and Sharing in the Philippine Highlands: Religion and Society among the Buid of Mindoro*. London: Athlone.

—— 1989 "Symbolic representations of tranquility and aggression among the Buid." Pages 60–78 in Howell and Willis 1989.

Gilje, Paul A. 1987 *The Road to Mobocracy: Popular Disorder in New York City, 1763–1834*. Chapel Hill: University of North Carolina Press.

Gillin, John 1934 "Crime and punishment among the Barama River Carib of British Guiana." *American Anthropologist* 36: 331–344.

Gilmartin, Christina 1990 "Violence against women in contemporary China." Pages 203–221 in Lipman and Harrell 1990.

Gilmore, David D. 1987a *Aggression and Community: Paradoxes of Andalusian Culture*. New Haven, CT: Yale University Press.

—— (editor) 1987b *Honor and Shame and the Unity of the Mediterranean*. Special publication of the American Anthropological Association, Number 22. Washington, DC: American Anthropological Association.

—— 1987c "Introduction: the shame of dishonor." Pages 2–21 in Gilmore 1987b.

Gilot, Françoise, and Carlton Lake 1964 *Life with Picasso*. New York: McGraw-Hill.

Ginat, Joseph 1987 *Blood Disputes among Bedouin and Rural Arabs in Israel: Revenge, Mediation, Outcasting and Family Honor*. Pittsburgh: University of Pittsburgh Press (in cooperation with the Jerusalem Institute for Israel Studies).

Ginnell, Laurence 1894 *The Brehon Laws: A Legal Handbook*. London: T. Fisher Unwin.

Girard, René 1972 *Violence and the Sacred*. Baltimore, MD: Johns Hopkins University Press, 1977.

—— 1986 *The Scapegoat*. Baltimore, MD: Johns Hopkins University Press.

—— 1987 "Generative scapegoating." Pages 73–105 in *Violent Origins: Ritual Killing and Cultural Formation*, edited by Robert G. Hamerton-Kelly. Stanford, CA: Stanford University Press.

Gluckman, Max 1963 "Gossip and scandal." *Current Anthropology* 4: 307–316.

—— 1965 *Politics, Law and Ritual in Tribal Society*. New York: New American Library.

—— (editor) 1972a *The Allocation of Responsibility*. Manchester: Manchester University Press.

—— 1972b "Moral crises: magical and secular solutions." Pages 1–50 in Gluckman 1972a.

Godard, Ellis 2003 "Reel life: the social geometry of reality shows." Pages 73–96 in *Survivor Lessons: Essays on Communication and Reality Television*, edited by Matthew J. Smith and Andrew F. Wood. Jefferson, NC: McFarland.

—— 2005 The Moral Order of Cyberspace: Social Structure and Conflict Management on the Internet. Unpublished doctoral dissertation, Department of Sociology, University of Virginia, Charlottesville.

Goffman, Erving 1956 "The nature of deference and demeanor." *American Anthropologist* 58: 473–502.

—— 1957 "Alienation from interaction." Pages 113–136 in Goffman 1967a.

—— 1959 *The Presentation of Self in Everyday Life*. Garden City, NY: Anchor.

—— 1961 *Asylums: Essays on the Social Situation of Mental Patients and Other Inmates*. Garden City, NY: Anchor.

—— 1963a *Behavior in Public Places: Notes on the Social Organization of Gatherings*. New York: Free Press.

—— 1963b *Stigma: Notes on the Management of Spoiled Identity*. Englewood Cliffs, NJ: Prentice-Hall.

—— 1964 "Mental symptoms and public order." Pages 137–148 in Goffman 1967a.

—— 1967a *Interaction Ritual: Essays on Face-to-Face Behavior*. Garden City, NY: Anchor.

—— 1967b "Where the action is." Pages 149–270 in Goffman 1967a.

—— 1969a "Expression games: an analysis of doubts at play." Pages 1–103 in *Strategic Interaction*. New York: Ballantine.

—— 1969b "The insanity of place." Pages 335–390 in Goffman 1971.

—— 1971 *Relations in Public: Microstudies of the Public Order*. New York: Basic Books.

Golczewski, Frank 1986 "Rural anti-Semitism in Galicia before World War I." Pages 97–105 in Abramsky, Jachimczyk, and Polonsky 1986.

Goldhagen, Daniel Jonah 1996 *Hitler's Willing Executioners: Ordinary Germans and the Holocaust*. New York: Vintage, 1997.

Golding, John 1998 "Simply himself." *New York Review of Books* 45 (May 14): 8–13.

Good, Kenneth (with David Chanoff) 1991 *Into the Heart: One Man's Pursuit of Love and Knowledge among the Yanomama*. New York: Simon & Schuster.

Goode, William J. 1963 *World Revolution and Family Patterns*. New York: Free Press.

Gorn, Elliott J. 1985 "'Gouge and bite, pull hair and scratch': the social significance of fighting in the Southern backcountry." *American Historical Review* 90: 18–43.

Gottfredson, Michael R., and Michael J. Hindelang 1979 "A study of *The Behavior of Law*." *American Sociological Review* 44: 3–18.

Gough, E. Kathleen 1960 "Caste in a Tanjore village." Pages 11–60 in *Aspects of Caste in South India, Ceylon and North-West Pakistan*, edited by E. R. Leach. Cambridge: Cambridge University Press, 1971 (first published 1960).

Gould, Roger V. 2003 *Collision of Wills: How Ambiguity about Social Rank Breeds Conflict*. Chicago: University of Chicago Press.

Gould, Stephen Jay 1987 *Time's Arrow, Time's Cycle: Myth and Metaphor in the Discovery of Geological Time*. Cambridge, MA: Harvard University Press.

Gouldner, Alvin W. 1960 "The norm of reciprocity: a preliminary statement." *American Sociological Review* 25: 161–178.

Granovetter, Mark S. 1973 "The strength of weak ties." *American Journal of Sociology* 78: 1360–1380.

Gray, Charles Edward 1972 "Paradoxes in Western creativity." *American Anthropologist* 74: 676–688.

Greenberg, David F. 1988 *The Construction of Homosexuality*. Chicago: University of Chicago Press.

Greenberg, Kenneth S. 1996 *Honor and Slavery: Lies, Duels, Noses, Masks, Dressing as a Woman, Gifts, Strangers, Death, Humanitarianism, Slave Rebellions, the Pro-Slavery Argument, Baseball, Hunting, and Gambling in the Old South*. Princeton, NJ: Princeton University Press.

Greene, Brian 1999 *The Elegant Universe: Superstrings, Hidden Dimensions, and the Quest for the Ultimate Theory*. New York: W. W. Norton.

Gregor, Thomas 1977 *Mehinaku: The Drama of Daily Life in a Brazilian Indian Village*. Chicago: University of Chicago Press.

———— 1985 *Anxious Pleasures: The Sexual Lives of an Amazonian People*. Chicago: University of Chicago Press.

———— 1990 "Uneasy peace: intertribal relations in Brazil's Upper Xingu." Pages 105–124 in Haas 1990.

Grimes, William 2009 "Arne Naess, Norwegian philosopher, dies at 96." *New York Times*. Online (January 14): http://www.nytimes.com/2009/01/15/world/europe/15naess.html.

Grimshaw, Allen D. 1962 "Factors contributing to color violence in the United States and Great Britain." Pages 254–269 in *Racial Violence in the United States*, edited by Allen D. Grimshaw. Chicago: Aldine, 1969.

Gross, Jan T. 2001 *Neighbors: The Destruction of the Jewish Community in Jebwadne, Poland*. Princeton, NJ: Princeton University Press.

Gross, Samuel, and Robert Mauro 1984 "Patterns of death: an analysis of racial disparities in capital sentencing and homicide victimization." *Stanford Law Review* 37: 27–153.

Gruber, Howard E. 1981 *Darwin on Man: A Psychological Study of Scientific Creativity*. Chicago: University of Chicago Press (second edition; first edition, 1974).

Grunfeld, Frederic V. 1979 *Prophets without Honour: Freud, Kafka, Einstein, and Their World*. New York: Kodansha International, 1996.

Gurr, Ted Robert 1970 *Why Men Rebel*. Princeton, NJ: Princeton University Press.

Gurvitch, Georges 1964 *The Spectrum of Social Time*. Dordrecht, Netherlands: Reidel.

Haas, Jonathan (editor) 1990 *The Anthropology of War*. New York: Cambridge University Press.

Hagan, William T. 1966 *Indian Police and Judges: Experiments in Acculturation and Control*. New Haven, CT: Yale University Press.

Haglunds, Magnus 2009 *Enemies of the People: Whistle-Blowing and the Sociology of Tragedy*. Stockholm: Acta Universitatis Stockholmiensis.

Haliczer, Stephen 1987a "The first holocaust: the Inquisition and the converted Jews of Spain and Portugal." Pages 7–18 in Halicer 1987b.

—— (editor) 1987b *Inquisition and Society in Early Modern Europe*. Totowa, NJ: Barnes & Noble.

Hall, Edward T. 1966 *The Hidden Dimension*. Garden City, NY: Anchor.

Hall, Jerome 1952 *Theft, Law, and Society*. Indianapolis, IN: Bobbs-Merrill (second edition; first edition, 1935).

Hall, Lesley, A. 1992 "Forbidden by God, despised by men: masturbation, medical warnings, moral panic, and manhood in Great Britain, 1850–1950." *Journal of the History of Sexuality* 2: 365–387.

Hallowell, A. Irving 1963 "American Indians, white and black: the phenomenon of transculturation." *Current Anthropology* 4: 519–531.

Hallpike, C. R. 1977 *Bloodshed and Vengeance in the Papuan Mountains: The Generation of Conflict in Tauade Society*. Oxford: Oxford University Press.

Hamilton, Annette 1981 "A complex strategical situation: gender and power in Aboriginal Australia." Pages 69–85 in *Australian Women: Feminist Perspectives*, edited by Norma Grieve and Patricia Grimshaw. Melbourne: Oxford University Press.

Hanawalt, Barbara A. 1979 *Crime and Conflict in English Communities: 1300–1348*. Cambridge, MA: Harvard University Press.

Hane, Mikiso 1982 *Peasants, Rebels and Outcastes: The Underside of Modern Japan*. New York: Pantheon.

Hare, E. H. 1962 "Masturbatory insanity: the history of an idea." *Journal of Mental Science* 108: 1–25.

Harfouche, Jamal Karam 1965 "The evil eye and infant health in Lebanon." Pages 86–106 in Dundes 1981a.

Harner, Michael J. 1972 *The Jívaro: People of the Sacred Waterfalls*. Garden City, NY: Anchor, 1973.

—— 1973a "Common themes in South American Indian yagé experiences." Pages 155–175 in Harner 1973b.

—— (editor) 1973b *Hallucinogens and Shamanism*. London: Oxford University Press.

Harper, Edward B. 1964 "Ritual pollution as an integrator of caste and religion." *Journal of Asian Studies* 23: 151–197.

Harper, Robert Francis (translator) 1904 *The Code of Hammurabi, King of Babylon: About 2250*. Chicago: University of Chicago Press.

Harrison, Frances 2007 "Iran ban on 'Western' hairstyles." *BBC News*. Online (April 29): http://news.bbc.co.uk/2/hi/middle_east/6605487.stm.

Hart, H. L. A. 1963 *Law, Liberty, and Morality*. Stanford, CA: Stanford University Press.

Haskins, George Lee 1960 *Law and Authority in Early Massachusetts: A Study in Tradition and Design*. Hamden, CT: Archon, 1968.

Hasluck, Margaret 1954 *The Unwritten Law of Albania*. Cambridge: Cambridge University Press.

Hay, Douglas 1975 "Poaching and the game laws on Cannock Chase." Pages 189–253 in *Albion's Fatal Tree: Crime and Society in Eighteenth-Century England*, edited by Douglas Hay, Peter Linebaugh, John G. Rule, E. P. Thompson, and Cal Winslow. New York: Pantheon.

Hayden, Tom 1967 *Rebellion in Newark: Official Violence and Ghetto Response*. New York: Random House.

Heard, J. Norman 1973 *White into Red: A Study of the Assimilation of White Persons Captured by Indians*. Metuchen, NJ: Scarecrow.

Heidegger, Martin 1952 *Being and Time: A Translation of* "Sein und Zeit." Albany: State University of New York Press, 1996 (seventh edition; first edition, 1927).

Heisenberg, Werner 1974 *Across the Frontiers*. Woodbridge, CT: Ox Bow, 1990.

Hekma, Gert 1991 "Homosexual behavior in the nineteenth-century Dutch army." *Journal of the History of Sexuality* 2: 266–288.

Held, David, and Anthony McGrew (editors) 2003 *The Global Transformations Reader: An Introduction to the Globalization Debate*. Cambridge, England: Polity (second edition; first edition, 2000).

Heller, Sarah-Grace 2004 "Anxiety, hierarchy, and appearance in thirteenth-century sumptuary laws and the *Roman de la rose*." *French Historical Studies* 27: 311–348.

Henry, Andrew F., and James F. Short, Jr. 1954 *Suicide and Homicide: Some Economic, Sociological and Psychological Aspects of Aggression*. Glencoe, IL: Free Press.

Hepworth, Mike, and Bryan S. Turner 1982a *Confession: Studies in Deviance and Religion*. London: Routledge & Kegan Paul.

———— 1982b "Introduction." Pages 1–15 in Hepworth and Turner 1982a.

———— 1982c "On the universality of confession: compulsion, constraint and conscience." Pages 66–84 in Hepworth and Turner 1982a.

Herdt, Gilbert H. 1981 *Guardians of the Flutes: Idioms of Masculinity*. New York: Columbia University Press.

———— 1984a "Ritualized homosexual behavior in the male cults of Melanesia, 1862–1983: an introduction." Pages 1–81 in Herdt 1984b.

———— (editor) 1984b *Ritualized Homosexuality in Melanesia*. Berkeley: University of California Press.

———— 1984c "Semen transactions in Sambia culture." Pages 167–210 in Herdt 1984b.

Herdt, Gilbert, and Robert J. Stoller 1990 *Intimate Communications: Erotics and the Study of Culture*. New York: Columbia University Press.

Herf, Jeffrey 2005 "The 'Jewish war': Goebbels and the anti-Semitic campaign of the Nazi propaganda ministry." *Holocaust and Genocide Studies* 19: 51–80.

——— 2006 *The Jewish Enemy: Nazi Propaganda during World War II and the Holocaust.* Cambridge, MA: Harvard University Press.

Herman, Judith Lewis (with Lisa Hirschman) 1981 *Father-Daughter Incest.* Cambridge, MA: Harvard University Press.

Herzfeld, Michael 1980 "Honour and shame: problems in the comparative analysis of moral systems." *Man* 15: 339–351.

Hiatt, L. R. 1965 *Kinship and Conflict: A Study of an Aboriginal Community in Northern Arnhem Land.* Canberra: Australian National University.

——— 1966 "A spear in the ear." *Oceania* 37: 153–154.

Hilberg, Raul 1985 *The Destruction of the European Jews.* New York: Holmes & Meier (revised and definitive edition; first edition, 1961). Three volumes.

Hinckeldey, Christoph (editor) 1980a *Criminal Justice Through the Ages: From Divine Judgment to Modern German Legislation.* Rothenburg, Germany: Mittelalterliches Criminalmuseum, 1981.

——— 1980b "History of crime and punishment." Pages 99–173 in Hinckeldey 1980a.

Hirschi, Travis 1969 *Causes of Delinquency.* Berkeley: University of California Press.

Hirschman, Albert O. 1970 *Exit, Voice, and Loyalty: Responses to Decline in Firms, Organizations, and States.* Cambridge, MA: Harvard University Press.

Hitler, Adolf 1925 *Mein Kampf.* Volume 1: *A Reckoning.* Boston: Houghton Mifflin, 1971.

——— 1926 *Mein Kampf.* Volume 2: *The National Socialist Movement.* Boston: Houghton Mifflin, 1971.

Hobhouse, Janet 1988 *The Bride Stripped Bare: The Artist and the Female Nude in the Twentieth Century.* New York: Weidenfeld & Nicolson.

Hobsbawm, E. J. 1959 *Primitive Rebels: Studies in Archaic Forms of Social Movement in the 19th and 20th Centuries.* New York: W. W. Norton, 1965.

Hoebel, E. Adamson 1940 *The Political Organization and Law-Ways of the Comanche Indians.* Memoirs of the American Anthropological Association, Number 54. Menasha, WI: American Anthropological Association.

———1954 *The Law of Primitive Man: A Study in Comparative Legal Dynamics*. Cambridge, MA: Harvard University Press, 1967.

——— 1969 "Keresan Pueblo law." Pages 92–116 in *Law in Culture and Society*, edited by Laura Nader. Chicago: Aldine.

Hoffmann, Banesh (with the collaboration of Helen Dukas) 1972 *Albert Einstein: Creator and Rebel*. New York: New American Library, 1973.

Hohfeld, Wesley Newcomb 1919 *Fundamental Legal Conceptions as Applied in Judicial Reasoning*, edited by Walter Wheeler Cook. New Haven, CT: Yale University Press.

Holmstrom, Lynda Lytle, and Ann Wolbert Burgess 1983 *The Victim of Rape: Institutional Reactions*. New Brunswick, NJ: Transaction (second edition; first edition, 1978).

Hoog, Michel 1989 *Cézanne: Father of 20th-Century Art*. New York: Harry N. Abrams, 1994.

Horwitz, Allan V. 1982 *The Social Control of Mental Illness*. New York: Academic Press.

——— 1984 "Therapy and social solidarity." Pages 211–250 in Black 1984c.

——— 2002 *Creating Mental Illness*. Chicago: University of Chicago Press.

Hosaka, Tomoko A. 2009 "For suicidal Japanese, help is finally at hand." *Yahoo!* Online (December 18): http://finance.yahoo.com/news/For-suicidal-Japanese-help-is-apf-4012329105.html?x=0&sec=topStories&pos=7&asset=&;ccode=.

Howard, Michael 1983 *The Causes of Wars*. Cambridge, MA: Harvard University Press.

Howell, Signe 1989 "'To be angry is not to be human, but to be fearful is': Chewong concepts of human nature." Pages 45–59 in Howell and Willis 1989.

Howell, Signe, and Roy Willis (editors) 1989 *Societies at Peace: Anthropological Perspectives*. London: Routledge.

Howkins, Alun 1979 "Economic crime and class law: poaching and the game laws, 1840–1880." Pages 273–287 in *The Imposition of Law*, edited by Sandra B. Burman and Barbara E. Harrell-Bond. New York: Academic Press.

Hubert, Henri 1905 *Essay on Time: A Brief Study of the Representation of Time in Religion and Magic*. Oxford, England: Durkheim Press, 1999.

Huffington, Arianna Stassinopoulos 1988 *Picasso: Creator and Destroyer*. New York: Avon, 1989.

Hughes, Diane Owen 1983 "Sumptuary laws and social relations in Renaissance Italy." Pages 69–99 in *Disputes and Settlements: Law and Human Relations in the West*, edited by John Bossy. Cambridge: Cambridge University Press.

Hughes, Geoffrey 1991 *Swearing: A Social History of Foul Language, Oaths and Profanity in English*. Oxford, England: Blackwell.

Hughes, Robert 1991 *The Shock of the New*. New York: Alfred A. Knopf.

Hume, David 1739 *A Treatise of Human Nature: Being an Attempt to Introduce the Experimental Method of Reasoning into Moral Subjects*. Garden City, NY: Dolphin, 1961.

Humphreys, Laud 1970 *Tearoom Trade: Impersonal Sex in Public Places*. Chicago: Aldine.

Hunt, Alan 1996 *Governance of the Consuming Passions: A History of Sumptuary Law*. New York: St. Martin's.

Hunter, James Davison 1991 *Culture Wars: The Struggle to Define America*. New York: Basic Books.

———— 1994 *Before the Shooting Begins: Searching for Democracy in America's Culture War*. New York: Free Press.

———— 2000 *The Death of Character: Moral Education in an Age without Good or Evil*. New York: Basic Books.

Huntington, Samuel P. 1996 *The Clash of Civilizations and the Remaking of World Order*. New York: Simon & Schuster.

Husserl, Edmund 1928 *On the Phenomenology of the Consciousness of Internal Time (1893–1917)*. Dordrecht, Netherlands: Kluwer Academic, 1991.

Ikegami, Eiko 1995 *The Taming of the Samurai: Honorific Individualism and the Making of Modern Japan*. Cambridge, MA: Harvard University Press.

Isaacson, Walter 2007 *Einstein: His Life and Universe*. New York: Simon & Schuster.

Jacobs, Janet Liebman 1989 *Divine Disenchantment: Deconverting from New Religions*. Bloomington: Indiana University Press.

Jacquard, Roland 2002 *In the Name of Osama bin Laden: Global Terrorism and the bin Laden Brotherhood*. Durham, NC: Duke University Press (revised edition; first edition, 2001).

Janik, Allan, and Stephen Toulmin 1973 *Wittgenstein's Vienna*. New York: Simon & Shuster.

Jeffers, Robinson 1928 "Hurt hawks." Page 45 in Jeffers 1963b.

—— 1934 "Letter to Sister Mary James Power." Page 189 in *The Wild God of the World: An Anthology of Robinson Jeffers*, selected by Albert Gelpi. Stanford, CA: Stanford University Press.

—— 1963a "Let them alone." Page 106 in Jeffers 1963b.

—— 1963b *Robinson Jeffers: Selected Poems*. New York: Vintage.

Jeffreys, M. D. W. 1952 "Samsonic suicide or suicide of revenge among Africans." *African Studies* 11: 118–122.

Jencks, Charles 1987 *Post-Modernism: The New Classicism in Art and Architecture*. New York: Rizzoli International.

Jennings, Francis 1975 *The Invasion of America: Indians, Colonialism, and the Cant of Conquest*. New York: W. W. Norton, 1976.

Jensen, Gary 2007 *The Path of the Devil: Early Modern Witch Hunts*. Lanham, MD: Rowman & Littlefield.

Judt, Tony 2001 "America and the war." *New York Review of Books* 48 (November 15): 4–6.

Jurgensmeyer, Mark 2000 *Terror in the Mind of God: The Global Rise of Religious Violence*. Berkeley: University of California Press.

Just, Peter 1991 "Going through the emotions: passion, violence, and 'other-control' among the Dou Donggo." *Ethos* 19: 288–312.

Kaeuper, Richard W. (editor) 2000 *Violence in Medieval Society*. Woodbridge, England: Boydell.

Kamen, Henry 1985 *Inquisition and Society in Spain*. London: Weidenfeld & Nicolson.

Kandinsky, Wassily 1937 "Interview with Karl Nierendorf." Pages 805–808 in Lindsay and Vergo 1982: Volume 2.

Kaplan, Joanna Overing 1975 *The Piaroa: A People of the Orinoco Basin, a Study in Kinship and Marriage*. Oxford: Oxford University Press. See also Overing, Joanna.

Karman, James 2001 *Robinson Jeffers: Poet of California*. Ashland, OR: Story Line (revised edition; first edition, 1995).

Kasson, John F. 1990 *Rudeness and Civility: Manners in Nineteenth-Century Urban America*. New York: Hill & Wang.

Katz, Jack 1988 *Seductions of Crime: Moral and Sensual Attractions in Doing Evil*. New York: Basic Books.

Keller, Bonnie B. 1978 "Marriage and medicine: women's search for love and luck." *African Social Research* 26: 489–505.

Kelly, David, and Sam Quinones 2008 "Engineer led solitary life marred by tragedy." *Los Angeles Times*. Online (September 17): http://articles.latimes.com/2008/sep/17/local/me-engineer17.

Kelly, John 2005 *The Great Mortality: An Intimate History of the Black Death, the Most Devastating Plague of All Time*. New York: HarperCollins.

Kelsen, Hans 1960 *Pure Theory of Law*. Clark, NJ: Lawbook Exchange, 2004 (revised and enlarged edition; first edition, 1934).

Kennedy, J. H. 1950 *Jesuit and Savage in New France*. New Haven, CT: Yale University Press.

Kent, Sarah 1985 "Scratching and biting savagery." Pages 3–12 in Kent and Morreau 1985b.

Kent, Sarah, and Jacqueline Morreau 1985a "Preface." Pages 1–2 in Kent and Morreau 1985b.

——— (editors) 1985b *Women's Images of Men*. London: Writers and Readers.

Kiefer, Thomas M. 1972 *The Tausug: Violence and Law in a Philippine Moslem Society*. New York: Holt, Rinehart & Winston.

Kimmelman, Michael 1989 "Unnerving art." *New York Times Magazine* (August 20): 40 ff.

Klor de Alva, J. Jorge 1991 "Colonizing souls: the failure of the Indian Inquisition and the rise of penitential discipline." Pages 3–22 in Perry and Cruz 1991.

Kluckhohn, Clyde 1944 *Navajo Witchcraft*. Boston: Beacon.

Knauft, Bruce M. 1985 *Good Company and Violence: Sorcery and Social Action in a Lowland New Guinea Society*. Berkeley: University of California Press.

——— 1990 "Melanesian warfare." *Oceania* 60: 250–311.

——— 1991 "Violence and sociality in human evolution." *Current Anthropology* 32: 391–428.

Knowles, Nathaniel 1940 "The torture of captives by the Indians of eastern North America." *Proceedings of the American Philosophical Society* 82: 151–225.

Koch, Klaus-Friedrich 1974 *War and Peace in Jalémó: The Management of Conflict in Highland New Guinea*. Cambridge, MA: Harvard University Press.

Kochman, Thomas (editor) 1972 *Rappin' and Stylin' Out: Communication in Urban Black America*. Urbana: University of Illinois Press.

Kolchin, Peter 1987 *Unfree Labor: American Slavery and Russian Serfdom*. Cambridge, MA: Harvard University Press.

Kopytoff, Igor 1961 "Extension of conflict as a method of conflict resolution among the Suku of the Congo." *Journal of Conflict Resolution* 5: 61–69.

Kposowa, Augustine J. 2000 "Marital status and suicide in the National Longitudinal Mortality Study." *Journal of Epidemiology and Community Health* 54: 254–261.

——— 2003 "Divorce and suicide risk." *Journal of Epidemiology and Community Health* 57: 993.

Krauss, Ellis S.; Thomas P. Rohlen; and Patricia G. Steinhoff (editors) 1984 *Conflict in Japan*. Honolulu: University of Hawaii Press.

Kristof, Nicholas D. 2008 "Terrorism that's personal." *New York Times*. Online (November 30): http://www.nytimes.com/2008/11/30/opinion/30kristof.html?_r=1&hp.

Kuhn, Philip A. 1990 *Soulstealers: The Chinese Sorcery Scare of 1768*. Cambridge, MA: Harvard University Press.

Kuhn, Thomas S. 1957 *The Copernican Revolution: Planetary Astronomy in the Development of Western Thought*. Cambridge, MA: Harvard University Press.

——— 1962 *The Structure of Scientific Revolutions*. Chicago: University of Chicago Press.

Kuspit, Donald 1987 *Fischl: An Interview with Eric Fischl*. New York: Vintage.

Labov, William 1972 "Rules for ritual insults." Pages 265–314 in Kochman 1972.

LaFave, Wayne R. 1965 *Arrest: The Decision to Take a Suspect into Custody*. Boston: Little, Brown.

La Fontaine, Jean 1963 "Witchcraft in Bugisu." Pages 187–220 in Middleton and Winter 1963b.

LaFree, Gary D. 1989 *Rape and Criminal Justice: The Social Construction of Sexual Assault*. Belmont, CA: Wadsworth.

Laing, R. D. 1959 *The Divided Self: An Existential Study in Sanity and Madness*. Middlesex, England: Penguin, 1965.

——— 1967 *The Politics of Experience*. New York: Ballantine.

Lambert, H. E. 1956 *Kikuyu Social and Political Institutions*. London: Oxford University Press.

Landau, Jacob M. 1961 "Ritual murder accusations in nineteenth-century Egypt." Pages 197–232 in Dundes 1991.

Langmuir, Gavin I. 1971 "Anti-Judaism as the necessary preparation for antisemitism." Pages 57–62 in Langmuir 1990b.

——— 1980 "The transformation of anti-Judaism." Pages 63–99 in Langmuir 1990b.

——— 1982 "Medieval antisemitism." Pages 301–310 in Langmuir 1990b.

——— 1984 "Thomas of Monmouth: detector of ritual murder." Pages 209–236 in Langmuir 1990b.

——— 1985 "Historiographic crucifixion." Pages 282–298 in Langmuir 1990b.

——— 1987 "Toward a definition of antisemitism." Pages 311–352 in Langmuir 1990b.

——— 1990a *History, Religion, and Antisemitism*. Berkeley: University of California Press.

——— 1990b *Toward a Definition of Antisemitism*. Berkeley: University of California Press.

Laqueur, Thomas W. 2003 *Solitary Sex: A Cultural History of Masturbation*. New York: Zone.

Lasch, Christopher 1978 *The Culture of Narcissism: American Life in an Age of Diminishing Expectations*. New York: W. W. Norton.

Leacock, Eleanor, and Richard Lee 1982a "Introduction." Pages 1–20 in Leacock and Lee 1982b.

────── (editors) 1982b *Politics and History in Band Societies*. Cambridge: Cambridge University Press.

Lebow, Richard Ned 2003 *The Tragic Vision of Politics: Ethics, Interests and Orders*. New York: Cambridge University Press.

Lebra, Takie Sugiyama 1984 "Nonconfrontational strategies for management of interpersonal conflicts." Pages 41–60 in Krauss, Rohlen, and Steinhoff 1984.

Lee, Richard Borshay 1969 "Eating Christmas in the Kalahari." *Natural History* (December): 14–22, 60–63.

────── 1979 *The !Kung San: Men, Women, and Work in a Foraging Society*. Cambridge: Cambridge University Press.

Leff, Gordon 1967 *Heresy in the Later Middle Ages: The Relation of Heterodoxy to Dissent, c. 1250–c. 1450*. Manchester: Manchester University Press. Two volumes.

LeGrand, Camille E.; Jay A. Reich; and Duncan Chappell 1977 *Forcible Rape: An Analysis of Legal Issues*. Seattle, WA: Battelle Law & Justice Study Center.

Le Guin, Ursula K. 1974 *The Dispossessed: An Ambiguous Utopia*. New York: HarperCollins.

Lemert, Edwin M. 1953 "An isolation and closure theory of naïve check forgery." Pages 99–108 in Lemert 1967b.

────── 1958 "The behavior of the systematic check forger." Pages 109–118 in Lemert 1967b.

────── 1962 "Paranoia and the dynamics of exclusion." *Sociometry* 25: 2–25.

────── 1967a "The concept of secondary deviation." Pages 40–64 in Lemert 1967b.

────── 1967b *Human Deviance, Social Problems, and Social Control*. Englewood Cliffs, NJ: Prentice-Hall.

Lepowsky, Maria 1991 "Gender in an egalitarian society: a case study from the Coral Sea." Pages 171–223 in *Beyond the Second Sex: New Directions in the Anthropology of Gender*, edited by Peggy Reeves Sanday and Ruth Gallagher Goodenough. Philadelphia: University of Pennsylvania Press.

Levin, Jack, and James Alan Fox 1985 *Mass Murder: America's Growing Menace*. New York: Plenum.

Le Vine, Robert A. 1959 "Gusii sex offenses: a study in social control." *American Anthropologist* 61: 965–990.

—— 1963 "Witchcraft and sorcery in a Gusii community." Pages 221–255 in Middleton and Winter 1963b.

Lévi-Strauss, Claude 1955 *Tristes Tropiques*. New York: Atheneum, 1970.

—— 1962 *The Savage Mind*. Chicago: University of Chicago Press, 1966.

Levy, Leonard W. 1993 *Blasphemy: Verbal Offense against the Sacred, from Moses to Salman Rushdie*. New York: Alfred A. Knopf.

Lewis, Bernard 1995 *Cultures in Conflict: Christians, Muslims, and Jews in the Age of Discovery*. New York: Oxford University Press.

Lewis, Leo 2006 "Nail that stuck up has been 'hammered down.'" *Financial Times*. Online (December 15): http://www.ft.com/cms/s/0/20299688-8bb1-11db-a61f0000779e2340.html.

Lewis, Oscar 1961 *The Children of Sánchez: Autobiography of a Mexican Family*. New York: Random House.

Liao, Kuang-sheng 1984 *Antiforeignism and Modernization in China, 1860–1980: Linkage between Domestic Politics and Foreign Policy*. Hong Kong: The Chinese University Press.

Liebow, Elliot 1967 *Tally's Corner: A Study of Negro Streetcorner Men*. Boston: Little, Brown.

Liliequist, Jonas 1991 "Peasants against nature: crossing the boundaries between man and animal in seventeenth- and eighteenth-century Sweden." *Journal of the History of Sexuality* 1: 393–423.

Lilla, Mark 1997 "The enemy of liberalism." *New York Review of Books* 44 (May 15): 38–44.

Lim, Tae-Seop, and Soo-Hyang Choi 1996 "Interpersonal relationships in Korea." Pages 122–136 in *Communication in Personal Relationships across Cultures*, edited by William B. Gudykunst, Stella Ting-Toomey, and Tsukasa Nishida. Thousand Oaks, CA: Sage.

Linderman, Gerald F. 1987 *Embattled Courage: The Experience of Combat in the American Civil War*. New York: Free Press.

Lindholm, Charles 1982 *Generosity and Jealousy: The Swat Pukhtun of Northern Pakistan*. New York: Columbia University Press.

Lindner, Evelin 2006 *Making Enemies: Humiliation and International Conflict*. Westport, CT: Praeger Security International.

Lindsay, Kenneth C., and Peter Vergo (editors) 1982 *Kandinsky: Complete Writings on Art*. Boston: G. K. Hall. Two volumes.

Lingat, Robert 1967 *The Classical Law of India*. Berkeley: University of California Press, 1973.

Lipman, Jonathan N., and Steven Harrell (editors) 1990 *Violence in China: Essays in Culture and Counterculture*. Albany: State University of New York Press.

Lipsett-Rivera, Sonya 1998 "A slap in the face of honor: social transgression and women in late-colonial Mexico." Pages 179–200 in *The Faces of Honor: Sex, Shame, and Violence in Colonial Latin America*, edited by Lyman L. Johnson and Sonya Lipsett-Rivera. Albuquerque: University of New Mexico Press.

Llewellyn, Karl N., and E. Adamson Hoebel 1941 *The Cheyenne Way: Conflict and Case Law in Primitive Jurisprudence*. Norman: University of Oklahoma Press.

Lofland, John 2003 *Demolishing a Historic Hotel: A Sociology of Preservation Failures in Davis, California*. Davis, CA: Davis Research.

Lofland, John, and Rodney Stark 1965 "Becoming a world-saver: a theory of conversion to a deviant perspective." *American Sociological Review* 30: 862–875.

Lofland, Lyn H. 1973 *A World of Strangers: Order and Action in Urban Public Space*. New York: Basic Books.

Lord, James 1993 *Picasso and Dora: A Personal Memoir*. New York: Farrar, Straus, Giroux.

Lucie-Smith, Edward 1984 *Movements in Art since 1945*. New York: Thames and Hudson, 1985 (revised edition; first published 1969).

Luckenbill, David F. 1977 "Criminal homicide as a situated transaction." *Social Problems* 25: 175–186.

Lundsgaarde, Henry P. 1977 *Murder in Space City: A Cultural Analysis of Houston Homicide Patterns*. New York: Oxford University Press.

Lyman, Stanford M., and Marvin B. Scott 1967 "Territoriality: a neglected sociological dimension." *Social Problems* 15: 236–249.

Macaulay, Stewart 1963 "Non-contractual relations in business: a preliminary study." *American Sociological Review* 28: 55–67.

MacCormack, Geoffrey 1996 *The Spirit of Traditional Chinese Law*. Athens: University of Georgia Press.

MacDonald, Robert H. 1967 "The frightful consequences of onanism: notes on the history of a delusion." *Journal of the History of Ideas* 28: 423–431.

Macfarlane, Alan 1970 *Witchcraft in Tudor and Stuart England: A Regional Study*. New York: Harper & Row.

MacKay, Angus 1972 "Popular movements and pogroms in fifteenth-century Castile." *Past & Present* 55: 33–67.

Mackinder, Halford J. 1919 *Democratic Ideals and Reality* (with additional papers edited by Anthony J. Pearce). New York: W. W. Norton, 1962.

Maddock, K. 1970 "A structural interpretation of the *mirriri*." *Oceania* 60: 165–176.

Magueijo, João 2003 *Faster Than the Speed of Light: The Story of a Scientific Speculation*. Cambridge, MA: Perseus.

Mailer, Norman 1957 "The white Negro: superficial reflections on the hipster." Pages 337–358 in *Advertisements for Myself*. New York: Putnam's, 1959.

——— 1995 *Portrait of Picasso as a Young Man*. New York: Warner, 1996.

Makarius, Raoul 1966 "Incest and redemption in Arnhem Land." *Oceania* 37: 148–152.

Makin, Kirk 2008 "Abusers who breach trust get shorter sentences, study shows." *Globe and Mail*. Online (October 29): http://www.theglobeandmail.com/servlet/story/RTGAM.20081029.wsentencing1030/BNStory/National/?page=rss&id=RTGAM.20081029.wsentencing1030.

Malinowski, Bronislaw 1948 *Magic, Science and Religion and Other Essays*. Garden City, NY: Doubleday.

Maloney, Clarence (editor) 1976a "Don't say 'pretty baby' lest you zap it with your eye—the evil eye in South Asia." Pages 102–148 in Maloney 1976b.

——— (editor) 1976b *The Evil Eye*. New York: Columbia University Press.

——— 1976c "Introduction." Pages v–xvi in Maloney 1976b.

Mandelbaum, David 1970 *Society in India*. Berkeley: University of California Press. Two volumes.

Mann, Michael 2005 *The Dark Side of Democracy: Explaining Ethnic Cleansing.* Cambridge: Cambridge University Press.

Manning, Helen 1969 *To Perish for Their Saving.* London: Victory.

Manning, Jason 2011 Suicide as Social Control: A Theoretical and Empirical Study. Unpublished doctoral dissertation. Department of Sociology, University of Virginia, Charlottesville.

Margalit, Avishai 2003 "After strange gods." *New York Review of Books* 50 (October 9): 29–32.

Markovits, Andrei S. 2007 *Uncouth Nation: Why Europe Dislikes America.* Princeton, NJ: Princeton University Press.

Marshall, Donald S. 1971 "Sexual behavior on Mangaia." Pages 103–162 in Marshall and Suggs 1971.

Marshall, Donald S., and Robert C. Suggs (editors) 1971 *Human Sexual Behavior: Variations in the Ethnographic Spectrum.* New York: Basic Books.

Marshall, Mac 1979 *Weekend Warriors: Alcohol in a Micronesian Culture.* Palo Alto, CA: Mayfield.

Marwick, Max 1970a "The decline of witch-beliefs in differentiated societies." Pages 379–382 in Marwick 1970c.

——— 1970b "Introduction." Pages 11–18 in Marwick 1970c.

——— (editor) 1970c *Witchcraft and Sorcery: Selected Readings.* Harmondsworth, England: Penguin.

Marx, Gary T. 1967 "The white Negro and the Negro white." *Phylon* 28: 168–177.

Marx, Karl, and Friedrich Engels 1888 *Manifesto of the Communist Party* (annotated English edition; first edition, 1848). Pages 1–41 in *Basic Writings on Politics and Philosophy: Karl Marx and Friedrich Engels,* edited by Lewis S. Feuer. Garden City, NY: Anchor, 1959.

Mason, Stephen F. 1962 *A History of the Sciences.* New York: Collier (revised edition; first published 1956).

Maull, Samuel 2008 "Hung jury declared in cat killer trial." *ABC News.* Online (September 26): http://abcnews.go.com/TheLaw/story?id=5894865&page=1.

Mauss, Marcel 1925 *The Gift: Forms and Functions of Exchange in Archaic Societies*. New York: W. W. Norton, 1967.

Maybury-Lewis, David 1974 *Akwẽ-Shavante Society*. New York: Oxford University Press.

McAleer, Kevin 1994 *Dueling: The Cult of Honor in Fin-de-Siècle Germany*. Princeton, NJ: Princeton University Press.

McCabe, James Dabney 1884 *The National Encyclopaedia of Business and Social Forms, Embracing the Laws of Etiquette and Good Society . . . 1883*. Philadelphia: National Publishing.

McCloskey, Deirdre 2008 "Hobbes, Rawls, Nussbaum, Buchanan, and all seven of the virtues." Paper presented to the Program in Political Philosophy, Policy, and Law, University of Virginia, Charlottesville. February 7.

McConaloque, James 2006 "EU criticizes Turkish law on 'insulting Turkishness.'" *Brussels Journal*. Online (July 19): http://www.brusselsjournal.com/node/1197.

McKnight, Brian E. 1973 "Sung justice: death by slicing." *Journal of the American Oriental Society* 93: 359–360.

McLuhan, Marshall 1964 *Understanding Media: The Extensions of Man*. New York: New American Library.

McMillen, Neil R. 1989 *Dark Journey: Black Mississippians in the Age of Jim Crow*. Urbana: University of Illinois Press.

McNeil, Legs, and Gillian McCain 1996 *Please Kill Me: The Uncensored Oral History of Punk*. New York: Grove.

McNeill, Sandra 1987 "Flashing: its effect on women." Pages 93–109 in *Women, Violence and Social Control*, edited by Jalna Hanmer and Mary Maynard. London: Macmillan.

McNeill, William H. 1976 *Plagues and Peoples*. Garden City, NY: Anchor.

McPherson, Miller; Lynn Smith-Lovin; and Matthew E. Brashears 2006 "Social isolation in America: changes in core discussion networks over two decades." *American Sociological Review* 71: 353–375.

Meggitt, Mervyn 1962 *Desert People: A Study of the Walbiri Aborigines of Central Australia*. Chicago: University of Chicago Press, 1965.

——— 1977 *Blood Is Their Argument: Warfare among the Mae Enga Tribesmen of the New Guinea Highlands.* Palo Alto, CA: Mayfield.

Meijer, M. J. 1985 "Homosexual offenses in Ch'ing law." *T'oung Pao: Revue Internationale de Sinologie* 71: 109–133.

Mernissi, Fatima 1975 *Beyond the Veil: Male–Female Dynamics in a Modern Muslim Society.* Cambridge, MA: Schenkman.

Merry, Sally Engle 1984 "Rethinking gossip and scandal." Pages 271–302 in Black 1984c.

——— 1990 *Getting Justice and Getting Even: Legal Consciousness among Working-Class Americans.* Chicago: University of Chicago Press.

Merton, Robert K. 1938 "Social structure and anomie." *American Sociological Review* 3: 672–682.

——— 1942 "The normative structure of science." Pages 267–278 in Merton 1973.

——— 1957 "Priorities in scientific discovery." Pages 286–324 in Merton 1973.

——— 1973 *The Sociology of Science: Theoretical and Empirical Investigations*, edited by Norman W. Storer. Chicago: University of Chicago Press.

Messenger, John C. 1968 "Types and causes of disputes in an Irish community." *Eire-Ireland: A Journal of Irish Studies* 3: 27–37.

——— 1971 "Sex and repression in an Irish folk community." Pages 3–37 in Marshall and Suggs 1971.

Messner, Steven F., and Richard Rosenfeld 1994 *Crime and the American Dream.* Belmont, CA: Wadsworth.

Michalski, Joseph H. 2003 "Financial altruism or unilateral resource exchanges? Toward a pure sociology of welfare." *Sociological Theory* 21: 341–358.

Middleton, John, and E. H. Winter 1963a "Introduction." Pages 1–25 in Middleton and Winter 1963b.

——— (editors) 1963b *Witchcraft and Sorcery in East Africa.* New York: Frederick A. Praeger.

Midelfort, H. C. Erik 1972 *Witch Hunting in Southwestern Germany, 1562–1684: The Social and Intellectual Foundations.* Stanford, CA: Stanford University Press.

——— 1994 *Mad Princes of Renaissance Germany*. Charlottesville: University of Virginia Press.

Miles, Barry 1989 *Ginsberg: A Biography*. New York: Simon & Schuster.

Mill, John Stuart 1859 *On Liberty*. London: Longman, Roberts & Green, 1869.

Miller, Arthur I. 2001 *Einstein, Picasso: Space, Time, and the Beauty That Causes Havoc*. New York: Basic Books.

Miller, Walter B. 1955 "Two concepts of authority." *American Anthropologist* 57: 271–289.

——— 1958 "Lower class culture as a generating milieu of gang delinquency." *Journal of Social Issues* 14: 5–13.

Miller, William Ian 1990 *Bloodtaking and Peacemaking: Feud, Law, and Society in Saga Iceland*. Chicago: University of Chicago Press.

Milner, Murray, Jr. 1994 *Status and Sacredness: A General Theory of Status Relations and an Analysis of Indian Culture*. New York: Oxford University Press.

——— 2004 *Freaks, Geeks, and Cool Kids: American Teenagers, Schools, and the Culture of Consumption*. New York: Routledge.

Minkowski, Hermann 1908 "Space and time." Lecture at 80th Assembly of German Natural Scientists and Physicians (September 21, Cologne, Germany). Pages 73–91 in *The Principle of Relativity: A Collection of Original Memoirs on the Special and General Theory of Relativity*, by Hendrik Antoon Lorentz, Albert Einstein, Hermann Minkowski, and Hermann Weyl. Mineola, NY: Dover, 1952.

Moffat, Alistair 1989 *Remembering Charles Rennie Mackintosh: An Illustrated Biography*. Lanark, Scotland: Colin Baxter Photography.

Mogar, Robert E. 1968 "Psychedelic states and schizophrenia." Pages 257–276 in Aaronson and Osmond 1970.

Mondrian, Piet 1919–20 "Natural reality and abstract reality: a trialogue (while strolling from the country to the city)." Pages 82–123 in *The New Art—The New Life: The Collected Writings of Piet Mondrian*, edited by Harry Holtzman and Martin S. James. Boston: G. K. Hall.

Monk, Ray 1990 *Ludwig Wittgenstein: The Duty of Genius*. New York: Free Press.

Moore, Wilbert E. 1963 *Social Change*. Englewood Cliffs, NJ: Prentice-Hall.

Moreno de los Arcos, Roberto 1991 "New Spain's Inquisition for Indians from the sixteenth to the nineteenth century." Pages 23–36 Perry and Cruz 1991.

Morrill, Calvin 1995 *The Executive Way: Conflict Management in Corporations.* Chicago: University of Chicago Press.

Morris, James 1972 "The final solution, down under." *Horizon* 14: 60–70.

Muir, Jim 2009 "Iraqi gay men face 'lives of hell.'" *BBC News.* Online (April 18): http://news.bbc.co.uk/2/hi/middle_east/8005420.stm.

Müller, Ingo 1987 *Hitler's Justice: The Courts of the Third Reich.* Cambridge, MA: Harvard University Press, 1991.

Mullin, Gerald W. 1972 *Flight and Rebellion: Slave Resistance in Eighteenth-Century Virginia.* New York: Oxford University Press.

Murdock, George Peter 1949 *Social Structure.* New York: Free Press.

Murgoci, Agnes 1923 "The evil eye in Roumania, and its antidotes." Pages 124–129 in Dundes 1981a.

Murphy, Robert F. 1957 "Intergroup hostility and social cohesion." *American Anthropologist* 59: 1018–1035.

Murray, John Allen (editor) 1942 *George Washington's Rules of Civility and Decent Behaviour in Company and Conversation.* New York: G. P. Putnam's Sons.

Myers, Fred R. 1988 "The logic and meaning of anger among Pintupi Aborigines." *Man* 23: 589–610.

Nader, Laura 1990 *Harmony Ideology: Justice and Control in a Zapotec Mountain Village.* Stanford, CA: Stanford University Press.

Nader, Laura, and Harry F. Todd, Jr. (editors) 1978 *The Disputing Process—Law in Ten Societies.* New York: Columbia University Press.

Naess, Arne 1995a "Equality, sameness, and rights." Pages 222–224 in Sessions 1995.

—— 1995b "Self-realization: an ecological approach to being in the world." Pages 225–239 in Sessions 1995.

Nandy, Ashis 1989 *The Tao of Cricket: On Games of Destiny and the Destiny of Games.* New Delhi: Viking.

Naranjo, Claudio 1973 "Psychological aspects of the yagé experience in an experimental setting." Pages 176–190 in Harner 1973b.

Nash, Gary B. 1974 *Red, White, and Black: The Peoples of Early America*. Englewood Cliffs, NJ: Prentice-Hall.

Neeley, Bill 1995 *The Last Comanche Chief: The Life and Times of Quanah Parker*. New York: John Wiley & Sons.

Netanyahu, Benzion 1995 *The Origins of the Inquisition in Fifteenth Century Spain*. New York: Random House.

—— 1999 *The Marranos of Spain: From the Late 14th to the Early 16th Century*. Ithaca, NY: Cornell University Press (third edition; first edition, 1966).

Newman, Katherine S. 1988 *Falling from Grace: The Experience of Downward Mobility in the American Middle Class*. New York: Vintage, 1989.

Nietzsche, Friedrich 1878 *Human, All-Too-Human*. Partially reprinted in *The Portable Nietzsche*, edited by Walter Kaufmann. New York: Viking, 1954.

Nirenberg, David 1996 *Communities of Violence: Persecution of Minorities in the Middle Ages*. Princeton, NJ: Princeton University Press.

Nohl, Johannes 1961 *The Black Death: A Chronicle of the Plague Compiled from Contemporary Sources*. London: Unwin (abridged edition; original edition, 1926).

Nye, Robert A. 1993 *Masculinity and Male Codes of Honor in Modern France*. New York: Oxford University Press.

O'Barr, William M. 1982 *Linguistic Evidence: Language, Power, and Strategy in the Courtroom*. New York: Academic Press.

Oberg, Kalervo 1934 "Crime and punishment in Tlingit society." *American Anthropologist* 36: 145–156.

Obeyesekere, Gananath 1975 "Sorcery, premeditated murder, and the canalization of aggression in Sri Lanka." *Ethnology* 14: 1–23.

Offer, Avner 1995 "Going to war in 1914: a matter of honor?" *Politics & Society* 23: 213–241.

Ohadike, Don C. 1996 "Igbo culture and history." Pages 236–257 in Achebe 2009.

Ohnuki-Tierney, Emiko 2002 *Kamikaze, Cherry Blossoms, and Nationalisms: The Militarization of Aesthetics in Japanese History*. Chicago: University of Chicago Press.

Olzak, Susan 1986 "A competition model of ethnic collective action in American cities, 1877–1889." Pages 17–46 in *Competitive Ethnic Relations*, edited by Susan Olzak and Joane Nagel. Orlando, FL: Academic Press.

——— 1992 *The Dynamics of Ethnic Competition and Conflict*. Stanford, CA: Stanford University Press.

O'Neill, Barry 1999 *Honor, Symbols, and War*. Ann Arbor: University of Michigan Press.

Opdyke, Irene Gut (with Jennifer Armstrong) 1999 *In My Hands: Memories of a Holocaust Rescuer*. New York: Alfred A. Knopf.

Orenstein, Henry 1965 *Gaon: Conflict and Cohesion in an Indian Village*. Princeton, NJ: Princeton University Press.

Organski, Abramo Fimo Kenneth, and Jacek Kugler 1980 *The War Ledger*. Chicago: University of Chicago Press.

Osmond, Humphrey 1970 "On being mad." Pages 21–28 in Aaronson and Osmond 1970.

Overing, Joanna 1989 "Styles of manhood: an Amazonian contrast in tranquility and violence." Pages 79–99 in Howell and Willis 1989. See also Kaplan, Joanna Overing.

Oyler, D. S. 1919 "The Shilluk's belief in the evil eye." Pages 78–85 in Dundes 1981a.

Paine, Robert 1967 "What is gossip about? An alternative hypothesis." *Man* 2: 278–285.

——— 1968 "Gossip and transaction." *Man* 3: 305–308.

Pais, Abraham 1991 *Niels Bohr's Times: In Physics, Philosophy, and Polity*. Oxford: Oxford University Press.

——— 1994 *Einstein Lived Here*. New York: Oxford University Press.

Pape, Robert A. 2005 *Dying to Win: The Strategic Logic of Suicide Terrorism*. New York: Random House, 2006.

Parsons, Talcott 1951a "Illness and the role of the physician: a sociological perspective." *American Journal of Orthopsychiatry* 21: 452–460.

—— 1951b *The Social System*. New York: Free Press.

Parsons, Talcott, and Renée Fox 1952 "Illness, therapy and the modern urban American family." *Journal of Social Issues* 8: 31–44.

Partington, Donald H. 1965 "The incidence of the death penalty for rape in Virginia." *Washington & Lee Law Review* 22: 43–75.

Patterson, Orlando 1982 *Slavery and Social Death: A Comparative Study*. Cambridge, MA: Harvard University Press.

Peppiatt, Michael 1996 *Francis Bacon: Anatomy of an Enigma*. New York: Farrar, Straus & Geroux.

Peristiany, J. G. (editor) 1966 *Honour and Shame: The Values of Mediterranean Society*. Chicago: University of Chicago Press.

Perry, Mary Elizabeth, and Anne J. Cruz (editors) 1991 *Cultural Encounters: The Impact of the Inquisition in Spain and the New World*. Berkeley: University of California Press.

Perutz, M. F. 1997 "A passion for science." *New York Review of Books* 44 (February 20): 39–42.

Peters, Edward 1985 *Torture*. New York: Basil Blackwell.

Peters, Emrys L. 1967 "Some structural aspects of the feud among the camel–herding Bedouin of Cyrenaica." *Africa* 37: 261–282.

Phillips, Scott, and Mark Cooney 2005 "Aiding peace, abetting violence: third parties and the management of conflict." *American Sociological Review* 70: 334–354.

Piaget, Jean 1932 *The Moral Judgment of the Child*. New York: Free Press.

Piliavin, Irving M., and Scott Briar 1964 "Police encounters with juveniles." *American Journal of Sociology* 70: 206–214.

Pinet, Hélène 1988 *Rodin: The Hands of Genius*. New York: Harry N. Abrams, 1992.

Pinker, Steven 2008 "The moral instinct." *New York Times Magazine*. Online (January 13): http://www.nytimes.com/2008/01/13/magazine/13Psychology-t.html?pagewanted=1.

Pitrè, Giuseppe 1889 "The *jettatura* and the evil eye." Pages 130–142 in Dundes 1981a.

Pitt-Rivers, Julian 1966 "Honour and social status." Pages 19–77 in Peristiany 1966.

—— 1977 "The moral foundations of the family." Pages 71–93 in *The Fate of Shechem or the Politics of Sex: Essays in the Anthropology of the Mediterranean*. Cambridge: Cambridge University Press.

Pocock, D. F. 1973 "The evil eye—envy and greed among the Patidar of central Gujerat." Pages 201–210 in Dundes 1981a.

Polanyi, Karl 1944 *The Great Transformation: The Political and Economic Origins of Our Time*. Boston: Beacon, 2001.

Poliakoff, Michael B. 1987 *Combat Sports in the Ancient World: Competition, Violence, and Culture*. New Haven, CT: Yale University Press.

Pollak, Michael 1982 "Male homosexuality—or happiness in the ghetto." Pages 40–61 in Ariès and Béjin 1982.

Pollock, Frederick, and Frederic William Maitland 1898 *The History of English Law: Before the Time of Edward I*. Cambridge: Cambridge University Press, 1968 (second edition; first edition, 1895). Two volumes.

Pomeroy, Sarah B. 1975 *Goddesses, Whores, Wives, and Slaves: Women in Classical Antiquity*. New York: Schocken.

Popham, Peter 2001 "Pakistan horrified by feudal husband's acid attack on beauty." *The Independent*. Online (September 2): http://www.independent.co.uk/news/world/asia/pakistan-horrified-by-feudal-husbands-acid-attack-on-beauty-667712.html.

Potter, Jeffrey 1985 *To a Violent Grave: An Oral Biography of Jackson Pollock*. Wainscott, NY: Pushcart, 1986.

Powers, Edwin 1966 *Crime and Punishment in Early Massachusetts, 1620–1692: A Documentary History*. Boston: Beacon.

Putnam, Robert D. 2001 *Bowling Alone: The Collapse and Revival of American Community*. New York: Simon & Schuster.

Quammen, David 1996 *The Song of the Dodo: Island Biography in an Age of Extinctions*. New York: Scribner.

Radcliffe-Brown, A. R. 1922 *The Andaman Islanders*. Glencoe, IL: Free Press, 1948.

Rand, Ayn 1943 *The Fountainhead*. New York: Penguin, 2005 (centennial edition).

—— 1961 "The objectivist ethics." Pages 1–34 in Rand 1964.

—— 1964 *The Virtue of Selfishness: A New Concept of Egoism*. With additional articles by Nathaniel Branden. New York: New American Library.

Rappaport, Ernest A. 1975 "The ritual murder accusation: the persistence of doubt and repetition compulsion." Pages 304–335 in Dundes 1991.

Rasmussen, Knud 1927 *Across Arctic America: Narrative of the Fifth Thule Expedition*. New York: Greenwood, 1969.

—— 1931 *The Netsilik Eskimos: Social Life and Spiritual Culture*. Report of the Fifth Thule Expedition, 1921–24. Volume 8, Numbers 1–2. Copenhagen: Gyldendalske Boghandel, Nordisk Forlag.

Read, Kenneth E. 1959 "Leadership and consensus in a New Guinea society." *American Anthropologist* 61: 425–436.

Reay, Marie 1953 "Social control amongst the Orokaiva." *Oceania* 34: 110–118.

Rediker, Marcus 2004 *Villains of All Nations: Atlantic Pirates in the Golden Age*. Boston: Beacon.

Redondi, Pietro 1983 *Galileo: Heretic*. Princeton, NJ: Princeton University Press, 1987.

Regan, Tom 1983 *The Case for Animal Rights*. Berkeley: University of California Press.

Regis, Ed 1987 *Who Got Einstein's Office? Eccentricity and Genius at the Institute for Advanced Study*. Reading, MA: Addison Wesley.

Reid, John Phillip 1970 *A Law of Blood: The Primitive Law of the Cherokee Nation*. New York: New York University Press.

Rejali, Darius M. 1994 *Torture and Modernity: Self, Society, and State in Modern Iran*. Boulder, CO: Westview.

Retzinger, Suzanne M. 1991 *Violent Emotions: Shame and Rage in Marital Quarrels*. Newbury Park, CA: Sage.

Richards, Audrey I. 1935 "A modern movement of witch-finders." Pages 164–177 in Marwick 1970c.

—— 1939 *Land, Labour, and Diet in Northern Rhodesia: An Economic Study of the Bemba Tribe*. London: Oxford University Press.

Richardson, Jane 1940 *Law and Status among the Kiowa Indians*. Seattle: University of Washington Press.

Richardson, John (with the collaboration of Marilyn McCully) 1991 *A Life of Picasso*. Volume 1: *1881–1906*. New York: Random House.

—— 1996 *A Life of Picasso*. Volume 2: *1907–1917*. New York: Random House.

—— 2007 *A Life of Picasso: The Triumphant Years, 1917–1932*. New York: Alfred A. Knopf.

Ridgeway, Cecilia L. 1983 *The Dynamics of Small Groups*. New York: St. Martin's.

Rieff, Philip 1959 *Freud: The Mind of the Moralist*. New York: Anchor, 1961.

—— 1966 *The Triumph of the Therapeutic: Uses of Faith after Freud*. New York: Harper & Row, 1968.

Rilke, Rainer Maria 1907 *Rodin*. Salt Lake City, UT: Peregrine Smith, 1979 (third edition; first published 1903).

—— 1952 *Letters on Cézanne*, edited by Clara Rilke. New York: International Publishing, 1985.

Robarchek, Clayton A. 1989 "Hobbesian and Rousseauan images of man: autonomy and individualism in a peaceful society." Pages 31–44 in *Societies at Peace: Anthropological Perspectives*, edited by Signe Howell and Roy Willis. London: Routledge.

Roberts, John M. 1976 "Belief in the evil eye in world perspective." Pages 223–278 in Maloney 1976b.

Robinson, Simon 2002 "Casting stones." *Time* (September 2): 36–37.

Roethlisberger, F. J., and William J. Dickson (with the assistance and collaboration of Harold A. Wright) 1939 *Management and the Worker: An Account of a Research Program Conducted by the Western Electric Company, Hawthorne Works, Chicago*. Cambridge, MA: Harvard University Press, 1956.

Rosen, Lawrence 1989 *The Anthropology of Justice: Law as Culture in Islamic Society*. Cambridge: Cambridge University Press.

Roth, Norman 1995 *Conversos, Inquisition, and the Expulsion of the Jews from Spain*. Madison: University of Wisconsin Press.

Rowe, William L. 1968 "The new Chauhans: a caste mobility movement in North India." Pages 66–77 in *Social Mobility in the Caste System in India: An Interdisciplinary Symposium*, edited by James Silverberg. *Comparative Studies in Society and History*, Supplement III. The Hague: Mouton.

Rubin, Barry, and Judith Colp Rubin 2004 *Hating America: A History*. New York: Oxford University Press.

Rubin, Jerry 1970 *Do It! Scenarios of the Revolution*. New York: Simon & Schuster.

Ruffini, Julio L. 1978 "Disputing over livestock in Sardinia." Pages 209–246 in Nader and Todd 1978.

Ruggiero, Guido 1980 *Violence in Early Renaissance Venice*. New Brunswick, NJ: Rutgers University Press.

Russell, Diana E. H. 1990 *Rape in Marriage*. Bloomington: Indiana University Press (expanded and revised edition; first edition, 1982).

Russell, Jeffrey Burton 1965 *Dissent and Reform in the Early Middle Ages*. Berkeley: University of California Press.

Russell, John 1979 *Francis Bacon*. New York: Thames & Hudson, 1985 (revised edition; first published 1971).

Ryan, Lyndall 1981 *The Aboriginal Tasmanians*. Vancouver: University of British Columbia Press.

Safranski, Rüdinger 1998 *Martin Heidegger: Between Good and Evil*. Cambridge, MA: Harvard University Press.

Sageman, Marc 2004 *Understanding Terror Networks*. Philadelphia: University of Pennsylvania Press.

Sahibzada, Mehnaz 1999 "The politics of rape in Pakistan: victim or criminal?" *GeoCities*. Online (Spring): http://www.geocities.com/capitolhill/parliament/3251/spring99/pakistan.html.

Sahlins, Marshall D. 1958 *Social Stratification in Polynesia*. Seattle: University of Washington Press.

Scheff, Thomas J. 1990 *Microsociology: Discourse, Emotion, and Social Structure.* Chicago: University of Chicago Press.

——— 1994 *Bloody Revenge: Emotions, Nationalism, and War.* Boulder, CO: Westview.

Scheff, Thomas J., and Suzanne M. Retzinger 1991 *Emotions and Violence: Shame and Rage in Destructive Conflicts.* Lexington, MA: Lexington.

Scheppele, Kim Lane 1988 *Legal Secrets: Equality and Efficiency in the Common Law.* Chicago: University of Chicago Press.

Schild, Wolfgang 1980 "The history of criminal law and procedure." Pages 46–98 in Hinckeldey 1980a.

Schneider, Jane 1971 "Of vigilance and virgins: honor, shame and access to resources in Mediterranean societies." *Ethnology* 10: 1–24.

Schoeck, Helmut 1955 "The evil eye: forms and dynamics of a universal superstition." Pages 192–200 in Dundes 1981a.

Schoetz, David 2008 "Daughter rejects marriage, ends up dead." *ABC News.* Online (July 8): http://abcnews.go.com/US/story?id=5322587&page=1.

Schultz, Magdalene 1986 "The blood libel: a motif in the history of childhood." Pages 273–303 in Dundes 1991.

Schuster, Ilsa 1983 "Women's aggression: an African case study." *Aggressive Behavior* 9: 319–331.

Schwartz, Richard D., and Jerome H. Skolnick 1962 "Two studies of legal stigma." *Social Problems* 10: 133–142.

Schwimmer, Eric 1984 "Male couples in New Guinea." Pages 248–291 in Herdt 1984b.

Sciutto, Jim 2008 "Holocaust survivor remembers pain of war." *ABC News.* Online (November 11): http://abcnews.go.com/WN/Story?id=6223066&page=1.

Scott, James C. 1985 *Weapons of the Weak: Everyday Forms of Peasant Resistance.* New Haven, CT: Yale University Press.

——— 1989 "Everyday forms of resistance." Pages 3–33 in Colburn 1989.

Scott, Joanna 1990 *Arrogance.* New York: Linden.

Selby, Henry A. 1974 *Zapotec Deviance: The Convergence of Folk and Modern Sociology*. Austin: University of Texas Press.

Senechal de la Roche, Roberta 1996 "Collective violence as social control." *Sociological Forum* 11: 97–128.

———— 1997 "The sociogenesis of lynching." Pages 48–76 in *Under Sentence of Death: Lynching in the South*, edited by W. Fitzhugh Brundage. Chapel Hill: University of North Carolina Press.

———— 2001a "The behavior of the dead." Paper presented at a session entitled "Beyond *The Behavior of Law*: Studies in Blackian Sociology," joint meetings of the International Sociological Association Research Committee on the Sociology of Law and the Law and Society Association, Central European University, Budapest, July 5.

———— 2001b "Why is collective violence collective?" *Sociological Theory* 19: 126–144.

———— 2004 "Modern lynchings." Pages 213–225 in Zahn, Brownstein, and Jackson 2004.

———— 2008 *In Lincoln's Shadow: The 1908 Race Riot in Springfield, Illinois*. Carbondale: Southern Illinois University Press (revised paperback edition; first published 1990).

Serpenti, Laurent 1984 "The ritual meaning of homosexuality and pedophilia among the Kimam-Papuans of South Irian Jaya." Pages 292–317 in Herdt 1984b.

Sessions, George (editor) 1995 *Deep Ecology for the 21st Century: Readings in the Philosophy and Practice of the New Environmentalism*. Boston: Shambhala.

Shafak, Elif 2007 *The Bastard of Istanbul*. New York: Penguin.

———— 2010 *The Forty Rules of Love*. New York: Viking.

Shakur, Sanyika (a.k.a. Monster Kody Scott) 1993 *Monster: The Autobiography of an L.A. Gang Member*. New York: Penguin, 1994.

Shamir, Ronen 1996 "Suspended in space: Bedouins under the law of Israel." *Law and Society Review* 30: 231–257.

Sharrock, David 2010 "Seven Muslims arrested over 'plot to kill cartoonist.'" *Times of London*. Online (March 10): http://www.timesonline.co.uk/tol/news/world/europe/article7055282.ece.

Shepard, Sanford 1968 "The present state of the ritual crime in Spain." Pages 162–179 in Dundes 1991.

Shermer, Michael 2002 *In Darwin's Shadow: The Life and Science of Alfred Russel Wallace*. New York: Oxford University Press.

Shively, Donald 1964 "Sumptuary regulation and status in early Tokugawa Japan." *Harvard Journal of Asiatic Studies* 125: 123–164.

Shostak, Margorie 1983 *Nisa: The Life and Words of a !Kung Woman*. New York: Vintage.

Simmel, Georg 1908 *The Sociology of Georg Simmel*, edited by Kurt H. Wolff. New York: Free Press, 1960.

——— 1923 "Conflict." Pages 11–123 in *Conflict and the Web of Group-Affiliations*. New York: Free Press, 1955.

Simonton, Dean Keith 1984 *Genius, Creativity, and Leadership: Historiometric Inquiries*. Cambridge, MA: Harvard University Press.

Sinclair, Andrew 1993 *Francis Bacon: His Life and Violent Times*. New York: Crown.

Singer, Peter 1990 *Animal Liberation*. New York: Avon (new revised edition; first published 1975).

Slezkine, Yuri 2004 *The Jewish Century*. Princeton, NJ: Princeton University Press.

Smelser, Neil J. 1959 *Social Change in the Industrial Revolution: An Application of Theory to the British Cotton Industry*. Chicago: University of Chicago Press.

Smith, Adam 1790 *The Theory of Moral Sentiments, or An Essay towards an Analysis of the Principles by which Men naturally judge concerning the Conduct and Character, first of their Neighbours, and afterwards of themselves*. Cambridge: Cambridge University Press, 2002 (sixth edition; first edition, 1759).

Smith, Cyril Stanley 1978 "Structural hierarchy in science, art, and history." Pages 9–30 in *On Aesthetics in Science*, edited by Judith Wechsler. Cambridge, MA: MIT Press.

Smith, R. Spencer 1976 "Voyeurism: a review of the literature." *Archives of Sexual Behavior* 5: 585–608.

Smolin, Lee 2006 *The Trouble with Physics: The Rise of String Theory, the Fall of Science, and What Comes Next*. Boston: Houghton Mifflin.

——— 2007 "The other Einstein." *New York Review of Books* 54 (June 14): 76–83.

Sombart, Werner 1911 *The Jews and Modern Capitalism*. New Brunswick, NJ: Transaction, 1982.

Sorli, Amrit 2004a "Mathematical time and physical time in the special and general theory of relativity." *General Science Journal*. Online (November 18): http://www.wbabin.net/physics/sorli.htm.

——— 2004b "Time is change." *Episteme: An International Journal of Science, History and Philosophy*. Online (Volume 8): http://www.dipmat.unipg.it/~bartocci/ep8/ep8-sorli.htm.

Sorokin, Pitirim A., and Robert K. Merton 1937 "Social time: a methodological and functional analysis." *American Journal of Sociology* 5: 615–629.

Spain, Daphne 1992 *Gendered Spaces*. Chapel Hill: University of North Carolina Press.

Spindel, Donna J. 1989 *Crime and Society in North Carolina, 1663–1776*. Baton Rouge: Louisiana State University Press.

Spooner, Brian 1970 "The evil eye in the Middle East." Pages 311–319 in M. Douglas 1970b.

Stack, Carol B. 1974 *All Our Kin: Strategies for Survival in a Black Community*. New York: Harper & Row.

Stack, Steven 1997 "Homicide followed by suicide: an analysis of Chicago data." *Criminology* 35: 435–454.

Stearns, Peter N. 1997 *Fat History: Bodies and Beauty in the Modern West*. New York: New York University Press.

Steele, Ian K. 1994 *Warpaths: Invasions of North America*. New York: Oxford University Press.

Stevens, John 1993 *Zen Masters: A Maverick, a Master of Masters, and a Wandering Poet*. Tokyo: Kodansha International, 1999.

Stewart, Frank Henderson 1994 *Honor*. Chicago: University of Chicago Press.

Stinchcombe, Arthur L. 1965 "Social structure and organizations." Pages 142–193 in *Handbook of Organizations*, edited by James G. March. Chicago: Rand McNally.

Stone, Christopher D. 1972 "Should trees have standing?—Toward legal rights for natural objects." *Southern California Law Review* 45: 450–501.

—— 2010 "Habeas corpus for animals? Why not?" *Washington Post*. Online (June 12): http://www.washingtonpost.com/wp-dyn/content/article/2010/06/11/AR2010061105310.html.

Stowe, Steven M. 1987 *Intimacy and Power in the Old South: Ritual in the Lives of the Planters*. Baltimore, MD: Johns Hopkins University Press.

Strehlow, C. 1907–20 *Die Aranda und Loritja-Stämme in Zentral-Australien*, edited by M. von Leonhardi. Frankfurt-am-Main: Veröffentlichungen des Völker-Museums.

Sulloway, Frank J. 1996 *Born to Rebel: Birth Order, Family Dynamics, and Creative Lives*. New York: Pantheon.

Sumner, William Graham 1906 *Folkways: A Study of the Sociological Importance of Usages, Manners, Customs, Mores, and Morals*. New York: New American Library, 1960.

Suplee, Curt 1989 "Berserk! Violent employees obsessed with revenge are turning the workplace into a killing zone." *Washington Post* (October 1): D1–D2.

Suttles, Gerald D. 1968 *The Social Order of the Slum: Ethnicity and Territory in the Inner City*. Chicago: University of Chicago Press.

Swanson, Guy E. 1960 *The Birth of the Gods: The Origin of Primitive Beliefs*. Ann Arbor: University of Michigan Press.

—— 1967 *Religion and Regime: A Sociological Account of the Reformation*. Ann Arbor: University of Michigan Press.

Sweet, James H. 1996 "Male homosexuality and spiritism in the African diaspora: the legacies of a link." *Journal of the History of Sexuality* 7: 184–202.

Sweet, Louise E. 1965 "Camel raiding of North Arabian Bedouin: a mechanism of ecological adaptation." *American Anthropologist* 67: 1132–1150.

Sylvester, David 1988 *The Brutality of Fact: Interviews with Francis Bacon*. New York: Thames & Hudson (third enlarged edition; first published 1975).

Szasz, Thomas S. 1960 *The Myth of Mental Illness: Foundations of a Theory of Personal Conduct*. New York: Paul B. Hoeber.

—— 1963 *Law, Liberty, and Psychiatry: An Inquiry into the Social Uses of Mental Health Practices*. New York: Macmillan.

Szép, Ernö 1945 *The Smell of Humans: A Memoir of the Holocaust in Hungary.* Budapest: Central European University Press, 1994.

Szpilman, Wladyslaw 1999 *The Pianist: The Extraordinary True Story of One Man's Survival in Warsaw, 1939–1945.* New York: Picador (first published 1945).

Tafel, Edgar 1979 *Years with Frank Lloyd Wright: Apprentice to Genius.* New York: Dover, 1985.

Talley, Colin L. 1996 "Gender and male same-sex erotic behavior in British North America in the seventeenth century." *Journal of the History of Sexuality* 6: 385–408.

Tanner, R. E. S. 1966 "Cattle theft in Musoma, 1958–9." *Tanzania Notes and Records* 65: 31–42.

Tavuchis, Nicholas 1991 *Mea Culpa: A Sociology of Apology and Reconciliation.* Stanford, CA: Stanford University Press.

Teitelbaum, Joel M. 1976 "The leer and the loom—social controls on handloom weavers." Pages 63–75 in Maloney 1976b.

Thomas, Keith 1970 "The relevance of social anthropology to the historical study of English witchcraft." Pages 47–79 in M. Douglas 1970b.

——1971 *Religion and the Decline of Magic.* New York: Charles Scribner's Sons.

Thornton, Russell 1987 *American Indian Holocaust and Survival: A Population History since 1492.* Norman: University of Oklahoma Press.

Trexler, Richard C. 1984 "*Correre la terra*: collective insults in the late Middle Ages." *Mélanges de l'École Française de Rome* 96: 845–902.

Tucker, James 1989 "Employee theft as social control." *Deviant Behavior* 10: 319–334.

——1993 "Everyday forms of employee resistance." *Sociological Forum* 8: 25–45.

——1999a *The Therapeutic Corporation.* New York: Oxford University Press.

—— 1999b "Therapy, organizations, and the state: a Blackian perspective." Pages 73–87 in *Counseling and the State*, edited by James J. Chriss. Hawthorne, NY: Aldine de Gruyter.

——2002 "New Age religion and the cult of the self." *Society* 39 (January/February): 46–51.

Tumin, Melvin M. 1952 *Caste in a Peasant Society: A Case Study in the Dynamics of Caste.* Princeton, NJ: Princeton University Press.

Turnbull, Colin M. 1961 *The Forest People: A Study of the Pygmies of the Congo.* New York: Simon & Schuster.

——— 1965 *Wayward Servants: The Two Worlds of the African Pygmies.* Westport, CT: Greenwood, 1976.

Turner, Bryan S. 1977 "Confession and social structure." Pages 39–65 in Hepworth and Turner 1982.

Uchendu, Victor C. 1965 "The Igbo world." Pages 225–235 in Achebe 2009.

Urbina, Ian, and Sean D. Hamill 2008 "As economy dips, arrests for shoplifting soar." *New York Times.* Online (December 22): http://www.nytimes.com/2008/12/23/us/23shoplift.html?_r=1&hp.

USA *Today* 2008a "Christians in India face attacks." Online (October 25): http://www.usatoday.com/news/religion/2008-10-25-india-attacks_N.htm.

——— 2008b "Santa gunman had lost job, wife before attack." Online (December 27): http://www.usatoday.com/news/nation/2008-12-27-santa-shooting_N.htm.

——— 2009 "Coach of 100-point win fired, says he's not sorry." Online (January 25): http://www.usatoday.com/sports/preps/basketball/2009-01-25-coach-fired_N.htm.

——— 2010a "Police in Denmark stop attack on controversial cartoonist." Online (January 1): http://www.usatoday.com/news/world/2010-01-01-danish-cartoonist-attack_N.htm.

——— 2010b "Survivor: Alabama university shooter fired suddenly." Online (December 16): http://www.usatoday.com/news/nation/2010-02-16-alabama-professor-shooting_N.htm.

Van Baal, J. 1984 "The dialectics of sex in Marind-Anim culture." Pages 128–166 in Herdt 1984b.

van der Meer, Theo 1991 "Tribades on trial: female same-sex offenders in late eighteenth-century Amsterdam." *Journal of the History of Sexuality* 1: 424–445.

van der Sprenkel, Sybille 1962 *Legal Institutions in Manchu China: A Sociological Analysis.* New York: Humanities.

van Eck, Clementine 2003 *Purified by Blood: Honour Killings amongst Turks in the Netherlands.* Amsterdam: Amsterdam University Press.

van Sommers, Peter 1988 *Jealousy.* London: Penguin.

Van Vechten, Carl 2007 *The Tiger in the House: A Cultural History of the Cat.* New York: New York Review Books (first published 1920).

Vaughan, Diane 1986 *Uncoupling: How Relationships Come Apart.* New York: Vintage, 1987.

Vera Institute of Justice 1977 *Felony Arrests: Their Prosecution and Disposition in New York City's Courts.* New York: Vera Institute of Justice.

Veyne, Paul 1982 "Homosexuality in ancient Rome." Pages 26–35 in Ariès and Béjin 1982.

Waley-Cohen, Joanna 1991 *Exile in Mid-Qing China: Banishment to Xinjiang, 1758–1820.* New Haven, CT: Yale University Press.

Waller, Richard D. 2003 "Witchcraft and colonial law in Kenya." *Past & Present* 180: 241–275.

Warner, W. Lloyd 1937 *A Black Civilization: A Social Study of an Australian Tribe.* New York: Harper.

Warren, Samuel D., and Louis D. Brandeis 1890 "The right of privacy." *Harvard Law Review* 4: 193–220.

Wattie, Chris 2007 "Dad charged after daughter killed in clash over *hijab.*" *National Post.* Online (December 11): http://www.nationalpost.com/news/story.html?id=159480.

Watts, Alan W. 1962 *The Joyous Cosmology: Adventures in the Chemistry of Consciousness.* New York: Vintage.

Waugh, Alexander 2008 *The House of Wittgenstein: A Family at War.* New York: Anchor, 2010.

Weber, David J. 1992 *The Spanish Frontier in North America.* New Haven, CT: Yale University Press.

Weber, Max 1904–05 *The Protestant Ethic and the Spirit of Capitalism.* New York: Charles Scribner's Sons, 1958.

——— 1915 *The Religion of China: Confucianism and Taoism.* New York: Free Press, 1951.

——— 1916–17 *The Religion of India: The Sociology of Hinduism and Buddhism*. New York: Free Press, 1958.

——— 1922 *The Sociology of Religion*. Boston: Beacon, 1963.

Weiermair, Peter 1987 *The Hidden Image: Photographs of the Male Nude in the Nineteenth and Twentieth Centuries*. Cambridge, MA: MIT Press, 1988.

Welsh, David 1969 "Capital punishment in South Africa." Pages 395–427 in *African Penal Systems*, edited by Alan Milner. New York: Frederick A. Praeger.

Westermeyer, Joseph J. 1972 "A comparison of amok and other homicide in Laos." *American Journal of Psychiatry* 129: 703–709.

Westfall, Richard S. 1980 *Never at Rest: A Biography of Isaac Newton*. Cambridge: Cambridge University Press.

White, Michael, and John Gribbin 1993 *Einstein: A Life in Science*. New York: Dutton.

Whitrow, G. J. (editor) 1967 *Einstein: The Man and His Achievement*. New York: Dover.

Wijayaratna, Mohan 1990 *Buddhist Monastic Life: According to the Texts of the Theravada Tradition*. Cambridge: Cambridge University Press.

Wijsen, Frans, and Ralph Tanner 2002 *"I Am Just a Sukuma": Globalization and Identity Construction in Northwest Tanzania*. Amsterdam: Rodopi.

Wikipedia: The Free Encyclopedia "Article 301 (Turkish penal code)." Online: http://en.wikipedia.org/wiki/Article_301_(Turkish_Penal_Code).

——— "George Hennard." Online: http://en.wikipedia.org/wiki/George_Hennard.

——— "Going postal." Online: http://en.wikipedia.org/wiki/Going_postal.

——— "Jante Law." Online: http://en.wikipedia.org/wiki/Jante_Law.

——— "Jewish deicide." Online: http://en.wikipedia.org/wiki/Jewish_deicide.

——— *"Jyllands-Posten* Muhammad cartoons controversy." Online: http://en.wikipedia.org/wiki/Jyllands-Posten_Muhammad_cartoons_controversy.

——— "McDonald's Massacre." Online: http://en.wikipedia.org/wiki/McDonald's_massacre.

———— "Mischling." Online: http://en.wikipedia.org/wiki/Mischling.

———— "Navajo people." Online: http://en.wikipedia.org/wiki/Navajo_people.

———— "Persecution of Baha'is." Online: http://en.wikipedia.org/wiki/Persecution_of_Bahá'ís.

———— "Robert-François Damiens." Online: http://en.wikipedia.org/wiki/Robert-François_Damiens.

———— "Roman Catholic sex abuse cases." Online: http://en.wikipedia.org/wiki/Roman_Catholic_sex_abuse_cases.

———— "Tall poppy syndrome." Online: http://en.wikipedia.org/wiki/Tall_poppy_syndrome.

———— "Virginia Tech massacre." Online: http://en.wikipedia.org/wiki/Virginia_Tech_massacre.

Williams, Daniel 2009 "Egypt forces Copts to hide as Muslims hit Swiss minaret ban." Bloomberg.com. Online (December 15): http://www.bloomberg.com/apps/news?pid=20601109&sid=axK5Voe2uZno&pos=15.

Williams, F. E. 1930 *Orokaiva Society.* London: Oxford University Press.

Williams, Jack K. 1980 *Dueling in the Old South: Vignettes of Social History.* College Station: Texas A & M University Press.

Williams, Linda S. 1984 "The classic rape: when do victims report?" *Social Problems* 31: 459–467.

Williamson, Joel 1980 *New People: Miscegenation and Mulattoes in the United States.* New York: Free Press.

Wilson, David Sloan 2002 *Darwin's Cathedral: Evolution, Religion, and the Nature of Society.* Chicago: University of Chicago Press.

Wilson, Margo, and Martin Daly 1993 "Spousal homicide risk and estrangement." *Violence and Victims* 8: 3–16.

Wilson, Monica Hunter 1951 "Witch-beliefs and social structure." Pages 252–263 in Marwick 1970c.

Wilson, Peter J. 1974 "Filcher of good names: an enquiry into anthropology and gossip." *Man* 9: 93–102.

Wilson, Simon 1980 *Egon Schiele.* Ithaca, NY: Cornell University Press.

Wilson, Stephen 1988 *Feuding, Conflict and Banditry in Nineteenth-Century Corsica*. Cambridge: Cambridge University Press.

Winans, Edgar V., and Robert B. Edgerton 1964 "Hehe magical justice." *American Anthropologist* 66: 745–764.

Wingfield, Marshall 1958 "Tennessee's Mormon massacre." *Tennessee Historical Quarterly* 17: 19–36.

Winter, Jana 2009 "Slaughter of foreigners in Yemen bears mark of Gitmo detainee, say experts." *Fox News*. Online (June 20): http://www.foxnews.com/story/0,2933,527868,00.html.

Winton, Richard; Andrew Blankstein; and Ari B. Bloomekatz 2009 "Los Angeles man kills his 5 children, wife, self." *Los Angeles Times*. Online (January 28): http://articles.latimes.com/2009/jan/28/local/me-children-killed28.

Winton, Richard; Evelyn Larrubia; and Kimi Yoshino 2008 "Father kills family and himself, despondent over financial losses." *Los Angeles Times*. Online (October 7): http://articles.latimes.com/2008/oct/07/local/me-porterranch7.

Wishman, Seymour 1981 *Confessions of a Criminal Lawyer*. New York: Penguin, 1982.

Woit, Peter 2006 *Not Even Wrong: The Failure of String Theory and the Search for Unity in Physical Law*. New York: Basic.

Wolf, Eric R. 1955 "Types of Latin American peasantry: a preliminary discussion." *American Anthropologist* 57: 452–471.

Wolfe, Tom 1975 *The Painted Word*. New York: Bantam, 1976.

Wolfgang, Marvin E. 1958 *Patterns in Criminal Homicide*. New York: Wiley, 1966.

Wolfgang, Marvin E., and Franco Ferracuti 1967 *The Subculture of Violence: Towards an Integrated Theory in Criminology*. London: Tavistock.

Wolfgang, Marvin E., and Marc Riedel 1975 "Rape, race, and the death penalty in Georgia." *American Journal of Orthopsychiatry* 45: 658–668.

Woodburn, James 1979 "Minimal politics: the political organization of the Hadza of North Tanzania." Pages 244–266 in *Politics in Leadership: A Comparative Perspective*, edited by William A. Shack and Perry S. Cohen. Oxford: Oxford University Press.

——— 1982 "Egalitarian societies." *Man* 17: 431–451.

Woodburne, A. Stewart 1935 "The evil eye in South Indian folklore." Pages 55–65 in Dundes 1981a.

Woodcock, George, and Ivan Avakumovic 1968 *The Doukhobors*. Toronto: Oxford University Press.

Woodhouse, Annie 1989 *Fantastic Women: Sex, Gender and Transvestism*. New Brunswick, NJ: Rutgers University Press.

Woods, Margo 1981 *Masturbation, Tantra and Self Love*. San Diego, CA: Omphaloskepsis.

Woodward, C. Vann 1974 *The Strange Career of Jim Crow*. New York: Oxford University Press (third revised edition; first edition, 1955).

Wyatt-Brown, Bertram 1982 *Southern Honor: Ethics and Behavior in the Old South*. New York: Oxford University Press.

Yngvesson, Barbara 1976 "Responses to grievance behavior: extended cases in a fishing community." *American Ethnologist* 3: 353–374.

—— 1978 "The Atlantic fishermen." Pages 59–85 in Nader and Todd 1978.

Yoshida, Teigo 1984 "Spirit possession and village conflict." Pages 85–104 in Krauss, Rohlen, and Steinhoff 1984.

Young, Michael W. 1971 *Fighting with Food: Leadership, Values and Social Control in a Massim Society*. Cambridge: Cambridge University Press.

Zahn, Margaret A.; Henry H. Brownstein; and Shelly L. Jackson (editors) 2004 *Violence: From Theory to Research*. Newark, NJ: LexisNexis/Anderson.

Zeid, Abou A. M. 1966 "Honour and shame among the Bedouins of Egypt." Pages 243–259 in Peristiany 1966.

Zerubavel, Eviatar 1985 *The Seven-Day Circle: The History and Meaning of the Week*. Chicago: University of Chicago Press.

—— 2006 *The Elephant in the Room: Silence and Denial in Everyday Life*. New York: Oxford University Press.

Zukav, Gary 1979 *The Dancing Wu Li Masters: An Overview of the New Physics*. New York: William Morrow.

Zwilling, Leonard, and Michael J. Sweet 1996 "'Like a city ablaze': the third sex and the creation of sexuality in Jain religious literature." *Journal of the History of Sexuality* 6: 359–384.

Name Index

A

Abbott, Jack Henry, 163n103, 175n110, 182n76
Abelson, Elaine S., 181n52
Abrahams, Roger D., 175nn104–5
Achebe, Chinua, 166n2, 177n153, 191n24, 196n3
Ackerknecht, Erwin H., 192n44
Aichelburg, Peter C., 154n12
Åkerström, Malin, 169n91
Alldritt, Leslie D., 163n109
Allen, Michael R., 160n59
al-Zarqawi, Abu Mussab, 174n78
Amherst, Lord Jeffrey, 105
Amos, Jonathan, 158n4
Anderson, Elijah, 67–68, 163n104, 172n51, 174n85, 175n103, 175nn106–7
Andrade, E. N. da C., 188n118
Anscombe, G. E. M., 157n58
Apollinaire, Guillaume, 114
Archimbaud, Michel, 187n99
Arendt, Hannah, 163n110, 163n119, 170n112, 193n65
Arensberg, Conrad M., 179n19

Ariès, Philippe, 160n51, 168n59, 169n84
Aristotle, 154n12, 157n58, 157n62
Arnold, Gina, 195nn111–12
Avakumovic, Ivan, 164n150
Axtell, James, 162n99, 192n39, 192nn42–43
Ayoub, Millicent R., 175n104
Azoy, G. Whitney, 170n8

B

Babb, Lawrence A., 162n94, 180n25
Bacon, Francis, 114, 187n99
Baden-Powell, Robert, 157n59
Bailey, George, 172n59, 174n74, 194n90
Bainton, Roland H., 186n61, 186n69
Balikci, Asen, 171n31, 178n163, 196n6, 196n8, 197n17, 197n27
Barber, Bernard, 188n111
Bardach, Janusz, 182n77
Barnard, George W., 167n39, 167n41
Barnes, J. A., 169nn98–99, 170n105, 170n108
Barnett, Stephen A., 175n104
Barrow, John, 115
Barth, Fredrik, 175n88, 179n21, 180n34

Barthel-Bouchier, Diane, 190n1, 198–99n51
Barton, Roy Franklin, 159n29
Baumgartner, M. P., 30, 38, 90, 160n44,
    162n86, 164n148, 165n1, 166n9, 166n20,
    167n26, 167n35, 178–79n1, 181n66, 197n33,
    197n35, 198n40, 198n46, 199n52, 199n59
Baxter, P. T. W., 179n9
Bay, Mia, 163n120
Bayley, David H., 163n102
Beals, Alan R., 182n93
Beattie, J. M., 160n42, 179n9, 181n49, 181n50
Beauvois, Daniel, 173n63
Becker, Howard S., 6, 155n22, 186n81
Beidelman, T. O., 161n76, 164n150, 166n3,
    171n20, 182n72, 185n47
Beirne, Piers, 161nn73–74, 161n77, 163n112,
    198n50, 199n58
Béjin, André, 169n90
Benedict, Ruth, 170n114
Berger, Brigitte, 175n94, 175n102
Berger, Peter, 175n94, 175n102
Bergesen, Albert, 182n75, 198–99n51
Bergson, Henri, 154n12, 155n19
Bernstein, Jeremy, 189n132
Bharati, Agehananda, 182n94
Biehl, Jody K., 192n48
bin Laden, Osama, 174n78
Bing, Léon, 174n85
Black, Donald, 153nn1–3, 154nn8–9, 155n19,
    155n24, 155nn27–28, 155n30, 155–56n32,
    156n36, 157nn55–56, 157n58, 158n67,
    158nn1–3, 160n42, 165n166, 165n1, 168n67,
    169n101, 170n1, 170n6, 171n28, 171n39,
    174n77, 174n82, 176n135, 176n139, 177n141,
    177n145, 177nn148–49, 177n177, 178–79n1,
    180n38, 180n40, 181n54, 182nn74–75,
    183n105, 183n1, 186nn78–80, 188nn110–11,
    188n114, 190n144, 190n151, 190n3, 197n35,
    198nn37–38, 198n46, 198n48, 199n52,
    199n60
Blackmun, Harry A., 198n39
Blankstein, Andrew, 176n128
Blau, Judith R., 155n29
Blau, Peter M., 155n29, 158n5
Blok, Anton, 175n87

Bloom, Paul, 157n49
Bloom-Katz, Ari B., 176n128
Blumberg, Rae Lesser, 153n4, 196n6
Blurton Jones, Nicholas G., 181nn55–56
Boehm, Christopher, 63, 171n27, 177n147,
    197n26
Bohr, Niels, 118, 190n143
Bok, Sissela, 164n141, 169n97
Bolton, Ralph, 180n38
Born, Max, 199n64
Boswell, John, 161n78, 168n63
Bourdieu, Pierre, 175n96, 185n49
Boyer, Paul, 171n23, 179n15
Bradshaw, Lisa, 168n72
Brandeis, Louis, 198n39
Braque, Georges, 113
Brashears, Matthew E., 197–98n36
Brenner, Reuven, 60, 74, 170n5, 171n38,
    176n117, 178n173, 181n58
Breslin, James E. B., 167n33, 168n65
Briar, Scott, 182n74
Briggs, Jean L., 150, 196n6, 199n56
Brinton, Crane, 176n130
Brison, Karen J., 64, 171n33, 178n162, 185n46
Bromley, David G., 194n91
Brooks, Juanita, 186n74
Browder, Chris, 183n103
Brower, David, 149, 198–99n51
Brown, Alison, 30, 162n93
Brown, H. Rap, 175n105
Brown, Julia S., 160n45
Brown, Richard Maxwell, 182n83, 182n87
Brownmiller, Susan, 159nn38–39, 160n41, 160n43
Brundage, James A., 169n95
Bruno, Giordano, 115
Bühler, Georg, 166n18, 180n41, 184n54
Bullough, Bonnie, 192n53, 193n54, 193n59
Bullough, Vern L., 192n53, 193n54, 193n59
Bunzel, Bessie, 168n70
Burbank, Victoria Katherine, 162n100,
    164n158, 164nn160–63, 167n23, 167n26,
    167n30
Burch, Ernest S., Jr., 196n8, 196n12
Burgess, Ann Wolbert, 159n15, 160nn41–42
Burtt, Edwin Arthur, 188n116

C

Cabanne, Pierre, 187nn85–88, 187n98
Campbell, Bradley, 155n30, 190n2, 199n60
Canetti, Elias, 165n183
Cantor, Norman F., 195nn96–97
Carone, Nicholas, 187n95
Catlin, George, 180n38
Cavan, Sherri, 163n125
Cézanne, Paul, 112
Chagnon, Napolean, 166n11
Chalk, Frank, 184n25, 184n30
Chamberlain, Lesley, 199n66
Chang, Iris, 160n43, 176n115
Chapell, Duncan, 160n42
Chernofsky, Erica, 168n67
Chevigny, Paul, 182n74
Choi, Soo-Hyang, 183n104
Christie, Nils, 157n60
Ch'ü, T'ung, 159n32, 177n146, 177n158, 181n54, 182nn68–69, 182n96, 183n107
Clastres, Pierre, 63, 171n28
Cleaver, Eldridge, 160n43
Clement VIII, Pope, 33
Cloward, Richard A., 155n29, 170n2
Cobain, Kurt, 136
Codere, Helen, 177n152
Cohen, Albert K., 75, 175n109, 176n122
Cohen, David, 176n116
Cohen, I. Bernard, 188n114, 188n120, 189n127, 189n130
Cohen, Lawrence E., 155n29, 197–98n36
Cohen, Mark R., 163n113, 191n19, 193n74
Cohen, Paul A., 192nn32–34
Cohn, Norman, 178n169, 178n174, 178n176, 186n66
Colburn, Forrest D., 181n51
Collins, Randall, 153n4, 182n75, 183n102, 186n80
Colson, Elizabeth, 46, 167n27, 171n40, 172nn43–44
Comini, Alessandra, 165n169
Comstock, Gary David, 160n54
Contreras, Jaime, 186n68
Cook, David, 183n3
Cook, Edward F., 187n94
Cook, Scott B., 185n32
Cooley, Charles Horton, 53, 169n104
Cooney, Daniel, 191n17
Cooney, Mark, 108, 127, 155n28, 157nn52–55, 166n22, 168n66, 174n84, 175n98, 175n102, 175n106, 176n139, 177n141, 185n43, 192nn46–47
Copernicus, Nicholas, 115, 190n144
Correll, DeeDee, 193n57
Coser, Lewis, 153n4
Courchesne, Shawn, 170n9
Coveney, Peter, 154n14, 154n16
Crawford, J. R., 171n120
Cressey, Donald R., 75, 176n120
Crick, Francis, 190n144

D

Dahrendorf, Ralf, 153n4
Dalí, Salvador, 113, 187n89
Daly, Martin, 45, 45–46, 47, 166n10, 166n22, 167nn38–40, 175n102
Damiens, Robert-François, 182n78
Damon, Arwa, 192n50
Darwin, Charles, 115, 116, 189n126, 190n144
Davidson, Nicholas, 163n113, 195nn98–99
Davies, James E., 75–76, 176n130
Davis, Joseph E., 198n46, 198n48
Davis, L. J., 198n46
Davis, Robert, 176n124
D'Emilio, John, 159n19
de Grazia, Edward, 165nn176–77, 165n179
de Laguna, Frederica, 177n151
Demos, John, 162n99, 179n15, 191n22, 191n24, 191n27, 192n40
Dentan, Robert Knox, 180n38
Denton-Edmundson, Matthew, 160n55
Desmond, Adrian, 188n124, 189n126, 189n128
De Soto, Hernando, 123
de Ste. Croix, G. E. M., 185n57, 186nn58–60, 191nn11–12
de Tocqueville, Alexis, 176n130
Devlin, Patrick, 156n43, 160n50, 198n39
Diamond, Jared, 150, 199n55, 199n57
Dick, Philip K., 189n138
Dickson, William J., 172n45

Dionisopoulos-Mass, Regina, 180n36
Di Stasi, Lawrence, 179n20
Dixon, Laura, 161n88
Dollard, John, 93, 158n6, 163n121, 175n102, 175n104, 175n105, 182nn88–89, 182nn91–92, 183nn111–12
Donaldson, Bess Allen, 180n25, 180n30
Dorell, Oren, 168n58, 175n90
Dorr, Lisa Lindquist, 159n24
Dorsman, Pieter, 172n53
Douglas, Jack, 49, 168nn69–70, 177nn156–57
Douglas, Mary, 156n46, 158n8, 162n90, 179n12
Dover, K. J., 161n61, 193n62
Doyle, Bertram Wilbur, 183n110
Drew, Katherine Fischer, 159n22, 159n28, 162n84, 166n19, 167n36, 177nn142–43, 180nn43–44
Driggs, Ken, 186n71
Dublin, Louis I., 168n70
du Boulay, Juliet, 170n106
Duker, Abraham G., 194n81
Dumont, Louis, 162nn91–92
Dundes, Alan, 173n65, 179n18, 179n20, 179n24, 180n33, 193n70, 194nn76–79, 194n81, 194n85
Durkheim, Émile, 76, 109, 153n5, 154n10, 155n22, 156n42, 160n46, 168n71, 176n131, 185n54, 196n1, 198nn45–46
Duvignaud, Jean, 162n99

E
Eccles, W. J., 191n22, 191–92n28
Eder, Donna, 163n128
Edgerton, Robert B., 169n75, 191n24
Edward I, King of England, 133
Eggen, Torgrim, 165n173
Einstein, Albert, 69, 115, 117, 135, 151, 154nn13–14, 154n17, 173n66, 189n134, 190n144, 193n68, 195n103, 199n65, 199n67
Einwohner, Rachel L., 176n11
Ejidike, Okey Martin, 166n2, 177n153, 199n53
Ekvall, Robert B., 180n38
Elias, Norbert, 38, 154n10, 164n149, 164n152, 165n181, 176n130, 183nn108–9, 187n105
Elison, George, 192nn29–31

Ellenzweig, Allen, 165n174
Ellis, Albert, 160n46
Elon, Amos, 68, 158n64, 163n115, 172nn58–59, 173n65, 173nn70–71, 174n74, 191nn15–16, 193n69, 195n94
Emerson, Robert H., 163n129, 163n131, 164n140, 166n5
Emmons, George Thornton, 177n151, 177n157
Engel, David M., 178–79n1, 198n38
Engels, Friedrich, 89, 153n4, 170n3, 181n55
Epstein, Joseph M., 159n27
Erikson, Kai, 153n5, 186n69
Estrich, Susan, 155n27, 157n51, 159n15
Evans-Pritchard, E. E., 164n150, 170n14, 178n160, 178n164, 199n58
Ewing, J. Franklin, 156n38
Eysenck, H. J., 188n111

F
Fallers, Lloyd A., 166n15
Faludi, Susan, 156n41
Farber, Leslie H., 189nn136–37
Farley, Maggie, 191n23
Farson, Daniel, 187n101
Favret-Saada, Jeanne, 171n25, 179n17
Feldman, Noah, 162n86, 164n159
Felson, Marcus, 155n29, 197–98n36
Ferdinand, King of Spain, 134
Ferracuti, Franco, 155n29, 174n83
Feuer, Lewis S., 154n14
Field, M. J., 190nn147–48
Finkelhor, David, 160n43
Fischl, Eric, 41
Fletcher, Connie, 156n40, 167n48
Fölsing, Albrecht, 193n68, 195n104,
Fordham, Signithia, 172nn48–50, 185n35, 192n45
Foucault, Michel, 169n78, 177n140, 182n78, 189n138, 190n145, 198n48
Fox, James Alan, 156n39, 176n129
Fox, Renée, 177n159
Frank, Tibor, 173n62, 189n134, 191n16
Frankena, William, 157n58
Frayser, Suzanne G., 166n9
Frazer, James G., 158n10, 162n94, 199n58

Frederick II, Holy Roman Emperor, 110
Freedman, Estelle B., 159n19
Freud, Sigmund, 173n66, 198n46
Fried, Jacob, 168n57, 168n61
Fry, Douglas P., 166n10, 196n5, 197n19
Fryer, Roland G., 172nn48–49
Fuchs, Stephan, 190n6
Fuller, Lon L., 157n58
Fussell, Paul, 185n49, 185n51

G
Gagarin, Michael, 161n61
Galileo Galilei, 115
Garfinkel, Harold, 155–56n32, 190n144
Garrison, Vivian, 179n19
Geertz, Clifford, 190n144
Gelfand, Michael, 170n11, 171n21, 174n80, 179n3, 199n53
Gernet, Jacques, 192n32
Gibson, Thomas P., 161n76, 171n32, 185n48, 196n12
Gilje, Paul A., 184n31
Gillin, John, 157n58
Gilmartin, Christina, 159n38, 182n71
Gilmore, David D., 31, 162n98, 164n157, 168n55, 171n41, 172n42, 174n84, 175n89
Gilot, Françoise, 167n32, 188n109
Ginat, Joseph, 161n67
Ginnell, Laurence, 177n144
Ginsberg, Allen, 38, 41
Girard, René, 160n46, 178n166, 178n174
Gleeson, Kathleen, 182n77
Gluckman, Max, 67, 157n62, 170n17, 170–71n18, 171n19, 171nn39–40, 172n47
Godard, Ellis, 167n25, 198n44
Godiva, Lady, 162n96
Goebbels, Joseph, 69
Goffman, Erving, 36, 50, 158n6, 158n9, 163n105, 163nn124–25, 164nn138–39, 165n182, 165n186, 169n74, 169nn77–78, 169nn80–82, 169n91, 170n111, 174n82, 176n134, 183n102, 190n151, 198n46, 198n48
Golczewski, Frank, 172n59
Goldhagen, Daniel Jonah, 173n65, 173n72, 173–74n73, 194n89

Golding, John, 187n99
Good, Kenneth, 196n15
Goode, William J., 153–54n7, 197n34
Gorn, Elliott J., 169n103, 175n94
Gosling, Nigel, 187n100
Gottfredson, Michael R., 155n24
Gough, E. Kathleen, 180n42
Gould, Roger, 153nn4–5, 174n84
Gould, Stephen Jay, 154n16
Gouldner, Alvin 166n7
Gowing, Lawrence, 187n101
Granovetter, Mark S., 176n137, 199n59
Gray, Charles Edward, 186n79
Greenberg, Clement, 113, 187n96
Greenberg, David, 160n58, 193n60, 193n61
Greenberg, Kenneth S., 53, 169n102
Greene, Brian, 154nn13–14
Gregor, Thomas, 164n145, 170n8, 184nn6–8, 196n11, 196n13, 196–97n16, 197n24, 197n28, 197n31
Gribbin, John, 173n67, 189n133
Grimes, William, 198–99n51
Grimshaw, Allen, 92, 182n83
Gross, Samuel, 198n38
Gross, Jan Tomasz, 194n89
Gruber, Howard E., 189n125, 189n129
Grunfeld, Frederic V., 173nn67–68
Gurr, Ted Robert, 176n130
Gurvitch, Georges, 154n10

H
Hagan, William T., 191n23
Haglunds, Magnus, 159n39, 165n1, 180n33
Haliczer, Stephen, 185n41, 186n65, 195n94, 195nn97–98
Hall, Edward T., 163n126
Hall, Jerome, 180n37
Hall, Lesley A., 161n79, 162n81
Hallowell, A. Irving, 192nn35–36
Hallpike, C. R., 65; 166n16, 169n76, 171n35
Hamill, Sean D., 176n121
Hamilton, Annette, 192n51, 197n31
Hanawalt, Barbara A., 159n15, 160nn42–43, 177n154, 180n45, 181n49
Hane, Mikiso, 163n109

Hare, E. H., 161n79, 162n80
Harfouche, Jamal Karam, 180n30
Harper, Edward B., 162n90, 161nn71–72
Harper, Robert Francis, 159n35
Harner, Michael J., 166n13, 190n155, 196n15
Harrison, Frances, 192n50
Hart, H. L. A., 156n44, 160n47
Haskins, George Lee, 166n20, 169n94
Hasluck, Margaret, 177n147
Hay, Douglas, 181n51
Hayden, Tom, 182n75
Heard, J. Norman, 184n11, 191n23, 191n25,
   192n35, 192nn37–38, 192n42
Heidegger, Martin, 59, 154n10, 173n70
Heisenberg, Werner, 189n142
Hekma, Gert, 160n53
Held, David, 198n44
Heller, Sarah-Grace, 183n100
Hepworth, Mike, 169n88, 169n95
Hennard, George, 156n39
Henry, Andrew F., 76, 170n2, 176nn118–19,
   176n132
Herdt, Gilbert H., 160n59, 161n60, 161n75
Herf, Jeffrey, 158n65, 173n72, 173–74n73
Herman, Judith Lewis, 160nn45–46
Herzfeld, Michael, 179n21
Hiatt, L. R., 164n160, 164n163, 165nn164–65,
   166n10
Highfield, Roger, 154n14, 154n16
Hilberg, Raul, 163n116, 163n118
Himmler, Heinrich, 34
Hinckeldey, Christoph, 160n48, 183n98, 191n10
Hindelang, Michael J., 155n24
Hirschi, Travis, 155n29
Hirschman, Albert O., 165n1, 198n40
Hitler, Adolf, 69, 132–33, 173–74n73, 189n134,
   194n88
Hobhouse, Janet, 165n170
Hobsbawm, E. J., 180n37
Hoebel, E. Adamson, 45, 157n58, 164n142,
   166n10, 166n12, 166nn14–15, 169n88,
   170n110, 177n146, 178n163, 191n26, 196n9,
   197n17
Hoffmann, Banesh, 189n131, 189nn133–34,
   199n65

Hohfeld, Wesley Newcomb, 157n48
Holstrom, Lynda Lytle, 159n15, 160nn41–42
Hoog, Michel, 187n83
Hooke, Robert, 188n120
Hooker, Joseph, 189n125
Horwitz, Allan V., 190n147, 190n151, 198n46,
   198n48
Hosaka, Tomoko A., 176n133
Howard, Michael, 181nn58–60, 181n64
Howell, Signe, 166n10, 184n6
Howkins, Alun, 181n51
Huffington, Arianna Stassinopoulos,
   167n31
Hughes, Geoffrey, 160n56, 183n98, 183n100
Hughes, Robert, 186n81, 187n84, 187n86
Hume, David, 5, 153n5, 154n11, 156n45
Humphreys, Laud, 160n52
Hunt, Alan, 95, 183nn98–101
Hunter, James Davison, 157n59, 165n180,
   168n65, 185n53, 198n43, 199n61
Huntington, Samuel P., 185n32
Hutchinson, Anne, 111
Huxley, Thomas, 189n127
Huygens, Christian, 116

I
Ikegami, Eiko, 174n84, 175n98
Isaacs, Reginald, 113, 187n97
Isaacson, Walter, 154n13, 173n67, 189n132,
   189n134, 195n104, 199nn64–65, 199n67
Isabella, Queen of Spain, 134

J
Jacobs, Janet Liebman, 162n99, 194n91
Jacquard, Roland, 174n78
Janik, Allan, 173n66
Jeffers, Robinson, 46, 188n110, 199n67
Jeffreys, M. D. W., 177n157
Jencks, Charles, 165n171
Jennings, Francis, 184n19, 184nn26–27,
   184n29, 191n22, 191n27
Jensen, Gary, 170n12, 178n182
Jesus of Nazareth, 107, 109–11, 118, 121, 125,
   130–33, 172n56, 185n56, 193n68
Joan of Arc, 128, 193n54

Jonassohn, Kurt, 184n25, 184n30
Joseph II, Austrian Emperor, 114
Judt, Tony, 174n78
Jung, Karl Gustav, 118
Jurgensmeyer, Mark, 183n3, 184n13
Just, Peter, 165n1, 169n85
Justinian, Roman Emperor, 26

K
Kaeuper, Richard W., 175n98
Kafka, Franz, 173n66
Kamen, Henry, 185n41, 195n94
Kandinsky, Wassily, 113, 187nn91–92
Kaplan, Joanna Overing, 162n101, 176n137, 178n162. See also Joanna Overing.
Karman, James, 167n24, 188n110
Kasson, John F., 163n126, 163n134, 165nn184–85, 190nn7–8
Katz, Jack, 155n29, 163n106, 180n38
Keller, Bonnie B., 167n29
Kellner, Hansfried, 175n94, 175n102
Kelly, David, 169n73
Kelly, John, 178n172, 178nn174–75
Kelsen, Hans, 156n47
Kennedy, J. H., 184n5, 191n28, 196n7, 197n25
Kent, Sarah, 165n175
Kiefer, Thomas M., 166n7
Kimmelman, Michael, 187n100
Klimt, Gustav, 40–41, 173n66
Klor de Alva, J. Jorge, 195n101
Kluckhohn, Clyde, 171n22, 179n4
Knauft, Bruce M., 158n10, 171n26, 178n161, 178n167, 179n10, 184n9, 196n4, 196n14, 197n23
Knowles, Nathaniel, 184n11
Koch, Klaus-Friedrich, 177n150, 177n157
Kochman, Thomas, 175nn104–5
Kolchin, Peter, 182n80
Kopytoff, Igor, 156n36
Kposowa, Augustine J., 168n71
Kristof, Nicholas D., 167n37
Kugler, Jacek, 89, 181nn61–63
Kuhn, Philip A., 185n45
Kuhn, Thomas S., 115, 188nn114–16
Kuspit, Donald, 165nn171–72

L
Labov, William, 175n104
LaFave, Wayne, 128, 193n55, 193n64
La Fontaine, Jean, 171n22, 185n47
LaFree, Gary D., 159n15
Laing, R. D., 54, 118, 170n113, 189n138, 190n146, 190n150
Lake, Carlton, 167n32, 188n109
Lambert, H. E., 164n150, 168n54
Landau, Jacob M., 194n79
Langmuir, Gavin, 130, 185n38, 193nn65–66, 193n68, 193nn70–72, 193n74, 194nn75–80, 194nn82–83, 194nn85–86
Laqueur, Thomas W., 161n79, 162n81
Larrubia, Evelyn, 176n127
Lasch, Christopher, 198n45
Lawrence, D. H., 41
Leacock, Eleanor, 171n26
Lebow, Richard Ned, 175n111
Lebra, Takie Sugiyama, 172n46
Lee, Richard B., 164n136, 169n86, 171n26, 171nn29–30, 181n55, 196n15, 197n19, 197nn21–22, 197n30
Leff, Gordon, 186n64
LeGrand, Camille E., 160n42
Le Guin, Ursula K., 181n57
Leibniz, Gottfried Wilhelm, 188n120
Lemert, Edwin M., 76, 156n34, 168n53, 169n91, 173–74n73, 176n134, 189n38
Lepowsky, Maria, 179n10, 196n15, 197n28
Lévi-Strauss, Claude, 160n58, 170n7, 176n138
Levin, Jack, 156n39, 176n129
LeVine, Robert A., 159n130, 179n11
Levy, H., 189n132
Levy, Leonard W., 191n10
Lewis, Bernard, 193n66, 195n99, 195n101
Lewis, Leo, 172n55
Lewis, Oscar, 175n91
Liao, Kyang-Sheng, 192n32
Liebow, Elliott, 181n56
Liliequist, Jonas, 161n75, 161n77
Lilla, Mark, 173n69
Lim, Tae-Seop, 183n104
Linderman, Gerald F., 176n114
Lindholm, Charles, 158n7, 164n155, 197n32

Lindner, Evelin, 174n81
Lindsay, Kenneth C., 187n91
Lingat, Robert, 162n90, 164n153, 166n18, 180n42
Lipsett-Rivera, Sonya, 159n16
Llewellyn, Karl N., 166n12
Lofland, John, 168n53, 198–99n51
Lofland, Lyn H., 158n9
Lord, James, 187n88
Louis XIV, King of France, 96
Louis XV, King of France, 96
Louis XVI, King of France, 96
Lucie-Smith, Edward, 187n98
Luckenbill, David F., 155n29
Lundsgaarde, Henry P., 157n53, 166n22, 167n42
Luther, Martin, 111, 132, 194n80
Lyman, Stanford M., 158n9

M
Macaulay, Stewart, 166n7, 198n38
MacCormack, Geoffrey, 177n158
MacDonald, Robert H., 161nn78–79
Macfarlane, Alan, 178n166, 179n4, 179nn15–16
MacKay, Angus, 185n39
Mackinder, Halford, 89, 181n60
Mackintosh, Charles Rennie, 114
Maddock, K., 164nn160–61, 165n163
Magueijo, João, 188nn112–13
Mahler, Gustav, 173n66
Mailer, Norman, 185n36, 187n90
Maitland, Frederic William, 158n9, 159n16, 177n154, 180nn47–48, 182n73
Makarius, Raoul, 164n158, 165n163
Makin, Kirk, 162n37
Malinowski, Bronislaw, 196n1
Maloney, Clarence, 179n18, 179n20, 179n22, 179n24
Mandelbaum, David, 161n72, 182nn93–94
Mann, Michael, 173n72, 194n89
Manning, Helen, 191–92n28
Manning, Jason, 168n71, 177n157
Margalit, Avishai, 167n34
Markovits, Andrei S., 157n57, 174nn75–76
Marshall, Donald S., 196n15

Marshall, Mac, 175n9
Marwick, Max, 171n19
Marx, Gary T., 185n36
Marx, 60, 89, 153n4, 170n3, 173n66
Mary, Mother of Jesus, 111
Mason, Stephen F., 188n117
Matisse, Henri, 113
Maull, Samuel, 167n34
Mauro, Robert, 198n38
Mauss, Marcel, 166n7
Maybury-Lewis, David, 178n168
McAleer, Kevin, 162n85, 175n100
McCabe, James Dabney, 190n7
McCain, Gillian, 195n112
McClellan, Catherine, 177n151
McCloskey, Deirdre, 157n58
McClure, W. P., 191n26
McConaloque, James, 190n9
McGrew, Anthony, 198n44
McKnight, Brian E., 182n68
McLuhan, Marshall, 148, 198n44
McMillen, Neil, 93, 182nn89–91
McNeil, Legs, 195n112
McNeill, Sandra, 164n146
McNeill, William H., 178nn169–70, 178n177, 178nn179–81, 184nn22–23, 184n25, 195n101
McPherson, Miller, 197–98n36
Meggitt, Mervyn, 159n31, 195n6
Meijer, M. J., 159n33, 161n63
Meitner, Lise, 199n64
Mernissi, Fatima, 162n99, 164n154, 164n156
Merry, Sally Engle, 165n1, 168n62, 171n39
Merton, Robert S., 52, 154n10, 154n12, 155n29, 169n92, 170n2, 188n120
Messenger, John C., 164n144, 170n107
Messner, Steven F., 170n2
Michalski, Joseph H., 199n52
Middleton, John, 170n14, 179nn12–13
Midelfort, H. C. Eric, 170n12, 179n4, 179n15, 190n149
Miles, Barry, 164n151, 165n178
Mill, John Stuart, 156n44
Miller, Arthur I., 154n13, 189n141
Miller, Henry, 41
Miller, Walter B., 155n29, 197n25

Miller, William Ian, 192n53
Milner, Murray, Jr., 158n8, 161n72, 162nn90–
91, 195n110
Minkowski, Hermann, 5, 154nn13–14
Modigliani, Amedeo, 41
Moffat, Alistair, 187n104
Mogar, Robert E., 190n152
Mohammed, 119, 190n5, 194n81
Mondrian, Piet, 135, 195n102
Monk, Ray, 162n82
Moore, James, 188n124, 189n126, 189n128
Moore, Wilbert E., 153–54n7
Moreno de los Arcos, Roberto, 195n101
Morreau, Jacqueline, 165n175
Morrill, Calvin, 185n52
Morris, James, 184n16, 184n18
Mozart, Wolfgang Amadeus, 114
Muir, Jim, 161n65
Müller, Ingo, 163nn116–17
Mullin, Gerald W., 182n80
Murdock, George, 160nn45–46, 166n9,
167n27
Murgoci, Agnes, 180n29
Murphy, Robert F., 184n10
Murray, John Allen, 163n126
Myers, Fred R., 197n20

N
Nader, Laura, 168n56, 168n64
Naess, Arne, 149, 198–99n51
Nandy, Ashis, 170n8
Napoleon I, French Emperor, 118
Naranjo, Claudio, 190n155
Nash, Gary B., 184nn25–26, 191n22
Neeley, Bill, 184n5, 192n41
Nerdrum, Odd, 41
Nero, Roman Emperor, 110
Netanyahu, Benzion, 185nn40–41, 195nn93–
94, 195nn96–97, 195nn100–1
Newman, Gustave, 167n39, 167n41
Newman, Katherine S., 75, 176n124
Newman, Roger K., 165n176
Newton, Isaac, 115–16, 188n120
Nicholas IV, Pope, 133
Nietzsche, Friedrich, 68, 151, 172n57

Nirenberg, David, 163n112, 163n114, 191n14
Nissenbaum, Stephen, 171n23, 179n15
Nohl, Johannes, 178n169, 178n171, 178nn173–
74, 178n176, 178n179
Nye, Robert A., 175n100

O
O'Barr, William M., 185n50
Oberg, Kalervo, 178–79n1
Obeyesekere, Gananath, 170n14
Offer, Avner, 176n113
Ogbu, John U., 172nn48–50, 185n35, 192n45
Ohadike, Don C., 191n24
Ohlin, Lloyd E., 155n29, 170n2
Ohnuki-Tierney, Emiko, 176n133
Olzak, Susan, 92, 182n84
O'Neill, Barry, 175n111, 176n112
Opdyke, Irene Gut, 183n113
Oppenheimer, J. Robert, 135
Orenstein, Henry, 162nn91–92
Organski, Abramo Fimo Kenneth, 89,
181nn61–63
Osmond, Humphrey, 190nn152–53
Overing, Joanna, 157n58. See also Joanna
Overing Kaplan.
Oyler, D. S., 180n28

P
Paine, Robert, 171n39
Pais, Abraham, 189n134, 190n143
Pape, Robert A., 158n67, 159n12, 174n75
Parsons, Talcott, 177n159
Partington, Donald H., 159n24
Patterson, Orlando, 159n39, 175n95
Pauli, Wolfgang, 135, 190n143
Peppiatt, Michael, 188n108
Peristiany, J. G., 174n84
Perutz, M. F., 199n64
Peters, Edward, 159n14, 177n147
Phillips, Scott, 155n28
Piaget, Jean, 197n33
Picasso, Pablo, 31, 46, 113, 114, 118, 154n13,
187n88
Piliavin, Irving M., 182n74
Pinet, Hélène, 187n103

Pinker, Steven, 157n48, 157n59
Pitrè, Giuseppe, 179n24, 180nn32–33
Pitt-Rivers, Julian, 168n55, 172n42,
    174nn82–84, 174n86, 175n89
Planck, Max, 189n134
Pocock, D. F., 179n21
Polanyi, Karl, 196n2, 197n29
Poliakoff, Michael B., 170n8
Pollak, Michael, 167n44
Pollock, Frederick, 158n9, 159n16, 177n154,
    180nn47–48, 182n73
Pollock, Jackson, 113
Pomeroy, Sarah B., 159n40
Popham, Peter, 167n37
Potter, Jeffrey, 187nn94–97
Powers, Edwin, 160n48
Putnam, Robert D., 197–98n36

Q

Quammen, David, 184n17
Quinones, Sam, 169n73

R

Radcliffe-Brown, A. R., 89, 166n15, 197n32
Rand, Ayn, 156n44, 157n61, 187n104
Rappaport, Ernest A., 194n82, 194n84
Rasmussen, Knud, 159n11, 161n76, 169n89,
    170n109, 196n8, 196n10, 197n17
Read, Kenneth E., 65, 171n36
Reay, Marie, 181n53
Rediker, Marcus, 181n50
Redondi, Pietro, 188n117
Regan, Tom, 198n50
Regis, Ed, 189n133, 195n104
Reich, Jay A., 160n42
Reid, John Phillip, 166n12, 177n146, 196n12
Rejali, Darius M., 182n79, 182nn81–82
Retzinger, Suzanne M., 167n35
Richards, Audrey I., 62, 170–71n18, 171n19
Richardson, Jane, 159n34
Richardson, John, 162n95, 167n32, 187n85, 189n141
Ridgeway, Cecilia L., 168n52
Riedel, Marc, 159n24
Rieff, Philip, 198nn46–47
Rilke, Rainer Maria, 187n103, 188n109

Robarchek, Clayton A., 197n18
Robert the Pious, King of France, 110
Roberts, John M., 179n18, 179n23
Robinson, Simon, 166n21
Rodin, Auguste, 114
Roethlisberger, F. J., 172n45
Rosen, Lawrence, 169n100
Rosenberg, Harold, 113
Rosenfeld, Richard, 170n2
Roth, Norman, 185n38, 191n14, 194n74,
    195n92, 195nn95–97, 195n101
Rothko, Mark, 46
Rowe, William L., 182n95
Rubin, Barry, 174nn75–76
Rubin, Jerry, 164n150
Rubin, Judith Colp, 174nn75–76
Ruffini, Julio L., 180n38
Ruggiero, Guido, 159nn17–18
Russell, Diana E. H., 156n40, 159n20,
    167nn45–47
Russell, Jeffrey Burton, 186nn62–63
Russell, John, 187n99
Ryan, Lyndall, 184n15, 184n18

S

Safranski, Rüdinger, 154n10, 173n70
Sageman, Marc, 168n53
Sahibzada, Mehnaz, 159n37
Sahlins, Marshall D., 162n89, 183n106
Sandermose, Aksel, 172n52
Scheff, Thomas J., 71, 153n5, 167n35, 174n81
Scheppele, Kim Lane, 164n143, 169n93
Schiele, Egon, 40
Schild, Wolfgang, 162n84, 177n146, 180n46
Schmitt, Carl, 69
Schneider, Jane, 180n38
Schoeck, Helmut, 179n20, 180nn25–26
Schoetz, David, 168n58
Schultz, Magdalene, 194n82
Schuster, Ilsa, 167nn28–29
Schwartz, Joseph E., 158n5
Schwartz, Richard D., 155–56n32
Schwimmer, Eric R., 160n59
Sciutto, Jim, 193n68
Scott, James C., 181n51, 181n66

Scott, Joanna, 165n168, 171n37
Scott, Marvin B., 158n9
Sedgwick, Adam, 189n129
Selby, Henry A., 179n8
Senechal de la Roche, Roberta, 92–93,
   155n28, 155n30, 156n35, 159nn25–26, 179n9,
   182nn85–87, 185n44, 196n1, 199n60
Serpenti, Laurent, 160n59, 161n60
Servetus, Michael, 111
Sessions, George, 198n50, 198–99n51
Shafak, Elif, 158n7, 186n77
Shakur, Sanyika, 156n41, 175nn107–8
Shamir, Ronen, 184n27
Shams of Tabriz, 186n77
Sharrock, David, 190n5
Shepard, Sanford, 194n82
Shermer, Michael, 189n126
Shively, Donald, 183n97
Short, James F., Jr., 76, 170n2, 176nn118–19,
   176n132
Shostak, Margorie, 197n19
Simmel, Georg, 51, 153n4, 158n6, 163n124,
   164n141, 169n83, 169n96, 169n98, 185n55
Simonton, Dean Keith, 189n139
Sinclair, Andrew, 187n100, 187n102, 188n108
Singer, Peter, 198n50
Skolnick, Jerome H., 155–56n32
Slezkine, Yuri, 68, 172n59, 173n60, 173n66, 174n74
Smelser, Neil, 153–54n7
Smith, Adam, 153n5, 156n43, 157n58
Smith, Cyril Stanley, 189n140
Smith, Joseph, 111
Smith, R. Spencer, 192n97
Smith-Lovin, Lynn, 197–98n36
Smolin, Lee, 135–36, 188n112, 195nn104–9
Socrates, 109
Sombart, Werner, 68, 173n61, 173n63, 174n74
Sorli, Amrit, 5, 154n15
Sorokin, Pitirim. 154n10, 154n12
Spain, Daphne, 161n75
Spindel, Donna J., 159n23, 182n80
Spooner, Brian, 179nn21–22, 180n30
Stack, Carol B., 176n137
Stack, Steven, 168n68
Stark, Rodney, 168n53

Stearns, Peter N., 185n51
Steele, Ian K., 184n28
Stevens, John, 199n63
Stewart, Frank Henderson. 174n84
Stinchcombe, Arthur L., 60, 170n4
Stoller, Robert J., 161n60
Stone, Christopher, 149, 198–99n51
Stowe, Steven M., 175n94, 175n99
Strauss, Richard, 114
Strehlow, C., 166n14
Sturrock, Mary Newbery, 187n104
Sulloway, Frank J., 115, 188n111
Sumner, William Graham, 183n4
Supler, Curt, 176n124
Suttles, Gerald D., 163n104, 163n127
Swanson, Guy E., 186n67, 196n1
Sweet, James H., 193n60
Sweet, Louise E., 180n38
Sweet, Michael J., 186n75, 193n60
Sylvester, David, 187n99
Szasz, Thomas S., 198n48
Szép, Ernö, 194n74, 194n89
Szpilman, Wladyslaw, 183n114

T
Tafel, Edgar, 187n104
Talley, Colin L., 193n61, 193n63
Tanner, Ralph, 170n13, 179n2, 179n14, 180n38
Tavuchis, Nicholas, 171n30
Teitelbaum, Joel M., 180n27
Tertullian, 122
Thomas, Keith, 178n166, 178n178, 179n4
Thornton, Russell, 184n22, 184n24, 184n30
Thucydides, 89
Toulmin, Stephen, 173n66
Trexler, Richard C., 162n99, 164n150
Tucker, James, 180n38, 181n66, 198n48
Tumin, Melvin M., 179n7
Turnbull, Colin M., 89, 164n145, 180n38,
   181nn55–56, 196n15, 197n21, 197n26, 199n56
Turner, Bryan S., 169n88, 169n95

U
Uchendu, Victor C., 169n87
Urbina, Ian, 176n121

V

Van Baal, J., 160n59, 164n135
van der Meer, Theo, 160n49, 160n53
van der Sprenkel, Sybille, 178–79n1
van Eck, Clementine, 161n66, 175n90
van Sommers, Peter, 166n8
Van Vechten, Carl, 199n58
Vaughan, Diane, 52, 168n60, 169n91
Vera, Herman, 167n39, 167n41
Vera, Maria I., 167n39, 167n41
Vergo, Peter, 187n91
Veyne, Paul, 161n62
Victoria, Queen of England, 116
von Treitschke, Heinrich, 74
Vonnegut, Kurt, 172n52

W

Waley-Cohen, Joanna, 182n70
Wallace, Alfred Russell, 189n126
Waller, Richard D., 169n79, 170n16
Warner, W. Lloyd, 164nn162–63, 165n164
Warren, Samuel A., 198n39
Wattie, Chris, 192n49
Watts, Alan, 119, 190n154
Waugh, Alexander, 177n155, 187–88n107
Weber, David J., 184nn20–21
Weber, Max, 111, 163n108, 163n110, 173n61,
    186nn75–76, 199n62
Weiermair, Peter, 165n174
Welsh, David, 159n24
Westermeyer, Joseph J., 156n37, 167n49
Westfall, Richard S., 188nn120–23
Weyland, Paul, 189n132
White, Michael, 173n67, 189n133
Whitrow, G. J., 189n132
Wijayaratna, Mohan, 161nn68–69, 161n78,
    166n4
Wijsen, Frans, 170n13, 179n2, 179n14
Williams, Daniel, 183n3
Williams, F. E., 181n53
Williams, Jack K., 175n93, 175n97, 175n99, 175n101
Williams, Linda S., 155n27, 157n51, 159n15
Williamson, Joel, 163n122, 175n99, 175n101
Willis, Roy, 166n10
Wilson, David Sloan, 184n12

Wilson, Margo, 45, 45–46, 47, 166n10, 166n22,
    167nn38–40, 175n102
Wilson, Monica Hunter, 169n79, 171n21,
    197n24
Wilson, Peter J., 171n39
Wilson, Simon, 165n168
Wilson, Stephen, 177n147
Winans, Edgar V., 169n75
Wingfield, Marshall, 186n72, 186n74
Winter, E. H., 170n14, 179n12
Winton, Richard, 176nn127–28
Wishman, Seymour, 169n100
Wittgenstein, Hans, 177n155
Wittgenstein, Konrad, 177n155
Wittgenstein, Ludwig, 78, 173n66, 177n155,
    187–88n107
Wittgenstein, Paul, 187–88n107
Wittgenstein, Rudolf, 78
Woit, Peter, 195n107
Wolf, Eric R., 179nn6–7
Wolfe, Tom, 186n81, 187n93
Wolfgang, Marvin E., 155n29, 166n22, 174n83
Woodburn, James, 165n1, 171n26, 196n5
Woodburne, A. Stewart, 180n31, 180n35
Woodcock, George, 164n150
Woodhouse, Annie, 193nn58–59
Woodward, C. Vann, 163n123
Woods, Margo, 162n83
Wright, Frank Lloyd, 114
Wyatt-Brown, Bertram, 178n165

Y

Yasmine, 49
Yllo, Kersti, 160n43
Yngvesson, Barbara, 38, 164n147
Yoshida, Teigo, 171n24
Yoshino, Kimi, 176n127
Young, Michael W., 65, 166n17, 171n34, 196n15

Z

Zeid, Abou A. M., 159n36
Zerubavel, Eviatar, 154n10, 163n128, 163n132
Zola, Émile, 41
Zukav, Gary, 188n115
Zwilling, Leonard, 186n75, 193n60

Subject Index

A

Abortion, 47, 49, 199n61

Accidents, 10, 27, 59, 62, 71, 77, 83, 85, 138, 146.
  See also Injury

Adultery, 21, 24, 25, 32, 44–46, 51, 53, 79, 133,
  141, 142, 162n99, 166nn8–10, 166n15,
  166n19, 167n34, 197n19

Afghanistan, 22, 39, 45, 72, 122

Africa and Africans, 3, 12, 27, 43, 46, 50, 61,
  62, 78, 84, 105, 106, 107, 173n72, 177n157.
  See also individual African countries

African-Americans, 3, 22, 23–24, 32, 34, 67–68,
  73, 92–93, 96, 106–107, 108, 126, 127, 139,
  156n35, 159n26, 174n85, 182n86, 183n111

Alcohol and alcoholism, 75, 78, 97, 119

Algeria and the Algerians, 72

Algonquin Indians, 123

Altruism, 177n57
  global, 150
  tribal, 150

America
  colonial, 23
  North, 125, 141, 143, 144
  See also United States and the Americans

American Civil War, 50, 74

American Revolutionary War, 50

Americas, the, 12, 123, 134, 184n22

Amok, running, 10, 48, 75, 78, 156nn38–39

Andalusia, 31, 39, 48, 65–66, 72, 171n41.
  See also Spain and the Spanish

Andaman Islanders, 89

Animals, non-human, 8, 21, 25, 28, 37, 46,
  49, 63, 65, 66, 77, 78, 80, 83, 87, 91, 95,
  96, 103, 110, 122, 125, 141, 142, 149, 150,
  151, 152, 155n20, 161n76, 168n65, 180n38,
  199n58. *See also* Bestiality

Anti-Americanism, 16, 70–71

Anti-Semitism, 16, 70, 101, 130, 132, 172n57,
  174n74, 191n16, 193n68, 194n81, 194n90.
  See also Holocaust; Jews and Judaism

Apache Indians, 104

Apology, 73, 74

Arabs, 106, 108, 132, 173n72, 194n81

Aran Islanders, 37

Architecture, 114

Aristocracy, nobility, and royalty, 30, 31, 38,
  72–73, 74, 82, 85, 91–92, 95–96, 165n166

Arson, 24, 80–81, 93, 110, 111, 191n24, 192n34

Art and artists, 5, 40–41, 101, 112–114, 117, 118, 135, 137, 144, 165n166, 165n168, 186n79, 186n82, 187nn88–89, 187n104, 187n106
overcreativity in, 112–114
Asia, 10, 12, 43, 50, 68, 80, 106, 107, 112, 198n37. *See also individual Asian countries*
Asian-Americans, 107
Assassination, 23, 48, 153n3, 186n77
Assault, 3, 8, 23, 24, 27, 28, 39, 40, 45, 46, 48, 67, 86, 87, 88, 90, 91, 91–92, 93, 94, 96, 97, 112, 122, 123, 144, 168n67
Assyrians, ancient, 24
Assimilation, cultural, 126–127
Athens, ancient, 24–25. *See also* Greece and the Greeks, ancient
Athletes and sports, 9, 60–61, 65, 67, 75, 83, 170nn6–8
Australia and the Australians, 28, 68, 191n23
Australian Aborigines, 31, 39–40, 45, 46, 106, 142, 144, 164n159, 164–165nn163–165, 191n23, 192n51, 196n6
Austria and the Austrians, 28, 40–41, 80, 114, 132, 187–188n107, 194n90
Authority, 4, 5, 63, 90, 120, 143, 146, 147, 155–156n32
Avoidance, xi, 43, 79, 102, 103, 107, 150, 153n3, 185n33, 198n40
Azande, 79, 178n160
Aztec Indians, 195n101

B

Babylonia, 12, 24, 198n41
Baha'is, 112
Baltic countries, 108
Bamberg Code, 88
Banishment, expulsion, and exile, 9, 43, 88, 91, 94, 102, 107, 111, 113, 121, 122, 132, 133, 134, 189n134
Basques, 50
Bedouin, 24, 27, 184n27. *See also* Arabs
Beggars and begging, 85, 108, 143
Belgium and the Belgians, 80, 158n46
Bemba, 62
Bengal. *See* India and the Indians

Berbers, 72
Bestiality, 25, 28, 33, 161n76
Bible, The, 12, 28, 77, 103, 109, 128
Birth, 5, 44, 85
Black Death, 16, 80–81, 178n182
Blasphemy, 17, 122, 176n146
Blinding, as social control, 23, 47, 88, 92, 125, 182n82
Blood libel, 131–132, 194n81, *See also* Anti-Semitism; Jews and Judaism
Body, human, 76, 109, 164n137, 182n68
decoration of, 144
depiction of, in art, 113, 114, 186n82, 187n89
obesity of, 109, 185n51
shape of, 109, 185n51
Botswana, 35, 51, 64, 142, 143, 197n19
Boycotts, 156n35
Brahmins, 28, 30, 38, 87
Bravery, 15, 72, 74
Brazil, 37, 45, 80, 103, 141, 142, 144, 166n9, 184n6
Brehon laws, 77. *See also* Ireland and the Irish
Brothers and sisters, 25, 31, 39–40, 61, 127, 160n45, 164–165n159, 165n163. *See also* Siblings
Buddhism and Buddhists, 27–28, 43, 111–112, 151
Buid, 64, 108, 161n76, 196n12
Burakumin, 32
Burglary, 22, 36, 74, 87, 88, 142, 145, 180n38
Burgundians, 23, 47, 77. *See also* Germanic tribes
Burning at the stake, 26, 33, 81, 110, 111, 115, 124, 131, 134. *See also* Death penalty
Business and business relationships, 5, 52, 60, 68–69, 173n63, 182n84

C

Canada and the Canadians, 123, 127, 140, 164n150, 191nn22–23
Cannibalism, 3, 79, 103, 110, 191–192n28
Castes, 28, 30, 32, 38, 140. *See also* Brahmins; Burakumin; Hindus and Hinduism; Jews and Judaism; India and the Indians; Untouchables

Castration, 23, 24, 97, 104, 177n146. *See also*
Mutilation
Catholics and the Catholic Church, 28, 48,
52, 81, 110–111, 115, 118, 123, 129–130, 132,
191nn22–24, 192n30, 193n68, 194n90
Celtic tribes, 12. *See also* Ireland and the Irish
Censorship, 40–41
Chad and the Chadians, 31
Chechnya and the Chechens, 50
Cherokee Indians, 196n12
Chewong, 103
Cheyenne Indians, 45
Children, 30, 42, 44, 48–49, 72, 92, 158n7,
162n86, 166n2, 168n71, 197n33
abandonment of, 48, 49, 168n63
conflict among, 30
death of, 84
kidnapping of, 16, 69, 103, 104, 123, 125, 131,
132, 184n17, 191n23
killing of, 16, 47, 69, 70, 97, 105, 118, 131, 132,
177n157, 184n26
misbehavior by, 90
neglect of, 49
punishment of, 23, 49, 90, 123
rape of, 23, 159n26
running away by, 49
sex with, 25, 26–27, 28, 141, 161n60, 162n87
China and the Chinese, 12, 16, 24, 27, 78, 80,
90, 94, 96, 105–106, 108, 112, 124–125,
177n146, 178n1, 181n54
Chinese-Americans, 107
Christianity and Christians, 3, 10, 16, 32–34,
69, 81, 101, 104, 107, 108, 109–111, 121, 122,
123, 124, 125, 130, 130–134, 144, 172n56,
173n63, 174n74, 186n61, 191–192n16,
192nn22–28, 192n34, 193–194n74, 195n94,
195n101
Class, social, 101, 109, 140, 153n4
Closeness, 7
cultural, 165n166
global, 148, 149, 159
over, 6, 137, 138–139, 145
relational, 44, 141, 155n28, 165n166
self, 147–148, 148, 149
social, 4, 6, 138–139, 140–144

tribal, 148, 150
under, 6, 137, 138–139
vertical, 165n166
Clothing, 29, 32–33, 37, 86, 93, 94–95, 101, 106,
108, 109, 123, 126, 144, 145, 175n90
stripping of, 23, 94, 123, 125, 144, 162n99,
183n97, 195n112
Colonies and colonialism, 102, 103, 104,
196nn2–3
Comanche Indians, 126
Communism, 60, 89, 174n74
Compensation, 9, 24, 29, 45, 77, 146, 180n38
Competition, 46, 60–61, 65, 143, 146
Confession, 52, 78, 80, 81, 178–179n1
Conflict, xi, 135
causes of, xii, 135, 153–154n7
definition of, 153n4
origin of, 5–11
theoretical formulations about, xi–xii, 3–4,
5–11, 22, 36, 44, 51, 60, 71, 82, 83, 89, 102,
109, 120, 121, 129, 138, 139
Congo, 10, 143
Conservatism, as cultural time, 130–133
Conversion, religious, 5, 11, 80–81, 108, 122–125,
131, 133, 134, 144, 168n53, 191nn13–6,
191nn22–24, 191–192n28, 192n34,
193–194n74, 195nn93–94, 195n101
as cultural time, 122–125
Creativity, 4, 5, 17, 186n79, 187n104. *See also*
Innovation
overcreativity, 112–117
Crime, xi, xii, 3, 5, 6, 9, 12, 91, 103–104, 110, 124,
128, 131, 132, 133, 138, 139, 153n6, 168n53
as social time, 6–11
causes of, 8–9, 11, 60, 74–75, 153n5, 176n130
See also individual types of crime
Criticism, as social control, xi, 3, 5, 35, 40, 42,
61, 64, 93, 107, 109, 114, 121, 127, 135
Cross-dressing, 128–129, 193n54
Crow Indians, 126, 180n38
Crucifixion, 3, 16, 110, 121, 124, 130, 131, 132.
See also Death penalty
Crusades, 130–131
Cuba and the Cubans, 104
Cultural distance, 4, 101, 120, 163n167

Cultural time, xii, 4, 5, 6, 7, 9, 11, 17, 99–136,
  137, 138, 156n96, 181n65
  conservatism as, 130–133
  conversion as, 122–125
  heresy as, 109–112
Culture, 12
  conflicts of, 106–108
  definition of, 3, 101
  gender as, 127–129
  insanity as, 117–119
  race as, 106–108
Cursing, as social control, 50, 90

D
Dangerousness, social, xi, 3, 39, 61, 85, 107,
  138, 143, 150, 173n73
Death, 5, 10, 76, 118, 137, 156n46, 176n138,
  178n162, 196n1
Death penalty, 9, 23–24, 26, 27, 28, 33, 36, 39,
  45, 47, 73, 78, 80, 81, 83, 87, 88, 90, 91,
  92, 109, 110, 111, 112, 115, 120, 122, 126,
  128, 131, 134, 145, 159n24, 163n111, 178n1,
  182n68, 186nn61–62, 193n54
Debt, 180n38
Deicide, 193n68
Denmark and the Danes, 121, 172n52
Desertion. See Leaving (a relationship)
Deviant behavior, xii, 3, 6, 7, 9, 43, 137, 153n1,
  154n23
Disasters, natural, 6, 10, 59, 122, 154n18
Disease, 6, 10, 16, 59, 71, 118, 144, 149. See also
  Epidemics; Health and illness
Dislike, 3, 13–15, 60, 68, 108–109, 129, 137, 138,
  154n18
Disrespect, 7, 71, 73, 90–91, 138, 139
Distance, social, 4, 138–139, 144–146, 154nn8–9
  cultural, 32, 101, 102, 120, 141, 155n30
  physical, 4
  relational, 4, 21, 23, 29, 145, 146, 155n30,
    158n1, 163n107 (see also Intimacy)
  vertical, 32, 59, 82, 141
Diversity, cultural, xi, 4, 5, 6, 7, 12, 16, 101, 120,
  138, 139–140, 147, 151, 198n43
  overdiversity, 6, 7, 14, 101–119, 120, 137, 138,
    139, 144, 191n13

right to, 147
  underdiversity, 6, 7, 14, 102, 120, 137, 139,
    191n13
Divorce, 4, 8, 25, 43, 44, 46, 46–50, 168n53,
  168n71, 197–198n36
Dou Donggo, 51
Doukhobors, 164n150
Drugs, illegal, and drug use, 75, 119,
  190n155
Duels and dueling, 29–30, 53, 73, 74

E
Eavesdropping, 35, 36
Ecuador, 45, 196n15
Egypt, and the Egyptians, 24, 132
Embezzlement, 11, 74–75
Employers and employees, 5, 11, 33, 43,
  66–67, 71, 75, 83, 109, 115, 147, 162n87,
  172nn45–46, 181n56. See also Job loss
Enemies, 3, 5, 53, 60, 65, 70, 103, 123–124,
  158n64, 160n43
England and the English, 21–22, 26, 28–29,
  30, 37, 41, 84, 88, 95, 103, 105, 114, 128,
  179n16, 187n99, 195n92
  medieval, 23, 78, 81, 88, 90–91, 107, 128, 131,
    132, 133, 160n43, 162n96
  See also Great Britain and the British
Epidemics, 52, 179n19. See also Disease;
  Health and illness
Equality, right to, 143. See also Inequality
Eskimos, 22, 51, 53, 64, 79, 141, 142, 143, 147,
  150, 161n76
Ethiopia, 106–107
Ethnicity and ethnic groups, 4, 7, 8, 9, 54–55,
  101, 106, 107, 108, 109, 144, 146, 147, 150,
  155n28, 163n107, 185nn34–37
Etiquette and manners, xii, 3, 6, 22, 34–36, 42,
  50–51, 54–55, 95–97, 101, 109, 121, 137, 146,
  183n111
Europe and Europeans, 12, 32, 38, 68, 69, 70,
  84, 102, 103, 104–105, 106, 107–108, 125,
  130, 131, 132, 133, 141
  medieval, 16, 38, 42, 72–73, 80–81, 87,
    110–111, 132, 140, 143, 150, 164n153, 198n41
  See also individual European countries

Exhibitionism, 17, 37, 42, 54–55
Exile. *See* Banishment, expulsion, and exile
Exposure
  and inequality, 38
  as intimacy, 36
  overexposure, 36–42, 164n137, 164n150, 165n167
  underexposure, 51–55
Expulsion. *See* Banishment, expulsion, and exile
Evil eye, 84–87, 179n19. *See also* Magic and sorcery

F

False accusations, xii, 14, 15–16, 69–70, 81, 83, 87, 103, 110, 111, 124–125, 131, 132, 138, 158nn63–64, 173n73, 195n93
Families, 6, 12, 13, 26, 89, 90–91, 95, 144, 145, 147, 150, 155n28, 196n5. *See also* Brothers and sisters; Divorce; Husbands and wives; Parents and children
  patriarchal, 22, 95, 158n7, 196n6
Famine, 52, 80, 122, 149, 179n19
Feudalism, 198n37
Feuds and feuding, xi, 49, 77, 150, 155n30
Fighting, xi, 153n3. *See also* Assault; Duels and dueling; Feuds and feuding; Warfare
Fines, 9, 87, 91, 94, 122
Foreigners, 4, 102, 103, 108, 125, 144, 150
Fornication, 25, 27. *See also* Sex
France and the French, 50, 63, 71, 73, 80, 81, 84, 91, 95, 103, 106, 112, 113, 114, 124, 125, 128, 130, 131, 132, 133, 141, 147, 150, 179n17, 191nn22–24
Freedom of expression, 12, 41, 137, 144, 147, 149
French Revolution, 96
Friends and friendship, xii, 5, 6, 12, 21–22, 23, 36, 37–38, 44, 51, 53, 59, 61, 76, 89, 102, 109, 139, 145, 155n28, 158n7

G

Gangs and gang members, 11, 31–32, 49, 73, 74, 75, 144, 150
Gebusi, 79, 80, 142, 143

Gender and gender relations, 26, 39, 44, 72, 86, 101, 109, 112, 139, 141, 146, 161n75, 164nn150–159, 165n165, 167n25, 167n37, 168n71, 174n85, 175n90, 178n161, 192n5
  as culture, 127–129
  gender conversion, 128–129
Generosity, 15, 64, 142, 171n22
Genocide, 3, 34, 69–70, 121, 149, 151, 158n3, 173n72, 194n90. *See also* Holocaust
Germany and the Germans, 3, 28, 29–30, 33–34, 68, 69, 71, 73, 80, 90, 95, 96–97, 106, 107, 114, 117, 118, 122, 127, 132, 155n30, 158n64, 173n72, 174n74, 189n134, 193n68, 194n90
  medieval, 87, 122, 130, 131, 132, 177n146
Germanic tribes, 12, 24, 29, 45. *See also* Burgundians; Lombards
Ghana, 118
Gisu, 171n22
Goodenough Island, 196n15
Gossip, xi, 6, 13, 14, 65–66, 79, 86, 171n41
Great Britain and the British, 89, 90, 104, 105, 124, 184n17, 196n3. *See also* England and the English; Scotland and the Scots
Greece and the Greeks, 53, 86
  ancient, 27, 74, 89, 129, 187n106, 198n37
Gusii, 24, 84

H

Hammurabi, Code of, 24
Happiness, right to, 148–149
Hawaii, 30, 95–96
Headhunting and headhunters, 45, 103
Health and illness, 3, 51–52, 62, 76, 79–81, 83, 85, 86, 104–105, 137, 171n24, 178nn160–162, 196n1. *See also* Disease; Epidemics
Hehe, 50
Heresy, 7, 9, 17, 109–112, 115, 116, 120, 133, 138, 139–140, 157n61, 186nn61–62, 186n77, 193n54
  as cultural time, 109–113
Hindus and Hinduism, 111–112, 156n48, 192n34
Hispanic-Americans, 107, 172n49
Holocaust, 34, 69–70, 80, 121, 133. *See also* Genocide; Jews and Judaism

Homelessness and the homeless, 8, 13, 77, 195n112

Homicide, xi, 3, 5, 7, 8, 10, 11, 13, 23, 27, 33, 43, 45, 47, 48, 49, 53, 61–62, 73, 75, 76–77, 80–81, 83, 84, 86, 90–92, 93, 94, 97, 102, 103, 104, 105, 108, 111, 123, 124, 125, 127, 128, 129–130, 131, 133, 134, 142, 143, 144, 150, 156n38, 157n58, 165n165, 166n2, 166n10, 168n58, 172n54, 175n90, 178n161, 184n17, 184n26, 186nn74–77, 191–192nn24–28, 192n34

Homosexuality and homosexuals, 17, 25, 26–27, 41, 47, 49, 67, 73–74, 128, 129, 156n43, 161n60

Honor, 15, 17, 71–74, 174n85, 175nn90–97

Host desecration, 132

Hunter-gatherers, 63–64, 89, 140–141, 171n26, 181n56, 196nn4–6

Hungary and the Hungarians, 68–69

Huron Indians, 141

Husbands and wives, 3, 8, 11, 22, 23, 24–25, 45–46, 47–48, 50, 78, 90–91, 128, 141–142, 158n7, 159n35, 166n10, 197–198n36

I

Ideas, 5, 14, 101, 115–117, 135, 144

Ifugao, 24

Igbo, 51, 78, 166n2, 191n24, 196n3

Illness. *See* Health and illness

Illinois Indians, 24, 102

Immigrants and immigration, 102, 105–106, 107–108, 127

Imprisonment, 9, 13, 24, 27, 28, 36, 41, 43, 95, 111, 112, 115, 133, 134, 155n32, 156n33, 178–179n1. *See also* Prisons and prisoners

Incest and the incest taboo, 17, 22, 25–26, 27, 79, 110, 160n45, 196–197n16

Independence movements, 50, 90

Indians, American, 102, 103, 104, 105, 123–124, 125, 126, 129, 141, 143, 144, 150, 162n99, 184n5, 184nn22–26, 191nn22–24, 197n25. *See also individual tribes*

India and the Indians, 12, 28, 30, 38, 45, 86, 87, 88, 89, 94, 105, 112, 151, 160n43, 166n9,

192n34. *See also* Brahmins; Castes; Hinduism and Hindus; Untouchables

Indonesia and the Indonesians, 51, 106

Inequality, xi, 4, 5, 6, 7, 8, 12, 59–81, 81–97, 138, 139, 140–141, 143, 144, 146, 171n26, 198n41. *See also* Equality; Inferiority; Stratification; Superiority

Inheritance, 59, 147

Injury, 16, 76, 77, 181n58. *See also* Accidents; Assault; Mutilation

Innovation
  overinnovation, 102, 109–119
  underinnovation, 121, 129–136
  See also Creativity

Inquisition, the, 110–111, 134, 186n65, 195n101

Insanity. *See* Mental illness

Insults, 3, 5, 71, 73, 74, 108, 113, 114, 122, 140, 164n150, 175n90, 175n105, 187n88, 190n9

Intimacy, xi, 4, 5, 6, 7, 11, 12, 21–55, 120, 140, 141–143, 146, 155n26, 158n7, 167n32, 168n53, 181n54, 183n111
  downward, 22, 38
  overintimacy, 6, 7, 14, 21–42, 137, 139, 142, 165n167, 186n82, 187n89
  right to, 141–143
  underintimacy, 6, 7, 14, 21, 43–55, 137–138, 139, 142, 171n22
  upward, 22, 38

Inuit. *See* Eskimos

Invasion, 22–23, 36, 96–97, 102, 144, 181n65

Involvement
  as intimacy, 22
  overinvolvement, 22–36, 164n137
  underinvolvement, 22, 44–51

Iran and the Iranians, 45, 86, 91, 112, 182n82, 192n50. *See also* Persia and the Persians

Iraq and the Iraqis, 27, 127

Ireland and the Irish, 28, 37, 53, 106, 108, 127, 187n99
  ancient, 77 (*see also* Celtic tribes)

Iroquois Indians, 123, 141. *See also* Mohawk Indians

Islam and Muslims, 3, 10, 12, 16, 22, 27, 31, 32–33, 39, 45, 47, 50, 70–71, 86, 101, 103, 108, 112, 121, 122, 123, 127, 130–131, 132,

139, 156n46, 158n67, 164n154, 169n100, 173n72, 174n79, 186n77, 190n5, 193–194n74, 194n81, 195n101. *See also* Arabs; *individual Islamic countries*
Israel and the Israelis, 27, 70, 168n67, 184n27
Israelites, ancient, 103, 130
Italian-Americans, 35
Italy and the Italians, 81, 95, 106, 134, 187n106
medieval, 80, 132, 162n99

J

Jains, 111–112, 151
Jalé, 78
Jante law, 68, 172n52
Japan and the Japanese, 3, 31–32, 54–55, 63, 67, 68, 72–73, 76, 94–95, 106, 171n24, 172n46, 176n133, 183n97, 192n30
Jews and Judaism, 3, 14–15, 16, 32–34, 68–70, 71, 80–81, 96–97, 101, 106, 107, 108, 109–110, 121, 122, 130–133, 133–134, 137, 156n46, 162n86, 164n159, 172n56, 173nn63–66, 173nn70–73, 174nn74–75, 182n86, 185n37, 185n56, 186n65, 189n134, 191n16, 193n68, 193n74, 194n77, 194n81, 194n90, 195nn92–94. *See also* Anti-Semitism; Holocaust
Jívaro, 45, 196n15
Job loss, 5, 8, 9, 10, 11, 14, 43, 48, 69, 71, 75. *See also* Employers and employees
Juvenile delinquency, 49, 75
Judges, 43, 90, 91

K

Kaguru, 62–63, 90, 108, 161n76
Kaingang, 166n9
Kenya and the Kenyans, 24, 48, 84, 191n23
Kikuyu, 48, 191n24
Killing. *See* Homicide
Kiowa Indians, 24
Koran, The, 27, 77, 123
Korea and the Koreans, 95, 106
Korean-Americans, 107
Kurds, 50
Kwakiutl Indians, 78
Kwanga, 79, 108

L

Latin America, 72, 83. *See also individual Latin American countries*
Law, xi, 3, 12–13, 83, 137, 145, 157n55, 198n37, 198n42
Lawsuits and litigation, xii, 36, 52, 60, 74, 79, 153n6
Lawyers, xi
Leaving (a relationship), 3, 7, 8, 11, 17, 43, 44, 45–50, 139, 145, 146. *See also* Divorce
Liability, 78, 157n56
collective, 80, 91
displaced, 156n36
strict, 157n56
subjective, 157n56
Lombards, 77. *See also* Germanic tribes
Looking
as deviant behavior, 30–32, 35
downward, 30
upward, 30
Loyalty, 15, 157n58
Luck, 61, 62
as social time, 10–11
Lying, 14, 17, 52–54, 169n100
Lynching, 24, 86, 150, 155n36. *See also* Homicide

M

Macah Indians, 65, 66
Magic and sorcery, 16, 50, 51, 61–63, 64, 65, 80, 108, 124, 125, 131, 178nn161–162, 179n6, 196n1. *See also* Witchcraft and witches
Malaysia, 65, 103, 142
Manners. *See* Etiquette and manners
Manu, Laws of, 45, 87, 181n54
Marriage, 5, 44, 51, 59, 139, 142, 159n16
between unequals, 28
forms of, 46, 167n27
inequality in, 47, 57, 158n7
interethnic and interracial, 32–33, 34, 125, 126
intimacy in, 22, 44, 46–47, 51, 139, 196–197n36 *See also* Husbands and wives

Massachusetts, colonial, 26, 63
Massacres, xii, 16, 92, 104, 105, 111, 125, 130–131, 158n64, 186n74, 194n81. *See also* Genocide; Homicide
Masturbation, 25, 28–29, 36, 40, 52
Mbuti, 89, 143, 196n15
McDonald's Massacre, 10, 75
Mediation, xi
Mehinaku Indians, 37, 141, 142, 143, 144, 184n6, 196–197n16
Melanesia, 103
Mexican-Americans, 32, 107
Mexico and the Mexicans, 48, 72, 84, 106, 195n101
Mental illness, 29, 31, 36, 37, 38, 51, 54, 76, 88, 113, 114, 117–119, 128, 148, 169n91, 189n138, 198n48. *See also* Paranoia
Micronesia, 72
Middle East, 70, 86, 107, 173n72, 174n74. *See also individual Middle Eastern countries and peoples*
Missionaries, 16, 65, 110, 111, 122, 123–125, 141, 143, 191nn22–24, 191–192n28
Mobility, vertical, 60–63, 65, 66–68, 76, 87, 90, 95, 138, 143, 146–147, 154n18, 179n17, 189n138
Modern time, 144–147
Mohawk Indians, 103, 126. *See also* Iroquois Indians
Moral time, xii, 4, 9, 11, 12, 17, 137–138, 145, 155n19, 155n20. *See also* Cultural time; Relational time; Vertical time
Morality, 138, 156nn44–46, 157n58
   global, 149–151, 198–199n51, 199n67
   modern, 144–147
   of closeness, 140
   of distance, 145
   origins of, xii, 11–17
   therapeutic, 148, 149, 198nn46–48
   tribal, 3, 126, 140–144
Monks, 27–28, 43, 108, 134, 151
Morocco and the Moroccans, 39, 169n100
Mormons, 111, 186n74
Mundurucú Indians, 103
Muslims. *See* Islam and Muslims

Mutilation, 24, 39, 45, 46, 47, 77, 88, 91, 92, 110, 122, 123, 124, 125, 127, 150, 163n111, 177n146, 182n68. *See also* Blinding, as social control; Castration

N
Nakedness, 40–41, 162n96, 164n150, 167n32, 186n82
   as relational time, 37–38
Natchez Indians, 197n25
Nations, xii, 3, 5, 6, 22–23, 60, 71, 74, 89–90, 181n65
Navajo Indians, 63, 102, 171n22
Nazis, 69, 70, 117, 122, 132, 174n74. *See also* Germany and the Germans; Holocaust; Jews and Judaism
Neighbors, 38, 50, 61, 62, 63, 83, 84, 86
New England, colonial, 45, 52, 95, 104, 123, 126, 129, 140,
New Guinea, 3, 24, 26–27, 35, 45, 50, 64, 65, 78, 79, 80, 106, 108, 142, 143, 150, 161n60, 178n161, 191–192n28, 196n15
New Zealand, 68
Netherlands, Holland, and the Dutch, 26, 68, 80, 105, 106
Nigeria and the Nigerians, 51, 78, 106–107, 108, 191n24, 196n3
Norms, 11. *See also* Rules
Norse law, 128
Norway and the Norwegians, 41
North Carolina, colonial, 23–24
Nuer, 79
Nuns, 23, 27–28
Nyoro, 84

O
Obscenity, 17, 37, 40–41, 164n150
Oceania, 12
Onanism. *See* Masturbation
Outlaws, 128
Opportunity, right to, 146
Organizations, 6, 12
Orokaiva, 88, 181n53
Ostracism, xi, 6, 65, 67, 78, 86, 135, 136
Ottawa Indians, 141

P

Painting and painters, 40–41, 46, 112–114, 135, 165nn166–168, 167n32, 168n65, 173n66, 198nn88–89

Pakistan and the Pakistanis, 22, 24, 39, 47, 72, 108, 127, 144, 160n43

Pamonkey Indians, 105

Paranoia, 76, 119, 173–174n73
  collective, 70, 71

Parents and children, 3, 11, 25, 27, 38, 41, 44, 47–48, 61, 78, 90, 127, 196–197n16

Pashtun, 22, 39, 72, 144

Pedophilia, 25, 28. *See also* Children, sex with

Peeping Toms, 31, 162n96

Perjury, 53

Persia and the Persians, 31, 86, 91–92, 186n77. *See also* Iran and the Iranians

Philippines and the Filipinos, 10, 24, 50, 64, 108, 161n76, 196n12

Piaroa Indians, 31, 176n137

Poaching, 88

Poets and poetry, 41, 46, 112, 114, 188n110, 199n67

Poland and the Poles, 69, 81, 96–97, 106, 108

Police, 24, 32, 40, 44, 90, 91, 97, 128, 129, 163n102
  complaints to, xi, 5, 25, 37, 38

Polynesia, 31

Pornography, 40–41

Portugal and the Portuguese, 124, 132, 134, 186n65

Postmodern time, 147–152

Poverty and the poor, 10, 74–76, 77, 85, 88, 143. *See also* Beggars and begging

Powhatan Indians, 105

Priests, 28, 52, 141

Prisons and prisoners, 23, 43, 73–74, 90, 91, 139, 151, 158n64; *see also* imprisonment

Privacy, 12, 137, 140, 142, 143, 146, 149, 151, 158n7, 199n61
  right to, 145–146

Property, 12, 137, 143, 145, 146, 147, 180n39
  confiscation of, 78, 94, 111, 112, 122, 133, 189n134
  damage and destruction of, 12, 65, 88, 91, 93, 111, 112, 117, 146

Prostitution, 25, 27, 33, 111

Protestant Reformation and Protestants, 81, 111, 118, 129–130, 132, 191–192n28

Pueblo Indians, 36, 123

Puerto Rico and the Puerto Ricans, 35, 107

Punishment, xi, 3, 5, 6, 13, 23, 156n33
  as social time, 9
  collective, 92
  See also specific kinds of punishment

Puritans, 52, 111, 123, 126, 140

Purity, right to, 144

R

Race and Racism, 17, 34, 146, 147, 159n24, 183n111, 185n33
  as culture, 106–108

Rape, 3, 4, 7, 9, 11, 13, 22, 23–25, 26, 36, 37, 44–45, 103, 104, 137–138, 139, 142, 145, 155nn25–26, 157n55, 159nn24–26, 160n42, 161n76, 177n146, 196n15
  as relational time, 23–25
  as social control, 26, 45, 47–48, 160n43
  between strangers, 9, 13, 23, 24
  between unequals, 23–24
  cultural, 123
  gang rape, 24, 45, 160n43
  marital, 23, 47–48

Rebellion, 7, 17, 90–92, 139, 157n61, 168n58
  as vertical time, 90–92

Relational distance. *See* Distance, relational

Relational time, xii, 4, 5, 6, 7, 9, 11, 17, 19–55, 117, 137, 137–138, 156n46, 173–174n73, 181n65
  nakedness as, 37–38
  rape as, 23–25

Religion, 4, 7, 8, 101, 109, 110, 121, 137, 138, 139–140, 144, 145, 146, 147, 149, 151, 154n10, 155n28, 163n107, 199n67. *See also individual faiths*

Revolution, 60, 75–76, 90

Ridicule, 3, 8, 64, 65, 66, 67, 113, 114, 115, 116, 128, 144, 184n6

Rights, right to, 149

Riots, 24, 90, 91, 92–93, 102, 107, 121, 133, 150, 155n28, 156n35, 159n26, 182n84

Robbery, 7, 11, 74, 87, 88, 180n38

Romania, 86

Romans, ancient, 27, 109–110, 122, 125, 130, 168n63, 172n54, 174n74
Rudeness, xii, 7, 12, 17, 36, 50, 137
Rules, xi, 3, 7, 12, 15. *See also* Norms
Russia and the Russians, 50, 113, 117

S
Sabotage, 23
Scandinavia, 68, 128; *see also* individual Scandinavian countries
Schools, 11, 61, 75, 123
　violence in, 48
　See also Students
Science and scientists, 3, 52, 69, 115–117, 118, 135–136, 137, 155n19, 187n104, 188n120, 189n126, 189nn134–135, 190nn143–144, 195n103
　overcreativity in, 115–117
Scotland and the Scots, 42, 81, 114
Sculpture, 114
Secrets and secrecy, 17, 36, 51–52, 169n91
Segregation, 24, 32–34, 39, 102, 107, 159n24, 174n74
Self, global, 149–153. *See also* Closeness, self
Self-injury. *See* Suicide
Semai, 142
Sex, 16, 22, 25–29, 31, 35, 36, 37, 40, 47–48, 52, 110, 124–125, 141
　interracial and interethnic, 33–34
　See also Adultery; Bestiality; Fornication; Homosexuality; Masturbation; Rape
Shamans, 84, 178n163
Shaming, 48, 88
Sharia law, 12
Shavante Indians, 80
Shetland Islands, 75
Shilluk, 86
Shona, 63, 83
Siblings, 27, 39–40, 61, 91. *See also* Brothers and sisters
Sicily and the Sicilians, 72, 86
Slavery and slaves, 23–24, 27, 53, 72, 76, 77, 79, 82–83, 87, 88, 90, 91–92, 95, 96, 103, 104, 105, 106, 110, 123, 133, 134, 139, 166n19, 171n26
Sin, 7, 52, 196n1

Social change, 5, 153n7
Social control, 3, 6, 9, 145, 153nn1–3, 155n23, 157n55, 181n66, 198n37
Social geometry, 138–140, 154n18, 155n30
Social space, 4, 5, 7, 9, 12, 15, 22, 37, 54, 59, 137, 138, 156n47, 157n61
Social time, xii, 3–4, 5, 6, 7, 11, 12, 13, 14, 15, 16, 81, 137, 144, 154nn10–18, 155nn26–28, 157n55, 186n77, 189n138, 196n1
　as moral time, 4
　as the origin of morality, 11–12
　crime as, 6–9
　definition of, 3–4
　geometry of, 138–140
　luck as, 10–11
　nature of, 4–5
　punishment as, 9
　See also Cultural time; Modern time; Postmodern time; Relational time; Tribal time; Vertical time
Soga, 45, 166n15
Somalia and the Somalis, 121
Sorcery. *See* Magic and sorcery
South Africa, 159n24
Soviet Union, 90
Space, physical, 4. *See also* Social space
Spain and the Spanish, 31, 39, 48, 50, 65–66, 72, 80, 81, 95, 104, 107, 111, 113, 123, 124, 130, 132, 134, 184n22, 186n65, 193–194n74, 194n81, 195nn93–94, 195n101
Sri Lanka, 50
Strangers, 5, 6, 7, 9, 10, 12, 13, 22, 23, 26, 31, 34, 36, 37, 38, 53, 75, 117, 139, 140, 144, 145, 147, 150, 157n55, 162n87, 174n74, 175n105
Stealing. *See* Theft
Stratification, social, 7, 26
　definition of, 59
　overstratification, 6, 14, 59–81, 137, 138, 139, 143, 189n135
　understratification, 6, 14, 60, 82–97, 137, 139
　See also Inequality
Students, 67, 147, 167n51
　high school, 25, 48
　college, 35, 36, 43
Sudan, 79, 86, 178n160

Suicide, 10–11, 24, 27, 28, 43, 46, 49, 76, 78, 81, 131, 142, 166n2, 167n24, 168n71, 176n133, 177nn155–157, 181n53
  murder-suicide, 8, 49, 75
Suku, 10
Sukuma, 83
Sumptuary laws. 94–95, 183n97
Superiority
  oversuperiority, 60–71, 178n161
  undersuperiority, 82–89
Swabian code, 88
Sweden and the Swedes, 28, 38, 41, 121
Switzerland and the Swiss, 80, 81, 95, 111

T

Taboos, 12, 25, 31, 51–52, 79, 162n90. *See also* Incest and the incest taboo
Tamils, 50
Tanzania, 50, 61–63, 83, 84, 90, 108, 161n76
Tarahumara Indians, 48, 49
Tasmania and the Tasmanians, 103–104, 184n17
Tattoos, 177n146, 181n54
Tauade, 50
Ten Commandments, 12, 45, 53, 85, 87, 90, 122, 167n34
Terrorism and terrorists, xi, 23, 48, 70–71, 150, 155n28, 155n30, 158n67
Thailand and the Thais, 178–179n1
Theft, 11, 12, 65, 74, 83, 87–89, 117, 139, 143, 157n58, 166n15, 180nn38–39, 181nn54–56, 189n137
Time
  biological, xii
  physical, xii, 4, 5, 154nn10–14
  See also Cultural time; Modern time; Postmodern time; Relational time; Social time; Tribal time; Vertical time
Tlingit Indians, 78, 82–83
Todas, 166n9
Tolerance, 12, 14, 15, 112, 120, 140, 144, 147
Tonga, 31
Torture, 3, 23, 24, 80, 81, 88, 91, 103, 108, 112, 115, 123, 124, 127, 132, 134, 144, 150, 151, 163n111, 192n30
Touching, as deviant behavior, 7, 22, 29–30, 108, 162nn86–87

  downward, 30
  upward, 30
Traditionalism
  overtraditionalism, 102–109
  undertraditionalism, 121–129
Transvestism. *See* Cross-dressing
Treason, 36, 125, 126–127
  cultural, 122, 123, 125, 126–127
  petty, 90–91
Trespassing, 7
Tribal societies, 12, 35, 45, 59, 63, 102, 140–144, 166n10. *See also individual tribes*
Tribal time, 140–144
Truk and the Trukese, 72
Tunisia and the Tunisians, 85
Turkey and the Turks, 27, 50, 106, 108, 122, 127, 158n7, 190n9

U

Uganda, 45, 84, 166n15, 171n22
Unemployed, the, 156n33. *See also* Job loss
United States and the Americans, 12, 14–15, 16, 23, 25, 26, 28, 29, 31, 34, 36, 41, 42, 45, 47, 49, 50, 53, 54, 61, 70, 74, 79, 88, 90, 102, 106, 107, 108–109, 112, 113, 114, 121, 128, 132, 140, 145, 146, 147, 158n67, 158n7, 160n42, 162n86, 162n99, 163n102, 164n150, 167n25, 169n100, 172n45, 174nn75–79, 176n133, 178–179n1, 181n56, 185n51, 189n134, 195n112, 196–197n36, 198n43
Untouchables, 28, 30, 38, 40, 94, 136
Utopias, 10, 89

V

Vandalism, 65, 75
Venezuela, 31, 45, 176n137, 178n162
Venice, Renaissance, 23. *See also* Italy and the Italians
Vertical time, xii, 4, 5, 6, 7, 9, 11, 57–97, 117, 137, 138, 155n32, 156n46, 159n13, 173–174n73, 181n65
  rebellion as, 90–92
  theft as, 87–89
  violence as, 76–78

Vietnam and the Vietnamese, 106
Vinatinai Islanders, 196n15
Violence, xi, 3, 6, 8, 17, 23, 45, 65, 68, 71, 73, 92,
    137, 142, 159n13, 166n10, 175n97, 175n105
    as vertical time, 76–78
    See also Assault; Death penalty;
        Homicide; Mutilation; Rape;
        Torture
Virginia, colonial, 105
Virtue, 15, 103, 157n58, 157n61
Voyeurism, 31

W
Warfare, xi, xii, 3, 22–23, 24, 50, 60, 71, 74,
    89–90, 103, 132, 149, 150, 153nn3–6
    germ warfare, 105
Wealth, 4, 12, 16, 59, 140, 176n137
    change in, 5, 74–76, 80, 176n130 (*see also*
        Mobility, vertical)
West Indies and the West Indians, 105, 106,
    107

Witchcraft and witches, 3, 16, 17, 43, 50,
    61–63, 69, 70, 71, 79–80, 82–87, 90, 108,
    118, 137, 143, 158n66, 161n76, 170n17,
    170–171nn17–19, 171n22, 178n160,
    178n182, 179n5, 179n16. *See also* Magic
    and sorcery
World War I, 16, 70, 71, 74, 89–90, 132, 158n64,
    187–188n107
World War II, 70, 71, 89, 176n133

X
Xingu Indians, 103

Y
Yanomamö Indians, 45

Z
Zaire, 89, 196n15
Zambia, 46, 62
Zapotec Indians, 48, 84
Zimbabwe, 63, 83